Foreign Protestant Communities in Sixteenth-Century London

ANDREW PETTEGREE

CLARENDON PRESS · OXFORD

1986

Oxford University Press, Walton Street, Oxford OX2 6DP

Oxford New York Toronto
Delhi Bombay Calcutta Madras Karachi
Petaling Jaya Singapore Hong Kong Tokyo
Nairobi Dar es Salaam Cape Town
Melbourne Auckland
and associated companies in
Beirut Berlin Ibadan Nicosia

Oxford is a trade mark of Oxford University Press

Published in the United States
by Oxford University Press, New York

British Library Cataloguing in Publication Data
Pettegree, Andrew
Foreign protestant communities in sixteenth-century London.
1. Calvinists—England—South East—History—16th century.
2. Calvinists—England—South East—Social conditions.
I. Title
305.6'42'0422   DA670.S63
ISBN 0-19-822938-0

Library of Congress Cataloging in Publication Data
Pettegree, Andrew
Foreign Protestant communities in sixteenth-century London.
(Oxford historical monographs)
Rev. version of a thesis (doctoral)—University of Oxford, 1983.
Bibliography: p.
Includes index.
1. Protestant churches—England—London—History—16th century.
2. Protestants—England—London—History—16th century.
3. London (England)—Church history.
4. London (England)—Foreign population—History—16th century.
I. Title.
BX4838.P48 1986   280'.4'09421   86-8663
ISBN 0-19-822938-0

Set by Litho Link Limited
Printed in Great Britain by
Billing & Sons Ltd
Worcester

Acknowledgements

This work is a revised version of a doctoral thesis submitted to the University of Oxford in the spring of 1983. During the course both of the initial research and subsequent revision I have received a great deal of help from many sources, and it is a pleasure to be able to acknowledge this assistance here. My first and greatest debt is to Joan Thirsk, who supervised my doctoral research, and has been a constant source of advice and encouragement since. I owe a great deal to her interests, insights, and (not least) vigorous editorial pencil. Alastair Duke has also given me a quite exceptional amount of help; my debt to his expertise in the field of Dutch Reformation studies will be readily apparent. In the early days of my research I benefited greatly from the opportunity to discuss my work with friends and colleagues in Oxford: Ian Archer, George Bernard, Susan Brigden, Cliff Davies, Stephen Gunn, Christopher Haigh, Jennifer Loach, and Philippa Tudor all at different times contributed comments or suggestions. Patrick Collinson and Paul Slack were sympathetic examiners, and encouraged me to press on with publication. I should also acknowledge the help given me by Irene Scouloudi, Secretary of the Huguenot Society of London, who made available to me the facilities of the Huguenot Library and gave me much shrewd advice.

After finishing my thesis in Oxford I was able to continue my research for two years in Germany thanks to a research award from the Stiftung F.V.S. of Hamburg. I am grateful to the Management Board of the Stiftung, and to Herr and Frau W. Koelle, Dr Heinold Fast, and Herr Hans Nitrowski for their generous hospitality during visits to German archives. The final stages of this book were completed in the congenial surroundings of Peterhouse, Cambridge, and I am grateful to the Master and Fellows for electing me to the Research Fellowship that made this possible. Mrs Pamela Stockham coped with the typing with great efficiency and dispatch. Finally, I would also like to acknowledge the help of the many friends, too numerous to name, whose interest in this work has helped sustain mine. To them and all those named above I am deeply grateful.

Peterhouse, Cambridge   ANDREW PETTEGREE
28 May 1985.

Contents

Abbreviations

Actes I	*Actes du Consistoire de L'Église Française de Londres, vol. i, 1560–1565,* ed. Elsie Johnson (Huguenot Society Publications, 38, 1937).
Actes II	*Actes du Consistoire . . ., vol. ii, 1571–1577,* ed. Anne M. Oakley (Huguenot Society Publications, 48, 1969).
APC	*Acts of the Privy Council of England,* ed. J. R. Dasent.
Archd. London	Guildhall Library, Archdeaconry Court of London Wills.
BHR	*Bibliothèque d'Humanisme et Renaissance.*
BL	British Library.
BRN	*Bibliotheca Reformatoria Neerlandica,* ed. S. Cramer and F. Pijper (The Hague, 1903–14).
BWPG	*Biografisch woordenboek van protestantsche godgeleerden in Nederland.*
Cal. Pat. Rolls	*Calendar of Patent Rolls.*
Cal. S. P. Dom., For., Span.,	*Calendar of State Papers Domestic, Foreign, Spanish.*
CO	*Joannis Calvini Opera,* ed. E. Cunitz and E. Baum (*Corpus Reformatorum,* 29–87, 1863–1900).
Coussemaker	E. de Coussemaker, *Troubles religieux du XVIᵉ siècle dans la Flandre maritime, 1560–1570* (Brussels, 1876).
Denizations	*Letters of Denization and Acts of Naturalization for Aliens in England, 1509–1603,* ed. W. Page (Huguenot Society Publications, 8, 1893).
DNB	*Dictionary of National Biography.*
Hessels	*Ecclesiae Londino-Batavae Archivum,* ed. J. H. Hessels (Cambridge, 1889–97).
HS	*Proceedings of the Huguenot Society.*
KL	J. M. B. C. Kervyn de Lettenhove, *Relations politiques des Pays-Bas et de l'Angleterre, sous le règne de Philippe II* (Brussels, 1888–1900).

KP I	*Kerkeraads-protocollen der Nederduitsche vluchtelingen-kerk te Londen, 1560–1563*, ed. A. A. van Schelven (Historisch Genootschap te Utrecht, 3rd series, 43, 1921).
KP II	*Kerkeraads-protocollen der Hollandsche gemeente te Londen, 1569–1571*, ed. A. Kuyper (Marnix Society, series 1, part 1, 1870).
L & P	*Letters and Papers Foreign and Domestic of the Reign of Henry VIII*, ed. J. S. Brewer (2nd edn., 1920–32).
Lasco Opera	*Joannis a Lasco Opera*, ed. A. Kuyper (Amsterdam, 1866).
London Comm.	Guildhall Library, Commissary Court of London Wills.
NAK	*Nederlandsch archief voor kerkgeschiedenis.*
NNBW	*Nieuw Nederlandsch Biografisch Woordenboek.*
OL	*Original Letters relative to the English Reformation*, ed. H. Robinson (Parker Society, 1846–7).
PCC	Public Record Office, Prerogative Court of Canterbury Wills.
PRO	Public Record Office.
Rep.	Corporation of London Record Office, Repertories of the Court of Aldermen.
Returns	*Returns of Aliens dwelling in the City and Suburbs of London*, ed. R. E. G. and E. F. Kirk (Huguenot Society Publications, 10, 1900–8).
STC	*Short-Title Catalogue of Books Printed in England, Scotland and Ireland, and of English Books Printed Abroad, 1475–1640*, ed. A. W. Pollard and G. R. Redgrave (2nd revised edn., 1976–1986).

Place of publication unless otherwise stated is London throughout.

List of Maps and Tables

Introduction

FOREIGN visitors to England in the last decades of the fifteenth
century commented with almost monotonous regularity on
one particular aspect of the English character: their dislike of
foreigners. Occasionally this hostility would boil over in violent
attacks on foreign workmen or merchants, but for the most
part Englishmen expressed their contempt for the foreigner in
more subtle ways. Foreign travellers were particularly struck
by the extraordinary self-satisfaction and insularity manifested
in the attitudes of their hosts. 'The English are great lovers
of themselves and of everything belonging to them', as one
Italian observed, 'they think there are no other men than
themselves, and no other world but England.'[1] In fairness,
most foreign commentators were prepared to make an exception for the gentry and nobility. They, after all, were the patrons of culture and the arbiters of taste, and in an age when
the most accomplished practitioners in the artistic and musical
world came from the Continent they, at least, showed themselves receptive to innovations from abroad. But reading these
travellers' tales and descriptions of England the overwhelming
impression is of an inward-looking and self-contained society
where any outsiders were regarded with suspicion. 'They have
an antipathy of foreigners', as our Italian source put it, 'and
imagine they never come into their island but to make themselves masters of it, and to usurp their goods.'[2]

In view of this quite dismal reputation, it must at first sight
seem somewhat surprising that during the course of the next
century such a large number of foreigners did 'come into their
island'; and that they were, on the whole, much better received

---

[1] *A Relation, or Rather a True Account of the Island of England*, ed. C. A. Sneyd (Camden
Soc., 37, 1857), p. 20. A remarkably similar opinion was expressed by a German
visitor to the court of Richard III. See W. D. Robson-Scott, *German Travellers in
England* (Oxford, 1953), p. 16.

[2] *Relation of England*, pp. 23–4. See also Andreas Franciscius, *Itinerarium Britanniæ*,
in *Two Italian Accounts of England*, ed. C. V. Malfatti (Barcelona, 1953), p. 36.

than the observations cited above might lead one to expect. In the first decades of the sixteenth century the immigration followed a traditional pattern, with foreign workmen and merchants coming to England in search of work or trade, as they had for centuries. But from about 1540 this existing community was reinforced by a growing number of foreigners who crossed the Channel for quite different motives: they were the first generation of religious refugees, the victims of an increasingly intense persecution in the Catholic lands of northern Europe. Probably as many as fifty thousand refugees settled in England during the course of the century, most of them in London or in the towns of south eastern England. By the end of Elizabeth's reign their presence in England had transformed the previously small and relatively stable foreign community. Some of the exiles soon returned to the Continent, but many remained, put down roots, and gradually became a part of English society. And their experiences seem to have been far removed from those which a previous generation of courtiers and diplomats had recorded in their travel books and dispatches. They clearly felt at home, and although there was a degree of friction between the immigrants and the native population, over the course of the century the host community also proved itself sufficiently open and flexible to accommodate this potentially disruptive but immensely invigorating new element.

This book is a study of this first Protestant refugee movement, and of the community that grew up around it in London during the course of the sixteenth century. At the centre of this community were the 'stranger churches', first established in 1550 to accommodate the fast growing number of Protestant refugees in the capital. These churches were from the beginning much more than purely religious institutions. Although founded to cater to the needs of the Reformed exiles, they quickly became the institutional centre of the whole foreign community of the city. This fact was crucial to their purpose and reputation for, as contemporaries were well aware, by no means all the foreigners who settled in England during the course of the sixteenth century were religiously motivated. The exiles joined a smaller but long-established foreign community in the capital, and other foreigners continued to come into London for more mundane reasons. Not the least remarkable

aspect of the foreign presence in London was the enormous
variety of experience it encompassed, from the Calvinist who
sought a temporary refuge from the heresy commission of
Philip II to the young apprentice who crossed the Channel in
search of work and ended up settled for life. But even for those
immigrants with little religious feeling, the stranger churches
were often of considerable importance. It is interesting to note
how many foreigners famous for their activities outside the
religious sphere: the inventor Acontius, the merchant historian
Emanuel van Meteren, the artists and scholars Marcus
Gheeraerts and Lucas de Heere, for example, still found their
lives in London inextricably bound up with the foreign
churches.[3] And the churches' ministers and elders found themselves involved in far more than simply the spiritual guidance
of their flocks; in fact in every aspect of society, social,
economic, and political where the immigrant presence made
itself felt.

A study which takes the stranger churches as its point of
departure thus inevitably touches on the issues which confronted the whole foreign community in London; and these
were issues which also went close to the heart of the most
serious problems which faced the governors of England in the
sixteenth century. It is an interesting measure of the impact
of the immigration in this period that so many of the groups
which formed and directed London opinion at some point
found themselves involved in the debate stimulated by the
arrival of the foreign refugees. For the governors of city and
state the foreign influx posed problems of control, but the more
entrepreneurially minded were not slow to recognize the attendant economic opportunities. For the more humble English
tradesmen the new arrivals appeared less as an economic
stimulus than as a threat to their livelihoods, and the new
churches quickly became the focus of their economic anxieties.
Protestant churchmen saw in the refugees the chance to
demonstrate solidarity with suffering co-religionists abroad;
the ambassadors of the Catholic powers saw only subversive
cells organizing in comfortable English exile for an assault on
their former homelands. All were agreed on one thing at least,

---

[3] Leonard Forster, *Janus Gruter's English Years* (1967), pp. 46–52. See also below,
pp. 173–4.

that the foreign communities in London were a potentially
unpredictable element, and in an age that valued stability
above change they had to be watched.

If so many shrewd and well-placed contemporary observers
saw the foreign community in this light, the historian may feel
encouraged in the conviction that the sixteenth-century immigration will bear rather closer examination than it has so far
received. This monograph represents a first attempt to assess
the impact of the refugee movement on English society, and
on the Reformation in England and on the Continent. In
writing it I have intended both to tell the story of the establishment of the stranger churches, and at the same time to
reflect something of the variety of the foreigners' interests and
experiences, and of the diversity of their influence. To this
extent the structure of the book reflects my feeling that a study
of the foreign community should turn in as many directions as
the foreigners did themselves. A strictly chronological
framework is maintained only for the first half; thereafter three
longer chapters (VII–IX) explore rather more thematically
the social, economic, and religious significance of the foreign
immigration in Elizabethan London and beyond. Perhaps
partly because the foreigners cannot be squeezed neatly into
any one category of historical scholarship, religious or political,
social or economic, the exile communities have not been the
object of much scholarly attention in England. This is true
both of the immigration in general and of the stranger churches
in particular. Most general histories of the English Reformation mention the stranger churches only in passing. Only the
more specialized studies of M. M. Knappen in his *Tudor
Puritanism* and W. K. Jordan on the reign of Edward VI concede the churches a measure of importance.[4]

Serious attention to the foreign church communities in Lon-
don has remained almost exclusively the preserve of foreign
historians. In 1950 the distinguished Dutch church historian
Jan Lindeboom was commissioned to write a history of the
Dutch church to celebrate its four hundredth anniversary. His
Austin Friars offers a useful general survey over a long time

---

[4] M. M. Knappen, *Tudor Puritanism* (1939), pp. 90–5; W. K. Jordan, *Edward VI,
The Threshold of Power* (1970), pp. 313–18; A. G. Dickens, *The English Reformation*
(1964), p. 239; G. R. Elton, *Reform and Reformation* (1977), p. 362.

period without in any way superseding the earlier work of A.
A. van Schelven, whose study of the Dutch exile communities
in England and Germany, *De Nederduitsche vluchtelingenkerken
der XVIe eeuw*, includes an authoritative account of the foundation and early years of the Dutch church in London. For the
French church nothing yet replaces Baron Fernand de Schickler's magisterial study, *Les Églises du Refuge en Angleterre*, published as long ago as 1892.[5] Mention should also be made of
the work of the German scholar Heinz Schilling and the Bel-
gian Philippe Denis, both of whom have turned their attention
to the London churches in order to illustrate a more general
thesis. Schilling's *Niederländische Exulanten* examines the effect
of the diaspora on the English and German towns in which
the Netherlanders settled. His treatment of London, though
useful for the contrasts he draws with the exiles' experience
in Germany, relies mostly on printed sources. Denis's concerns
are more narrowly theological, though his examination of disputes in the London foreign churches as examples of the conflict between unorthodox and orthodox strands in Calvinism
offers some fascinating vignettes of community life in the age
of confessional growth.[6]

None of these works, with the exception of Schilling's comparative study, attempts to put the exiles into an economic
context, perhaps understandably in view of the authors' preoccupations as church historians. But one might have expected
economic historians to have shown a more lively awareness
of the importance of the immigration for the development of
English crafts and industry. Here again, however, interest in
the immigrant contribution has been slight. For a view of the
general significance of the immigration one is still forced to
turn back to William Cunningham's *Alien Immigrants to England*,
first published in 1897, or even to the hagiographical account
of *The Huguenots* by the Victorian apostle of self-help, Samuel
Smiles. One recent book, Robin Gwynn's *Huguenot Heritage*,

[5] J. Lindeboom, *Austin Friars, History of the Dutch Reformed Church in London, 1550–1950*
(The Hague, 1950); A. A. van Schelven, *De Nederduitsche vluchtelingenkerken der XVIᵉ
eeuw in Engeland en Duitschland* (The Hague, 1909); F. de Schickler, *Les Églises du Refuge
en Angleterre* (Paris, 1892).

[6] Heinz Schilling, *Niederländische Exulanten im 16. Jahrhundert* (Gütersloh, 1972);
Philippe Denis, 'Les Églises d'étrangers à Londres jusqu'à la mort de Calvin' (unpublished mémoire de licence, Liège Univ., 1973–4), and articles cited below.

begins the task of assessing the influence of the immigration over a long period though, as his title suggests, Dr Gwynn is concerned only with the French immigrants rather than the numerically and (in the sixteenth century) economically more significant Dutch.[7] For particular crafts and trades, only the occasional monograph such as Eleanor Godfrey's excellent study of *The Development of English Glassmaking* explores in any detail the importance of foreign expertise in the technical advances made in the sixteenth century. In the case of most branches of industry, however, there is often nothing to supplement the useful articles published over the years in the *Proceedings* of the Huguenot Society of London, a mine of information on every aspect of the immigrant presence.[8] The present work does not aspire to be a comprehensive survey of the economic influence of the exile movement, but it will, it is hoped, make some contribution to a recognition of the refugees' innovatory role in industry and trade, which was at the time such an important factor in determining the attitude of the English government towards the foreign immigration.

Although the religious immigration of the sixteenth century has not been the object of much scholarly attention in this country, the materials available for such a study are both extensive and fairly accessible. The French and Dutch churches in London have both preserved a substantial body of records (those of the Dutch church deposited in the Guildhall Library). The best of these sources, including most of the records relating to the churches' early years, have now been published, beginning with the magnificent collection of the correspondence of the Dutch church edited by J. H. Hessels. Two volumes of the consistory minutes of both the French and Dutch congregations have also appeared in print, together with the surviving registers of baptisms and marriages, and, for the Dutch church, the surviving membership lists. These last are printed, together with all the subsidy listings of foreigners and the official surveys of the alien population, in the

---

[7] Samuel Smiles, *The Huguenots* (1867); Robin Gwynn, *Huguenot Heritage* (1985).

[8] E. S. Godfrey, *The Development of English Glassmaking, 1560–1640* (Oxford, 1975); Lionel Williams, 'Alien Immigrants in relation to Industry and Society in Tudor England', *HS*, 19 (1952–8), 146–69; Mark Girouard, 'Some Alien Craftsmen in Sixteenth and Seventeenth Century England', *HS*, 20 (1958–64), 26–35.

four volumes of the *Returns of Aliens* published by the Huguenot Society of London.[9]

These sources, the product both of the government's careful regulation of the strangers' comings and goings and of the foreign congregations' own meticulous organization, form the basis of this study. But much valuable information concerning the stranger community may also be gleaned from other independent sources, for instance the records of local and central government. I have found the records of the City of London (principally the Letter Books and Repertories of the Court of Aldermen) particularly valuable for what they reveal of relations between the strangers and the local population. In addition two sources not previously exploited in work of this sort have proved especially rewarding: Company Records, and Wills. My analysis of the churches' appeal to different sections of the foreign population in Chapter IV is based on surviving Company Records for occupational groups in which foreigners were particularly active, while the 250 foreign wills discovered for this period have been used extensively in the second half of this work.

The sources used here do not exhaust all possible approaches to the study of London's foreign population. Almost any category of English record could provide some information about foreigners, although the search for stray references in many types of document would be long and laborious. These considerations have precluded any use of legal records. I did explore the possibilities which parish registers appeared to offer for an examination of relationships between foreigners and English residents at a local level, but unfortunately London parishes with good early records turned out not to be those in which large numbers of foreigners were settled. But this may well prove a fruitful source for students of London at a slightly later period, or for a study of provincial foreign communities. I have also confined my attention almost exclusively to the two largest foreign Protestant communities, the Dutch- and the French-speaking. Much smaller groups of Italians and

[9] J. H. Hessels, *Ecclesiae Londino-Batavae Archivum, Epistulae et Tractatus* (Cambridge, 1889–97). Cited as Hessels. Consistory minutes cited as *Actes I, Actes II, KP I*, and *KP II*. See below, Ch. VII n. 3. *Returns of Aliens dwelling in the City and Suburbs of London*, ed. R. E. G. *and* E. F. Kirk (*Huguenot Society Publications*, 10, 1900–8).

Spaniards were also present in the capital, and for a time the Protestants amongst them enjoyed the privilege of meeting together in their own separate churches. These tiny communities on the fringes of the main foreign churches are certainly not without interest, although the materials available to the student do not compare with those for the larger stranger churches. It is to be hoped that there will one day be a study of the Italian community in Elizabethan London, of which the Italian church formed a somewhat enigmatic part.[10] But rather than allow this small and rather untypical group of merchants and intellectuals to occupy a disproportionate amount of space here, I have been content to resign the Italian church to other hands. For the Spanish congregation, which met for a few years at the beginning of Elizabeth's reign, the reader is referred to the excellent biography of its minister, Casiodoro de Reina.[11]

---

[10] Most of the names on one surviving list of members of the Italian church are not obviously Italian. *Returns*, i. 387–8. See Patrick Collinson, *Archbishop Grindal, 1519–1583* (1979), p. 148. The church does seem to have been, as Professor Collinson remarks, 'a curiously mixed society'.

[11] A. Gordon Kinder, *Casiodoro de Reina* (1975).

I

The Foreign Community Before 1547

WITH the foundation of the stranger churches in the summer of 1550 foreign Protestants settled in London had for the first time a place to meet and worship in their own languages and according to their own rites. In this respect the establishment of the churches was an important milestone for London's foreign community, but the presence of a substantial body of foreigners in the capital was not in itself a new phenomenon. On the contrary, foreign merchants and workmen had been making their homes in the city for several centuries, and were an established part of the London scene. Merchants who plied their trade between England and the Continent necessarily spent long periods in London, and could generally count on a welcome; the most prosperous of them, the great international merchants, enjoyed close and privileged relations with the English crown. But perhaps more surprisingly, large numbers of foreign workmen were also comfortably settled in the city, and native-born Londoners were fully accustomed to their presence. It was indeed extremely important for the first generation of foreign Protestant refugees that they were able to join a well-established and settled foreign community in the city, and many of these foreign residents of an earlier generation would give the foreign churches sturdy support in their first difficult years. Before moving on to discuss the first stirrings of Protestantism in the stranger community it is therefore worth casting an eye over the distinctive foreign presence in the capital in the decades before the foundation of the churches, and describe briefly a foreign community that was as stratified and various as the rest of London society.

The richest and most influential of the foreigners settled in medieval London were the alien merchants, amongst whom the Italians occupied a position of special eminence.[1] The

[1] Cunningham, *Alien Immigrants*, pp. 69 ff.; M. Giuseppi, 'Alien Merchants in England in the Fifteenth Century', *Transactions of the Royal Historical Society*, 9 (1895),

expulsion of the Jews by Edward I in 1290 had given the Italians the opportunity to make their financial services indispensable to the English Crown, and in the intervening centuries the leading Italian merchant families had succeeded in cornering a substantial proportion of London's import and export trade. Most of the larger merchants houses retained permanent representatives in London, often young men serving a form of apprenticeship before returning to their native lands. Economically sophisticated and socially self-contained, the Italian merchant community was rightly regarded as a commercial and financial aristocracy within the stranger community; more recently, however, the pre-eminence of the Italians had been challenged by merchants from the Low Countries and North German cities, known collectively in the confusing contemporary parlance as 'Doche'.[2] The most prominent of these northern traders were the merchants of the Hanse, who by the judicious use of political power in the later years of the fifteenth century had established a trading position more privileged even than that of English merchants.[3] In the last decade of the fifteenth century as many as eighty Hanseatic merchants were resident in London, mostly quartered in the monastic privacy of the Hanse headquarters in Dowgate Ward, the Steelyard. The privileges of the foreign merchants were, inevitably, deeply resented, and as the English merchant community grew in power and influence during the sixteenth century their position came under sustained attack. By 1547 the power of the Hanse was on the wane, but it was still a force to be reckoned with, and the same might be said of the Italians. In the early decades of the sixteenth century foreign merchants still controlled almost half of London's export trade, and had successfully preserved their near monopoly over certain categories of imports.[4] As surviving subsidy returns make clear,

75–98. On the Italian community see particularly M. E. Bratchel, 'Alien Merchant Communities in London, 1500–1550' (Cambridge Univ. Ph.D. thesis, 1974).

    [2] Germans were sometimes referred to as 'Almayns' but the distinction between 'Almayns' and 'Doche' was not clearly or consistently made.
    [3] Philippe Dollinger, *The German Hansa* (1970), pp. 305–10.
    [4] Bratchel, 'Alien Merchant Communities', pp. 161–2, 393–4; Dollinger, *Hansa*, pp. 312–20.

the merchants had also maintained their position as a monied élite within the alien community.

The foreign merchants were the most visible and influential members of the stranger community, but they were easily outnumbered by more humble artisans and craftsmen settled in the capital. It seems unlikely that merchants and brokers made up more than 10 per cent of the substantial body of more than two thousand foreigners enrolled to pay the special alien subsidy of 1440; the rest would have been engaged in more mundane trades.[5] The presence of such a large body of foreign workmen in London at this early date may come as something of a surprise in view of subsequent protests by London craftsmen at the threat posed to their livelihoods by recent immigration. In fact foreign artisans had long been accustomed to cross the Channel in search of work in England and by the sixteenth century many skills and trades were closely associated with foreign expertise. A settlement of Flemish weavers in the fourteenth century had made an early and crucial contribution to the development of English weaving techniques, and two centuries later large numbers of strangers still made a living in this and the associated trades of dyeing, tailoring, and haberdashery. Many of London's hat- and felt-makers were foreign, as were a large proportion of the city's glovers. More foreigners were employed in the tanning and working of leather than in any other occupation. Half of London's coopers were foreign, a consequence of the close association of this craft with beer-brewing, which had been introduced into England by north German immigrants in the fourteenth century. At least half of the larger breweries in London were still owned by Germans or Dutchmen in the sixteenth century, and English brewers also depended for a large part of their skilled work-force on immigrant labour.[6]

Even before the arrival of the first Protestant refugees these earlier generations of foreign immigrants had earned a reputation for high quality workmanship which was the envy of

[5] Sylvia Thrupp, 'Aliens in and around London in the Fifteenth Century', in A. E. J. Hollaender and William Kellaway (eds.), *Studies in London History* (1969), 251–72.
[6] See the introduction by W. Page to *Denizations*, pp. xlii–li; Smiles, *Huguenots*, pp. 95–130. Also Ch. IV, below.

native craftsmen. The growing demand for luxury goods in the early sixteenth century, when it was not satisfied by imports, was met largely through the labours of foreign masters settled in England. Edward III had invited three Dutch clockmakers to settle in London, and foreign craftsmen retained a reputation for unrivalled skill in the making of precision instruments. A large proportion of London's goldsmiths were foreigners, and Henry VIII's foreign cutler was probably only the most successful exponent of an occupation in which foreigners played an important role. Whilst Englishmen in the intervening centuries had fully mastered the art of making high-quality broadcloths, Londoners still looked to foreign weavers for the new fabrics and for luxury items, the silks, linens, and tapestry, which were in increasing demand. Nowhere, of course, was the foreign contribution more explicit than in the archetypal new industry, printing.[7] Foreign masters owed their welcome and prosperity to the growing consumer demand for quality and choice, and when once England's rulers began to take an interest in the promotion of certain branches of domestic industry the clear superiority of Continental techniques forced them to look abroad for skilled workmen. The government of Henry VIII showed a tentative interest in economic projects, particularly when they offered the possibility of reducing the kingdom's dependence on potentially hostile regimes for munitions and raw materials. In 1528 a royal agent in Nuremberg was looking for a skilled master to help develop the mining industry in England, a quest which led to the appointment later in the year of Daniel Hochstetter as 'Surveyor and Master of all the mines in England and Ireland'. Royal initiatives also resulted in the establishment of foundries for the making of ordnance manned by workmen specially brought from abroad.[8]

The large number of foreign workmen settled in the capital did not pass unnoticed by other foreign visitors to London. Here, wrote Nicander Nicius, who came to London in 1545

---

[7] See below, pp. 84 ff.

[8] *L & P*, IV, ii. 4639, 5110; Lionel Williams, 'Alien Immigrants in Relation to Industry and Society', 147–9. See also B. G. Awty, 'The Continental Origins of Wealden Ironworkers, 1451–1544', *Economic History Review*, 2nd Series, 34 (1981), 524–39.

in the retinue of the Emperor's ambassadors, 'there dwell men from most of the nations of Europe, employed in various mercantile arts; such especially as regard the working of iron and other metals, added to which they execute with surprising skill the weaving of woollen cloths and richly embroidered tapestry'.[9] But although the search for well-qualified specialists occasionally brought foreign workmen to England from as far afield as Italy and Central Europe, most of the foreign craftsmen settled here came from the lands directly across the Channel. The great bulk of the foreign workmen enrolled to pay the special alien subsidies of the fifteenth century were classified as 'Doche', that is to say mostly Dutch-speaking residents of the Low Countries, also sometimes known to Englishmen as 'Flemings'.[10] By the middle decades of the sixteenth century, however, large numbers of French speakers had settled in the capital. By no means all of these French-speaking immigrants were from France itself. Many were from the French-speaking or 'Walloon' provinces of the Netherlands, and when in the second half of the sixteenth century religious persecution in the Netherlands reached its peak these Walloons far outnumbered refugees from France in the London French church.[11] It must be said, however, that the London officials who compiled the surveys of the alien population were not concerned with such fine distinctions, and Walloons are found in records variously described as French, 'subjects of the King of Spain', or even 'Dutch'.[12] For the sake of simplicity the two foreign churches will be referred to throughout this work as French and Dutch, but it should be kept in mind that a large proportion of the French church's members were in fact from the Low Countries, and that many members of the Dutch church came from Flanders and Brabant and other areas not now part of the Netherlands.

The skill and industry of these early immigrants brought many of them wealth, which inevitably also aroused the resentment of English craftsmen who felt threatened by their success.

[9] *The Second Book of the Travels of Nicander Nucius of Coreyra*, ed. J. A. Cramer (Camden Society, 17, 1841), p. 9.
[10] Thrupp, 'Aliens in London', 259.
[11] See below, ch. VIII n. 173.
[12] For instance see *Returns*, ii. 53.

The frustrations of the English artisans boiled over into occasional violence. When Wat Tyler led his peasant bands into the City in 1381 the strangers were the first to suffer, and some dozens of Flemings were dragged from the sanctuary of the city churches and summarily executed. The merchants of the Hanse were saved only by the security of the Steelyard, but a century later even this protection proved ineffective when a rioting mob attacked and completely gutted the Hanse headquarters.[13] The most famous anti-stranger riot was that of 'Evil May-Day' in 1517. Roused by an inflammatory preacher, several hundred apprentices took to the streets in search of foreigners, and a strong show of royal force was necessary to restore order.[14]

Occasional outbursts of violence of this sort must have been extremely alarming for the stranger merchants; nevertheless, they are hardly indicative of a general climate of hostility towards aliens resident in London. More characteristic expressions of native anxieties were the frequent demands that the business activities of the strangers should be more closely controlled, and largely as a result of this agitation, the seventy years before the foundation of the stranger churches saw the development of a code of law which severely circumscribed the conditions under which the strangers could work. The first statute, enacted during the short reign of Richard III, was directed principally at the Italian merchant community, but it also turned its attention to the large number of foreign artisans in the city, who were now forbidden to employ other strangers as apprentices or to sell goods by retail.[15] Subsequent statutes of 1523 and 1529 reinforced the control of the London companies over foreigners working in the capital and extended their authority to the suburbs where many of the foreigners congregated.[16] These three statutes together also established significant economic advantages for those foreigners prepared to seek the privileged status of 'denizens'. By the statute of

[13] Smiles, *Huguenots*, pp. 464–6; Giuseppi, 'Alien Merchants in England', 80; R. B. Dobson, *The Peasants' Revolt of 1381* (1970), pp. 162, 175, 188–9, 201.

[14] Martin Holmes, 'Evil May Day, 1517: the Story of a Riot', *History Today*, 15 (1965), 642–50.

[15] 1 Richard III c. 9.

[16] 14/15 Henry VIII c. 2; 21 Henry VIII c. 16.

1483 only denizens were in future to set themselves up as handicraftsmen, and the statute of 1529 excluded denizens from the prohibition on foreigners keeping a shop or chamber for carrying on their craft. A consolidating statute of 1540 confirmed previous legislation and established the right of denizens to lease property, a privilege otherwise reserved to merchants who intended to reside in England for only a short time.[17]

In the wake of this legislation many of the foreign workmen who had settled in England permanently found it expedient to take the oath of loyalty and pay the fees necessary to obtain a patent of denization. In the first three decades of Henry VIII's reign over 500 new denizens were enrolled, and a further 400 secured patents after the passage of the 1540 Act.[18] In 1544 almost three thousand new denizens were registered, although this owed more to security considerations than any strong economic motive on the part of the strangers involved. In May of that year, with the King about to embark on an invasion of France, all non-denizen Frenchmen were ordered to take out a patent of denization or quit the realm, and large numbers preferred to register and remain.[19] These three thousand (not all of whom lived in London) were very much the stable core of the stranger population, as most of the more transient French residents probably left the country in the twenty days allowed for by the terms of the proclamation. Many of those who chose to remain had already been in England thirty years or more.[20] Denizens, however, were still at a considerable disadvantage as compared with native-born Englishmen: they were forbidden to take other strangers as apprentices (and might employ only two foreign journeymen), and a statute of 1531 confirmed that denizens were to continue to pay the alien rate of tax, normally double.[21] In London the 'custom' of the city, limiting the right to ply a trade to those free of one of the guild companies, was a further limitation

---

[17] 32 Henry VIII c. 16.
[18] *Denizations*, p. liii.
[19] *Tudor Royal Proclamations*, ed. P. L. Hughes and J. F. Larkin (1964–69), i. 326.
[20] For example see *Denizations*, pp. 36–7 (William Bullande, Denys Burshall, James Busshop).
[21] 22 Henry VIII c. 8, confirming 1 Henry VII c. 2.

upon the benefit of denizen status, and it is not surprising that many foreign handicraftsmen opted not to go through the costly and time-consuming process of obtaining a patent. From the reiterated complaints of English tradesmen and the repetition of statutory provisions it is clear that restrictions on foreign workmen were easier to enact than to enforce, and many new arrivals in London managed to make a comfortable living oblivious of the government's attempts to regulate their activities. Indeed, the fact that many long-term foreign residents were enrolled in the wake of the proclamation of 1544 is itself revealing; evidently they had not felt before that their business activities were limited by their status as aliens.

Foreigners, then, were an established and generally prosperous element of the city population long before the arrival of the first generation of Protestant refugees. As a proportion of the total population of the city, however, the alien presence should not be overestimated. Though the number of foreigners in the capital grew steadily through the first half of the sixteenth century, so too did the population of the city as a whole.[22] Sixteen hundred aliens paid subsidy in 1485, a reduction from the peak of 1440 but still a considerable number; by 1541 this total had risen to 2,500, sufficient evidence in itself of a considerable increase in the stranger population during the first half of the sixteenth century.[23] Subsidy returns, though, invariably under-estimate the number of foreigners in the city. Apart from exemptions granted to privileged groups, such as the Hanse merchants, only adult males were liable for subsidy, and a degree of avoidance and non-registration was inevitable on the fringes. Where both subsidy returns and surveys of the whole alien population survive from approximately the same date later in the century these suggest that the subsidy figures need to be scaled up two or two and a half times to get an

[22] The best estimates of London's population in the sixteenth century suggest that it grew from about fifty thousand in 1500 to between seventy and ninety thousand in mid-century. Roger Finlay, *Population and Metropolis* (Cambridge, 1981), p. 51; G. D. Ramsay, *The City of London in International Politics at the Accession of Elizabeth Tudor* (Manchester, 1975), p. 33.

[23] Sylvia Thrupp, *The Merchant Class of Medieval London* (Michigan, 1948), p. 50; *Returns*, i. 30–68.

idea of the total population.[24] On this basis the number of foreigners in London seems to have grown from a minimum of three thousand at the beginning of the sixteenth century to something like five or six thousand by the end of Henry VIII's reign, amounting to between 5 and 8 per cent of the city's total population. Curiously, more strangers paid subsidy in 1541 than would do so in 1549, a time when contemporaries thought that the number of strangers in the capital was increasing rapidly.[25] A similar disparity between official figures and popular rumour will be apparent in the Elizabethan period, suggesting that reports of enormously inflated numbers of strangers in the capital should be seen more as indications of concern at their presence than realistic estimates of the extent of the immigration.[26]

Although the foreigners did not make up a particularly large proportion of the population, their impact was proportionally greater because of their tendency to congregate in certain areas of the city. 'Tottenham has turned French' had passed into a proverb by the early years of Henry VIII's reign, and the suburbs of Southwark and St Katherine's both had long-established concentrations of foreigners: over four hundred aliens were enrolled to pay subsidy in Southwark in 1549 and one hundred and fifty in St Katherine's.[27] Unfortunately it is not possible to say what proportion of the total population this represented in these two densely populated suburbs. Because English citizens were exempt from subsidy payments if they possessed less than twenty shillings' worth of moveable goods, whereas aliens were polled, a comparison of the numbers of Englishmen and strangers enrolled for each subsidy is not particularly revealing. For the city itself, however, the existence of a second quite separate series of statistics does make it possible to be rather more precise about the relative density of immigrants living in different parts of the city. The Chantry

[24] The subsidy returns of 1559/64 have 1770 alien names, and 4544 aliens were found in the survey of the stranger population in 1563. Similar ratios from later in the century were 2160 : 4079 (1576/1581), 1911 : 5242 (1599/1593). These figures are from I. Scouloudi, 'Alien Immigration and alien communities in London 1558–1640' (London Univ. MSc(Econ) thesis, 1936).

[25] *Returns*, i. 136–90.

[26] See below, pp. 279–80.

[27] Smiles, *Huguenots*, p. 108; *Returns*, i. 141–7, 154–6.

Certificates of 1548, a survey compiled to record the property
that would accrue to the crown on the dissolution of the chan-
tries in 1547, record, almost incidentally, the number of 'houslings' (or communicants) in each of the London parishes. Since
the 1549 subsidy theoretically registered all male strangers
over the age of twelve (who were liable to a poll tax), a simple
division of the number of 'houslings' should enable a reasonably accurate comparison to be made between the total adult
male population of each ward and the number of strangers
recorded in the subsidy returns.[28] The result of this calculation
is shown on the accompanying map. It will be seen that the
highest concentrations of strangers were to be found in the
poorer east end of the city and down by the waterfront. Only
in Langborne Ward, where most of the stranger goldsmiths
lived, were aliens settled in any numbers in the prosperous
central areas of the city. The largest concentrations were either
outside the city walls in Southwark, St Katherine's, or East
Smithfield, or in the small intra-mural liberties: in the liberty
of St Martin-le-Grande the strangers made up half the population.

These long-established foreign quarters gave London's
stranger community an air of stability which may to some
extent have masked the transitory nature of much of the foreign
population. Merchants came and went in the course of their
business, and artisans also had a tendency to cross back and
forth: not all who came in search of work settled, and many
returned to their homelands for short periods to visit relatives
or buy materials for their trades, or in the case of servants on
completion of an apprenticeship. London's foreign community
was in many respects a very open one, and this helps to explain
why, when the impact of Luther's protest began to make itself
felt in England, the foreign residents of the capital were
amongst the first to respond. The constant interchange of
merchants and craftsmen between England and the cities of
northern Europe meant that the foreigners settled in London
quickly learned of the new ideas circulating abroad, and the
English authorities were soon faced with worrying manifesta-

[28] *London and Middlesex Chantry Certificates, 1548*, ed. C. J. Kitching (London Record
Society, 16, 1980). For a more detailed explanation of these calculations see my short
note, 'The Foreign population of London in 1549', *HS*, 24, no. 2 (1984), 141–6.

tions of sympathy for the new heresies. In 1522 Wolsey's commissioners examined Adam Dolveyn, a Dutchman, who acknowledged responsibility for the publication of a book with notes by the Dutch spiritualist thinker Cornelius Hoen. Dolveyn was forced to abjure again in 1526 when he was found in possession of Luther's works in Dutch translation.[29] Foreigners also played an important role in the dissemination of heretical ideas amongst the English population, particularly through their trade in forbidden books. In 1526 an Englishman, John Pykas, confessed to having bought Tyndale's New Testament from a Lombard in London, and two years later another arrested reformer claimed to have been offered two hundred copies of an English Testament by a Dutchman in the city. Tyndale's first patron Humphrey Monmouth also later confessed to having made use of a member of London's foreign community, in this case a sympathetic merchant of the Steelyard, to send money to the reformer.[30]

By the end of the 1520s the English authorities were making strenuous efforts to stem the flow of Protestant literature into the capital, and the Hanse merchants, many of whom came from cities which went over to the Reformation during these years, did not escape unscathed. In 1526 Wolsey, alerted by the abrupt discontinuation of the regular Mass celebrated by the Hanse merchants in their local parish church, bore down on the Steelyard to investigate. Four merchants admitted to having brought in Lutheran books and submitted to correction, and the following year two of the German merchants were forced to abjure and do penance alongside Robert Barnes in St Paul's.[31] The Steelyard was raided on two further occasions in 1527 by Chancellor More, again on the lookout for Lutheran books, but thereafter the merchants were left largely undisturbed. Once the King had embarked on his divorce proceedings the possibility always existed that he would be forced to turn to the German Lutherans for support, and even the conservative reaction of Henry's last years brought no recurrence of government interference.

---

[29] *L & P*, iii (ii).823, iv (ii).1481; John F. Davis, *Heresy and Reformation in the South-East of England, 1520–1559* (1983), p. 44.

[30] Davis, op. cit., pp. 58, 59, 64.

[31] *L & P*, iv (i). 1962; Davis, op. cit., p. 46.

By this time there were in any case more worrying manifestations of heresy amongst London's foreign residents than the
discreet Lutheran sympathies of the Hanse merchants. About
1532 anabaptist heresies made their first appearance in England, and by 1535 the authorities were sufficiently alarmed by
the growing numbers of sectaries in the capital to take drastic
action. A proclamation in March ordered all foreign sectaries
to leave the realm within twelve days on pain of death, and
when in June twenty-five members of an anabaptist cell in the
capital were apprehended all those who refused to recant their
errors were executed.[32] All the victims of this repression were
Dutch, and during these years anabaptist heresies remained
largely confined to the immigrant community. That the
English authorities were seriously concerned at the extent of
sectarian support is certain enough: in the spring of 1535 the
conduct of the rulers of the anabaptist 'kingdom' of Münster
had scandalized even the Protestant princes of northern Germany, and after the fall of the city in June it was rumoured
that many of the surviving anabaptists were planning to take
refuge in England.[33] The flurry of activity in 1535 did not in
the event signal the start of a sustained campaign against the
foreign sectaries in London. A new spate of rumour provoked
a second proclamation and a commission to search out anabaptists in 1538, but the achievements of the commission were
modest: four Dutchmen burned in 1538 and two who died in
1540 (together with one Englishman) were the last anabaptist
victims of the reign.[34]

Much as one may pity the wretched individuals who fell
victim to these proceedings, there is no evidence that the
sporadic repression of Henry's reign acted as much of a deter-
rent to foreign Protestants who contemplated taking refuge in
England. Persecution, such as it was, was much less severe
than on the Continent: in Amsterdam, for instance, no fewer
than 157 were executed in 1535 in the wake of an abortive
rising in support of the anabaptists in Münster, and many

[32] *Tudor Royal Proclamations*, i. 227; I. B. Horst, *The Radical Brethren* (Nieuwkoop,
1972), pp. 37–95.

[33] Horst, op. cit. p.71.

[34] *Tudor Royal Proclamations*, i. 270; Horst, op. cit., pp. 85–93.

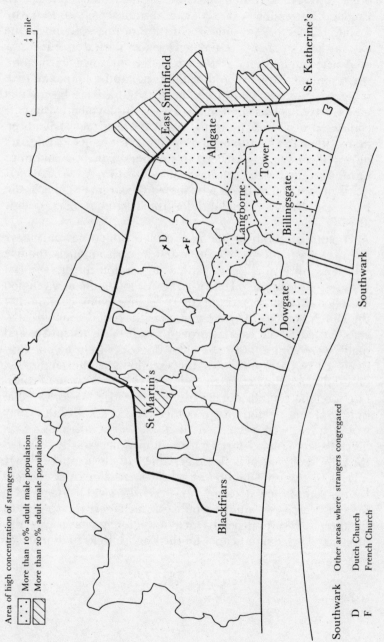

The Distribution of London's Foreign Population in 1550.

Area of high concentration of strangers

More than 10% adult male population

More than 20% adult male population

Southwark Other areas where strangers congregated

D Dutch Church
F French Church

East Smithfield

Aldgate

Langborne

Tower

Billingsgate

St. Katherine's

Southwark

Dowgate

St Martin's

Blackfriars

0   ¼ mile

other towns took similar measures against the sectaries.[35] In England repression was too arbitrary and sporadic to create a similar effect. A graphic illustration of this is found in the extraordinary career of Gualter Delenus, Professor of Hebrew at Amsterdam, who was forced to flee the town in 1535 on suspicion of complicity in the failed anabaptist coup, and took refuge in England. Far from being troubled for his radical views, Delenus was soon in the king's employment, where he continued until the end of the reign.[36] There must have been many other less distinguished foreign Protestants in England during these years who were able to pursue their occupations untroubled by lay or ecclesiastical authorities. As we shall see, a fair proportion of those who joined the stranger churches in 1550 had lived in England for the best part of a decade already.[37]

To sum up, both orthodox Protestant doctrines and more radical views had made substantial inroads amongst the five thousand or so foreigners settled in London during the last decades of the reign of Henry VIII. Although the new religion attracted little support from the Italian merchant community, the Dutch and North German merchants and the foreign arti-sans settled in the capital proved much more receptive, and many were committed to the new doctrines from a compara-tively early date. Yet with the exception of the anabaptist group dispersed in 1535, there is no evidence that the Protes-tant foreigners made any attempt to meet together for worship during Henry's reign, nor was there any possibility that they would have been permitted to do so. The gathering of an officially recognized foreign community necessarily awaited the radical change of policy that came with the death of Henry VIII and the introduction of a Protestant church settlement by his son. When it came, however, the establishment of a foreign church community would be much more than a reward for the patience and persistence of the foreigners; it was also an event of some significance for the English Reformation itself.

[35] Horst, op. cit., p. 73.
[36] See below, p. 50.
[37] Below, p. 81.

II

The Foundation of the Stranger Churches

THE death of Henry VIII in January 1547 aroused widespread expectation, both in England and on the Continent, of the introduction of a Protestant Reformation. Government was soon firmly in the hands of the young King's uncle, the Protector Somerset, and an initial relaxation of the repressive penal statutes of the late King was accompanied by clear indications that the regime would favour the new religion.[1] Foreign Protestants settled in the capital were soon aware of the more favourable climate of opinion, and from early in the reign a steady flow of new refugees testified to England's fast-growing reputation as a safe and hospitable refuge. The accession of Edward VI came at a timely moment for the international Protestant community. Since making peace in 1544 both Francis I and Charles V had intensified persecution of reformers in their lands, and the death of Francis in March 1547 brought no respite for French Protestants; under the new king, Henry II, the persecution reached its climax with the promulgation of a series of new edicts against heresy and the creation of the notorious *chambre ardente*.[2] In the Netherlands the repression of 1544–5 dealt the small Protestant communities a blow from which a decade later they had hardly recovered.[3] When, in April 1547, the Emperor Charles V inflicted a decisive defeat on the League of Protestant Princes at Mühlberg, it seemed that even in Germany the Protestant cause was under serious threat.[4] Small wonder that beleaguered Continental reformers followed events in England with keen interest, and that

[1] W. K. Jordan, *Edward VI: The Young King* (1968), pp. 155–81.
[2] R. J. Knecht, *Francis I* (Cambridge, 1982), pp. 404 ff.; N. M. Sutherland, *The Huguenot Struggle for Recognition* (1980), pp. 36–44; F. C. Spooner, 'The Reformation in Difficulties', in *New Cambridge Modern History*, ii (1958), pp. 221–4.
[3] J. Decavele, *De Dageraad van de Reformatie in Vlaanderen* (Brussels, 1975), i. 322, 433–4; Van Schelven, *Vluchtelingenkerken*, pp. 4–11, 22–3.
[4] Franz Lau and Ernst Bizer, *A History of the Reformation in Germany* (1969), pp. 201 ff.

increasing numbers of more humble Protestants sought safety across the Channel.

Encouraged by their reception and by the growing evidence of widespread sympathy for the new religion in the capital, groups of foreigners probably began to meet together for worship on an informal basis from early in the reign. By the end of 1548 they were sufficiently confident of their position to embark on the organization of a formal church community. In December of that year the exiled Italian reformer Bernardino Ochino was persuaded to write on behalf of the 'Germans' in the capital to invite the distinguished German minister Wolfgang Musculus, then in exile in Zurich, to come to London as their minister.[5] In the event Musculus proved reluctant to abandon Germany, so that the refugees were still searching for a suitable minister in the summer of 1549 when they turned to Martin Bucer for assistance. Bucer in turn referred the problem to Albert Hardenberg in Bremen, and from his letter it is clear that although, as Ochino had informed Musculus, there were now as many as five thousand 'Germans' in the capital, the refugee congregation was about six or eight hundred strong. The specification that the minister should speak 'the language of Brabant' reveals that this was a community of refugees from the Netherlands, rather than Germans in the modern sense.[6]

Although a permanent minister had still not materialized, by the summer of 1549 the Dutch exiles in the capital were clearly gathering together for worship on a regular basis. Both Paul Fagius in April and Francis Dryander in June remarked on the existence of a 'German' church in letters to friends abroad.[7] By the end of the year the French-speaking refugees had also organized some sort of a community. In August 1549 Bucer and three other leading foreign theologians in England petitioned the Privy Council on their behalf.[8] Both congregations, however, still lacked both suitable buildings in which to meet and official recognition: the foundation of a formal church with the privilege of worship by its own liturgy was

[5] *OL*, i. 336.
[6] *OL*, ii. 539–40.
[7] G. C. Gorham, *Gleanings of a few scattered ears during the period of the Reformation in England, 1533–1588* (1857), p. 78; *OL*, i. 352.
[8] J. Strype, *Memorials of Archbishop Cranmer* (Oxford, 1848–54), iii. 697.

achieved only in the summer of 1550.[9] Although in the latter
half of 1549 the foreign refugees pressed confidently on with
the organization of their communities, it was by no means a
matter of course that the privilege of separate worship would
be granted, and a powerful faction within the hierarchy of the
new English Church remained resolutely opposed to the concession. By the time of the official foundation of the foreign
churches in 1550 the strangers' cause had in fact become bound
up with far more fundamental issues, concerning not only their
own privileges, but also the whole nature of the Protestant
Reformation in England. Specifically, the events surrounding
the foundation of the stranger churches in 1550 can be seen
as part of a concerted effort to effect a substantial revision of
the 1549 Prayer Book, and introduce into England a radical
Reformed polity on the Swiss model. To see why this should
be so it is necessary to turn back and consider the progress of
the English Reformation in the years before the churches'
foundation.

Foreign theologians had from the beginning of the reign
played an important role in events as the new government set
about the institution of a Protestant form of worship. They
found in England a generous patron in the Archbishop of
Canterbury, Thomas Cranmer, who, freed from the patient
discretion imposed upon him whilst Henry VIII still lived,
now revealed himself as a committed Protestant. To Cranmer,
the difficulties experienced by Protestants abroad represented
something of an opportunity. In particular, as the Protestant
free cities of Germany reluctantly recognized the implications
of the Emperor's victory at Mühlberg and accepted the
Augsburg Interim, Cranmer saw his chance both to offer England as a refuge for the distinguished reformers hounded out

[9] In the first period of their existence the French and Dutch congregations were
part of one foundation and technically one church; the correspondence of the reformers
at this time usually refers to a singular 'stranger church'. But although Lasco was
superintendent of both communities and they shared a common liturgy, the French
and Dutch congregations used separate buildings from the outset and had their own
ministers and consistory: to all intents and purposes they were from the start two
churches, as they officially became after 1559. Here the correct singular form will be
used in discussing the establishment in 1550 and describing common institutions in
Ch. III, but otherwise the two communities will generally be treated as separate
churches.

of their pulpits and, at the same time, to harness the best brains to the task of creating a Protestant state in England. Throughout 1547 and 1548 he worked assiduously to bring about a cherished scheme of his, a conference in England to unite the Protestant confessions through the establishment of a core of agreed doctrine, and in particular to settle the vexed question of the Lord's Supper.[10] Both Melanchthon in Wittenberg and Calvin in Geneva responded somewhat equivocally to Cranmer's invitation and the plan came to nothing, but England's obvious attractiveness both as a refuge and as a new field for reforming endeavour outside the hardening lines of division in Germany brought several front-rank reformers to England: Peter Martyr and Bernardino Ochino in 1547, Francis Dryander, and for a short time, John a Lasco in 1548, and most important, after Strasburg's acceptance of the Interim in 1549, Martin Bucer and Paul Fagius.

The terms in which Cranmer expressed his aims seemed to justify the hopes of those who looked for the speedy institution of a radically reformed liturgy and church order in England. In 1548, for example, Cranmer had written to John a Lasco: 'We are desirous of setting forth in our churches the true doctrine of God, and have no wish to adapt it to all tastes, or to deal in ambiguities; but laying aside all carnal considerations, to transmit to posterity a true and explicit form of doctrine agreeable to the rule of the sacred writings.'[11] His progress towards this end was watched with particular concern by Henry Bullinger, Zwingli's successor at Zurich and the leading figure in the Swiss Reformation. Bullinger's importance amongst the second generation leaders of the reformation has been somewhat obscured for historians by the subsequent emergence of Calvin and Geneva as a major international force. But in 1547 Calvin was still very much preoccupied with domestic problems, whereas Bullinger was already a reformer of considerable international reputation and stature.[12]

---

[10] Cranmer's letters to Continental reformers in *OL*, i. 16–22. See also Lasco to Hardenberg, 19 July 1548; Gorham, *Gleanings*, p. 52.

[11] *OL*, i. 17.

[12] André Bouvier, *Henri Bullinger . . . le successeur de Zwingli* (Paris, 1940), p. 35. On Calvin's problems at Geneva see G. R. Potter and Mark Greengrass, *John Calvin* (1983), pp. 85–91; E. W. Monter, *Calvin's Geneva* (New York, 1967), pp. 65–92.

A loyal band of former pupils and friends kept Bullinger closely in touch with events in England, and the Zurich reformer exercised a powerful influence over the subsequent course of events.

To Bullinger and his associates the 1549 Prayer Book was a grave disappointment. Cranmer's bold words to Lasco may well have represented his genuine aims at this time, but the English government had to face the political reality of a still largely conservative nation and the real risk that rapid progress towards Protestantism would provoke an angry reaction from the Emperor.[13] Bullinger's correspondents had some appreciation of the constraints that held the English government back, but could find little good to say about the 1549 Order. The Prayer Book did mark a decisive shift towards a Protestant form of worship, but this was obscured by a pervasive discretion which left ambiguity and an air of compromise. The Book retained many of the trappings of the old Mass, such as the canon, traditional vestments, the altar, candles, chrism, and a prayer for the dead, but, worst in the eyes of the reformers, a form of words was retained in the central communion order which might carry an interpretation of a real presence in the sacraments: 'whosoever shall be partakers of this holy communion, may worthily receive the most precious body and blood of thy son Jesus Christ'.[14] The guarded hopes of many reformers soon turned to outright criticism of the book. In March 1549 Francis Dryander lamented that 'some puerilities have still been suffered to remain' in the planned order, but expressed confidence that they would soon be amended. Of the end result he could only say 'the book speaks very obscurely', with 'great absurdity'.[15] To the urgent reformers of Zurich this was hardly the true, explicit, and unambiguous doctrine Cranmer had promised.

Bullinger's correspondents in England were inclined to blame the disappointment of their hopes on the foreign theologians closest to Cranmer at this time, principally Peter Martyr and Martin Bucer. In reporting the introduction of the Prayer

---

[13] M. L. Bush, *The Government Policy of Protector Somerset* (1975), pp. 119–23.
[14] *First and Second Prayer Books of Edward VI* (Everyman's Library, 1913), p. 223.
[15] *OL*, i. 350–1.

Book to Bullinger the English merchant Richard Hilles lamented that the English authorities were not as yet inclined to adopt the Zurich rites for the administration of the sacraments, and then added significantly: 'nor do I doubt but that master Martin Bucer and the other learned men from Germany and Italy ... teach ... that there is no occasion for it, and perhaps even, that it is not becoming'.[16]

In focusing their resentments on Martyr and Bucer the Zurich faction misunderstood and misrepresented the position of the two reformers on the 1549 Prayer Book. Peter Martyr, a distinguished Italian refugee whom Cranmer had established in 1547 as Regius Professor at Oxford, believed in 1550 that many things still remained to be done. He regretted that the worldly prudence of some was putting obstacles in the way of further reform and in a black moment could write that very little in religion had so far been accomplished.[17] Bucer too would provide an extensive list of criticisms of the 1549 Prayer Book at Cranmer's request, many of which were reflected in the changes effected by the 1552 Book.[18] In 1549 Martyr and Bucer were distinguished from the Zurichers rather by their readiness to accept the politic considerations that caused the English government to proceed with caution than by an enthusiastic acceptance of the theology of the 1549 Book. Nevertheless important theological points were at issue between them and the more radical Swiss. Martyr, after five years as his guest in Strasburg, probably accepted Bucer's eucharistic doctrine in 1547, and Bucer was a resolute defender of a sacramental Real Presence.[19] Bucer's determined efforts to effect a compromise between the Lutherans and the Swiss reformers had earned him the suspicions of both parties, and the ambiguities of his own views caused him to be distrusted not only by Bullinger, but also by the personally more sympathetic Calvin.[20] His resolute opposition to the sacramental

---

[16] *OL*, i. 266.

[17] *OL*, ii. 478, 481–2, 485.

[18] C. Hopf, *Martin Bucer and the English Reformation* (Oxford, 1946), pp. 55–98.

[19] Hopf, ibid. pp. 41–51. Bucer to Calvin, August 1549, Gorham, *Gleanings*, pp. 99–108. Martyr would later come round to a view of the Eucharist much nearer to that of the Swiss reformers. See his letter to Bullinger, Jan. 1550, *OL*, ii. 478.

[20] Calvin to Farel, July 1550: 'I have heard nothing of Bucer except that he seems rather pliant to some. . . . Whether he affords any occasion for [this prejudice] or

symbolism of Zurich doctrine, which laid stress on the Communion as a memorial and the bread and wine as seals of God's promise, brought him an antipathy which bordered on vituperation from Bullinger's admirers in England, and when Strasburg's submission to the Emperor made Bucer's departure from the City inevitable the Zurichers watched his movements with increasing alarm. Cranmer, blithely unconcerned by the divisions between the continental theologians he admired, was quick to invite Bucer and his loyal lieutenant Paul Fagius to England. 'Bucer and Fagius have been dismissed', reported one of Bullinger's correspondents in Strasburg; 'may the Lord preserve our England from both of them.'[21] Within one month, however, both were in England. In April 1549 Hooper reported 'Peter Martyr and Bernardine so stoutly defend Lutheranism, and there is now arrived a third, (I mean Bucer) who will leave no stone unturned to obtain a footing.' By the end of the month Hooper was gloomily convinced that Cranmer was acting under Bucer's influence.[22]

Running through much of this correspondence is the unflattering assumption that Cranmer had no fixed doctrinal views and was susceptible to the nearest influence: Bullinger's correspondents chronicle with extreme care who was at Lambeth, when.[23] No doubt this did Cranmer a grave injustice; Cranmer's profound grasp of the theological issues of the day has been amply demonstrated by modern scholarship, and it is now evident that Cranmer already inclined to a distinctly Reformed sacramental doctrine by 1549.[24] But this was far from obvious from the 1549 Prayer Book, and for those of Bullinger's supporters dissatisfied with the Book and distrustful of the Archbishop the way forward was clear: Zurich must

---

not, I cannot tell'. *Letters of John Calvin*, ed. J. Bonnet (Edinburgh, 1855–7), ii. 262–3, *CO*, xiii. 605. See also Calvin to Bucer, Oct. 1549, Gorham, *Gleanings*, p. 117. On Bucer's ecumenical efforts see Heinrich Bornkamm, 'Martin Bucer, der dritte deutsche Reformator' in *Das Jahrhundert der Reformation* (Göttingen, 1966), 88–112.

[21] *OL*, ii. 651.

[22] *OL*, i. 61, 64.

[23] The *Original Letters* contain thirty-five references to Cranmer. See C. H. Smyth, *Cranmer and the Reformation under Edward VI* (Cambridge, 1926), pp. 49–50.

[24] Peter Brooks, *Thomas Cranmer's Doctrine of the Eucharist* (1965), pp. 38–60.

have its own men close to the centre of power. Central to this design were John Hooper and John a Lasco. Heralded by the Zurichers as the 'Future Zwingli of England', Hooper was the leading English disciple of the Swiss Reformation.[25] His outspoken Reformed views had forced him to leave England in 1544 and during his five-year exile Hooper had become a confirmed exponent of the austere doctrine and liturgy of Zurich, with its exclusion of altars, images, and church music. Hooper did not make an immediate return to England on Edward's accession, preferring to promote the Zurich Reformation in print whilst remaining in the city, and his English friends became increasingly impatient for the return of such a 'true friend of the liberties of the church and commonwealth of Zurich, and their defender from every calumny'.[26] Hooper finally returned to England in May 1549 and immediately became a figure of great influence. His London sermons and lectures drew large and enthusiastic crowds and the Protector, to whom Hooper had shrewdly dedicated one of his Zurich works, the *Declaration of Christ and his Office*, took him into his household.[27] The fall of Somerset brought hardly a check to Hooper's progress; the Earl of Warwick also seemed keen to advance him and he quickly won the confidence of the young King. By the spring of 1550 Hooper was fast becoming the most influential cleric at Court.

Hooper, in his turn, was equally urgent in his hopes that John a Lasco would soon return to England.[28] Lasco, who seems to have exerted a strong influence on everyone who came into contact with him, was a firm if somewhat independent admirer of Bullinger and Zurich.[29] He had been one of the leading foreign theologians to respond to Cranmer's invitation to England in 1548 but had returned to his post at Emden early in 1549. By 1550, however, it was clear that Emden would no longer resist the imposition of the Interim,

---

[25] There is no biography of Hooper. See Smyth, *Cranmer and the Reformation*, pp. 95–9; *DNB*, xxvii. 304–6.

[26] Dryander to Bullinger, 25 Mar. 1549, *OL*, i. 350. The description was Stumphius's, *OL*, ii. 462. For Hooper's works printed in Zurich (*STC* 13741, 13745, 13746) see *Early Writings of Bishop Hooper* (Parker Society, 1843), pp. 1–430.

[27] Bush, *Protector Somerset*, p. 108.

[28] Hooper to Bullinger, 26 Apr. 1549, *OL*, i. 61.

[29] See below, pp. 48, 70.

and Lasco turned once more towards England. He arrived in May, and immediately threw himself with energy into the strangers' affairs. Already in the spring of 1550 the stranger community had made a formal approach to the government for the provision of buildings in which they might worship. The petition was presented by Francis Bertie, a prominent member of the stranger merchant community, who had enlisted the aid of the Duchess of Suffolk and the King's two schoolmasters, Cooke and Cheke.[30] According to Ruytinck, the first historian of the Dutch community, the decision was taken to hand the former church of the Austin Friars over to the strangers, but when Lasco returned to England this had not been done. Rumours were rife that Lasco would be the superintendent of a new foreign church, but in June Martin Micron was still preaching to the Dutch congregation in a private house.[31]

On his arrival in England Lasco went straight to Lambeth, where he remained close to Cranmer during the crucial weeks leading up to the grant of the church. On 1 June Peter Martyr noted that Lasco was living with the archbishop and was aware that he would most likely preside over the Dutch church, and the next week Martin Faber recorded having met Lasco at Lambeth and having engaged him in a friendly debate over sacramental doctrine.[32] By the end of the month Lasco was confident of success. On 25 June he wrote to Bucer anticipating that the business of the church would soon be concluded, and on 29 June the grant of Austin Friars to the strangers was recorded in the King's Journal.[33] The charter which confirmed Lasco's superintendency and named the church's first ministers followed a month later, on 24 July.[34]

These were stirring times for John Hooper also. In February 1550 he had been appointed to preach the Lenten sermons

[30] Lindeboom, *Austin Friars*, p. 6, quoting Symeon Ruytinck, *Gheschiedenissen ende Handelingen die voornemelick aengaen de Nederduytsche Natie*, ed. J. J. van Toorenenbergen (Marnix Society, Series III, Part I, 1873), p. 12.

[31] Utenhove to Bullinger, 29 June 1550, in F. Pijper, *Jan Utenhove* (Leiden, 1883), appendix, p. lxviii. Utenhove reported that Micron was preaching 'inter privatos parietes'.

[32] *OL*, ii. 483; Gorham, *Gleanings*, pp. 149–50.

[33] Gorham, *Gleanings*, pp. 156–7; *Chronicle and Political Papers of King Edward VI*, ed. W. K. Jordan (1966), p. 37.

[34] The Charter is printed in Lindeboom, *Austin Friars*, pp. 198–203.

before the King and Court, and took the opportunity to make swingeing criticism of the clerical vestments retained in the Prayer Book and the oath prescribed by the Ordinal.[35] Hooper's remarks brought down upon him the wrath of Archbishop Cranmer, but no action was taken until Hooper's appointment to a bishopric in May brought matters to a head. Hooper refused to be consecrated in the prescribed vestments and so declined the appointment. Such a refusal was an offence against the Act of Uniformity and Hooper was summoned before the Privy Council. To the surprise of his own supporters Hooper emerged victorious and on 15 May was granted permission to be consecrated without the offensive vestments.[36] His fellow bishops were appalled, and sharply contested the decision. Whilst Lasco pursued the interests of the strangers at Lambeth, Hooper defended his position at Court, and two months later, on 23 July, secured a reaffirmation of the Council's decision in his favour.

Close attention to the chronology and events of the months which saw the emergence of the stranger church suggest two important observations about the circumstances of its foundation. The first is the significance of Lasco's contribution to the negotiation. The strangers had had powerful advocates at Court before, but with Lasco established close to Cranmer, he was able to secure not only the grant of Austin Friars already mooted, but also a charter which confirmed his own superintendency and an important measure of freedom from outside interference for the church. Both represented important victories for the Zurich faction, as not only they recognized: Bucer too had seen that the issue of who led the strangers in London might have a much wider impact than merely on the community itself. In August 1549 he had been invited to help provide a minister for the gathering Dutch community, and in a letter to Hardenberg had expressed the hope that someone might be found who agreed with him on Eucharistic doctrine. 'If the brother whom you may send', he wrote, 'is in the habit of explaining the Mystery of the Eucharist in the

---

[35] The best reconstruction of these events is J. H. Primus, *The Vestments Controversy* (Kampen, 1960), pp. 5–12. See also John Opie, 'The Anglicising of John Hooper', *Archiv für Reformationsgeschichte*, 59 (1968), 150–77.

[36] Primus, *Vestments Controversy*, p. 11; *APC*, iii. 31.

words of Scripture, he will be the more acceptable on this account, as acknowledging that the Lord gives himself to us in the Eucharist . . . I could wish such a one to be sent as would have at heart a reverence for the Mysteries, without which discipline and communion of the brethren in Christ cannot be restored.'[37] Bucer, however, missed his chance, and by the spring of 1550 he sensed that the tide was moving against him. Under persistent attack from the Zurichers he became exasperated and morose, and his letters to Calvin are full of plaintive complaints against those who accused him of being too pliant.[38] 'The Zurich people', he wrote in April, 'have here many and great followers.'[39] Lasco's return in May clinched the issue of who would lead the Church.

If Lasco's influence exercised a decisive effect, so too did the parallel progress of Hooper's cause. The emergence of the stranger church coincided with the highest point of Hooper's precarious triumph in the Council, and there can be no doubt that Hooper's agitation for consecration on his own terms and the establishment of the stranger church were closely connected. Hooper took a lively interest in the strangers' petition, and as his cause prospered so too did theirs. By the end of June both seemed to have prevailed. On 29 June, the same day that the grant of the stranger church was concluded, Hooper reported to Bullinger his own apparent success: he had been able to take his bishopric on terms which freed him from the defilement of all superstition.[40] By the first week in July both Hooper and Lasco had received Letters Patent for their new offices, Hooper as Bishop of Gloucester and Lasco as superintendent of the foreign churches.[41] Hooper's opponents rallied to have him called before the Council on 20 July, but he was once again triumphant: after a personal intervention by the King, Northumberland instructed Cranmer on 23 July to permit Hooper to be consecrated on his own terms.[42] The strangers received their charter securing the liberties of their church the next day.

[37] Gorham, *Gleanings*, p. 121.
[38] Calvin to Farel, 19 Aug. 1550, *Letters of Calvin*, ii. 267.
[39] Gorham, *Gleanings*, p. 142.
[40] *OL*, i. 86–90.
[41] On 27 June and 3 July. Rymer, *Foedera*, xv. 238, 240.
[42] Primus, *Vestments Controversy*, pp. 11–12.

Hooper had not been too preoccupied with his own affairs to involve himself directly in the strangers' petition. Early in June he had met Lasco and twelve leading members of the Dutch community for a conference which lasted all day.[43] The first ministers of the Church were a tightly-knit group, and Hooper was already well acquainted with most of them. Lasco himself was a personal friend, as was his loyal lieutenant Jan Utenhove, and the Dutch minister, Martin Micron. Micron had studied with Hooper in Zurich, and lived for a time in his house in London. One of the French ministers, Vauville, had recently married the maid of Hooper's wife.[44] The appointment of Vauville, along with Perussel (a former associate of Utenhove from the Canterbury community), to minister to the French congregation is probably the clearest indication of Hooper's involvement and influence, as there were other, rather more distinguished, French ministers in London at the time who might reasonably have expected the appointment.[45] In the summer of 1550 Hooper's influence was at its zenith, and it seemed for a moment as if his agitation for a radical revision of the 1549 Prayer Book might carry all before it. 'Never before in our time', wrote Richard Hilles at the end of June, 'has there been such hope of the advancement of the pure doctrine of the gospel, and of the complete subversion and rooting up of antichristian ceremonies and traditions.'[46]

It is important to understand the heady atmosphere of June 1550 when considering the remarkable freedom granted the strangers to regulate their own affairs. Their leaders freely confessed that this was greater than they had either asked or dared hope for.[47] The charter laid down that 'There may be by the ministers of the Church of the Germans and other

---

[43] Hessels, ii. 29–31.

[44] See below, pp. 49–54.

[45] Peter Alexander, the former chaplain to the Queen of Hungary had preached to the French congregation and was involved in the petition on their behalf. See below, p. 36. Valérand Poullain was in London and without employment. K. Bauer, *Valérand Poullain* (Elberfeld, 1927), p. 132. The French minister John Veron was also in England, and not yet rector of St Alphage, Cripplegate. *DNB*, xx. 283; Philippe Denis, 'John Veron: the First Known French Protestant in England', *HS*, 22 (1970–6), 257–63.

[46] *OL*, i. 269.

[47] Utenhove to Calvin, 23 Aug. 1550, *CO*, xiii. 628–9; Pijper, *Utenhove*, pp. 64–6; Lindeboom, *Austin Friars*, p. 7.

foreigners, an uncorrupt interpretation of the most Holy Gospel and administration of the sacraments according to the word of God and apostolic observance'.[48] It was certain that this uncorrupt interpretation would be modelled on the Continental church with which Lasco was most in sympathy, that of Zurich.[49] Most important of all was the freedom from interference by the English authorities which was granted to the strangers. The Mayor, bishops, and judges were all enjoined to permit them 'freely and quietly to practice, enjoy, use, and exercise their own rites and ceremonies and their own peculiar ecclesiastical discipline, notwithstanding that they do not conform with the rites and ceremonies used in our kingdom, without impeachment, disturbance, or vexation of any of them.'[50]

The charter in effect anticipated, in the midst of an English Church still only partially reformed, a radical Protestant community whch by its very existence would serve as a constant spur to further reform in the English Church itself. As Lasco was later to write, 'We thought in effect that encouraged by this example the English Churches themselves would be aroused to return to the apostolic worship in all its purity.'[51] Small wonder that Hooper interested himself so much in the strangers' cause: the establishment of a model Reformed community and his own struggle against the clerical vestments were essentially two aspects of the same effort, to free the English Church from the vestiges of popery and urge it towards a more complete Reformation. It was largely because the opponents of their endeavours could also recognize the connection that the early months of the new Church would be so fraught with difficulty.

If the strangers were astonished at the independence granted them by their charter, they might equally have remarked the generosity of the grant by which the church was established. Lasco's patent granted him the substantial salary of £100 per annum to be paid by the English government.[52] The grant of

---

[48] Lindeboom, *Austin Friars*, p. 201.

[49] See below, pp. 68–71.

[50] Lindeboom, *Austin Friars*, p. 202.

[51] Lasco to the King of Poland, 6 Sept. 1555. *Lasco Opera*, ii. 10. Quoted in F. A. Norwood, 'The Strangers' "Model Churches" in Sixteenth Century England', in *Reformation Studies*, ed. F. H. Littell (Richmond, Va., 1962), 184.

[52] *Cal. Pat. Rolls Edward VI*, iii. 316; Rymer, *Foedera*, xv. 238.

the church of Austin Friars was also a very considerable gift, enhanced by the Council's undertaking to see to its repair before it was handed over. The Austin Friars, rebuilt in 1354 on the site of an original foundation of 1253, was the largest friary church in England.[53] It was the centre of a large complex of buildings and possessed a fine steeple; its numerous monuments had earned it the title of the Westminster Abbey of the City. On the dissolution of the priory in 1538 much of the site had been granted out to courtiers, but the main body of the church remained empty until the nave and aisles were granted to the strangers in 1550.[54] The community was in addition granted the use of the churchyard and two houses in the precincts for its ministers.[55] Austin Friars was an appropriate as well as a generous gift; the most cosmopolitan of the religious houses, it had long been a meeting-place for the stranger merchant community, and still had a room known as Lumbardshall.[56] The grant of such a large and prominent city church was an ostentatious gesture of goodwill towards the stranger community, and a measure of the favour they enjoyed in these months.

Austin Friars was originally intended for all the strangers, but it quickly became clear that this would prove an inconvenient arrangement. During the negotiations for the establishment of the church the French community had had to take a less prominent role than their Dutch brethren, as until March 1550 England and France were at war. The French had to be watchful that their interests were not forgotten. Lasco had much closer links with the Dutch community, and according to a later account the French were indebted to Peter Alexander, the distinguished French exile and pensioner of Cranmer, who managed to insert a mention of 'other foreigners' into the draft

---

[53] The following remarks are based on J. T. C. Van Dulken, *The Dutch Church, Austin Friars*, pamphlet in the Guildhall Library (pam. 4206); Lindeboom, *Austin Friars*, pp. 11–13. See also J. Stow, *Survey of London*, ed. C. L. Kingsford (Oxford, 1971), i. 177.

[54] Although the City had attempted to buy the church, offering a thousand marks for the property in 1539. (Van Dulken, op. cit.)

[55] Ruytinck, *Gheschiedenissen*, p. 32.

[56] Thrupp, 'Aliens in London', 263. Many of the Flemings murdered by the peasants in 1381 had sought sanctuary in Austin Friars, but were dragged out and butchered. Dobson, *Peasants' Revolt*, p. 175.

petition on behalf of the Dutch.[57] When it became apparent that Austin Friars could not in fact accommodate both Dutch and French communities, a solution to the problem was worked out at a conference of twelve representatives of each congregation at Lasco's house in Bow Lane. The strangers sought and obtained permission from the Privy Council to rent the former hospital of St Anthony on Threadneedle Street from the Dean and Chapter of Windsor, and Austin Friars was then resigned to the Dutch on condition that they would share the rent and the cost of repairing St Anthony's for the use of the French. This was only fair as Austin Friars was handed over as a gift fully repaired, whereas the Chapel of St Anthony, unused since 1543, was in a dilapidated state.[58]

The lease for the French church was signed on 16 October, but by that time the stranger community was already experiencing serious problems. It soon became clear that the liberties granted to the strangers in their charter would not easily be secured in practice. A first note of alarm appeared in Micron's letter to Bullinger reporting the establishment of the church. 'Some of the bishops, and especially the Bishop of London', he wrote, 'are opposed to our design; but I hope their opposition will be ineffectual.'[59]

The strangers were initially surprised and puzzled by the opposition of Nicholas Ridley, Bishop of London. A sincere and conscientious reformer, Ridley had been frequently commended by Bullinger's correspondents for his zealous stewardship of his diocese.[60] For an explanation of Ridley's hostility, however, one need look no further than his resolute opposition to Hooper on the issue of vestments, for Ridley's opposition to Hooper was based on a point of principle that could equally well embrace the stranger church. Ridley argued that if the vestments were things indifferent (as Hooper had acknowledged in the Council meeting of 15 May) then they might properly be retained and enforced by church and state. It was essentially an argument that the church had the right

---

[57] *Actes II*, p. 108.

[58] Ibid. G. B. Beeman, 'The Early History of the Strangers' Church, 1550–1561', *HS*, 15 (1934–7), 271–2.

[59] *OL*, ii. 568.

[60] *OL*, i. 79, 185, 187–8, 323.

to preserve unity and order against Hooper's defence of the right of the individual conscience. However desirable further change might be towards full reformed simplicity, it was for the church authorities to regulate the change; to allow the claim of the individual to exercise scruples was to open the door to any number of interpretations of biblical instruction, and ultimately (as Ridley was not slow to point out) to the glorious variety of anabaptism.[61]

If Hooper's refusal to accept the prescribed vestments undermined the authority of government to establish a uniform order of religion, so too did a licensed independent church in the heart of Ridley's own diocese.[62] The close association of the strangers' cause with Hooper, so recently a source of strength, soon seemed likely to prove their undoing. Defiantly defending himself in front of the Privy Council, Hooper challenged his opponents to submit to the judgement of the Apostolic Church or present-day churches faithful to the apostolic example.[63] The nearest such church was the community which Lasco was carefully building in conformity to the apostolic model, and such a reminder to Ridley of the stranger church's significance in the present dispute was, to say the least, tactless.

The spectacle of a church established in his diocese yet outside his control may well have spurred Ridley to the resolute opposition he presented to Hooper's stand. Required by Cranmer to consecrate Hooper in accordance with the Council instruction of 24 July, Ridley flatly refused to use any other form of consecration than that prescribed by Parliament.[64] When Hooper returned to the Council and secured a reaffirmation of their instruction Ridley temporized, and then hurried to the Council to put his case in person. This he did so effectively that Hooper, appearing in the Council Chamber in his turn, found that his views were hardly even given a hearing.

---

[61] On the points at issue between Hooper and Ridley see Primus, *Vestments Controversy*, pp. 16–34. The most detailed treatment of adiaphora is Bernard J. Verkamp, *The Indifferent Mean; Adiaphorism in the English Reformation to 1554* (Athens, Ohio, 1977).

[62] Ridley later wrote to Grindal that he would have forced Lasco's church to conform in 1550. *Works of Bishop Ridley* (Parker Society, 1841), p. 534.

[63] Primus, *Vestments Controversy*, p. 31.

[64] This paragraph follows Micron's detailed and accurate summary of events for Bullinger, *OL*, ii. 567.

The tide had turned against him with ominous implications which the strangers were quick to realize.

Micron's letters to Bullinger expressed first frustration, then alarm. By the end of August the community had still not secured possession of Austin Friars. Ironically the very generosity of the bequest proved a source of obstruction and delay, for when Lasco asked for the key to the church to be handed over he was told by the Lord Treasurer, Paulet, that it would reflect dishonourably on the King's gift to hand the church over before the repairs, being undertaken at royal expense, were complete. Lasco suspected a deeper motive for the delay and these suspicions were confirmed when the Lord Treasurer went on to ask why the strangers chose to have different ceremonies from those used by the English Church, since these were not repugnant to the word of God. He concluded by demanding that the foreigners should either adopt the English ceremonies or disprove them.[65]

The strangers thought that the Lord Treasurer had been put up to this by Ridley, and no doubt the arguments were those of the bishops, but Paulet had his own reason to resent the strangers' title to Austin Friars. He had acquired extensive rights in the property since the dissolution of the monasteries and probably had designs also on that part of the building made over to the strangers.[66] Paulet was a dangerous enemy for the strangers, a conservative in religion and influential on the Council, but Lasco managed to overcome his obstruction by acquiring the use of another church until the Austin Friars was grudgingly handed over in December.[67] In the meantime, however, Hooper's cause had taken a decided turn for the worse. After Ridley had been asked to present his case to the Council there were further bitter exchanges in the meeting of 19 October, from which Ridley emerged with the Council's support.[68] This had grave implications for the strangers. 'We have discovered', wrote Micron to Bullinger on the 20th, 'that the whole of the King's council are inclined to side with the bishops in this controversy about the vestments against master

[65] Micron to Bullinger, postscript of 31 Aug. 1550, *OL*, ii. 569.
[66] Lindeboom, *Austin Friars*, p. 13.
[67] *OL*, ii. 570.
[68] Opie, 'Anglicising of John Hooper', 169.

Hooper. In addition to this the privileges of our German church are in the greatest danger. By canvassing and persuasion the bishops have procured from the King's council that we are not to enjoy the free use of the sacraments, but must be fettered by the English ceremonies, which are intolerable to all godly persons.'[69]

Micron's denunciation of the 'intolerable' ceremonies of the English Church illustrates how the struggle against the vestments was becoming increasingly radicalized as both sides became entrenched. Faced with Ridley's argument that if the vestments were indifferent they could legitimately be enforced, Hooper had changed his tack and now condemned the vestments as popish remnants which could in no circumstances be retained.[70] Such an argument might have almost universal application against any institution to which Hooper and his friends objected. The widening implications of the dispute were clearly apparent, but Hooper's intemperance had by now brought general condemnation of his stand. Canvassed by both sides, Peter Martyr and Martin Bucer gave opinions which ultimately defended the right of the civil power to regulate clerical dress.[71] Neither ultimately wished to see the vestments retained, but Bucer in particular was persuaded that Hooper's defiance was a greater evil than the vestments themselves. Cranmer, faced with what was now a major challenge to his authority, was already inclined to back Ridley (as his leading questions to Bucer show), and the lay support that Hooper had enjoyed had dwindled away: crucially, by October Northumberland had lost patience with his tiresome protégé, and urged Hooper to conform for the sake of the unity of the church.[72]

The leaders of the stranger church alone were steadfast in their support for Hooper. Lasco threw himself into the controversy with characteristic energy. During the heated debates of October 1550 he wrote three times to Bucer at Cambridge, suggesting in his first letter that the foreign theologians might

---

[69] *OL*, ii. 573.

[70] Primus, *Vestments Controversy*, p. 18.

[71] Primus, op. cit., pp. 43–59; Hopf, *Bucer*, pp. 131–7.

[72] Primus, op. cit., p. 45; Hopf, *Bucer*, p. 133. Opic, 'Anglicising of John Hooper', 165.

put out a joint statement of opinion on the vestments. On 26 October Lasco had to apologize for assuming Bucer's agreement without consulting him first, but urged Bucer strongly to give Hooper his support. When Bucer in a characteristically long and involved reply rejected Lasco's appeal, Lasco accused him in a third letter of missing the point.[73] Lasco expounded his own view in a treatise in which he argued, as Hooper was now doing, that vestments were not indifferent, and could not be retained in a true Church. His tests of true adiaphora were so strikingly similar to the conditions laid down by Hooper in his notes presented to the Council as to suggest close co-operation between them.[74] Things indifferent, he argued, must be of manifest commodity to the church, grounded in Scripture, and void of tyranny binding mens' consciences. Vestments he excluded on all these grounds as they served only to obscure Christ (and were therefore not of manifest commodity), whereas the example of Christ and his disciples allowed for no distinctions of dress. Against Ridley Lasco argued that an appeal to authority was no legitimate defence of garments as authority could not be invoked to defend a practice harmful to the church.

In addition to this treatise Lasco made a further direct appeal to Cranmer, but his intemperate denunciation of vestments as things brought by Antichrist, not free but utterly intolerable, was hardly likely to win the archbishop's approval, more particularly as Hooper had now moved to outright defiance of the Council.[75] Confined to his house for his refusal to yield, Hooper was forbidden to preach or publish, but he disobeyed in what Peter Martyr described as 'unseasonable and too bitter sermons'. His publication of a defence of his views in December 1550 was the last straw and Hooper was confined to Cranmer's house. Even so Lasco's support was

---

[73] These letters, unknown to Kuyper, are printed in Hopf, *Bucer*, pp. 148–67. The first two are reprinted by J. P. Pollet, *Martin Bucer, Études sur la correspondance* (Paris, 1958), pp. 273–80 with notes and corrections. Bucer's letter to Lasco is printed in Strype, *Eccesiastical Memorials* (Oxford, 1822), II, ii. 444–55.

[74] Lasco's opinion is in *The Fortress of Fathers, ernestly defending the purity of Religion* (Emden, 1566), *STC* 1040. See Primus, *Vestments Controversy*, pp. 37–9. Hooper's notes to the Council are printed in the *Journal of Theological Studies*, 44 (1943), 194–9. See Verkamp, *Indifferent Mean*, pp. 72–5.

[75] Primus, *Vestments Controversy*, pp. 40–3, 60–4.

unwavering, and it seems it may by now have been Lasco, rather than Hooper himself, who was the major obstacle to a settlement. In a revealing letter Peter Martyr described to Bucer a visit he had paid to Hooper whilst Hooper was incarcerated in Cranmer's house at Lambeth.[76] After their first meeting Martyr had some hope of breaking down Hooper's determination, and Hooper asked him to come back after dinner. But in the meantime some other person had access to Hooper, and Martyr on his return found him once more obstinate and defiant. This 'other', whom Martyr describes as 'the leader of the farce', seems to have been Lasco, and reinforced by his persuasions Hooper rebuffed Martyr's pacific urgings at two further conferences.

By now, however, the Council was determined to secure Hooper's compliance and on 27 January 1551 he was confined to the Fleet Prison. It was ordered that he was to be allowed to confer with no one but the ministers of the prison, and, deprived of the sustaining support of his remaining sympathizers, within two weeks Hooper submitted.[77] On 8 March he was finally consecrated. The stranger leaders were loud in their regrets, but from the point of view of their community Hooper's capitulation was timely. In the spring of 1551 food shortages in the capital triggered a wave of anti-stranger feeling and demands for their expulsion. Lasco's uncompromising support for Hooper risked alienating the strangers' remaining friends in the Council and amongst the governors of the city who were their sole protection from this hostility.[78] But Lasco seems to have been impervious to wider considerations of this sort. Even after Hooper's submission he directed another letter to the King castigating the vestments as the whorish trimmings of the papacy.[79] Lasco's contributions to the vestments controversy manifested all the intemperance which made him such an uncomfortable guest throughout his career. Ridley's antipathy, too, was slow to die, and as late as October 1552 Lasco had to appeal to the Council for help against local officials who were trying to force strangers to attend English

[76] Gorham, *Gleanings*, p. 233.

[77] *APC*, iii. 199–200.

[78] See below, p. 83. *Cal. S. P. Span.*, x. 265. Utenhove to Bullinger, 9 Apr. 1551, *OL*, ii. 586.

[79] Strype, *Ecclesiastical Memorials*, II. ii. 34–6.

parish churches. The Council ordered Lasco and Ridley to confer to solve the problem, and by the spring of 1553 Micron could finally report to Bullinger that the church was flourishing.[80]

The same letter contained news of another important development. Micron reported to Bullinger that 'no foreigner is now eligible for the rights of an English citizen without having made a confession of faith to the ministers of the foreign churches'. It was evidently envisaged that in future only foreigners who joined the stranger communities would be permitted the privileged status of denizens. There is no sign that this regulation was ever actually enforced, but the fact that a scheme of this sort should have been mooted is evidence enough that attitudes to the churches were not influenced by religious considerations alone. The economic potential of the Continental refugees was beginning to be appreciated, and the more far-sighted English statesmen were quick to recognize that the stranger churches might play an important role in the economic regulation of the foreign community. The Lord Protector, Somerset, had himself sponsored a scheme to plant a colony of French Protestant weavers at Glastonbury. The project was designed to revive a district of declining cloth manufacture through the introduction of advanced continental techniques, and the weavers were organized in a religious community under the French reformer Valérand Poullain.[81] The recognition that economic self-interest could be served by aiding the London strangers was not a decisive motive at the time of the churches' foundation in 1550. Economic considerations played a much more important role a decade later at the time of the churches' restoration under Elizabeth. But it is worth noting that the man who would play a leading role at that time, William Cecil, was already regarded by the strangers as one of their most reliable friends during the Edwardian period.[82]

If such economic motives for assisting the strangers were as yet only beginning to be grasped, one other more immediate

---

[80] *APC*, iv. 160–1; *OL*, ii. 581.
[81] Jordan, *Threshold of Power*, pp. 318–21; J. Thirsk, *Economic Policy and Projects* (Oxford, 1978), pp. 35–6; Bauer, *Poullain*, pp. 148–58.
[82] See below, p. 137.

and pressing consideration was undoubtedly of considerable significance in persuading the Council of the advantage in permitting the strangers their own churches. The King's Journal recorded that a church was granted to the strangers for 'avoiding all sects of Anabaptists and suchlike'.[83] The relaxation of controls on Edward's accession had led to a bewildering proliferation of heresies, much to the embarrassment of the government, and also of the Reformed preachers who feared their views might be tainted by association with these often uneducated free-thinkers. In March 1549 Latimer drew attention to the extent of sectarian activity in a sermon preached before the King, and by June even the pugnacious Hooper was seriously alarmed by the growing confidence of the anabaptists who, as he reported to Bullinger, flocked to his sermons in great numbers and gave him trouble with their contentious interruptions.[84] A powerful commission to search out heretics was appointed in April and succeeded in forcing several Londoners to recant anabaptist errors at St Paul's, but although Cranmer took the lead in pursuing these firm measures the government's action seems to have proved largely ineffective. Joan Bocher, who refused to abjure her errors and was condemned to death, boasted that 'a thousand in London were of her sect', and by the spring of 1550 the problem was if anything worse. Hooper wrote to Bullinger in June of the 'frenzy' of anabaptist activity in Essex and Kent, and the government was finally forced to take drastic measures to control the sects. In May 1550 Joan Bocher was executed, and a new campaign against sectarian error was set in motion.[85]

It was clearly envisaged that the new stranger churches would play their part in eliminating sectarian views. As we have seen, in the Henrician period anabaptist heresy had been almost exclusively confined to the Dutch immigrant community in London, and although by 1550 a strong native strand had emerged, unorthodox opinions were certainly widely disseminated amongst the foreign residents of the capital. No doubt the foreign ambassadors exaggerated when they urged

---

[83] *Chronicle of Edward*, p. 37.

[84] *Sermons by Hugh Latimer* (Everyman's Library, 1906), p. 130. Hooper to Bullinger, 25 June 1549, *OL*, i. 65.

[85] Jordan, *Threshold of Power*, pp. 326–9; Horst, *Radical Brethren*, pp. 97–111; *OL*, i. 87.

the Council to prohibit further immigration on the grounds that most of the newcomers were fugitives from justice or sectaries, but their charges were not entirely groundless: in May 1550 the strangers' leaders were themselves arguing that the establishment of a stranger church would help them regulate the opinions of their fellow countrymen.[86] The argument that the new churches would help control heresy amongst the strangers was undoubtedly of great weight in securing the necessary consensus of support for the granting of the strangers' charter. Lasco and his colleagues were well aware of this and strove conscientiously to discharge their obligations. The struggle against the sectaries would take up much of the ministers' attentions in the first years of the churches' life.[87]

Weighty political considerations thus urged the granting of the privileges for which Lasco and Hooper were lobbying so energetically in the summer of 1550. Arguments of this kind must have made it easier to persuade sceptics of the advantages in permitting the strangers their own churches, but the sectarian challenge was only one of the stranger ministers' priorities; even whilst establishing the institutions of the church and organizing the new community the foreign ministers never lost sight of the ambitious aim that their community should serve as a model of the best Reformed practice, and influence the course of further reform in the English Church. The progress made towards these various goals before the dispersal of the community in 1553 must be considered in the next chapter.

---

[86] *Cal. S. P. Span.*, x. 254; *OL*, ii. 560–1.
[87] Below, pp. 62–6.

III

Early Years

Lasco and his colleagues wasted no time in organizing their new community. Even before the church at Austin Friars had been handed over to the strangers, the work of establishing the institutions and ministry of the church had begun. Micron preached for the first time on 21 September, and on 5 October the Dutch community elected four elders to assist the ministers in the government of the church. A week later four deacons were elected to care for the community's poor.[1] Soon the superintendent and ministers were turning out a steady stream of doctrinal and liturgical works, both for the use of the community itself, and to justify the new churches to a wider audience.

Few of the churches' records from these early years have survived. On the dispersal of the communities in 1553 the charter was taken abroad and carefully conserved, but of the churches' first registers only a single membership list of the Dutch community is still extant. The minutes of the consistory of both the French and Dutch communities have also disappeared, rendering impossible a detailed study of the care and control exercised by the churches over their members.[2] Our knowledge of how the churches functioned in the first years of their existence, therefore, relies heavily on the ministers' published works, together with occasional references to progress and problems in letters to continental reformers.

Yet even from these limited sources a picture emerges of the steady development of the churches' institutions in the months and years after their foundation. The ministers' liturgical works and particularly the complete church order published in exile in 1554 tell us much about the daily life of the young community, and its problems; it is also clear that Lasco's

[1] *OL*, ii. 570–1.
[2] For a survey of the churches' role in the community during the Elizabethan period see below, Ch. VII.

wider preoccupations remained very much in view, and this chapter will conclude with an assessment of how far the strangers' leaders were successful in their stated objective of influencing the course of further development in the English Church. But first it is worth taking a closer look at the distinguished group which made up the first leaders of the stranger churches. For if much of enduring worth was achieved in three short years in the face of often daunting problems, then this was essentially the achievement of the tight and capable group that made up the churches' first ministers and elders.

Lasco was quick to acknowledge his debt to his colleagues in the work of establishing the institutions of the church, but the charter in appointing him superintendent did no more than recognize his pre-eminence as a major international reformer. John a Lasco, Baron of Poland, seemed destined from an early age for a distinguished church career.[3] Brought up in the household of his uncle the Primate of Poland, Lasco travelled extensively in his youth and took full advantage of the educational opportunities available to a young man of wealth and good family. It was during one such trip that Lasco paid an extended visit to Erasmus at Basle, and the great humanist clearly found the young Pole a charming guest. 'He is a true pearl', he told one correspondent, 'and so unassuming and free from arrogance, although he is one day called to fill one of the highest offices in his native land.'[4]

After his return to Poland in 1535 Lasco was appointed Archdeacon of Warsaw; further preferment seemed inevitable, but in 1538 he abruptly departed his native land and returned to Germany. Two years later he married, thus publicly proclaiming his conversion to Protestantism. In 1540 he settled in Emden in East Friesland, and although he initially declined to serve as minister (on the grounds that he knew no German) in 1543 he accepted the office of superintendent of the churches of the territory. Lasco now embarked on both a vigorous reform

---

[3] On Lasco see H. Dalton, *Johannes a Lasco* (Gotha, 1881); G. Pascal, *Jean de Lasco* (Paris, 1894); B. Hall, *John a Lasco, A Pole in Reformation England* (Friends of Dr Williams's Library, 25th Lecture, 1971); *BWPG*, v. 592–612; *DNB*, xxxii. 158; *Lasco Opera*.

[4] *Opus Epistolarum Des. Erasmi Roterodami*, ed. P. S. Allen *et al.* (Oxford, 1906–58), vi. 186.

of the local churches and a voluminous correspondence with other established reformers. Bucer, Calvin, and Bullinger were all eager to welcome as a brother such a distinguished convert, and with Bullinger in particular Lasco struck up an enduring friendship.[5] The necessary reforming measures in Emden were carried through in the face of determined opposition from both Catholics and sectaries. Local churches were stripped of their images and several organizational improvements introduced which were later to find their echo in London. Four laymen were appointed as elders to assist the ministers, sharing with them the power to excommunicate offenders, and a weekly conference of ministers introduced (the *coetus*) for the discussion of doctrine and regulation of the ministers' conduct. Finally Lasco compiled a catechism and confession of faith to provide a clear statement of the new doctrine of the church.[6]

Lasco's activity inevitably stirred up resentment and opposition. On one occcasion he was forced temporarily to resign his office as superintendent, and the publication of the Augsburg Interim made his position still more insecure. In July 1548 Lasco gratefully accepted an invitation from Archbishop Cranmer to come to England, but this first visit proved to be of short duration. Lasco was mainly occupied with negotiations on behalf of a group of German princes for a Protestant League against the Emperor, and when his diplomatic activities bore no immediate fruit he returned to the Continent taking with him a gratuity of £50 from the Privy Council and a letter from Cranmer to Melanchthon.[7] There was now, however, no longer a place for him at Emden. The Emperor, fully aware of Lasco's activity on behalf of the Protestant princes, made his expulsion an absolute condition of the acceptance of a religious compromise put forward by the court of East Friesland in the wake of the Interim, and the Countess Anna reluctantly accepted the inevitability of Lasco's departure.[8] After a brief stay in Hamburg, Lasco turned once

---

[5] Bullinger endorsed Lasco's first letter 'John a Lasco, most noble baron of Poland, ... particular friend of Erasmus and legate of the King of Poland.' *Lasco Opera*, ii. 569.

[6] *Lasco Opera*, i. 481–556, ii. 342–475; Richard Kruske, *Johannes a Lasco und der Sacramentsstreit* (Leipzig, 1901), pp. 53–70; Hall, *John a Lasco*, pp. 23–9.

[7] Cranmer to Lasco, 4 July 1548. *OL*, i. 16–18; Pascal, *Jean de Lasco*, pp. 201–4; *Cal. S. P. For. Edward VI*, no. 253; *APC*, ii. 244; Cranmer to Melanchthon, *OL*, i. 22.

[8] Lasco to the Duke of Prussia, 21 Oct. 1549. *Lasco Opera*, ii. 634.

more towards England. With Martyr and Bucer established in the universities, Lasco's stature and experience made him a natural choice for the task of establishing an ordered church amongst the stranger community in London. The charter appointed him to the same office that he had discharged with such evident success at Emden.

In addition to appointing Lasco as superintendent over both French and Dutch communities the charter named the churches' first ministers, Francis Perussel and Richard Vauville for the French congregation and Martin Micron and Gualter Delenus for the Dutch. They were men of very diverse talents, but all would serve the community with distinction. Martin Micron (Micronius), a native of Ghent, had practised medicine in Basle before taking up his ministry.[9] In 1548 he visited Zurich in the company of John Hooper, where Micron, like Hooper, became strongly committed to the theology of Zurich and its minister Henry Bullinger. In London Micron would be one of Bullinger's most regular correspondents, chronicling with particular care the troubles of his friend Hooper at the time of the establishment of the stranger church.[10]

In March 1549, when Hooper left Zurich to return to England, Micron accompanied him and for a time lived in Hooper's household in London; from about the beginning of 1550, however, he was also serving as minister to the gathering Dutch community.[11] On the official foundation of the church Micron was confirmed as minister, and as his colleague Delenus devoted himself mostly to study and teaching, the main burden of the preaching ministry fell on Micron. At an early stage consideration was given to finding another minister to share his pastoral duties, and by 1553 Delenus's son Peter had been appointed to serve the community in this capacity.[12]

---

[9] In 1549 he published a medical textbook, *In libros de placitis Hippocratis et Platonis argumenta*. Decavele, *Dageraad*, i. 328. On Micron see J. H. Gerretsen, *Micronius* (Nijmegen, 1895); *NNBW*, ix. 678.

[10] *OL*, ii. 557–82.

[11] Gerretsen, *Micronius*, p. 7; Utenhove to Bullinger, 29 June 1550. Pijper, *Utenhove*, appendix p. lxviii.

[12] Lasco to Hardenberg, 12 Dec. 1550. *Lasco Opera*, ii. 644. At one point Utenhove described Micron as the sole minister of the church. *OL*, ii. 587. For Peter Delenus as minister see below, p. 115.

In the meantime, however, Micron proved a willing and industrious worker, not only in his preaching but also in the assistance he gave Lasco in establishing the liturgy of the church. His two most important contributions, the *Kleyne Catechismus* and *Christlicke Ordinancien*, were adapted from Lasco's longer Latin catechism and church order, but in neither case did Micron slavishly follow Lasco's originals in producing Dutch versions for the use of the community itself.[13] Micron also found time during these years to produce a long tract on the Eucharist, attacking Catholic theology and repudiating anabaptist error.[14] In exile in Mary's reign Micron played an important role in helping to establish the exile communities in both Emden and Frankfurt before settling in Norden in East Friesland, where he remained as minister to his death in 1559.

Micron's colleague, Gualter Delenus, was a man of a very different stamp: first and foremost a distinguished scholar, Delenus had already been in England for a decade by the time of the establishment of the church.[15] In an otherwise tightly-knit group Delenus was something of an outsider, and was probably not personally known to the other leaders of the stranger community at the time of his appointment as minister. Originally from Brabant, Delenus had (like Lasco and Utenhove) studied at Louvain before taking up an appointment in 1533 as a teacher of Hebrew and Greek in Amsterdam. Forced to flee the town after the anabaptist insurrection of 1535, Delenus took refuge in England, and by 1539 he was in the King's service: the preface to the Latin New Testament which he published in 1540 described him as the King's *biblioscopus*.[16]. The New Testament was dedicated to Henry on the

---

[13] *De Kleyne Catechismus, oft kinderleere* (1552). *STC* 15260.7. Modern edition in *Quellen zur Geschichte des Kirchlichen Unterrichts*, ed. J. M. Reu, viii (Gütersloh, 1924), 1149–70; *De Christlicke Ordinancien de Nederlantscher Ghemeinten Christi* (Emden, 1554). *STC* 16571a. Modern edition, ed. W. F. Dankbaar (The Hague, 1956).

[14] *Een claer bewijs, van het recht gebruyck des nachtmaels Christi* (1552). *STC* 17863.3. Modern edition in *BRN*, i. 437–563.

[15] On Delenus see H. F. Wijnman, 'Wouter Deelen', *Jaarboek Amstelodamum*, 27 (1930), 43–65; J. Trapman, 'Delenus en de Bijbel', *NAK*, 56 (1975–6), 95–113; H. J. de Jonge, 'Caro in Spiritum', in I. B. Horst etc. (eds.), *De Geest in het geding* (Alphen, 1978), pp. 145–68; *BWPG*, ii. 424–7; *NNBW*, i. 703–4.

[16] Librarian, or possibly censor. De Jonge adopts a further suggestion of Wijnman

occasion of his marriage to Anne of Cleves, and Delenus later presented manuscripts to both Henry and Edward VI.[17] He seems to have continued in royal employment after the accession of Edward, and it was probably to royal patronage that he owed his appointment to the stranger church.[18]

The New Testament of 1540 is a tribute to Delenus's erudition; his annotations show that he altered Erasmus's vulgate in more than six hundred places after collation with Greek manuscripts, and Delenus's colleagues in the Dutch community would show the greatest respect for his learning both in London and in exile; Utenhove described him as 'vir trium linguarum undiquaque doctissimus', and looked to Delenus for assistance with his Dutch Bible project in Emden, particularly in the collation of the Old Testament with the Hebrew.[19] In London Delenus was not particularly active in the ministry, but he did share with Lasco the weekly Latin sermon preached in the Dutch church, expounding the Old Testament whilst Lasco dealt with the New.[20] The doubts about his orthodoxy, first raised in Amsterdam, were never quite stilled, and in 1553 criticisms by Delenus of the church's Confession of Faith caused trouble in the church.[21] But Delenus was not an anabaptist, as the pungent criticism of the separatists in his manuscripts make clear. In his treatment of Genesis 1.3, with which he opened his course of lectures, Delenus vigorously denounced the anabaptist doctrine that Christ took no flesh of the Virgin.[22]

In his dispute with the other ministers Delenus was brought to admit that he had erred, and no further trouble was reported: Delenus was rather more capable than his colleagues of keeping himself to himself, as he had demonstrated in preserving

---

that Delenus may have been employed to select books for the king's library from the libraries of dissolved monasteries. De Jonge, 'Caro in spiritum', pp. 149–50; Horst, *Radical Brethren*, p. 75.

[17] *Novum testamentum latinum* (1540), *STC* 2799. Wijnman, 'Wouter Deelen', 56; Trapman, 'Delenus en de Bijbel', 102.

[18] *Literary Remains of King Edward VI*, ed. J. G. Nichols (Roxburghe Club, 1857, lxxiv), p. ccxvi.

[19] *Simplex et Fidelis Narratio*, *BRN*, ix. 148; Hessels, ii. 50.

[20] *OL*, ii. 587.

[21] See below, pp. 64–5.

[22] Trapman, 'Delenus en de Bijbel', 102.

position and favour for several years under Henry VIII. His colleagues retained their genuine respect for his learning, and after joining them in exile Delenus would be one of the first to return to England in 1559, where he fell victim to the plague of 1563.

The two ministers appointed for the French community were both former monks, but otherwise men of very different character. Francis Perussel, a native of Orléans, had entered a local monastery before moving to Paris, where he was won over to the Reformation in 1542.[23] He dissembled his views with some care and it was not until 1545 that action was taken against him. He was then accused of having preached heretical sermons in several Paris churches and in 1546, having defended himself and denied the charges for a year, Perussel fled to Geneva. Calvin seems to have had a (perhaps justifiably) low opinion of Perussel's constancy at this time, and finding a cool reception in Geneva Perussel soon moved on to Basle.[24] By 1548 he was in Canterbury, where he assisted Utenhove in the foundation of the French church before moving to London to take up his appointment as minister.

Perussel was an able theologian; in London he published a long theological work, the *Summa Christianae Religionis*, and later, in 1561, he was an active participant at the Colloquy of Poissy.[25] On the dissolution of the London church in 1553 Perussel's services were much in demand, and after a period as minister of the French church in Wesel, Perussel was called to Frankfurt as Poullain's successor.[26] Perussel remained a figure of controversy to the last; the French church at Wesel was closed down by the town council after two turbulent years under Perussel's supervision, and new disputes arose after his arrival in Frankfurt. By 1562 Perussel was serving as chaplain

---

[23] On Perussel see F. W. Cross, *History of the Walloon and Huguenot Church at Canterbury* (Huguenot Society Publications, xv, 1898), pp. 6–8; E. & E. Haag, *La France Protestante* (1st edn., Paris, 1846–59), viii. 202; Schickler, *Églises du Refuge*, i. 55–6.

[24] Calvin to Falais, 23 Nov. 1547: 'I hope that God will teach him to give up his many affectations. I pray you on your part to try to hold him lest he fall away; for God is able to mould him so as to render him fit for his service.' *CO*, xii. 636.

[25] *Summa Christianae Religionis* (1551). STC 19783. Haag, *La France Protestante*, viii. 202.

[26] Bauer, *Poullain*, pp. 246, 261. Perussel also received an invitation to minister to the French church at Emden. *CO*, xv. 886–8.

to Condé, with whom he was captured at the battle of Dreux.[27]

Perussel's colleague in London, Richard Vauville, was a much less contentious figure: Valérand Poullain described him as 'a man truly perfect in Christian piety', and in contrast to Perussel he remained in friendly contact with Calvin.[28] Vauville had been active as a reformer in both Bourges and Strasburg before he moved to London, where he became an intimate of the family of John Hooper; in June 1550 he married Joanna, Anne Hooper's maid.[29] Poullain speaks of Vauville as the first minister of the French church, so he was probably serving the community from the time of its first informal gatherings in 1549. In 1553 Vauville seems to have sailed north with Lasco and Micron, but in 1555 he was called to the ministry in Frankfurt, where his pacific spirit was sorely needed in a community wracked by internal dissension. Vauville, however, was unable to effect the desired reconciliation as he fell a victim to the plague within a few months of his arrival.[30]

The first ministers by no means exhausted the talent at the disposal of the community; the elders who served with them in the consistory also included several figures of note. The Dutch community initially elected four elders, and one may assume that the French (whose registers are lost) probably did likewise; as the church grew the Dutch later found it necessary to increase this number to ten.[31] Lasco's commentary on the institutions of the church makes clear that he regarded the elders as true colleagues in the ministry. The elders took no part in the ministry of the Word or sacraments, but shared full authority for the government of the community, in spiritual as in temporal things.[32] The elders would have been expected to play a full part in establishing the liturgy and institutions of the church, and as a group were well qualified for this task.

---

[27] Haag, *La France Protestante*, ii. 452.

[28] *Pollanus, Liturgia Sacra*, ed. A. C. Honders (Leiden, 1970), p. 33; Schickler, *Églises du Refuge*, i. 56.

[29] *OL*, i. 108, ii. 565. Pijper and Lindeboom both suggest that Joanna married Martin Micron, but this is a misreading of the first of the above references. Pijper, *Utenhove*, p. 33; Lindeboom, *Austin Friars*, p. 15.

[30] Bauer, *Poullain*, pp. 186, 238–41.

[31] Micron, *Ordinancien*, ed. Dankbaar, p. 37; *Returns*, i. 202.

[32] *Forma ac Ratio* (below, p. 57), *Lasco Opera*, ii. 51.

The most distinguished of the elders was undoubtedly
Lasco's friend and colleague, Jan Utenhove.[33] A member of
one of the foremost burgher families of Ghent, Utenhove had
been an early convert to the Reformation. In 1543 he was
implicated in the performance of a heretical play and forced
to abandon his homeland, though not before he had successfully removed a large proportion of his property into exile.[34]
Utenhove settled in Strasburg, where he met Bucer and Martyr, and on the promulgation of the Interim in 1548 he quickly
followed Martyr across the Channel to England. In England
Utenhove was Cranmer's guest at Canterbury, and seems to
have been the moving spirit behind the foundation of the
French church there, the first such community in England.[35]
Returning to the Continent early in 1549, Utenhove met
Hooper and Micron, then on their way to England, and Hooper
gave Utenhove a letter of introduction to Bullinger in Zurich.
Utenhove made an extremely favourable impression on the
Zurich reformer and whilst in Zurich he embraced whole-hear-
tedly the sacramental theology of his hosts.[36] From Zurich
Utenhove visited Geneva briefly before returning to England
late in 1549.

In London Utenhove lodged with Hooper, and on Hooper's
appointment to the bishopric of Gloucester planned to accompany him to his new diocese; his own election as an elder of
the Dutch church, however, frustrated this intention.[37]
Utenhove was soon at work on the liturgies of the church. He
translated both the Emden catechism and Lasco's *Compendium
doctrinae* into Dutch for the use of the church, and provided
Poullain with a French translation of Lasco's opinion of attendance at the Mass for his edition of Musculus's *Temporiseur*.[38]
These years also saw the publication of the first of Utenhove's
Dutch metrical psalm translations, which were to absorb much
of his energies until his death; by 1553 he had completed

[33] On Utenhove see Pijper, *Utenhove*; Decavele, *Dageraad*, i. 80–85; *NNBW*, ix.
1145–8; *DNB*, lviii. 78.

[34] Decavele, *Dageraad*, i. 80–2, 208–9.

[35] Pijper, *Utenhove*, pp. 28–32; Cross, *Huguenot Church at Canterbury*, pp. 1–10.

[36] J. ten D. Koolman, 'Jan Utenhoves Besuch bei Heinrich Bullinger im Jahre
1549', *Zwingliana*, 14 (1974–8), 263–73; Pijper, *Utenhove*, p. 39; *OL*, i. 56.

[37] *OL*, ii. 565, 572.

[38] *Le Temporiseur* (1550), *STC* 18311. According to Poullain, Utenhove suggested
the project to him in the first place. Bauer, *Poullain*, pp. 135–6.

versions of all the psalms regularly used in the week's services.[39] Utenhove spent his own fortune freely in the publication of these Reformed works, and seems to have experienced financial difficulties in later years in consequence; much must have been lost as a result of the disastrous failure of his new Dutch Bible, a project on which Utenhove embarked in exile in Emden, and for which he enlisted the help of his London colleagues Micron and Delenus.[40] In 1559, his enthusiasm undimmed by hardship or disappointment, Utenhove returned to London. Unquestionably now the leading figure of the stranger community, Utenhove was content to remain an elder of the Dutch church. He died in 1566, still in office, anxious that his death should not frustrate the imminent publication of a complete edition of his psalms.[41]

Less is known of Utenhove's colleagues, but several at some point left evidence of their commitment to the Reformed cause. Hermes Backerel acted as the schoolmaster of the community in London, and his departure to Emden with the other leading members of the community in 1553 was the beginning of a distinguished career as an itinerant preacher in the Netherlands.[42] He twice subsequently visited England but did not settle; his colleague Anthony Ashe, on the other hand, was one of the first to return in 1559, arriving within six months of Elizabeth's accession to petition for the restoration of the church's privileges.[43] Four of the elders are known to have been religious refugees: Backerel and Utenhove, and two of those newly appointed when the number of elders was raised to ten, Josias Dauwe, a priest, and the printer Gilles van der Erve. Van der Erve, like his fellow elder Nicholas van den Berghe (the printer Nicholas Hill), would demonstrate his zeal for the Reformed cause in exile, turning out a stream of Protestant publications directed at the English market.[44]

[39] S. J. Lenselink, *De Nederlandse Psalmberijmingen* (Assen, 1959), pp. 250–314. No copies survive of the collections of ten and twenty-five psalms published in 1551, but there is a fragment containing four of these early translations from 1552. *STC* 2738.7.

[40] *KP I*, p. 95; Hessels, ii. 50, 63. On the Bible project, see also below, p. 90.

[41] His will contains detailed instructions for the publication of the Psalter. London Comm. 1566 (15, fo. 243).

[42] *NNBW*, ii. 57–8; Decavele, *Dageraad*, i. 376–7.

[43] On Ashe see below, pp. 97–9, 134–6.

[44] *APC*, iv. 250; Decavele, *Dageraad*, ii. 66, 102, 106. On the printers see below, pp. 88–90.

The elders seem to have been men of substance. Both Utenhove and Backerel left behind considerable property when they left Flanders, yet neither was without resources in England. Anthony Ashe was a prosperous silkweaver, and Harmon West, the fourth of the original elders, was marked on subsidy returns as 'master'.[45] Although generally amongst the more prosperous members of the church, in other respects the elders fully reflected the diversity of experience within the stranger community. Whereas the four religious exiles were obviously newcomers in Edward's reign, three of the elders, Ashe, West, and Nicholas Hill had been in England since at least 1541. It is a measure of their commitment to the Reformed faith that all these elders abandoned established and comfortable situations in London to join the church in exile. Ashe in particular had much to lose, and Utenhove left a considerable portion of his goods in the hands of an English merchant, which he later found it difficult to recover.[46]

As striking as the Reformed commitment of these first elders of the Dutch church is their high level of education, including as they did a schoolmaster, two printers, and a priest, as well as the highly literate master-weaver Anthony Ashe, and Utenhove, as distinguished a linguist and scholar as any of the strangers. The elders were well equipped for an active role in establishing the institutions of the church, and it is clear that Lasco and his ministers made good use of their talents. In January 1551 Lasco was able to tell Bullinger that the Confession of Faith would be published with the unanimous consent of all his colleagues, and the title-page of Micron's Dutch version of the complete church order, the *Christlicke Ordinancien*, explicitly states that it was established in the community with the agreement of the ministers and elders, 'der Dienaren ende Ouderlinghen'.[47]

The *Christlicke Ordinancien* was not published until after the church's dissolution on Mary's accession in 1553,[48] and it was

---

[45] *Returns*, i. 35.
[46] *Cal. S. P. Dom.*, *1547–80*, p. 144 (Petition of 11 Dec. 1559).
[47] *Lasco Opera*, ii. 646; Gorham, *Gleanings*, p. 225; Micron, *Ordinancien*, p. 31.
[48] 'Buyten Londen' (i.e. Emden), 1554. *STC* 16571a.

not until 1555 that Lasco finally published his description of the forms of worship and government of the church. Lasco's work, *Forma ac Ratio tota ecclesiastici Ministerii, in peregrinorum, potissimum vero Germanorum Ecclesia: instituta Londini*,[49] was not a liturgy but a longer exposition of the liturgical forms and customs of the church: it was a work of polemic designed to answer critics of the community and give wider publicity to what Lasco thought of as a complete order for a model Reformed community. Lasco was revising the *Forma ac Ratio* up to the time of its publication, and it has been open to doubt how far it represents the real practice of the church during the first years of its existence. There is, however, considerable evidence that the institutions and liturgical forms described were, by and large, functioning in the community before its dispersal in 1553. In June 1553 Lasco had written to Bullinger that he was on the verge of publishing his account of the church's institutions, and Micron's *Ordinancien* appeared so soon after his arrival in Emden as to leave little time for revision.[50] From other references in the ministers' correspondence, and the early publications produced for the use of the church, a picture emerges of the steady development of the community's institutions in the months and years after its foundation. In January 1551 Lasco reported to Bullinger that the church would soon publish its Confession of Faith, and he enclosed several copies for Bullinger's perusal. This was the *Compendium doctrinae de vera unicaque Dei et Christi ecclesia*, and 1551 saw the publication both of this and a Dutch translation by Utenhove for the benefit of the members of the church.[51] The *Compendium doctrinae* appended a provisional form of prayers used in the community at their main Sunday service, and a note at the end of Utenhove's translation promised that

---

[49] Frankfurt, 1555. *STC* 16571. *Lasco Opera*, ii. 1–283. A French translation, *Toute la forme et maniere du ministere ecclesiastique . . .* was published in the following year at Emden. *STC* 16574.

[50] *Lasco Opera*, ii. 674, Gorham, *Gleanings*, p. 296.

[51] *Lasco Opera*, ii. 646, Gorham, *Gleanings*, p. 225; *Compendium doctrinae*, *STC* 15263; *Een Kort begrijp der leeringhe van de warachtige ende eenighe Ghemeynte Gods ende Christi*. The two are printed in parallel in *Lasco Opera*, ii. 285–339. No copy of the 1551 edition of the *Kort begrijp* survives. See Lindeboom, *Austin Friars*, p. 16.

a full account of the ceremonies of the church would be published soon. This did not appear, but in April 1551 Lasco could inform a correspondent that an order for the celebration of the Eucharist would soon be introduced.[52] In December of the same year Lasco reported to the Duke of Prussia the institution of a 'discipline' in the church.[53]

Lasco was probably here referring to a church order rather than specifically an order for ecclesiastical discipline; his letter seems to suggest that the institutions and liturgy of the church were largely complete by the end of 1551, a supposition that receives strong support from the recent discovery of two small French liturgies in the Bodleian Library, Oxford. Entitled *La forme des prieres ecclesiastiques. Avec la maniere d'administrer les sacramens* and *Doctrine de la penitence publique*, both describe the rites of the French church and both were published during its Edwardian life, in 1552.[54] The *Forme des prieres* contains the prayers to be used by the church on different occasions, beginning with the main Sunday service and adding prayers to be used in time of plague or war. The book also contains orders for baptism, communion, marriage, and the election of elders and deacons. In contrast to Lasco's *Forma ac Ratio* which is largely descriptive, this book was clearly actually intended for use in church. The second pamphlet is smaller, containing only an order for public repentance (a characteristic institution of Lasco's church), and for the celebration of Holy Communion. This second communion order is not identical with that in the *Forme des prieres* in the arrangement of the prayers, but it is more detailed and corresponds closely to the order described by Lasco in the *Forma ac Ratio*. On occasion the prayers in the two French works are so nearly identical as to suggest that they were different translations prepared for the convenience of the French community of a common (probably Latin) original.

The discovery of the *Forme des Prieres* makes clear that the main institutions of the foreign churches were all functioning by 1552 in much the form described by Lasco. The lengthy

---

[52] 'Usum sacramentorum purum ac legitimum brevi per gratiam Dei habituri sumus.' *Lasco Opera*, ii. 651.

[53] *Lasco Opera*, ii. 666.

[54] *STC* 16572.3, 16572.7.

discursive passages of the *Forma ac Ratio* reflect Lasco's concern to justify the institutions of the community, constructed as far as possible after the model of the early apostolic church: the church order, however, is also the form of worship for a working church, and is infused throughout by the practical spirit which was an important aspect of Lasco's organizational talent.

The central acts of worship for the foreign churches were the two Sunday services.[55] These services, at nine in the morning and two in the afternoon, gave pride of place to the ministry of the Word. After an opening psalm a passage was read from Scripture on which the minister would then preach for an hour. Lasco laid down that the reading should be only as much as could be dealt with in an hour, but long enough to avoid falling into the papist error of taking a text out of context.[56] The Creed, the Ten Commandments, and the General Confession were said at the morning service, but in the afternoon they were omitted in favour of a public exposition of some part of the catechism. Both Sunday services ended with prayers and the chanting of a psalm, using in the Dutch church Utenhove's new metrical versions. The prayers focused on the particular needs and debts of gratitude of the stranger community. Prayers for the universal church were followed by prayers for the King, for the Council (that they might be moved to complete the abolition of Antichrist here begun), and for the City of London. In a reference to the troubles of the times the strangers also prayed that the people might remain in obedience. The strangers' own homelands were not forgotten, with prayers for 'the churches under the cross'.[57]

Marriage, baptism, or the celebration of Holy Communion took place after the conclusion of the prayers during the main Sunday service. No registers of marriages and baptisms survive from these early years, but it is clear, both from the extant French orders and from Delenus's criticisms of the baptismal rite in 1553, that the institutions were functioning by this time, notwithstanding the early opposition of the bishops.[58] Lasco's order provided for a monthly communion, alternating between

---

[55] *Lasco Opera*. ii. 81–91; *Toute la Forme*, pp. 37–48.
[56] *Lasco Opera*, ii. 81; *Toute la Forme*, p. 38.
[57] *Lasco Opera*, ii. 87–90; *Toute la Forme*, pp. 44–7; Micron, *Ordinancien*, pp. 64–5.
[58] See below, p. 64.

the Dutch and French churches.[59] The mode of celebration demonstrates both Lasco's determination to return to the pure model of the apostolic church and the practicality which runs through the whole order. Communion was to be taken seated round the communion table as a faithful re-enactment of the Last Supper, but as each group came to the table a gap was to be left opposite the minister so that the whole congregation might see.[60] The celebration was preceded by a lengthy process of self-examination, repentance, and reconciliation. Notice of the coming celebration was given fifteen days in advance so that those intending to receive could first examine their consciences and settle any disputes with their brethren. That church members took this duty seriously is demonstrated by the rash of disputes that came before the consistory in the days before the monthly communion in the Elizabethan period.[64]

Those church members who could not settle their differences could not simply stay away, as only the sick were excused attendance.[62] This obligation to come to communion was highly significant, as it meant that the communion was not only a liturgical high-point, but also a bi-monthly (in the Elizabethan church monthly) opportunity to scrutinize the conduct of the membership. A new list of communicants was drawn up for each celebration, and the elders held a special gathering the day before to debar any they thought unfit to take part.[63] Only those who had signed the community's Confession of Faith were allowed to attend the communion service; for this central rite the community was limited to the gathered church of those of known doctrinal orthodoxy. By 1553 those wishing to be admitted to the communion had in addition to undergo a public examination on the essentials of their faith. The examination, a series of forty questions and answers, is printed as part of the *Forma ac Ratio*, and was published separately in 1553 in a Dutch translation as *Een korte ondersoeckinghe*

[59] The communion order is described in *Lasco Opera*, ii. 122 ff.; *Toute la Forme*, pp. 88ᵛ ff.; Micron, *Ordinancien*, pp. 80–105.

[60] *Lasco Opera*, ii. 163; *Toute la Forme*, p. 142ᵛ.; Micron, *Ordinancien*, p. 100.

[61] For example, *Actes I*, pp. 20–2.

[62] *Lasco Opera*, ii. 160; *Toute la Forme*, p. 139ᵛ.

[63] *Lasco Opera*, ii. 137; *Toute la Forme*, p. 108ᵛ.

des gheloofs, over de ghene die haer tot der Ghemeynte begheven willen.[64]

The church thus demanded of its members a high degree of understanding, or at least awareness, of the doctrine of the community. The ministers lost no opportunity to improve the standard of the religious education of the membership, and special emphasis was laid on the training of the children of the community. Catechismal training took place regularly during the Sunday afternoon service in the presence of the whole community.[65] The afternoon sermon was limited to half an hour so that the rest of the hour allotted to the ministry of the Word could be given over to an examination of the older children on the essentials of their faith. The catechism used in the Dutch church was Lasco's Emden catechism, translated by Utenhove and published in 1551 by the press of a member of the church, Steven Mierdman.[66] Each week the minister expounded some portion of the catechism and examined the older children, assembled on benches in front of him, on their understanding of it. The catechism was a long and thorough work, and it was clearly expected that the adults present would also benefit from the exercise.

A doctrinal exposition of such complexity was clearly unsuitable for younger children, but from 1552 they were provided with Micron's shorter catechism.[67] This was still a formidable tract with over 130 questions and answers, and, if children were expected to learn the responses by heart, the catechism is an eloquent testimony to the capacity of children in the sixteenth century for rote learning.[68] The *Forma ac Ratio* made provision for a twice-yearly enrolment of children of members of the community who had reached the age of five to ensure

[64] *Lasco Opera*, ii. 127–35, 477–92. The edition of 1553 is known only from an annotation to a surviving copy of the 1561 edition, *STC* 18812. See *Lasco Opera*, i. xcix-c. An English translation was published in 1556, *STC* 17864. In the revised *STC* it is incorrectly suggested that this is a translation of the *Claer Bewijs*. (See note 14, above.) The Dutch edition is printed in *Quellen zur Geschichte des Kirchlichen Unterrichts*, viii. 1170–6 and in Micron, *Ordinancien*, pp. 83–94.

[65] *Lasco Opera*, ii. 98; *Toute la Forme*, p. 57.

[66] *De catechismus, oft kinder leere, diemen te Londen is ghebruyckende*, *STC* 15260. *Lasco Opera*, ii. 342–475.

[67] *STC* 15262a. (See note 13, above.)

[68] Phillippa Tudor, 'Religious Instruction for Children and Adolescents in the Early English Reformation', *Journal of Ecclesiastical History*, 35 (1984), 391–413.

that all were embarking on religious instruction. On these occasions the younger children would then be put through the ordeal of public examination of their progress. These younger children (who were obviously thought something of a nuisance and so were settled on their benches before the service began) were catechized in church only on these twice-yearly occasions; ordinarily the responsibility was left to their schoolmasters and parents in their home districts.[69] This suggests that there must have been small schools for Dutch children in different parts of the city, but in addition the church established its own school, probably in the precincts of the church, with Hermes Backerel as schoolmaster.[70] With such thorough training it was expected that children would be ready to come forward for confirmation at the age of fourteen. The educational aspect of the church functioned smoothly in these early years. Appended to the first membership list of the Dutch church is a list of thirty-one boys and nine girls who were successful in making their responses to the catechism on 7 June 1551. Heading the list were Lasco's three eldest children, Joannes, Hieronymus, and Barbara.[71]

With the two catechisms and the Confession of Faith the ministers had established a carefully-graduated hierarchy of instruction for the members of the church, but their desire to improve the educational standards of church members was only part of the explanation for this concentration on doctrinal education. As important was the ministers' concern to protect the community from false doctrine. The ministers clearly perceived their church as an embattled minority in the stranger community, and in their correspondence laid frequent emphasis on the scale of the problem posed by the proliferation of false doctrine amongst the foreigners. Before the charter had been granted Micron was arguing the importance of preaching in Dutch 'to guard against the heresies which are introduced by our countrymen', and a year later he described in detail to Bullinger the Arian error which presented the most stubborn opposition to the church's doctrine.[72] The publica-

---

[69] *Lasco Opera*, ii. 80–1, 94–5, 96; *Toute la Forme*, pp. 36ᵛ., 52ᵛ., 55.
[70] Micron, *Ordinancien*, p. 37.
[71] *Returns*, i. 210.
[72] *OL*, ii. 560, 574.

tions of the church ministers were all expected to play their part in combating these influences. Lasco asserted in his *Forma ac Ratio* that a catechism was necessary as never before as the church was so full of sects, and one of the responses made by new members coming to the communion explicitly rejected the anabaptist error regarding the Virgin Birth.[73]

In their concern for the churches' doctrinal orthodoxy, the ministers did not neglect a wider evangelical role in the stranger community. It was not to be forgotten that a major factor in persuading the government of the utility of a stranger church was the hope that the church would bring the sects under control, and the ministers pursued this mission with energy. The evangelical purpose of the church was reflected in the primacy given to the ministry of the Word: many more strangers seem to have attended services at Austin Friars than were full members of the church,[74] and the rites of the gathered church were not allowed to dislodge the preaching of the Gospel from pride of place. A key role in both the defence of orthodoxy in the community and positive evangelism was played by the mid-week service known as the 'prophesy'. At this weekly exercise church members could raise doubts and objections stimulated by the preaching on Sunday, and the minister would then explain his teaching. 'This arrangement', as Micron explained, 'in some measure represses the heretical and confirms the ignorant in the christian doctrine.' Lasco, too, saw the primary purpose of the prophesy as to fortify the faith of church members, but he also hoped that the exercise could win over many formerly attracted by ignorance to the sects.[75] The prophesy was one of the distinctive institutions of Lasco's community, and attracted a good deal of attention. One of the first German travellers to leave an account of a visit to England, the student Josua Maler, attended a prophesy at Austin Friars whilst he was in London, and was deeply impressed.[76]

---

[73] *Lasco Opera*, ii. 94, 130; *Toute la Forme*, pp. 52, 98ᵛ; Micron, *Ordinancien*, p. 87.
[74] Below, pp. 66, 78.
[75] *OL*, ii. 575; *Lasco Opera*, ii. 102–3; *Toute la Forme*, p. 63.
[76] W. D. Robson-Scott, 'Josua Maler's visit to England in 1551', *Modern Language Review*, xlv (1950), 346–51.

Taking the mid-week exercise with the catechism and preaching, Micron could with justice claim that the church was exerting every effort to combat heresy.[77] It must therefore have come as something of a shock that the first serious challenge to the doctrine of the church came from within its own ranks; indeed from one of the church's own ministers. ·

Lasco always hoped that his church would have a wider influence than purely on the stranger population alone, and to this end he instituted a series of mid-week scriptural lectures in Latin to accompany the prophesy in Dutch. Lasco himself lectured on the New Testament, and the Old Testament lecture was entrusted to Gualter Delenus.[78] This was entirely appropriate as Delenus was a Hebrew scholar of repute, but his lectures unexpectedly became the centre of controversy when Delenus used them to make pungent criticisms of the doctrine of the church. He questioned the function of godparents at baptism, denounced the practice of kneeling at communion, and declared that the article on the descent into Hell ought to be removed from the Confession of Faith.[79]

Delenus had not consulted his colleagues before making these remarks, and they reacted sharply. His criticisms had worrying implications, that concerning godparents in particular raising an issue which would erupt into a divisive controversy later in the church's life.[80] Lasco's church order made clear that ministers were to be subject to the discipline like all other members, and it was probably in the weekly assembly of the ministers and elders that Delenus's case was dealt with.[81] He was brought to admit that he had erred, and the quarrel was patched up. But it left its mark: Micron, writing to Bullinger in 1553, recorded that the Latin lectures had been suspended since the previous August, ostensibly because of the death of Lasco's wife (though he was now remarried and in good health). And when a new edition of the catechism was published in 1553 a further seven questions were added, all

[77] *OL*, ii. 575.
[78] *OL*, ii. 587.
[79] Lasco's account of the quarrel in a letter to Bullinger, *Lasco Opera*, ii. 676–7. See also Lindeboom, *Austin Friars*, p. 19; Van Schelven, *Vluchtelingenkerken*, pp. 74 ff.
[80] See below, pp. 243 ff. The strictures on kneeling at communion must have been directed at the English practice as the strangers took the sacrament seated.
[81] *Lasco Opera*, ii. 223–36; *Toute la Forme*, pp. 221–39.

in connection with the article on the descent into Hell which Delenus had wanted removed.[82]

The dispute with Delenus showed the leaders extremely sensitive when the doctrine of the church was challenged and danger loomed that they might be tarnished by a hint of anabaptist error. The same sensitivity may in part explain the drastic action in the case of George van Parris.

If the catechisms and preaching represent the positive aspect of the defence of orthodoxy, then the ecclesiastical discipline allowed a more negative control. It was envisaged as a system as much of moral as of doctrinal regulation, and Lasco laid down a carefully graduated system of Christian admonition and brotherly reproof before any recalcitrant sinner finally came before the ministers and elders.[83] If he remained unrepentant in the face of repeated warnings and urgings he would be excommunicated from the body of the church, but this drastic action was to be taken only so that he might ultimately be reconciled. While he was excommunicated, the brethren were to lose no opportunity to bring the erring member back to obedience, and the return of a penitent was celebrated in a major service of thanksgiving.[84]

The ecclesiastical discipline as thus envisaged by Lasco was a sensitive and flexible institution of salvation as well as regulation. In practice, however, it could be imposed with an inexorable determination, and in at least one case, had a tragic end. The King's Journal for April 1551 records that 'a certain Aryan of the strangers, a Dutchman, being excommunicated by the congregation of his countrymen, was after long disputation condemned to the fire'. Van Parris's error was to deny the Trinity, acknowledging only God the Father as true God. He was condemned after meticulous investigation by the heresy commission headed by Cranmer with Coverdale acting as interpreter for the prisoner, who spoke no English.[85] The part played by the Dutch ministers in all this is unclear. Van Parris, a surgeon, does not appear on the register of members

---

[82] *OL*, ii. 581; *BWPG*, ii. 424. The 1553 edition of the catechism is *STC* 15260.5.

[83] The *Forma ac Ratio* describes the system of ecclesiastical discipline in great detail. *Lasco Opera*, ii. 170–239.

[84] Ibid., ii. 208–22; *Toute la Forme*, pp. 202–20ᵛ.

[85] *Chronicle of Edward*, p. 58; Jordan, *Threshold of Power*, p. 330.

of the church, although he was made a denizen at the same
time as many of the first church members.[86] The correspondence of the church leaders maintains an embarrassed silence
on the subject. Although the denunciation of Van Parris
reflected no great credit on the Dutch community, many of
whose members were themselves refugees from persecution,
the difficulties of the ministers' position may be appreciated.
Anabaptism was a charge quickly raised by those who
defended the English Church establishment against those who
favoured further reformation. The independent stranger
churches, whose leaders had resolutely supported Hooper in
his struggle to further the reform of the English Church, shared
his vulnerability to this charge. The strangers, too, had the
additional handicap that their churches were easily tarnished
by association with the foreign sectaries, over which, in reality,
they had no control, as the church discipline could be applied
only to those who joined voluntarily. To guard the church
against such calumny Lasco suggested that the home parishes
of church members should be noted in the register. The English
ministers could then be informed which of the strangers in
their parish were members of the foreign congregations, to
prevent other foreigners spreading false doctrine under colour
of membership.[87]

The churches' concern to protect themselves from sectaries
could bring tragic consequences, but the more positive aspect
of the ministry also had its successes. There is at least one
well-documented example of the persuasive powers of Lasco
and his colleagues in the life story of Jooris van der Katelene,
later published by Micron in exile.[88] Van der Katelene was
an engraver who came to England as a youth. He attended
the services of the Dutch church from the first, initially remaining inclined to Catholicism but gradually coming to accept
the church's teaching. He then joined the church, and by
assiduous attendance at the preaching and prophesy educated
himself sufficiently to be able to explain the doctrine of the

[86] On 29 Oct. 1550. *Cal. Pat. Rolls Edward VI*, iii. 249.
[87] *Lasco Opera*, ii. 136. The Dutch register carried out this intention only partially.
See below, p. 82.
[88] *Een waerachteghe Historie van Hoste (gheseyt Jooris) vander Katelyne* (Emden, 1555).
Modern edition, *BRN*, viii. 187–253.

church to others. He was particularly persistent in his efforts to convert anabaptists, whom he visited in their homes in order to show them the error of their beliefs. On the accession of Mary he chose exile with the church leaders, taking with him his pregnant wife and household. Van der Katelene met an untimely end when he was apprehended on a visit to his native town of Ghent in 1555 and burnt for heresy.

It is extremely rare to have such an account of the conversion of an ordinary member of the community, but van der Katelene's experience was certainly not unique. Two reformers who were later to play a crucial role in the development of Dutch Calvinism, Guy de Brès and Peter Dathenus, were both in England during these years, and probably had their first formal religious education as young men in Lasco's London community.[89] Their cases and that of van der Katelene are a timely reminder that those who became committed Protestants whilst members of the London churches were probably as important an element of the Edwardian congregations as those Protestant exiles who were Cranmer's original concern. For the ministers of the churches the regulation of opinion within the stranger community was an ambitious undertaking. But clearly much had been achieved in the three short years before Edward's death.

The work of conversion and control in the stranger community was one important aspect of the mission of the stranger churches in their early years, but it was not for this alone that Lasco and his colleagues had established and publicized the 'model' institutions of their community. The ministers certainly hoped that their churches would have a wider influence and in particular, as Lasco later explained, act as a spur to further reform in the English Church. The extent to which these hopes were realized in the case of the Edwardian Reformation will be considered shortly, but first it is necessary to identify rather more precisely what were the influences that would be mediated through the liturgy and institutions of the stranger churches. It will be clear from the foregoing discussion

---

[89] *NNBW*, ii. 367 (Dathenus), vii. 196 (Brès); Theodor Ruys, *Petrus Dathenus* (Utrecht, 1919), pp. 12–16.

that the institutions of the new church were to some extent
moulded by the particular circumstances and problems of the
community in London. But Lasco and his colleagues drew on
other Reformed church orders in compiling their own, and it
was their explicit intention to present in the institutions and
liturgy of their church a living model of the best reformed
practice. What then were the Continental models which most
influenced the London ministers in drawing up their church
order and which, they hoped, would be transmitted through
their liturgy to the English Church?[90]

In the preface to his *Forma ac Ratio* Lasco would later write
that the ministers used as their models for the London church
order the orders of the refugee churches at Strasburg and
Geneva. The Geneva order with which he was familiar was
probably the *Forme des prieres et chantz ecclesiastiques* of 1542, and
the Strasburg order was also easily to hand, having recently
been published in London by Valérand Poullain, minister of
the French church at Glastonbury.[91] Both church orders were
the work of John Calvin, but one must be cautious about
attributing too much to his influence. The general orientation
of the London community was much less strongly towards the
doctrine and practice of the Geneva reformer than the use of
two of his orders as models would seem to imply. Lasco's was
an eclectic spirit and he drew heavily both on his own experience and on wide reading; his borrowings from other sources
suggest that his more fundamental debt was to the great reformers of an earlier generation, particularly Martin Bucer and
the Zurich ministers Zwingli and Bullinger. Calvin's Strasburg
and Geneva orders were in any case very largely based on
Bucer's earlier Strasburg works, and where Lasco's London
order differs from Calvin in points of detail it is often because
he has returned to the earlier Bucerian model: the words of
institution at the Eucharist, for example, were taken from a

---

[90] For a more detailed discussion of the relationship between the London order
and other Reformed church orders see A. Sprengler-Ruppenthal, *Mysterium und Riten
nach der Londoner Kirchenordnung der Niederländer* (Cologne, 1967). See also Sprengler-
Ruppenthal's introduction to the German edition of Micron's *Ordinancien* in *Die
evangelischen Kirchenordnungen des 16. Jahrhunderts*, ed. E. Sehling, vii (Tubingen, 1963),
552–78.

[91] *Lasco Opera*, ii. 50; *Liturgia Sacra, STC* 16566; Sehling, *Kirchenordnungen*, 558–9.

Strasburg order of 1537.[92] Bucer's most profound influence on
the London church is evident in the emphasis placed in the
London order on the exercise of ecclesiastical discipline. In
the London order the use of the discipline was developed along
with the ministry of the Word and the sacraments as a third
hallmark of the true Church; Calvin in contrast named only
the latter two.[93]

It might seem something of an irony that Lasco leaned so
heavily on the work of a man whose influence in England he
and his associates distrusted so profoundly. Yet Lasco never
lost his respect for Bucer's formidable learning, and their differences over eucharistic doctrine and ecclesiastical vestments
did not prevent Lasco turning to Bucer for advice as he set
about establishing the institutions of his new church.[94] A
further major influence was undoubtedly Lasco's experiences
in Emden, where like Bucer in Strasburg, Lasco had faced a
serious challenge from lively anabaptist groups: the emphasis
both men placed on community discipline and the education
of the laity may be attributed to this shared experience.[95] The
London order bore several marks of Lasco's sojourn in Emden.
The regular meetings of ministers and elders in the consistory
and the weekly gathering of ministers (*coetus*) were institutions
tried and tested in East Friesland, but here the London order
also exhibited signs of a more fundamental debt to Zwingli
and the Reformation in Zurich. The *coetus* was in origin a Zurich
institution, and one of the most striking innovations of the London church, the prophesy, also developed from a Zurich model.
From 1525 the Zurich professors had expounded the scripture
before the students and the people, and in London this became
an opportunity for the preachers to defend their Sunday sermon.[96] Calvin definitely opposed such a practice. He would
have nothing more than weekly bible readings by the preachers
in the presence of the laity (*congregations*).[97]

[92] Dankbaar in Micron, *Ordinancien*, p. 22.
[93] Sprengler-Ruppenthal, *Mysterium und Riten*, pp. 18–19; Sehling, op. cit., 559–65.
[94] Lasco to Bucer, 12, 26 Oct. 1550. Hopf, *Bucer*, pp. 149, 164.
[95] Sehling, op. cit., 553–8; Bornkamm, 'Martin Bucer', 90–8.
[96] Sehling, op. cit., 569–71. Dankbaar in Micron, *Ordinancien*, pp. 17–19.
[97] This was much nearer the form adopted in the French community. See
below, p. 71.

Whilst the characteristic institutions of the London community thus diverged sharply from the Calvinist models, the doctrinal emphasis was very definitely much closer to that of the Zurich church. Lasco, Micron, and Utenhove all accepted and expounded the sacramental theology of Zurich in their writings, stressing the primary importance of the eucharist as a remembrance.[98] The doctrine of the new church had the same emphasis. The communion is defined as an ordinance of Christ by which his saving death is visibly announced to us; the bread and wine remind us of his body and blood. This is not, however, a bare remembrance. The institution is not only a sign of the infinite generosity of Christ, but in itself a seal of our relationship with Christ; through the sacrament of communion all true believers become one flesh with Christ.[99] This refinement of the starkness of Zwinglian sacramental theology followed the Continental developments which had resulted in a common understanding between the leading Swiss churches in the *Consensus Tigurinus*. Lasco welcomed the Consensus and published it with his lectures pleading for an end to disputes on the nature of the sacrament. As the *Forma ac Ratio* asserted, consideration of God's infinite mercy demonstrated in Christ's death offered far more profound consolation than debating whether the bread contained the substance of Christ's body.[100]

The affinities of the new church to Zurich are hardly to be wondered at. Lasco, Micron, and Utenhove had all been at Zurich and all corresponded with Bullinger; it was to him as a friend and mentor that the trials and triumphs of the London community were first reported. Their relations with Calvin were much more distant. Utenhove had made a brief visit to Geneva in 1549, and faithfully kept Calvin abreast of development on his return to London,[101] but Calvin's relations with Lasco were cool. On one occasion Calvin confided to Farel his misgivings at the extent of Lasco's influence in London.

---

[98] For instance Micron in his *Claer Bewijs*, Utenhove in his *Rationes Quodam*, Lasco in his London lectures. Gerretsen, *Micronius*, pp. 108–10; Pijper, *Utenhove*, p. 39.

[99] *Lasco Opera*, ii. 133, 140, 147, 156; *Toute la Forme*, pp. 103, 112ᵛ, 133ᵛ.

[100] *Brevis et dilucida de sacramentis ecclesiae Christi tractatio*, STC 15259. Printed in *Lasco Opera*, i. 97–232; ibid. ii. 149–50; *Toute la Forme*, 124ᵛ–5.

[101] Koolman, 'Utenhoves Besuch', 270–1.

The impetuosity of the London superintendent was entirely foreign to Calvin's temperament, and there were also theological differences: Lasco for his part made clear that although he had the greatest respect for Calvin he could not accept his doctrine of predestination in all its severity.[102]

Such influence as Calvin had in London was more evident in the French community. The French congregation for the most part used the liturgies established by Lasco for the whole stranger church,[103] but Lasco's order was always intended to leave room for variety and the practice of the French community did differ in several respects. The French adopted a different form for the mid-week prophesy, favouring an exposition of a passage of scripture by the assembled ministers and elders rather than the discussion of the doctrine of the Sunday sermon practised by the Dutch. Lasco approved the variety, arguing that both exercises were necessary in the church, and they took place on different days so that the many strangers who spoke both French and Dutch could profit from both.[104] Yet Calvin would certainly not have approved the Dutch model, and the fact that the French adopted an exercise less prone to controversy may have reflected his influence. Lasco's catechism, too, never appeared in a French translation, suggesting that the French congregation probably used the Geneva catechism. An edition was published in London in 1552, and the only extant copy is bound with the two French liturgies in the Bodleian Library. A year before an edition of Calvin's Geneva New Testament had been printed in London in French.[105] The *Forme des Prieres* also prints several prayers used only in the French church (on Sunday afternoons and weekdays) which are not found in Lasco's order, and these begin with an assertion of the Calvinist doctrine of predestination.[106]

Calvin's adherents in London caused the ministers some difficulties during the church's early years. In 1553 Lasco

---

[102] *CO*, xiii. 655; *Lasco Opera*, ii. 676.

[103] See above, p. 58. The Spanish ambassador reported also that the Confession of Faith had been published by both communities together. *Cal. S. P. Span.*, x. 261.

[104] *Toute la Forme*, pp. 64ᵛ–65ᵛ.; *Lasco Opera*, ii. 104–5.

[105] *Le catechisme de Genéve*, STC 4391; *Le Nouveau Testament*, STC 2957.8; B. Chambers, 'The First French New Testament Printed in England?', *BHR*, 39 (1977), 143–8.

[106] *Forme des Prieres*, p. 10: 'Merciful Father, you have from the beginning elected and adopted your children . . .'.

wrote to Bullinger that he and one of his colleagues had been
denounced before the *coetus* for teaching doctrine different from
that of Calvin. The complaint was raised by the minister of
the small Italian community, Florio, himself in trouble for a
serious moral dereliction; Lasco asked Bullinger to entreat
master Calvin 'not to give rash credit to anything concerning
me, until he shall have had knowledge of the whole matter
from myself'.[107] The previous year Lasco had made a direct
appeal to the Geneva reformer when a serious dissension was
raised in the French church by sympathizers of Calvin. A
newcomer condemned certain of the practices of the London
church which he found different from those of Geneva. Calvin's
name was invoked in support of these criticisms, so Lasco
wrote to inform him of the dispute. Calvin's response was a
letter to the whole French congregation, sharply reproving
those who raised dissension by making 'an idol of me, and a
Jerusalem of Geneva'. He urged the protesters to obey the
rule of the church, even if, in his discussion of the issues raised,
he cautiously endorsed the protesters' criticisms.[108]

  The defensive tone of Calvin's letter indicates a real reluctance to be involved in the affairs of the stranger community
in London at this time. Clearly Calvin did not regard the
London community as a part of his sphere of interest, and the
influence of the Genevan reform on the institutions and doctrine of the church in this early period was extremely limited.
Much the same could be said of Calvin's influence on the
Edwardian Reformation in general. While he followed events
with interest he was not well-informed.[109] The contrast with
Bullinger is striking. Whilst Bullinger was quick to respond
to Hooper's suggestion that he should dedicate the publication
of one of his works to an English notable, Utenhove had some
trouble persuading Calvin to do likewise; when he finally
agreed to do so he returned to Utenhove a revealing enquiry
as to what he should say in his dedication.[110] The evidence

  [107] *Lasco Opera*, ii. 676; Gorham, *Gleanings*, p. 297; Dalton, *Lasco*, pp. 412–13.
  [108] *CO*, xiv. 362–5; Gorham, *Gleanings*, pp. 283–6. Lasco's letter is lost.
  [109] Calvin directed less than a dozen letters to England during the reign of Edward
VI. Albert-Marie Schmidt, *Calvin, Lettres Anglaises* (Paris, 1959).
  [110] *CO*, xiii. 627. On Bullinger's dedication of volumes of his sermons to Edward
VI and the Marquis of Dorset see W. Hollweg, *Heinrich Bullingers Hausbuch* (Neukir-
chen, 1956), pp. 152–5. Also *OL*, ii. 406–7. 415.

from the stranger community should warn against the danger
of over-estimating the influence of the Genevan reform in England at this early stage. Calvin's own position in Geneva was
not entirely secure until after 1553, and for much of Edward's
reign he was under something of a personal shadow following
the death of his wife. A considerable growth in the European
influence of Calvin may be identified during the course of the
1550s, a change that was reflected in the much closer links
with Geneva after the churches' refoundation in 1559.[111]

The doctrine of the London community was thus stamped
by a marked affinity to the Reformation of Zurich, and the
influence the ministers sought to exercise on the English Reformation was very much in this direction. It is important,
though, not to forget the large element of originality in Lasco's
church order. None of the Reformed church orders which
Lasco made use of placed such stress on the participation of
lay members of the community in the election of ministers and
elders and in the discussion of doctrine. No doubt this marked
democratic tendency reflected the priorities of the community
in London and Lasco's own experiences in Emden, but the
personal preferences of the superintendent played their part,
for Lasco was both an original thinker and a strong personality.
The large element of lay participation reflected Lasco's determination to create a community which faithfully reflected the
practice of the primitive church, but in this respect his
painstaking work was not particularly influential, and no subsequent Reformed church order was prepared to concede so
large a measure of control to members of the community.[112]
It is fair to say that Lasco's talent was fundamentally organizational rather than theological: theologically he was heavy-
handed and not always clear-headed, and one may suspect
the guiding hand of Micron steering the church towards a safe
orthodoxy of doctrine.[113] It was Lasco's organizational talent

[111] Below, pp. 151, 163–4. See also my essay, 'The London Exile Community and the
Second Sacramentarian Controversy', forthcoming in *Archiv für Reformationsgeschichte*.
[112] A. van Ginkel, *De Ouderling* (Amsterdam, 1975), pp. 178–83.
[113] A first doctrinal work from Lasco's time at Emden was so unfavourably received
by his fellow reformers that it was never published. Hall, *John a Lasco*, pp. 26, 28.
The respective contributions of Lasco and Micron to the *Forma ac Ratio* and *Ordinancien*

that commended him as superintendent to the English
authorities: his attempts to intervene more generally in the
affairs of his hosts were generally unappreciated and largely
counter-productive. An examination of the strangers' efforts
to accelerate the progress of reform in England is a story of
bold endeavour rather than of any great success.

The English authorities recognized Lasco as one of the most
distinguished of their foreign guests, and were prepared to
make use of his undoubted abilities. In 1552 Lasco was
included in the commission of thirty-two entrusted with the
revision of ecclesiastical law, a distinction accorded to only
two of the foreigners.[114] Thus encouraged, Lasco did not hesitate to offer his advice and opinions. He continued to argue
the case against the vestments long after Hooper had given
way, and used the Latin lectures at Austin Friars to expound
the Zurich view of sacramental doctrine. The lectures were
published in 1552 with a dedication to the King, and Lasco
was also responsible for the publication of one of Bullinger's
own tracts on the eucharist.[115] The practice of the stranger
church was also intended to stimulate further reform in the
English Church, and the *Forma ac Ratio* contains several
implicit criticisms of the practice of the English Church. The
long exposition of the church's preference for taking communion seated, for instance, was probably mainly intended for
English ears.[116]

For all Lasco's enthusiasm the influence of the stranger
church on the course of the English Reformation, whether by
example or exhortation, was ultimately modest. The 1552
Prayer Book did make substantial changes of the sort advocated by the ministers of the foreign churches, but this is not

and the relationship between the two works raise complicated questions. The suggestion that both were based on an earlier Latin draft of the church order gained added
credence from the discovery of the two French orders (see p. 58). Micron himself
would later write that it was Utenhove who first translated the Latin order into
Dutch. Micron, *Ordinancien*, p. 37. See further Sehling, *Kirchenordnungen*, pp. 571–6.

[114] *Chronicle of Edward*, p. 110. Peter Martyr was the other.
[115] H. Bullinger, *Absoluta de Christi domini et catholicae eius ecclesiae Sacramentis tractatio*
(1551), *STC* 4042.4. For Lasco's lectures see note 100, above.
[116] *Lasco Opera*, ii. 116–22; *Toute la Forme*, pp. 81–88ᵛ. See also Lasco to Cranmer,
Aug. 1551, *Lasco Opera*, ii. 657.

to say that these changes were their responsibility. Several other influential figures, including Martin Bucer and Peter Martyr, had also pressed for an extensive revision of the 1549 Prayer Book, and the changes effected closely reflected the detailed criticisms of the First Book made by Bucer in his *Censura*, submitted to the English government at Cranmer's invitation.[117] Several institutions and practices of which the advanced reformers did not approve were retained in the 1552 Book, and the issue of whether further changes should be made to bring the Book into line with the practice of the Swiss churches was to prove deeply divisive in exile during Mary's reign.[118] But in 1552 the biggest furore was caused by the retention of kneeling to receive communion, a practice which the strangers' order firmly rejected. The protests of the Reformed led to the addition of the Black Rubric to the new book (explaining that kneeling implied no adoration of the sacrament), a victory of sorts but one usually attributed to the influence of Knox rather than to Lasco and his colleagues.[119] The insertion of the Black Rubric angered Cranmer, who had argued strongly against it, but that the Reformed were ultimately forced to accept a practice which they regarded as idolatrous even with this reservation was a significant re-assertion of the government's right to regulate the practices of the church. In this respect the defeat inflicted on Hooper and his allies over clerical vestments had proved crucial. Hooper and Lasco had made their stand, first for the rights of the individual conscience, then for the prescriptive power of scripture in matters of church order and doctrine. Their failure to prevail represented both an assertion of the role of the state in religious affairs and, in the long term equally significantly, an assertion of the right of the English Church to develop independently of Continental models. In practical terms the change was reflected initially only in comparatively subtle differences, but

[117] Hopf, *Martin Bucer*, pp. 55–98.

[118] (William Whittingham), *A Brief Discourse of the Troubles begun at Frankfurt* (1574), STC 25442. Modern edition 1846; Jasper Ridley, *John Knox* (Oxford, 1968), pp. 189–214.

[119] Ridley, *Knox*, pp. 106–9; Richard Greaves, 'John Knox, the Reformed Tradition, and the Sacrament of the Lord's Supper', *Archiv für Reformationsgeschichte*, 66 (1975), 246–7.

the pattern was set for the future development of the English Church.

In the long run the London church order exercised a much more profound influence on the Reformed church in the Netherlands than on the English church.[120] That is not to say that the institutions of the stranger church might not, given time, have had an impact in England; but time was against them, and in the few short years of the communities' first existence English churchmen were probably more impressed by the strangers' turbulence, the manner of their lobbying, and their internal wrangles, than by the liturgy they had established. In this respect Lasco's insistent pressure probably rebounded to the strangers' disadvantage. The experience of the Edwardian period would not encourage a repetition of the experiment of an independent church, and the privileges of the foreign community would be severely curtailed when the churches were refounded in 1559.

[120] Below, Ch. VIII.

IV

The Stranger Churches and the Foreign Community

THE foundation of the stranger churches evoked an enthusiastic response from London's foreign community. Observers reported large crowds at Austin Friars, and the Dutch congregation soon had to increase the size of their consistory to cope with the increased burdens brought by growing numbers.[1] It is difficult to offer more than an informed estimate of the actual number who joined the two churches during the Edwardian period. The one surviving register for members of the Dutch congregation lists 489 members (of which 135 were women and children), and although the list was added to as time went on, the register was certainly not kept up to date until the end of the reign.[2] By 1553 the Dutch church probably had twice as many members as are listed in the register; as early as April 1551 the Spanish ambassador reported that more than a thousand had been seen at Austin Friars at one time, so this may be a conservative estimate.[3] No statistical evidence of any sort survives for the size of the French congregation, but in the Elizabethan period the French and Dutch churches were always roughly the same size,[4] so it is probable that the two congregations together grew from something approaching seven hundred adult male members in 1550–1 to about double

[1] Micron, *Ordinancien*, p. 37.

[2] Dutch Register, Guildhall Library MS 7402. Printed in *Returns*, i. 201–9. The names of several reformers known to have been members of the church (Dathenus, Winghen, van Meteren, van der Katelene) do not appear on the register. See also note 3, below.

[3] *Cal. S. P. Span.*, x. 278–9. Of the 34 Dutch names on a partial list of those who took ship with Lasco in 1553 (see Ch. V n. 23), 15 are recorded in the register and 19 are not, which offers some support for the suggestion that the church approximately doubled in size. *BRN*, ix. 89–90.

[4] According to the survey of 1568, 1,910 foreigners belonged to the Dutch church and 1,810 to the French. *Returns*, iii. 439. In 1593 the figures were 1,376 and 1,344 respectively. *Returns of Strangers in the Metropolis, 1593, 1627, 1635, 1639*, ed. I. Scouloudi (Huguenot Society Publications, 57, 1985), p. 90.

that number by the end of the reign. Taking into account wives and children, the church communities must have numbered something between three and four thousand by 1553.

Clearly this was nothing like the total size of London's foreign community. There were already more than five thousand foreigners settled in the capital before 1547 and this number increased steadily during the next six years. In 1553 Henry Bullinger believed that there were as many as fifteen thousand foreign refugees in England, and although no great reliance should be placed on his estimate the chances are that by end of the reign there were at least ten thousand foreigners settled in the city and its suburbs.[5] On this reckoning the members of the French and Dutch churches would have made up less than half the total foreign population of the capital, a proportion roughly in line with that revealed by the comprehensive surveys of the alien community later in the century.[6] Of course, the influence of the churches would not necessarily have been confined to those who became full members of the community. Van der Katelene's account of his own conversion is evidence that foreign residents who were not members of the churches attended their services, and not all who shared his curiosity would have followed his example and subsequently embarked on the intensive doctrinal instruction which preceded admission to full membership of the congregation. It is quite probable that many foreigners of genuinely Reformed sympathies may have baulked at the public scrutiny of their beliefs necessary before they could be admitted to membership of the church, and other long-established foreign residents may simply have felt well settled in their parish churches, and for this reason ignored the foreign communities.[7]

Even allowing for a substantial number of foreigners generally sympathetic to the new institutions who decided, for various reasons, not to join, there must still have been large

[5] Bullinger to Calvin, Aug. 1553. *CO*, xiv. 598. Since the reformers talk of there being more than 5,000 'Germans' in the capital during Edward's reign, an estimate of double this number for the total stranger population seems very plausible. *OL*, i. 336; Gorham, *Gleanings*, p. 78.

[6] 2,823 foreigners were recorded in 1568 as going either to English parish churches or to no church at all, as against 3,720 who attended the French and Dutch churches (about 55%). *Returns*, iii. 439.

[7] For example, the printer Reyner Wolf. See below, pp. 93–4.

numbers of foreigners in London who had little or nothing to do with the foreign churches. On the basis of the figures presented above, as many as half London's foreign population fell into this latter category. In some respects (as will be suggested in a later chapter[8]) the new churches acted as a focus for the communal life of the whole foreign community, but in the short term their impact on different sections of the stranger community seems to have been very varied. An analysis of the surviving membership list of the Dutch congregation suggests that the churches won adherents amongst all groups within the foreign community, including those long settled in England. But, equally clearly, the new institutions exercised a much stronger appeal to some groups within the foreign population than to others: a detailed examination of three occupational groups, for instance, shows a wide disparity between their levels of commitment to the new institution. Although there can never be a simple explanation of why some strangers joined the churches and others did not, it may well be possible to suggest some factors, vocational, locational, or broadly socio-economic, that influenced the different reactions of individuals to the stranger churches.

The stranger churches were ostensibly founded in 1550 to succour the victims of continental persecution, and naturally strangers newly arrived in England since 1547 made up a considerable proportion of the membership of the new churches. The best indication of this is the evidence of enrolled patents of denization where they are recorded for members of the Dutch congregation listed in the surviving register of the church. A patent of denization is recorded for 62 of the 351 male members of the church, and of these 39 received their patents in the great enrolment which coincided with the church's foundation. The new denizens were almost all recent arrivals in England.[9] Not all of them need necessarily have come to England for religious reasons, but a group who certainly were refugees may be identified with the help of the

---

[8] Below, Ch. VII.

[9] *Cal. Pat. Rolls Edward VI*, iii. 248–52. Hardly any of these new denizens can be found in subsidy returns before 1547.

records of the heresy commission in Flanders.[10] At least 24 members of the Dutch congregation had fled to England after investigation or condemnation by the commission. These included four of the elders, and two deacons, William de Vischer, a rich carpet-manufacturer who fled from Oudenaarde in 1550, and Paul van Winghen who followed him across the Channel two years later.[11] Both would play a prominent role in the life of the church after the dissolution of the London community in 1553, and the same can be said of two other educated refugees who were content to join the church in London without holding any office. Gerard Mortaigne had studied in Louvain before the discovery of an incriminating letter at the house of a friend forced him to flee to London. In 1553 he joined the other leading members of the church in Emden, where he was made an elder of the church in 1557.[12] Karel de Koninck was a priest near Ghent before his conversion to the Reformation. In England he lived with Bucer in Cambridge, and on the latter's death in 1551 evidently moved south to London, where he earned a living as a schoolmaster. Although forced to leave London in the spring of 1554, de Koninck scorned a safe asylum at Emden, and in 1557 he was apprehended and executed at Bruges.[13] Some of the refugees abandoned a considerable property in the Netherlands when they fled to England. Jan Baccau and Hermes and Peter Bruggeman all left a house or piece of agricultural land in Ronse, and only Peter Bruggeman succeeded in bringing with him enough to be accounted a householder in London.[14]

The 39 new denizens and 24 Flanders refugees must substantially understate the proportion of the church's members who were new arrivals during Edward's reign. Many of the names on the Dutch church register cannot be identified in other records, and it is likely that many of these were recent immigrants.[15] There were doubtless other refugees from Brabant,

---

[10] Decavele, *Dageraad*, vol. ii.

[11] Ibid., i. 382, ii. 192, 204.

[12] Ibid., i. 96–8, ii. 150.

[13] Ibid., i. 325–7, ii. 94.

[14] Ibid., i. 541; *Returns*, i. 213.

[15] Some will have escaped detection because of gaps in the records, or because their names have been altered to forms which cannot reliably be matched to the names in the Dutch register. The subsidy returns and denization rolls which provide

Holland, and northern France. Nevertheless, the church also drew a substantial number of its members from amongst those foreigners who had been in London for some years.

Three of the Dutch elders had been in London since at least 1544, and the same can be said of 21 of the 89 ordinary members of the congregation for whom a subsidy payment or patent of denization has been traced.[16] Many of these longer-term residents were amongst the most prosperous members of the church. Anthony Godfrey, a broker who had been in England since 1539, was assessed on goods worth £20 for the subsidy of 1549, as was the shoemaker Jan Schauwe.[17] Another shoemaker, Jan van Cuelen, who had been in England since 1544, was assessed at £40.[18] The hatmakers Jan Martens and Ruth Langor were assessed at £15 and £25 respectively, and the tailor Nicholas Janson and the joiner Vincent Naghel at £10 each; all had been in England since 1544.[19] If one bears in mind that it was possible to have a reasonable living and be assessed for subsidy on as little as £2,[20] and that well-to-do gentry were assessed at £20 on land, then these established Dutch craftsmen were rather more than comfortably well off. Of the 70 members of the Dutch church for whom a subsidy payment can be traced, 43 paid on £3 or more, whilst only 21 paid a poll tax on the minimum assessment of twenty shillings. On the evidence of subsidy returns the more prosperous members of the foreign community made up a substantial proportion of the Dutch congregation, and 102 members of the church were registered on a separate list as the church's 'householders'.[21]

---

much of the information used in this survey were compiled by local English officials, who were sometimes quite baffled by foreign names. The name of Hubert d'Anvillier, a French typecaster, appears in English records in eleven different forms (listed in E. J. Worman, *Alien Members of the Book Trade* (1906), pp. 13–14). With common names (Jansen, Johnson) it has not been assumed that a person mentioned in a subsidy list is identical with the member of the church unless corroborating evidence is available (profession or place of residence).

[16] For the elders see p. 56, above.
[17] *Returns*, i. 161, 185.
[18] Ibid., i. 106.
[19] Ibid., i. 142, 143, 223, 225. Evidence for length of residence, ibid., i. 31, 341, 467; *Denizations*, p. 136.
[20] See below, p. 88.
[21] *Returns*, i. 211–14.

If church members were often long-established in London, they were also well integrated in the London trade structure. In the case of 260 of the first members of the Dutch congregation their occupations are known, either because they are marked in the church register or because their names have been identified on company records.[22] Most seem to have worked in traditional crafts or trades. The largest group worked in clothing and shoemaking: some 45 were tailors and 50 shoemakers and cobblers; another 16 made hats and gloves. 37 worked in woodwork crafts, mostly as joiners, boxmakers, and coopers, and another 8 were basket-makers. Amongst 30 metalworkers were 10 cutlers and 12 goldsmiths, these last being the most prominent representatives of aliens serving the luxury and consumer market with which they would increasingly be associated. In this category the six glassmakers and most of the seventeen weavers should also be mentioned; the fifteen members of the printing trade also worked in a new industry in which foreign expertise made a marked contribution.

Most church members, though, followed traditional trades in which they would have been in direct competition with English tradesmen. Inevitably they aroused some hostility, and it is not surprising that most church members reacted in traditional ways, by making their homes in the liberties or outside the city walls. 230 members of the Dutch church have their place of residence marked on the register, or have been traced in subsidy returns. By far the biggest group (77) lived in Southwark, and another 70 outside the city: 40 to the east in East Smithfield, St Katherine's, and Whitechapel, and 30 to the west, mostly in Faringdon Ward Without. Strangers came to the church from as far afield as Westminster and Stepney. Inside the city walls major concentrations are found only in the Liberty of St Martin's, a traditional haunt of aliens, where 20 church members lived, and in the three wards at the east end of the city, Aldgate, Tower, and Langborne. In all the rest of the city there were only another 22 church

[22] 230 have their occupation marked in the register. In a few cases a servant living in the house of another member is assumed to be an apprentice carrying on the same trade.

members, while some central wards had none at all. The members of the church settled almost entirely in areas with established concentrations of foreign residents,[23] and even the more substantial strangers seem to have had no wish to move away from their fellow-countrymen into the more exclusive parts of the city. Those with substantial business operations would often presumably have wished to stay close to a plentiful supply of foreign workmen.

The geographical concentration of church members around and outside the city walls helps to explain why the foundation of the churches made such an impact. When strangers flocked to Austin Friars and to the French church in Threadneedle Street, both situated in Broad Street Ward in the prosperous heart of the city, Englishmen were made aware of concentrations of aliens where few if any had been seen before. The effect was to stimulate a wave of hostile rumours of vast numbers of strangers in the city, and the foreigners were easy scapegoats for the high prices and food shortages experienced in the capital after two bad harvests.[24] In the spring of 1551, a time of particular tension and rumbling discontent, a deputation of citizens made a formal complaint to the Lord Mayor against the strangers, and a plot to attack the foreigners was nipped in the bud by the city authorities.[25] It was being put about that there were forty or fifty thousand strangers in London, but this, as the Imperial ambassador was aware, was an absurd exaggeration. The true figure, as Scheyfve judiciously remarked, was nearer a tenth of this total.[26]

It was thus an important aspect of the impact of the stranger churches, as Scheyfve realized at the time, that they made the stranger population more visible. Strangers came to the foreign churches from all parts of London, and the congregation included representatives of most of the trades in which numbers of foreigners were active. So much is clear from the first Dutch register, but the register on its own can give no very clear idea of how typical the individuals who joined the church

[23] See above, p. 18.
[24] *Cal. S. P. Span.*, x. 218–19.
[25] *Chronicle of Edward*, p. 59; *Cal. S. P. For., Edward VI*, pp. 119–20; *APC*, iii. 256–7.
[26] *Cal. S. P. Span.*, x. 278–9. It is interesting that when rumours of vast numbers of aliens in the capital began circulating again in the 1560s, the figure mentioned was again forty thousand. See below, p. 279.

were of the groups within the foreign population to which they belonged. A more suggestive picture emerges when one compares the information available from the register with what is known of all the foreigners active in certain trades. An analysis of complete trade groups, in so far as this is possible, makes clear that the church evoked a very different response in different sections of the alien community, both in the number who joined the church and in the reaction of members to its dissolution in 1553.

A study of this sort is severely restricted by the patchy nature of surviving records. It is frustrating, for instance, that no company records exist which would allow us to assess what proportion of the total number of alien shoemakers working in London were the fifty who joined the church. Usable records do exist, however, for weavers, coopers, and for the printing trade, and large numbers of aliens were at work in all these occupations. Printing, the archetypal new industry, relied heavily on foreign expertise, and whilst weaving was of course long-established in England there was a tradition of employing foreign workmen. In the sixteenth century the superiority of their techniques for the manufacture of light cloths and luxury fabrics brought renewed interest in harnessing the skills of these foreign artisans in London. No such technical innovation was connected with the making of barrels, but the involvement of foreign workmen was the result of the close association of cooperage with beer-brewing, and brewing was certainly an occupation in which foreigners were important innovators. By examining what we know of the individuals listed in these occupational records, it is possible to say something of the measure of commitment of each of these groups to the new foreign churches.

The domination of the English book trade by imported works from the major Continental printing centres was only gradually broken during the first half of the sixteenth century.[27] Not until

---

[27] These general remarks are based on M. E. Kronenberg, 'Notes on English Printing in the Low Countries', *The Library*, 4th ser., ix (1928–9), 139–63; Patricia M. Took, 'Government and the Printing Trade', (London Univ. Ph.D. thesis, 1979); E. Gordon Duff, *A Century of the English Book Trade* (1948). See also Colin Clair, 'Refugee Printers and Publishers in Britain during the Tudor Period', *HS*, xxii (1970–6), 115–26.

1540 or 1550 were English presses able to satisfy domestic demand for works such as liturgies, and even during the reign of Edward purchasers continued to look abroad for serious works of scholarship. The development of a native industry to compete with these high-quality imports relied heavily on foreign expertise, and by the middle of the century there was an established tradition of foreign printers' setting up in London. Caxton's own press passed on his death to his Alsatian assistant Wynkyn de Worde, who by the time of his death in 1535 had printed nearly 800 books, mostly in London and most using Caxton's familiar device and initials.[28] The first printers to establish a press in London, William de Machlinia and John Lettou, were both foreigners. Richard Pynson, King's Printer from 1508 to 1529, was a Norman by birth, and John Reynes, the prosperous stationer and bookbinder active in London for over thirty years until 1544, was a native of the Low Countries.[29] Some of the first Protestant works printed in London were the work of immigrant printers. James Nicholson, a native of the Low Countries resident in Southwark, began his career by publishing in 1535 the first edition of the English Bible printed at Zurich by Froschauer, for which he printed titles and prefatory material. In 1537 and 1538 he printed further editions of the Bible and Coverdale's New Testament, one of the latter being edited by John Hollybush, a refugee stationer probably identifiable as the Antwerp printer Jan van Ruremond.[30]

The relaxation of controls on the accession of Edward VI brought a great upsurge of demand for books, and particularly for works of religious polemic. The number of printers working to meet this demand increased rapidly, and much of the extra capacity was provided by foreign craftsmen. Some seventy foreigners were active in the printing trade during Edward's reign.[31] The majority of these were Dutch journeymen, several employed by the leading London English printers Grafton,

---

[28] Duff, *Century*, pp. 173–4.
[29] Ibid., pp. 92, 97, 126–7, 135–6.
[30] Ibid., pp. 110–11, 141–2.
[31] They are listed in an appendix to Took, 'Government and the Printing Trade'. The information is derived from Worman, *Alien Members of the Book Trade*.

Whitchurch, Singleton, and Day.[32] The printers were served by a variety of foreign stationers, typefounders, and (mostly French) bookbinders. Of the fifty or so Dutchmen working in the trade fifteen were members of the Dutch church, and these included all three independent Dutch printers who set up in London during Edward's reign, and another, Gilles van der Erve, who would be an important printer of Reformed works in exile.[33]

Three Dutch printers, Walter Lynn, Nicholas Hill, and Stephen Mierdman, were between them responsible for a considerable proportion of the religious literature which poured off the presses during Edward's reign. They repay close attention, because in their books one has the comparatively rare phenomenon of a personal expression of religious feeling from an ordinary member of the Church. This is particularly so in the case of Walter Lynn, who was responsible for the publication of twenty-one titles between 1548 and 1550, almost all of them Protestant works.[34] It seems unlikely that Lynn had his own press (almost all his editions are marked as being for him by another printer), but Lynn as publisher often provided a letter to the reader or a dedication. There are dedications to King Edward and his sister the Princess Elizabeth, Somerset and his wife the Duchess Anne, and Archbishop Cranmer.[35] All express Lynn's confidence in the power of the printed word to spread the Gospel and banish popery. I wish all men would read it, he says of his *Dialogue between a Christian Father and his Son*, 'to put away their new errors (grounded upon the Romish rock) by the knowledge of the old faith that is builded upon the foundations of the prophets and Apostles'.[36] Lynn had an entrepreneur's awareness of the strength of demand for Protestant tracts, and searched out for publication a diverse selection of devotional and exhortatory works from Continental sources.

[32] Worman, ibid., pp. 14, 25, 62, 70.

[33] *Returns*, i. 202–9. Marked as printer (drucker) or as a servant to a known printer (Mierdman, Hill, Day).

[34] For Lynn see Duff, *Century*, pp. 95–6; Worman, *Alien Members*, pp. 37–8.

[35] *STC* 4079, 4626 (Edward VI); 17115 (Edward VI and Protector Somerset); 16982 (Princess Elizabeth); 17117, 17119, 24223.5 (Duchess of Somerset); 20843 (Cranmer).

[36] *The True Belief of Christ and His Sacraments, set forth in a dialogue between a Christian Father and his Son* (1550). Dedication, Sig. Aiii., *STC* 24223.5.

Even personal misfortune could be turned to ultimate good, as when Lynn published a collection of the scriptural texts that had helped him overcome the sorrow of a bereavement, to which he added two sermons of Luther on the same subject.[37] In this compilation and his dedications Lynn appears as author as well as publisher, but his most important personal contribution was probably as a translator. In his dedication to *The Three Books of Chronicles*, a history of 300 folios which he translated from the Latin, Lynn described himself as 'one that spendeth all his tyme in the setting forth of books in the English tongue'.[38] Nine of Lynn's books are his own translations, either from Latin or German, among them works by Luther and Bullinger which he made available in English for the first time.[39]

Lynn came to England from Antwerp in about 1540 and settled in Billingsgate Ward.[40] He prospered quickly, and by 1547 had built up a comfortable capital.[41] Lynn clearly felt at home in England: one of his translations, Bullinger's sermon on magistrates and obedience, Lynn presented to Edward VI in consideration of the 'great benefits I have received of this your Majesty's realm of England which hath so many years nourished and succoured my poor life hitherto'.[42] Lynn enjoyed some measure of official patronage, for, in addition to the protection of his exclusive right to the religious works which he published, he was also entrusted with the publication of two editions of Cranmer's catechism. Possibly in recognition of his services as a publisher of Reformed works, in 1549 Lynn was licensed to import 800 tuns of wine and woad from France

[37] *A brief collection of all such texts of scripture as declare the happy estate of them that be visited with sycknes* (1549), *STC* 17119.

[38] *STC* 4626. Sig. *ii.

[39] Luther, *STC* 16964, 16982, sermons appended to *STC* 17119, 21826.6; Bullinger, *STC* 4079, 17117.

[40] He paid subsidy on goods assessed at 20*s.* in 1541. *Returns*, i. 61. Lynn was made a citizen of Antwerp on 21 Nov. 1533. See Colin Clair, 'On the Printing of Certain Reformation Books', *The Library*, 5th Ser., 18 (1963), 280 n. 1. He was probably the Wouter van Lin who printed three books at Antwerp in 1533–4. See Worman, *Alien Members*, p. 38.

[41] He was assessed on goods worth £10 in 1549, and was one of the householders of the Dutch church. *Returns*, i. 161, 214.

[42] *STC* 4079, Dedication, Sig. Aii.

or Spain.[43] The profits to be made by shipping merchandise seem to have been sufficient to allow Lynn to wind up his publishing business, for after 1550 no further editions appeared bearing his distinctive emblem. By 1553 Lynn probably felt sufficiently separated from the printing trade not to fear reprisals from the Marian regime, and he chose not to follow the leaders of the Dutch church into exile.[44] He lived on undisturbed in Billingsgate Ward until his death some time before 1571.[45]

None of the other alien printers matches Lynn as an initiator of projects, nor in the garrulous enthusiasm of his dedications; all three, however, leave evidence of the sincerity of their support for the Reformed religion. Nicholas Hill (van den Berghe) printed thirty-six editions between 1547 and 1553, almost all of them Protestant works.[46] In 1552 and 1553 he was entrusted with the printing of the catechisms of the Dutch church, of which he was himself an elder.[47] Hill had been in England for some years before the establishment of the stranger church, and took out letters of denization in 1544.[48] He settled outside the city to the west in St John Street, and was assessed for subsidy in 1549 at forty shillings. In 1550 Hill's assessment was reduced to twenty shillings, but he must nevertheless have been a man of some substance as he employed two assistants on his presses and appeared in the householder list of the church.[49] In 1553 he was particularly busy, with at least eleven

---

[43] *STC* 5993, 5994. *Cal. Pat. Rolls Edward VI*, ii. 238. Licence to Walter Lynne of London, Stacyoner.

[44] Although he had been sufficiently committed to the church to have his daughter catechized. *Returns*, i. 210.

[45] The 1571 return of aliens has 'Annys Lin, widow' marked in Billingsgate Ward. Walter had been alive in 1567. *Returns*, i. 331, 443.

[46] For Hill see Duff, *Century*, pp. 72–3; Worman, *Alien Members*, pp. 30–1; H. F. Wijnman, 'Grepen uit de Geschiedenis van de Nederlandse Emigrantendrukkerijen te Emden', I, *Het Boek*, 36 (1963–4), 162–3. Duff thinks that Hill's name was crossed out in the register because he died before 1553, but in fact his name was removed from the main list when he was elected an elder. The same happened with other elders (see Roland Honaer, *Returns*, i. 208).

[47] *STC* 15260.5, 15260.7; *Returns*, i. 202 (Nicholas van der Berghe).

[48] *Denizations*, p. 124 (Nicholas Hilles, printer).

[49] Paul Seghers marked 'drucker, met Nicholais', and Peter de Cupere marked 'met Nicholais de prentere.' Urban van Coelen marked Smithfield, 'bouckprenter' was probably a third assistant. He is almost certainly Urban Lynyng, who was a servant of Hill in 1549. *Returns*, i. 157, 208, 209. See also below, p. 92. Subsidy and Householder list, *Returns*, i. 157, 200, 213.

titles coming from his press, but on the accession of Mary he dismantled his substantial operations and abandoned his established position in England to follow the other leading members of the Dutch church into exile. Hill set up his press once again in Emden, where he continued to print the works of his London colleagues under the pseudonym Cornelius Volckwinner, as well as a great number of works in English.[50] These, mostly works of Reformed propaganda with fantastic colophons, included works by Ridley, Cranmer, and Knox, and were clearly intended for clandestine distribution in England. Hill died in March 1557, sincerely regretted by his former London colleagues. His widow would return to England on the re-establishment of the Dutch church in 1559.[51]

On Hill's death his press passed to another former member of the Dutch church in London, Gilles van der Erve.[52] Unlike Hill, van der Erve was a new arrival in London in Edward's reign, having fled there after investigation by the heresy commission in Flanders. In London van der Erve became a deacon of the Dutch church, and was later elected to serve alongside Hill as elder.[53] He took out letters of denization, but seems not to have run his own press in London as no editions survive which bear his name. Possibly he worked for Hill, as he seems to have done during the first years of the exile in Emden.[54] Van der Erve was one of the first group to leave London on

[50] *STC* 16571a, 17863.5. F. Isaacs and A. F. Johnson, in identifying Volckwinner as a pseudonym of Ctematius, attribute all these productions of Hill's Emden press to van der Erve. But Wijnman demonstrates convincingly that Volckwinner was Hill (Collis = heuvel, berg; νικαω = winnen; λαοσ = volk) and that Hill founded the Emden printing-house in which van der Erve initially assisted him. See Wijnman, 'Emigrantendrukkerijen te Emden', I, 162 n. 2; F. Isaacs, 'Egidius van der Erve and his English Printed Books', *The Library*, 4th ser., 12 (1931–2), 336–52; A. F. Johnson, 'English Books Printed Abroad', *The Library*, 5th ser., 4 (1949–50), 274; *KP I*, p. 257 n. 1.

[51] Mortaigne to Utenhove, 11 Apr. 1557: 'Our former printer Nicholas has died here'. Also Winghen to Utenhove, 13 Apr. 1557. Hessels, ii. 59, 63. Vidua Nicholai Bergensis, calcographi, cum suis orphanis. *Returns*, i. 209.

[52] For van der Erve see Duff, *Century*, p. 44; Worman. *Alien Members*, pp. 18–21; Wijnman, 'Emigrantendrukkerijen te Emden', I and II, *Het Boek*, 37 (1964–6), 121–51.

[53] Decavele, ii. 106; *Returns*, i. 202 (Gilles vand Herue, Diaconus. Egidius vander Erve, Senior).

[54] *Denizations*, p. 88 (Gilles Ander Ersen). Worman is incorrect in suggesting that the 1552 editions of the *Claer Bewijs* and *Kleyne Catechismus* might have been printed by van der Erve. The former was printed by Mierdman and the latter by Hill. *STC* 15260.7, 17863.3. Wijnman, 'Emigrantendrukkerijen te Emden', I, 162–3.

the dissolution of the church in 1553. He sailed with the church leaders from Gravesend, and made the hazardous and tortuous journey through Denmark to Emden with them. In December 1553 the leaders of the church were summoned by the Council of Copenhagen to explain their eucharistic doctrine, and in the absence of the ministers at Court, van der Erve was one of the leading members of the consistory sent to represent the church.[55] In Emden he would once again serve on the consistory as an elder, and prove a loyal supporter of the London ministers even at some financial peril to himself. Even before Hill's death, their press had been heavily involved in Utenhove's project for a new Dutch Bible. When Hill died, van der Erve, now printing as Gellius Ctematius, was saddled with the whole responsibility for the work, which, though published in a large edition in 1556, proved quite unsaleable.[56] For a time it seemed as if van der Erve might be bankrupted by this disaster; his press was still not running at full capacity eighteen months later, and he was forced to recover his financial position with an edition of the unorthodox Liesveldt Bible favoured by anabaptists. Although forced to this project by financial stringency, van der Erve was an orthodox supporter of the doctrine of the church (he is known to have said that he would have strangled Hendrik Niklaes of the Family of Love with his bare hands), and he continued to serve the church leaders loyally despite his experience with Utenhove's Bible: 1558 saw reprints of three of the London church's publications, and two new volumes of Utenhove's psalms.[57]

The commercial and critical failure of Utenhove's Bible was all the more marked as a result of the success of a rival edition of the same year published by the other Emden printing house of Mierdman and Galliart.[58] Stephen Mierdman was another who had made the trek from London to Emden in 1553; this

[55] Utenhove, *Simplex et Fidelis Narratio, BRN,* ix. 83, 90.

[56] Wijnman, 'Emigrantendrukkerijen te Emden', I, 142. 2,500 copies were printed, but Utenhove's insistence on what he regarded as linguistic purity found favour with no one except his close associates. See also Jan Weerda, 'Eine Denkschrift Godfried van Wingens an den Emder Kirchenrat gegen die Gheilliaert-Bibel von 1556', *NAK*, 31 (1940), 107.

[57] Wijnman, 'Emigrantendrukkerijen te Emden', I, 142 ff., II, 151; Worman, *Alien Members*, p. 20.

[58] Wijnman, 'Emigrantendrukkerijen te Emden', I, 146.

indeed was his second exile, as he had been forced to leave a thriving business in Antwerp when he first came to London.[59] In Antwerp Mierdman had initially worked in partnership with his brother-in-law Matthew Crom, from whom he took over the direction of the press at about the same time as he was admitted to the freedom of the city in 1543. He was already a committed Protestant, and his press was soon given over to publishing works of the Reformed religion, including a substantial number of vernacular works destined for clandestine importation into England.[60] Some time between 1546 and 1549 Antwerp became too dangerous, and Mierdman was forced to remove to London.[61] He settled in Billingsgate, close to Lynn, for whom much of his early English work was printed. Mierdman must have brought some capital with him as he was assessed on a fairly substantial £5 worth of goods in 1549. More importantly, he was also able to bring much of his printing equipment with him.[62] Mierdman's London press was soon extremely busy. He employed at least three men, and produced nearly fifty editions between 1548 and 1553. Almost all of these were Protestant works, and his monopoly rights to these editions were protected by a patent of July 1550.[63] Mierdman printed works in Latin, French, and Dutch, as well as in English, including commissions for Perussel, Poullain, and the leaders of the Dutch church, for whom Mierdman printed the first edition of the catechism and two of Lasco's Latin works.[64] He joined the Dutch church and was made

[59] For Mierdman see Duff, *Century*, p. 105; Worman, *Alien Members*, pp. 44–7; Colin Clair, 'On the Printing of Certain Reformation Books', 275–87.

[60] H. F. Wijnman, 'De Antwerpse herformingsgezinde drukker Mattheus Crom en zijn naaste omgeving', *De Gulden Passer*, 40 (1962), 105–24; Clair, 'Reformation Books', 276–8; *Short Title Catalogue of Books Printed in the Netherlands and Belgium in the British Museum* (1965), p. 245; *Belgica Typographica, 1541–1600* (Nieuwkoop, 1968–80), i. 508, ii. 367.

[61] Mierdman's shop in Antwerp was made over to his sister-in-law in 1546, but he is not found in London records before 1549, and the revised *STC* persists in locating editions published by Mierdman in 1547 and 1548 in Antwerp. Probably he did not come to England until shortly before 1549. Wijnman, 'Mattheus Crom', 118; Clair, 'Reformation Books', 285–6; *STC* 17789, 18877.

[62] *Returns*, i. 161. The fact that Mierdman brought much of his printing materials with him to England explains the confusion over the date of his arrival in England, as there is no difference in type between his London and Antwerp work. Clair, 'Reformation Books', 278; ibid., 'Refugee Printers', 123.

[63] *Cal. Pat. Rolls Edward VI*, iii. 314; *Returns*, i. 207, 209.

[64] *STC* 15259, 15260, 15263, 16566, 19783.

denizen with many others of the first members in October 1550. Amongst the works he printed for his fellow church members was a violent attack on the papacy, *Den Val der Roomscher Kercken*. Mierdman has sometimes been credited with the authorship of this polemic, though it seems in fact to be a translation from an English original.[65] Mierdman was quick to quit England on the dissolution of the London church, and by 1554 he had set up his printing operations anew in Emden. There he concentrated on the production of a Dutch version of the Liesveldt Bible, the success of which would add greatly to van der Erve's problems after the débâcle of the Utenhove Bible. Mierdman died in 1559, and his press passed to his partner, Johan Galliart.

These four Dutch printers, Lynn, Hill, Mierdman, and van der Erve, were between them responsible for a considerable proportion both of the religious literature produced during Edward's reign, and of the clandestine Protestant propaganda directed towards England during the reign of Mary. All gave personal testimony of their devotion to the Reformed faith, Lynn in his writings, the others, perhaps more eloquently, in their withdrawal into exile with the church in 1553 and their activities once there. Much less is known of the journeymen-printers who joined the church. Many are no more than names on the Dutch church register. Paul Seygar, one of Hill's apprentices, had previously worked for Whitchurch. He took out letters of denization at the time of the church's establishment, but then disappears from the records.[66] The fact that so many of the journeymen-printers cannot be traced in records after 1550 suggests that some at least accompanied the master printers into exile. One at least is known to have done so: Urban Lyning, another of Hill's journeymen, became a citizen of Emden in 1557. He came back to England with the church at the beginning of Elizabeth's reign but soon returned to the Continent, and in 1571 is found printing for Plantin at

---

[65] *STC* 21307.3, modern edition, *BRN*, i. 391–420. The British Library Catalogue gives Mierdman as the author, but Pijper in his introduction for the *BRN* demonstrates conclusively its English origin.

[66] Worman, *Alien Members*, p. 61; *Returns*, i. 208; *Denizations*, p. 218.

Antwerp.[67] Only one of the Dutch journeymen-printers who joined the church is known to have remained in England during Mary's reign. Jacob Wolfaert, a compositor with Grafton, joined the church but is marked in the return of aliens of 1571 as having been in England since the first year of Edward VI's reign.[68] The Dutch printers most likely to have remained in England were those who had not joined the church. Conrad Miller, a servant of Gypkin in 1549, was admitted a brother of the Stationers' Company before 1556. He remained, and prospered: by 1564 he was assessed on a prosperous £5 worth of goods.[69]

At least one independent Dutch printer, Reyner Wolf, did not join the Dutch church. A native of Gelderland, Wolf arrived in England about 1530, and by the time of the church's foundation had already made for himself a substantial position in London society. Wolf originally traded as a bookseller; he was made a denizen in 1533, and a member of the Stationers' Company in 1536.[70] Wolf frequently travelled to the Frankfurt Book Fair, and in 1539 he was entrusted with letters to the King's emissary in Germany, Christopher Mont. He began to print in 1542, and was responsible for the first book published in England in Greek. His expertise in this field was recognized when he was appointed King's Printer in Latin, Greek, and Hebrew, with an annuity of twenty-six shillings and eightpence in 1547.[71] By 1547 Wolf was a wealthy man, owning a row of shops which he had built on the site of the old charnel-house near St Paul's. Perhaps this is why he baulked at subjecting himself to the discipline of the stranger church, although he seems to have been a firm Protestant. He carried letters between Bullinger and his London correspondents, and though he remained in England during Mary's reign he seems to have

---

[67] Worman, *Alien Members*, pp. 12, 38; Duff, *Century*, pp. 96, 161; Wijnman, 'Emigrantendrukkerijen te Emden', I, 157–60. Wijnman shows that Urban van Coelen and Urban Lynyng were the same person, which Worman and Duff both doubted.

[68] Worman, op. cit., pp. 71–2; *Returns*, ii. 45.

[69] Worman, op. cit., p. 47; *Returns*, i. 314.

[70] For Wolf see Worman, op. cit., pp. 72–3; Duff, *Century*, pp. 171–2; C. Sayle, 'Reynold Wolf', *Transactions of the Bibliographical Society*, 13 (1913–15), 171–92; *Denizations*, p. 255.

[71] *Cal. Pat. Rolls Edward VI*, i. 187.

printed little.[72] On Elizabeth's accession his patents were renewed, and his press was busy once again. He was four times master of the Stationers' Company between 1559 and his death in 1573.

Measuring the commitment of French members of the printing fraternity to Protestantism is inhibited by the absence of a surviving French church register. Probably more Frenchmen worked in the trade than are now known to us. But several who would be members of the French church under Elizabeth were in London before 1553, suggesting that they were probably also members of the church in the earlier period.[73] Isaac de Bruges and Thomas Hacket were two of the many French bookbinders working in London at this time. Their trade was protected by a statute of 1534 forbidding the importation of books already bound,[74] and Hacket at least flourished. A long-term resident in London, Hacket married an Englishwoman and took out letters of denization in 1544; by 1549 he was paying subsidy on goods worth £5.[75] Isaac de Bruges seems to have been an Edwardian arrival, as he took out letters of denization in October 1550, and so too were Giles Godet and Hubert d'Anvillier. Godet, who became a denizen in 1551, is marked in 1562 as a printer, though there is no sign of his having worked independently in the Edwardian period. D'Anvillier, who arrived in 1553, was a type-founder.[76]

These four Edwardian residents who appear in the Elizabethan church seem to have taken their chance and remained in England during Mary's reign. In the case of d'Anvillier and Godet their faith was not proof against changed circumstances, and both were later required to make an act of public penitence for having attended Mass. Godet was admitted a brother of the Stationers' Company during Mary's reign, in 1555.[77] Isaac de Bruges's wife also performed an act

---

[72] *OL*, ii. 609. Wolf printed only three volumes during Mary's reign, compared to 29 between 1547 and 1553. *Handlist of English Printers, 1501–1556*, ed. E. G. Duff, *et al.*, 3 (1905).

[73] Identified from the French petition of 1561. *Returns*, i. 288–92.

[74] 25 Henry VIII c. 15, m. 2.

[75] *Denizations*, p. 114; *Returns*, i. 185.

[76] *Denizations*, pp. 62, 64, 107.

[77] *Actes I*, p. 15; *Transcript of the Registers of the Company of Stationers of London, 1554–1640*, ed. E. Arber, 1 (1865), p. 37.

of penitence though there is no record of de Bruges himself having done so; he did testify early in Elizabeth's reign that he had been in Rouen at some point, and so may have left London for a time, though the Return of Aliens for 1571 suggests that he has been in England for twenty years.[78]

It is impossible to know, in the absence of a church register, how many French printing workers went abroad in 1553 not to return. Certainly the one independent French printer is found in no English records after 1553. Thomas Gualtier, like Lynn and Hill, had been in England some years before Edward VI's accession.[79] In 1544 a 'Thomas Walter' was assessed for subsidy in Faringdon Ward Without at twenty shillings and this was probably the printer. He took out letters of denization in the same year, and according to his patent he was married to an Englishwoman.[80] Between 1550, when Gualtier began printing, and 1553, fifteen editions are known to have originated from his press, almost all of them Protestant works. Gualtier had a close association with the French church, of which presumably he must have been a member. The French liturgies, the Geneva catechism, and two editions of the Bible in French were all printed by Gualtier for their use.[81] In 1552 Lasco wrote a letter to Cecil on his behalf asking that Gualtier be entrusted with the printing of a French edition of the 1552 Prayer Book for the benefit of the French-speaking Channel Islands. This request was granted and Gualtier was licensed in December 1552, bringing out the required volume in the next year.[82] Gualtier disappears in 1553, and one must assume that he, like his Dutch colleagues, followed the leaders of his church into exile. It should come as no surprise that the foreign printers settled in London during Edward's reign manifested so impressive a commitment to the new religion; their English counterparts were hardly less closely identified with

[78] *Actes I*, pp. 36, 37; *Returns*, ii. 61.

[79] Duff, *Century*, p. 53; Clair, 'Refugee Printers', 117–18.

[80] *Returns*, i. 96; *Denizations*, p. 100 (Thomas Galtyer).

[81] *STC* 2957.8, 2957.9, 4391, 16572.3, 16572.7; B. Chambers, 'Thomas Gualtier strikes again . . . and again?', *BHR*, 41 (1979), 353–8.

[82] Strype, *Cranmer*, ii. 647–8; idem, *Memorials*, II, ii. 251; *Le livre des prieres communes*, *STC* 16430. See also D. N. Griffiths, 'French Translations of the English Book of Common Prayer', *HS*, 22 (1970–6), 91–3.

Protestantism, and many printed little or nothing during Mary's reign.[83] The foreign printers were also deeply committed to the stranger churches. Several held consistorial office, and the master printers took their opportunity to do the churches valuable service both in England and in exile.

The craft of weaving was traditionally one in which foreign workmen had been employed in large numbers. As early as the fourteenth century Edward III had encouraged the settlement of Flemish weavers in England, stimulating what would later become a familiar round of complaints from native weavers, charges by the foreigners of intimidation, and royal mediation. In the mid-sixteenth century foreign workmen were again in demand. The government, with the Lord Protector leading the way, was turning its attention to improving the quality of cloths woven in England and attempting to introduce the weaving of finer cloths and silks. In 1547 the Privy Council arranged that Bretons skilled in the weaving of poldavies should be brought to England to teach Englishmen their art, and shortly thereafter Somerset established his colony of French weavers at Glastonbury producing worsteds in the superior French style.[84] The London Weavers' Company too was showing a new interest in foreign skills: in 1551 it regulated for the first time the pay of journeymen silk-weavers, and a steady stream of foreign weavers was admitted to the Company during the reign.[85]

The accounts of the Weavers' Company survive intact for the period 1547 to 1553, and from them the names of some thirty foreigners who were admitted to the Company during this period may be identified.[86] From 1547 to 1551 twelve aliens were enrolled, paying a variety of fees. Three paid £2 for the freedom of the Company, and others smaller sums for their 'upset'; one other stranger paid £1 to become a 'free brother'. As a result it is not altogether clear what sum an alien was expected to pay at this time in order to purchase

[83] Took, 'Government and the Printing Trade'.
[84] Frances Consitt, *The London Weavers' Company* (Oxford, 1933), Ch. 2; *APC*, ii. 109; See also above, p. 43.
[85] Consitt, op. cit., pp. 128, 229.
[86] Printed in Consitt, op. cit., pp. 234–85. See Table 1.

entry to the Company, but in 1552 the Company's attitude towards the foreigners achieved clearer definition. A new rate of twenty-five shillings was established for 'admission into the Hall', and all eighteen aliens who entered the Company in the next two years paid this sum.[87] Furthermore, this new rate seems to have been established exclusively for strangers. The admission of these strangers to membership of the Weavers' Company during Edward's reign was clearly the result of a conscious change of policy on the part of the Company, as previously few foreigners had been admitted. The new climate encouraged several foreign weavers who had been in England for some years to seek entry to the Company. Mercy Byssmore and William Merchant purchased admission in 1552, but both had been in England since at least 1544; Gilles Barre was admitted in 1553, but had been in England since 1536.[88] Both Anthony Ashe and William Cowbridge who became Freemen in 1548 had been in England since 1541, and John Lache entered the Company twelve years after he is first recorded in London in 1537.[89] These six weavers active in London during Henry's reign were all, judging from their subsidy assessments, substantial citizens, yet only Ashe is mentioned in the Company accounts before 1547.[90]

All these six Henrician residents had presumably previously worked outside the Company, as many foreign weavers continued to do during Edward's reign. Of the seventeen weavers marked in the Dutch church only seven joined the Company, the rest all being journeymen who presumably could not afford the necessary fees to become free of the Company.[91] That these journeymen were able to continue to work suggests that the enrolment of foreigners in the Company was not the result of an aggressive drive against unauthorized competition, but

[87] Occasional discrepancies occurred when payments were made by instalments: William Norry paid 26s. 6d. over four years, whilst Mercy Byssmore was 8d. light when he finished paying off his fee. Consitt, op. cit., pp. 271 (Mowre), 276, 277, 279, 282 (Norry), 267, 271, 280 (Byssmore).

[88] *Returns*, i. 98 (Marse Bysue); *Denizations*, pp. 39, 169. Gilles Barre, *Returns*, i. 57, 437; *Denizations*, p. 15.

[89] *Returns*, i. 50, 52, ii. 97.

[90] Consitt, *Weavers' Company*, p. 247.

[91] Marked in Dutch register as 'wever', 'lynewever', or as servant to a known weaver (Ashe). *Returns*, i. 202–9.

rather indicated a desire to harness the skills of the foreigners by accommodating them within the Company. This favourable disposition towards the foreigners was further evidenced by the Company's willingness to allow them to pay their entry fees by instalments. Of the thirty who joined the Company no fewer than ten did so. These ten were generally men of modest means, and significantly five of them were attempting during the same period to have themselves enrolled as denizens. A patent of denization seems to have cost about £4 or £5,[92] and to find such a large sum on top of the cost of entry to the Company would have stretched their resources considerably. It is no wonder that the aliens often took advantage of the Company's readiness to allow them to buy themselves in by easy stages.

It must be said that more aggressive measures on the part of the Company might well have been doomed to failure in any case. It is possible to identify the place of residence of twenty-four of the thirty strangers who joined the Company and all of them had set up their looms outside the city or in the Liberty of St Martin-le-Grande. Five were to be found in the Liberty, ten in Southwark, three in Faringdon Ward Without, two in Westminster, and one each in Lambeth, Whitechapel, St Katherine's, and Bishopsgate Without.[93] The weavers in the Dutch church who had not joined the Company, not surprisingly, seem also to have worked in the suburbs. Try as they might the companies could never establish effective control over these areas. The weavers, at least, chose instead to encourage aliens to join the Company on roughly equal terms.

The foreign weavers who joined the Company, though often not rich men, seem to have been a religiously conscious group. At least sixteen of the thirty were members of the foreign churches, and given that the majority of the names are French and no list of the French church exists for the Edwardian period, probably as many as two-thirds were in fact members of the stranger churches. Most prominent amongst them was

[92] *Cal. S. P. Span.*, x. 265.
[93] See Table 1. The information is derived from the Dutch register of 1550, the French petition of 1561, and subsidy returns.

the formidable Anthony Ashe, who was one of the first elders of the Dutch church and after exile in the reign of Mary would return as one of those entrusted with securing the churches' restoration. When he chose exile in 1553 he gave up a position of some importance in the Weavers' Company, of which he was a freeman and Assistant Warden.[94] One of the deacons of the Dutch church was also a weaver, though unlike Ashe, Jasper Camber was probably a new arrival in Edward's reign. He set up in 1550 in Southwark where by 1552 he was employing two servants, one of them Jan Baccau, a fugitive from the Heresy Commission in Flanders.[95] Daniel Laute was another religious refugee who arrived in London in 1550. He apparently did not leave the Continent penniless, however, as he is marked in the Dutch church list as a householder and supported in his house two other church members, including his fellow exile the deacon Paul van Winghen.[96] In 1553 Laute, like Ashe, would return to the Continent, accompanied by his wife and three children.[97]

Although no French church register survives for Edward's reign, seven of the weavers are identifiable from a list of 1561 as members of the French church.[98] These included the deacon Nicholas Binet, and Nicholas Wilpin, elected deacon in 1560 but dismissed after having been seen drunk in the streets, a judgement which Wilpin contested with some acrimony.[99] None of the seven is listed amongst those who performed an act of penitence in 1559 for having attended Mass in Mary's reign, and it seems likely that most of them went abroad with the Church in 1553. Two of these French weavers, James Russell and Anthony Wilpin, are known to have been in Emden, where they were admitted as citizens in 1555. At the request of John a Lasco they were exempted from payment of the usual fees.[100]

---

[94] Consitt, *Weavers' Company*, p. 229.
[95] *Denizations*, p. 40; *Returns*, i. 239, 240; Baccau, Decavele, *Dageraad*, ii. 72.
[96] Decavele, *Dageraad*, ii. 134; *Denizations*, p. 148 (Daniel Lowte); *Returns*, i. 205, 208 (Hans de Swaerte, Paul van Wynghen, met Daniel Lante), 212.
[97] List in *BRN*, ix. 89 (Daniel Lauthen).
[98] *Returns*, i. 288–92.
[99] *Actes I*, p. 6. See below, p. 190.
[100] Emden, Stadtarchiv, Bürgerbücher, vol. 2 fo. 6.

Like all such professional groups the weavers reflected a variety of religious and economic experience. Not all the Edwardian arrivals joined the church, and, of the longer-term residents, some like Ashe, Gilles Barre, and Melchior Nicholson joined the new church, whilst others like John Lache and Govert Lambertson took advantage of the new economic climate to take out letters of denization and join the Weavers' Company whilst remaining aloof from the stranger churches. But that a group of thirty should contain at least sixteen church members, four of whom held office in the French or Dutch community, reflects an unusual degree of commitment to the foreign churches, and one which contrasts strongly with the experience of another trade group, the coopers.

It is doubtful whether the Weavers' Company was as interested in the foreign weavers' religious commitment as in their economic potential. The indications are that those who joined fulfilled the Company's expectations in this latter respect. For those for whom we have specific information, we know that at least three of the thirty were silk-weavers, and four 'fringeweavers'; one was a ribbonmaker, one a lacemaker, and four were linen-weavers.[101] It was in the making of these finer and more specialized fabrics that foreigners possessed the most pronounced superiority, and with the development of consumer demand for a greater diversity of products on the market it was these skills that Englishmen were most anxious to learn. Just as important was the fact that some of the foreign weavers brought with them capital as well as skill. Although the frequency of payment of entry fees by instalments has already been remarked, it is equally significant that many newly arrived foreign weavers could find the money for the considerable double outlay of entry to the Company and the purchase of letters of denization. Thirteen of those buying into the Company in 1552 and 1553 paid their twenty-five shillings in one lump sum, and nine of these became denizens at about the same time. It is doubtful whether they could have generated surplus cash from income in such a short time and many,

---

[101] The information comes from the Dutch register and the French petition. In addition one may note that Nicholas Wilpin was described in his will as a 'maker of parchement lace'. Archd. London 1564 (3, fo. 130).

refugees or not, must have been able to bring capital with them to England.[102] At least one of these new arrivals, Jasper Camber, was employing two other weavers within two years of his arrival in England; men who thus combined capital resources with new skills would have been doubly welcome to the Company.

The foreign coopers present an entirely different picture, although cooperage was also a trade in which foreign workmen were well-established. It was inevitably closely associated with beer-brewing, an art introduced into England by Flemings at the end of the fourteenth century and for a long time exclusively practised by them.[103] A list of beer-brewers summoned before the Common Council in 1549 includes ten strangers amongst the twenty-five brewers named, and a further eight, though themselves English, employed alien workmen.[104] Beer and ale were part of the staple diet in sixteenth-century London, the more so as there were no reliable supplies of clean fresh water. In 1549, a time of food shortages and social unrest, the Common Council was prepared to advance the brewers £700 to ensure that they had sufficient stocks of malt to last a month, and the Council showed a concern for the maintenance of supplies of beer second only to their anxiety for the provision of wheat.[105] The brewers fulfilled a vital role in the supply of the London market and prospered as a result, and as barrels were as vital as the beer the coopers were able to share in this prosperity. The independence of the craft was protected by a statute of 1531 forbidding the brewers to make their own barrels (though they could employ one or two coopers to mend barrels), and so coopers clustered in large numbers around the large brewhouses outside the city walls in East Smithfield and Southwark or down by the river in Dowgate Ward.[106]

A substantial proportion of these coopers were foreign, and they were already well established in the Coopers' Company

---

[102] The question of how much capital refugees brought with them is discussed below, pp. 224–5.

[103] G. Elkington, *The Coopers, Company and Craft* (1933), pp. 240–1.

[104] Rep. 12 i., fo. 121b.

[105] Ibid., fo. 126, 129.

[106] 23 Henry VIII c. 4.

Table 1. Stranger Weavers in the Weavers' Company, 1547–1553

	Admitted to Company			Type	Place of Residence[3]	First in England[4]	Denizen[5]	Subsidy	Church
	in	as[1]	pays[2]						
Anthony Ashe	1548	Freem.	£2	silkweaver	Bish. Wo.	1541	d.	1547 £10	D.
Gilles Barre	1553	Hall	25s.	silkweaver	Far. Wo.	1536	1541	1549 £30	Fr.
Remens Belvoys	1552	Hall	25s.				1550		Fr.
Nicolas Bennet	1552	Hall	(25s.)	fringemaker	St Mart.		1550	1549 40s.	
John Beoval	1549	upset	(40s.)		Westm.				D.
Peter Bumer	1553	Hall	25s.	linenweaver	Southw.		1551	1552 £6	
Robert Bustard	1548–9	Bro.	(20s.)		Southw.			1549 20s.	
Mercy Byssmore	1549–52	upset	(24/4)	ribbonweaver	St Mart.		1544	1549 £8	
Jasper Camber	1552	upset	25s.	linenweaver	Southw.		1550	1552 £5	D.
William Cowbrege	1548	Freem.	£2		St Mart.	1541		1549 £7	
John Furrens	1553	Hall	25s.		Lambeth				
Barbara Herman	1548		1s.					1549 20s.	
John Johnson	1548	Freem.	£2						
John Lache	1551	upset	(15s.)		Southw.	1537	1549	1551 20s.	
Govert Lambertson	1549	upset	8s.		Westm.	1538		1549 20s.	
Daniel Laute	1552	Hall	25s.	linenweaver			1550		D.
William Merchant	1552	Hall	25s.	fringemaker	St Mart.		1552		Fr.
John Mays[6]	1551	Hall	25s.	fringemaker			1544		
John Moryne	1551	upset	(14s.)		St Mart.				
William Norry	1550–3	upset	(26/6)	fringemaker	St Mart.		1550	1549 £5	Fr.
Melchior Nicholson[7]					Southw.	1545	1544	1549 £10	D.
Harry Permerayne	1546–8	upset	(13/4)		Southw.		1544	1549 £4	D.
John Poffleet	1551–3	upset	(25s.)		White Ch.		1550		D.
Francis Russell	1552	Hall	25s.	linenweaver	Southw.		1550	1552 20s.	
James Russell	1552	Hall	25s.		Southw.		1550	1552 40s.	Fr.

Honor Seneschal	1553	Hall	25s.	silkweaver	Southw.		1551	1552 £3	Fr.
Paul Testelet	1552–3	upset	(25s.)	fringemaker	Far. Wo.	1547	1550	1549 8d.	Fr.
Anthony Wilpin	1553	Hall	25s.		Southw.		1551	1551 £3	Fr.
Nicholas Wilpin	1552	Hall	25s.	lacemaker			1550		Fr.
Henry Vicars	1548	Freem.	£2		St Kath.		1550	1549 40s.	

Notes:

1. Freem. = Freeman; Hall = Admission to Hall; Bro. = Free Brother.
2. A bracketed entry indicates payment by instalments.
3. Bish. Wo. = Bishopsgate Ward Without; Far. Wo. = Faringdon Ward Without; St Mart. = St Martin-le-Grande.
4. An entry has been made in this column only when it is known that a stranger was in England before he became a denizen.
5. A d. indicates that a stranger was known to be a denizen from a later survey but that no patent has been found.
6. John Mays paid a further 15s. later in the year for his 'upset'. The total (40s.) probably made him a Freeman.
7. Melchior Nicholson is known to be a member of the Company as he contributed to a Company levy in 1550, but no entry has been found for him.

by 1547. The Company accounts list by name those who paid quarterage to the Company of whom a dozen were 'stranger householders' according to the account of 1531.[107] From 1541 Dutch journeymen were also enrolled, and by 1547 some 25 per cent of those paying quarterage to the Company were strangers, rising to 35 per cent in 1552 and a peak of 40 per cent in 1555.[108] This sharp increase did not necessarily represent large-scale immigration under Edward VI: of the seventeen coopers added to the list of denizen householders between 1548 and 1553, many had been in England for some years before they joined the Company. The increase in numbers enrolled followed steady efforts on the part of the Company to control unauthorized competition. The accounts for 1531 contain an item for entertaining certain Dutch coopers to breakfast when they came to bear witness against some of their countrymen for setting up shop without authorization.[109] A statute of the same year empowered the Company to control alien workmen in their craft and search for them up to two miles outside the city walls, and the accounts for 1539 show the Coopers exercising this right with a thorough search of the alien coopers working in East Smithfield and St Katherine's Lane to see how many of them were denizens. In 1552 one Jasper Cromwell was fined £1 for working in strangers' cellars in the night 'to the slander of the Company'.[110]

Relations between the Company and the Dutch coopers seem however to have been generally fairly harmonious. The statute of 1524 laid down that one substantial alien of the craft should be present at any search of alien premises, and it was probably as a result of this provision that the Coopers' Company established a separate warden for the alien coopers. Many of the Dutch householders took a turn in this office and are marked as such as in the quarterage accounts. The more substantial Dutch coopers seem indeed to have been fully integrated in the life of the Company. They contributed towards the cost of a suit in Parliament against the brewers in 1541,

---

[107] Guildhall Library, Coopers Company Accounts, MS 5606, i., fo. 12.
[108] 40/158 in the Company in 1547, 77/218 in 1552, and 135/335 in 1555.
[109] Coopers Company Accounts, i., fo. 22ᵛ.
[110] 23 Henry VIII c. 4, following general statute 14/15 Henry VIII c. 2. Coopers Company Accounts, i. fos. 61ᵛ., 173.

and helped equip six soldiers for the French expedition of 1544. During the reign of Edward the Dutch contributed to the city's levy for the provision of corn, and to the Company's collection for the poor.[111]

The Dutch coopers were, then, already playing a full part in the Company's affairs by 1547, and an analysis of the individuals listed in the quarterage accounts illustrates how small an impact the religious changes of mid-century made on the alien workers in this craft. Some thirty-two Dutch coopers were listed as denizen householders during Edward's reign; large numbers of journeymen were also listed, but these tended to pay quarterage rather more erratically and are less frequently found in other records such as subsidy returns. The householders, however, were a stable and prosperous group.[112] Those already members of the Company in 1547 had often been so since the 1530s; in some cases they had been in England since the 1520s. Even of those added to the householders' list between 1548 and 1553 few seem to have been new arrivals in England. Some like Henry Stone and Hubert Williamson had previously been journeymen members of the Company (both since 1541). Others like Nicholas Gumport, who first paid quarterage in 1552 yet was made a denizen in 1541, had presumably previously worked outside the Company. At least twenty-three of the thirty-two stranger householders in the Company had been in England since at least 1541. Their prosperity was equally marked. Almost all the householders paid subsidy on goods assessed at £5 or more and many employed at least one apprentice; for several of the longest-established alien coopers their subsidy assessment amounted to £30 or £40.

This settled and prosperous community showed little interest in the stranger churches. Only four of the thirty-two Dutch householders joined Lasco's community, three of whom had been in England for a decade already. The fourth was Martin Derkinderen, who apparently arrived in England in 1550. None of the Dutch coopers who paid quarterage as journeymen in their trades appear in the Dutch church register

---

[111] Coopers Company Accounts, fos. 81, 100, 142ᵛ., 168.
[112] See Table 2.

and there were only ten coopers in the Church all told (including several servants who do not appear in the Company
records).[113] This low level of religious commitment contrasts
sharply with the two occupational groups previously discussed,
and the real enthusiasm even of those who did join Lasco's
community is open to doubt. Henry Muskyn, the most substantial Southwark cooper, joined the Church, but worked on
unaffected by its dissolution in 1553, paying his quarterage throughout Mary's reign. Perhaps more surprisingly,
so did Roland Boghaert, another long-time member of the
Company who became a deacon of Lasco's Church. He did
not join the other church leaders in exile and continued to pay
his quarterage until he disappeared from the Company
records in 1556. Leonard Hughens was another church member who continued in the Company throughout Mary's reign
and into Elizabeth's, as did the only Edwardian arrival
amongst the cooper householders to join the church, Martin
Derkinderen.

No disappearances from the quarterage lists in 1553–5 point
to a return of coopers to the Continent on religious grounds.
Of the twenty-seven Edwardian householders still paying
quarterage in 1552–3 all but two were still doing so in 1554,
and most were to be found in London throughout Mary's
reign. More surprising still is the high measure of continuity
amongst the Dutch journeymen coopers. Of the fifty-three
journeymen listed in 1552–3 only two are not found in subsequent accounts; of the seventy-seven listed in 1553–4 only
three then disappear from the records.[114] This is a striking
measure of continuity, not only because one would expect a
greater degree of mobility amongst non-denizen journeymen,
but because these more humble coopers had to deal not only
with the implications of a change of religion on Mary's accession, but also with the proclamation of 1554 ordering all foreign
artisans who were not denizens to depart the realm.[115] The
proclamation seems, however, to have had an effect quite contrary to that intended, as the numbers of journeymen enrolled

---

[113] *Returns*, i. 202–9, marked 'cuper'.
[114] Coopers Company Accounts, i. fos. 165 (1552–3), 180 (1553–4), 191 (1554–5).
[115] *Tudor Royal Proclamations*, ii. 31–2.

moved steadily up from 77 in 1553, to 89 in 1554, reaching a peak of 115 in 1555.[116] It is unlikely that this swollen roster represented new arrivals in England. More probably, coopers already in England sought in the wake of this proclamation to legitimize their position by joining the Company.

The Coopers' Company certainly had little to gain by the rigid enforcement of this proclamation which would have meant the loss of a high proportion of its skilled work-force. Only three days after its publication the beer-brewers applied to the Common Council of the city for assistance in petitioning the Chancellor for a further explanation of the proclamation as it affected their foreign servants. A counter-application by an English brewer decided the Council that they would not support the request of the brewers for special concessions, but an order of the Council of 1556 forbidding the employment of foreigners specifically exempted brewing from its provisions.[117] Coopers probably enjoyed a similar protection though they are not specifically mentioned in the order. It was probably clear to contemporaries, as it is to us, that the coopers were hardly the seditious aliens against whom the proclamation of 1554 was aimed.

Why then were the coopers as a group so blithely unconcerned by religious change? Why, indeed, did the foreign coopers show so little interest in the stranger churches, in marked contrast to the enthusiastic response of the weavers and leading printers? The answer may lie partly in the nature of the occupation, and partly in the locality where the different groups settled. Studies of the impact of the Reformation in local communities in France suggest that whereas the Reformed religion drew its adherents from rich and poor in numbers roughly proportional to their distribution in the population at large, certain occupational groups were definitely over-represented in the Protestant movement. These were generally occupations involving a high degree of skill, some new technology or new claim to prestige, or where the trade occupation was only recently arrived in the locality and thus less well integrated

---

[116] Coopers Company Accounts, i. fos. 181, 191, 202.
[117] Rep. 13 i, fo. 126ᵛ., 127ᵛ; Corporation of London, Letter Book R, fo. 93ᵛ.

in the traditional trade structure.[118] Applying these broad categories to the occupational groups under discussion, it does seem that a very plausible explanation for the different behaviour of the printers, weavers, and coopers can be constructed. Printing was the archetypal new industry, and as we have seen, the foreign weavers who joined the Weavers' Company generally made cloths new to England or high-status products such as silks. Their superior products made them a craft élite. Moreover, there was the additional significant impulse of technical innovation brought by new immigrants, many of them from the industrial villages of the Flanders Westkwartier where the Reformation had made an early and profound impact. The coopers on the other hand were a well-established group, working in a time-honoured craft calling for little product differentiation or technical improvement. Many of the coopers at work in Edward's reign were long-term survivors from a pre-Protestant age; so too were some of the weavers and printers, but whereas both these other groups were reinforced by numbers of genuine religious refugees the coopers migrating in Edward's reign were not noticeably tainted by religious enthusiasm either.

Geography may also have played its part in determining the divergent experiences of the different craft groups. Whilst the weavers tended to be scattered around the suburbs, the coopers were heavily concentrated in East Smithfield, where foreigners seem to have enjoyed a separate community life to a much greater extent than they did elsewhere around London. Something of this is evident from the wills of the stranger coopers dying in East Smithfield during the period under study. Commitment to the stranger community as a whole is much less marked amongst these coopers than with other foreign testators. Only two of the eleven coopers whose wills have been identified left money to the poor.[119] Most of their wills were simple affairs made in the presence of their friends and disposing of property to wives and children. The witnesses

---

[118] N. Z. Davis, 'Strikes and Salvation at Lyons', *Archiv für Reformationsgeschichte*, 56 (1965), 48–64, reprinted in *Society and Culture in Early Modern France* (1975), pp. 1–16; Philip Benedict, *Rouen during the Wars of Religion* (Cambridge, 1981), pp. 71–94.

[119] Adam Derkinderen and Leonard Nicholas. Archd. London 1563, 1570 (3, fos. 42ᵛ., 261ᵛ.).

were often other local coopers: Hubert Williamson, an Edwardian householder and member of the Company since 1541, witnessed the wills of three of his friends and colleagues between 1555 and 1563.[120] The local curate was present on only three occasions, and a minister of the Dutch church only once.[121]

Coopers leaving wills in East Smithfield kept their distance from other London strangers, but were not necessarily economically isolated. Eight of the eleven were members of the Coopers' Company. The strangers in East Smithfield were often, moreover, important figures locally. When the parishioners of St Botolph's Without Aldgate were in dispute with the farmer of the tithes of the parish in 1550, their two representatives before the Common Council were both strangers, Giles Harrison and Anthony Anthony, the two most substantial of the local brewers.[122] Secure and rather separated in East Smithfield, the coopers pursued a trade long associated with alien workmen, and prospered. With no product diversification or new technology to open up the craft to a new influx from the Continent, the coopers were never subjected to the neighbourly pressure that might have helped the stranger churches make deeper inroads. The Company having established solid control over the alien coopers by mid-century, they were left to pursue their time-honoured craft generally oblivious to the religious and economic upheavals of the time.

The charter had anticipated a wide field for the missionary efforts of the stranger churches and this expectation was fully borne out by the fact that only about half the alien population joined the new communities. The churches had a very different impact on different sections of the community, but this was

---

[120] Henry Stone (1555), John Strong (1562) and Leonard Nicholas. Archd. London (2, fo. 156, 3, fos. 6ᵛ, 42ᵛ.).

[121] Robert Hearse, curate of St Botolph's Without Aldgate witnessed the wills of Cornelius Lambertson (1568), Henry Johnson (1570), and Arnold Johnson (1576). Archd. London (3, fos. 216, 242ᵛ., 4, fo. 76ᵛ.). Peter Delenus witnessed the will of James Williamson. Ibid., 1553 (2, fo. 104ᵛ.).

[122] Rep. 12 i. f. 216ᵛ. The eight members of the Company were Leonard Nicholas, John Strong, Mark Adams, Archd. London 1566 (3, fo. 176); Cornelius Lambertson, Stephen Pasman, ibid., 1569 (3, fo. 225ᵛ.); James Williamson, Henry Stone, and Rauf Egerton, ibid, 1561 (3, fo. 6ᵛ.). The exceptions were Henry Johnson, Adam Derkinderen, and Arnold Johnson.

Table 2. Dutch Cooper Householders in the Coopers' Company, 1547–1553

	First in Company	Householder	Leaves Company[1]	Place of Residence	First in England[2]	Denizen	Subsidy	Church
Henry Muskyn	by 1531	by 1547	1559	Southwark			1547 £45	D.
Roland Boghaert	by 1531	by 1547	1556	Eastsm. F.			1549 £20	D.
Harry Nerskyn	1532	by 1547	1550	Eastsm. F			1549 £15	
James Williamson	1537	by 1547	d. 1553	Eastsm. F	1535	1535	1549 £9	
John Cowper	1538	by 1547	1554	St Kath.	1524			
John Peterson	1541	by 1547	1560	Eastsm. F	1525	1544	1549 £8	
Christian Paules	1541	by 1547	1552	Eastsm. F			1549 £8	
Peter Ricardes	1541	by 1547	1551	Southwark			1549 £20	
Mark Adams	1543	by 1547	a. 1560	Eastsm. F	1540		1540 £9	
Gyllam Segar	1541	by 1547	1557	Southwark			1551 £16	
Anthony Wesyll	1541	by 1547	1560	Eastsm. F		1541	1549 £3	
James a Barke	1541	1547	a. 1560	St Kath.			1550 £10	
John Tuer	1541	by 1547	1560	Eastsm. F			1549 £8	
Peter Coke	1547	1547	a. 1560	Southwark	1540		1549 £8	
Cornelis Hubertson	1541	1547	1551	Eastsm. F			1549 £10	
George Williamson	1545	1548	1554	Far. Wo.			1550 £40	D.
Leonard Hughens	1541	1548	a. 1560	Southwark			1551 £6	
Harry Stone	1541	1548	1556	Eastsm. F			1549 £6	
Hubert Williamson	1541	1550	a. 1560	Eastsm. F			1549 £5	

Name						
Anthony Lambert		1550	a. 1560	Southwark	1551	1549 £5
Angel Anthony	1541	1550	a. 1560	Eastsm. F	1541	1549 £5
John Strong		1550	a. 1560	Eastsm. F	1550	
Garrett Edwards		1550	a. 1560	Southwark	1550	1551 £4
John Selles	1541	1550	a. 1560	St Kath. 1542	1544	
Peter Johnson		1551	1552		1550	D.
Martin Derkinderen		1551	1558			
Nicholas Gumport		1551	1555	Southwark	1550	1552 £30
Cornelis Lambert		1551	a. 1560	Eastsm. F	1541	
Anthony Derickson		1552	a. 1560		1551	
Peter Polyard		1552	a. 1560	Eastsm. F	1551	
Edward Peterson	1542	1553	1559	Dowgate	1551	1549 4 os.
John Johnson	1545	1552	1560		1541	

Notes:

1. 'a. 1560' indicates that the Cooper was still a member of the Company in 1560 and subsequently.

2. An entry has been made in this column only when it is known that a stranger was in England before he became a denizen.

by no means a simple dichotomy between rich and poor, or even between long-established residents and recent refugees. Some of the strangers who came to England during Edward's reign after the church's foundation did so for traditional economic reasons, and had little intention of subjecting themselves to the discipline of the church, whilst many strangers resident in England before 1547 now revealed Protestant sympathies which had perforce previously remained concealed. Although many of the churches' members were poor artisans and servants Lasco could rely on the support of some of the more substantial of London's foreign residents, and many of these would be prepared to abandon a prosperous security to follow him into exile in 1553.

It was not to be expected that the lead given by the ministers in 1553 would be followed by all London's foreign population. Those that had come for purely economic reasons, and had not joined the church, had no need to feel threatened when Mary's accession brought the church's existence to an abrupt end. For many even of the church's members the prospect of a new exile was an unhappy one, and for these the change of government provided an acute test of their commitment to the new faith.

V

The Stranger Community during the Reign of Mary

By the spring of 1553 the foreign churches had overcome their initial difficulties, and the ministers could look forward to a bright future. Writing to Bullinger in February, Micron reflected with enthusiasm on the flourishing condition of the London communities, and hoped that the continued work of himself and his colleagues might lead eventually to the eradication of heresy in the stranger community.[1] The strangers' leaders seem to have had little idea of the impending threat to their own survival. Writing in June, Utenhove's principal concern was to secure from Zurich the dispatch of a spiced cake. He mentioned in passing that the King had been in some danger from a severe cough, and that it was doubted whether he would be fit again before the end of the summer.[2] In fact, as those closer to the King already realized, his condition was much more serious.[3] Within a month he was dead, and the strangers had lost their patron and protector.

Edward's death seems to have reduced Bullinger's correspondents to a shocked silence, and no letters written by Lasco, Micron, or Utenhove survive from the time of Mary's accession to their departure from England. In consequence, it is impossible to know what attitude the strangers took to the attempted coup on behalf of Jane Grey. Lasco and his colleagues were probably sympathetically disposed towards the pious young Protestant who shared their admiration for Bullinger and the Zurich reform, but they seem to have waited on events as no active role in the plot was ever alleged against them.[4] Even

---

[1] *OL*, ii. 581.

[2] *OL*, ii. 592–4.

[3] Cf., for instance, Sir John Cheke's letter to Bullinger written the same day. *OL*, i. 141.

[4] Lady Jane and her father both corresponded with Bullinger, and Bullinger dedicated a volume of his sermons to Grey during Edward's reign. *OL*, i. 3–11. See also above, Ch. III, n. 110.

so, the foreign ministers were soon marked out as one of the most serious potential impediments to the restoration of Catholicism. Before the end of July the Spanish ambassadors had brought to the Queen's attention the large number of foreign sectaries lurking in her kingdom, and over the following weeks they wasted no opportunity to urge on her the necessity of expelling such potentially disruptive elements forthwith. The ambassadors added weight to their persuasions by alleging, as Scheyfve had to Paget in the previous reign, that many of the foreign refugees were fugitives from justice in their own land, and their representations were backed by similar advice from the Emperor.[5] In consequence, although the first proclamation of the new regime in matters of religion seemed generally moderate and irenic, the strangers were amongst the first to feel the effects of the changed religious climate. By 16 August the foreign ministers had been forbidden to preach, and this may well have marked the end of services in Austin Friars and Threadneedle Street. At the beginning of September the Privy Council also took action to break up Poullain's community at Glastonbury.[6]

By this time the leaders of the stranger churches had apparently already accepted the inevitability of a new exile. The Spanish ambassadors were aware that the strangers were making plans to leave before the end of August; their information must have come from a good source as they suggested quite accurately that the Dutch would be heading towards Denmark.[7] A further three weeks passed before the necessary preparations for departure were complete. The problem of suitable transport was solved when two Danish ships were discovered to be lying in the Thames. These were quickly chartered for the voyage, and on 17 September Lasco and 175 of his church, all for whom room could be found, embarked at Gravesend. With Lasco went many leading members of both communities including Utenhove and two of the ministers, Micron and Vauville. After a short service of dedication,

---

[5] *Cal. S. P. Span.*, xi. 118, 169, 179, 194.
[6] *Tudor Royal Proclamations*, ii. 5–8; *Cal. S. P. Span.*, xi. 173; *APC*, iv. 341.
[7] *Cal. S. P. Span.*, xi. 188.

and to the accompaniment of psalm-singing from those left behind, the strangers set sail for Denmark.[8]

Those who had found no place on the ships made their way back to London. Some quickly succeeded in organizing their departure by other routes. The majority were reported to be heading in the direction of Flushing and Zeeland, whence many passed on to Emden and Germany; those who could arrange no passage direct from London travelled from the Channel ports. The Privy Council had no desire to obstruct the movement of foreigners out of the capital, and early in September the mayors of Dover and Rye were instructed to allow French Protestants free passage on their way back to the Continent. (The Spanish ambassadors thought that the French would head for Geneva.[9]) The steady flow of foreigners out of London must have accounted for a large proportion of the members of the stranger churches, yet other church members clearly entertained some initial hopes that they might be able to remain in London. Karel de Koninck moved outside the city in the hope that he might be able to live undisturbed and keep his school open, and other church members may have done likewise.[10] Both communities had left behind ministers to care for those who remained: Francis Perussel for the French, and Peter Delenus, by now sharing the duties of his ageing father, for the Dutch.[11] They were joined in London by Valérand Poullain, who had journeyed to the capital with the rump of his Glastonbury community and now lingered through the autumn, attending in the meanwhile the Westminster disputation staged by the government between the champions of the old faith and the beleaguered defenders of Protestantism.[12] Although the foreign churches were shut up the ministers probably hoped to carry on some sort of services in a private house.

This, however, was not the intention of the government, which made energetic efforts to shift those foreign Protestants who lingered in the city. Gardiner related to Renard with some

---

[8] Utenhove, *Simplex et Fidelis Narratio, BRN*, ix. 39–40.
[9] *Cal. S. P. Span.*, xi. 188, 199; *APC*, iv. 349.
[10] Decavele, *Dageraad*, i. 326.
[11] *Simplex et Fidelis Narratio, BRN*, ix. 40.
[12] Bauer, *Poullain*, pp. 168–70.

relish his own method of hastening them on their way.[13] When he heard that one of the preachers was still in London he summoned him to appear before him, expecting that the minister, fearing the Tower, would make his escape. He intended to employ this stratagem to coax Cranmer's client, Peter Alexander, into exile; if he were bold enough to obey the summons he was to be told that the Emperor and the King of France were about to demand the extradition of their subjects. Alexander was too distinguished a figure to pass unnoticed, but lay members of the congregation were also by no means secure. According to a later report in the French consistory minutes Bonner, the Bishop of London, was in possession of the list of foreign Protestants in the city, and made strenuous efforts to apprehend them. The list was compiled with the help of a French informer, and both communities seem to have been imperilled by former friends prepared to betray them to the authorities.[14]

The mounting difficulties took a steady toll of those strangers who had initially elected to remain in England, and in the last months of 1553 more drifted back to the Continent. In December Parliament repealed the Edwardian settlement and the Mass was officially restored. This seems to have been the signal for Poullain to abandon London. With the remnant of his Glastonbury community he set off for Antwerp, whence they journeyed on to Wesel before finding a safe refuge in Frankfurt where a church was provided for their use.[15] Perussel seems also to have left London at about this time.[16] Gualter and Peter Delenus remained, but they too were feeling the strain. In a letter to Lasco in February 1554 Peter Delenus spoke of the great and increasing dangers of their situation, and at about the same time he set out the arguments for and against remaining in London in a series of notes which have

---

[13] *Cal. S. P. Span.*, xi. 217.

[14] *Actes I*, pp. 22, 23. See also Delenus's letter in Gorham, *Gleanings*, pp. 311–13 and Hessels, ii. 40: We have as many enemies as hairs on our head, as many Judas Iscariots, false brothers, and false prophets.

[15] Bauer, *Poullain*, pp. 170 ff.

[16] Perussel, *Historia de Wesaliensis Ecclesiae dissipatione*, printed in *Frankfurtische Religions-Handlungen* (Frankfurt, 1735), i. 278–89.

survived in the Dutch church archive.[17] By this time he clearly doubted whether there was any point in lingering in England unless some sort of community could continue to meet.

Delenus wrote in the aftermath of Wyatt's rebellion, the events of which worsened the already uncomfortable position of the strangers.[18] The rising in Kent and abortive attempts to raise an armed protest against Mary's foreign marriage in other parts of the country left the regime badly shaken. The loyalty of London was in doubt to the last moment and the Queen and her advisers needed little convincing that the foreign Protestants who remained in the capital were in large measure responsible for its unreliability. In the tense days before the outbreak of the rebellion Renard believed that the foreigners were going from house to house encouraging sedition, and in consequence he thought that the foreign preachers would be expelled even before the crisis point of the revolt was reached. Renard's report proved somewhat premature, but within a week of the collapse of the rebellion the Privy Council had decided on a general expulsion of the foreign refugees. On 17 February a proclamation was issued ordering all seditious and non-denizen aliens to depart.[19] The influence of the Spanish envoy may well be discernible, for the proclamation repeated his frequently urged argument that the foreigners included a 'multitude' fleeing for horrible crimes committed in their native lands; all such strangers 'commerant and lingering' to teach heresies were given twenty days to depart the realm. The proclamation singled out for special mention 'preachers, printers, and booksellers', and seems to have been successful in inducing the last of the foreign ministers to quit the capital. Gualter and Peter Delenus must have left soon after its publication, as within ten days of the expiry of the twenty-four allowed for departure they had arrived in Hamburg.[20] There they, and the band of thirty who accompanied them, met up with the main body of the community

---

[17] Gorham, *Gleanings*, pp. 311–13; Hessels, ii. 40–4. The notes are written on the back of a letter to Delenus from John Foxe.

[18] On Wyatt's rebellion see D. M. Loades, *Two Tudor Conspiracies* (Cambridge, 1965), particularly pp. 67–74.

[19] *Cal. S. P. Span.*, xii. 31, 39; *Tudor Royal Proclamations*, ii. 31–2.

[20] Utenhove, *Simplex et Fidelis Narratio, BRN*, ix. 148.

who had taken ship with Lasco, and the two groups travelled on together to Emden. Their departure marked the end of the attempt to maintain an official church community in London.

Renard reported the capital much quieter after the proclamation of February, and it is quite possible that a considerable number of strangers left London on its publication.[21] Apparently, though, even without the hope of continued meetings some former members of the foreign churches preferred to take their chance and ride out the storm in London. This suggestion requires further elaboration, not least because it has generally been assumed by historians that the members of the London churches quickly followed their ministers back to the Continent, and that most of them found a new home in the German exile communities, the Dutch in Emden, and the French in Wesel and Frankfurt.[22] Yet a search of local records in these three German exile centres has revealed surprisingly little evidence of a large-scale influx from London. If, as has been suggested, the combined strength of the two London church communities was in the region of 4,000 by 1553, the 175 men, women, and children who sailed with Lasco and eventually found their way to Emden represent only a small proportion of this substantial number.[23] Other church members made their own way to Emden, yet only two dozen names familiar from the London Dutch community are to be found in Emden records, either in the consistory records of the church or in the list of new citizens of the town.[24] The new church at Wesel, although it elected Perussel as minister, seems to have numbered few of his former London community amongst its members, and the Frankfurt church was established initially for

---

[21] *Cal. S. P. Span.*, xii. 126.

[22] D. M. Loades, *The Reign of Mary Tudor* (1979), p. 152; Schilling, *Niederländische Exulanten*, pp. 84–8; Van Schelven, *Vluchtelingenkerken*, pp. 104 ff., 287. Wilhelm Neuser, 'Die Aufnahme der Flüchtlinge aus England in Wesel (1553) und ihre Ausweisung trotz der Vermittlung Calvins und Melanchthons', in *Weseler Konvent, 1568–1968* (Düsseldorf, 1968), 28–49.

[23] See above, p. 78. An incomplete list of those who sailed with Lasco is printed in *BRN*, ix. 89–90.

[24] Emden, Stadtarchiv, Bürgerbücher, i. fos. 98–9ᵛ., ii. 3 ff.; Archiv der evangelische reformierte Kirche, Kerkeraadsprotokollen, vol. 1 (1557–1562).

Poullain and the remnant of his Glastonbury church, rather than for refugees from London.[25]

Most of the members of the London churches who made their way back to the Continent probably returned to their former homes in Flanders and Brabant rather than to the German exile towns. Some are known to have been in Antwerp, and returning exiles in the Flanders towns of Bruges and Ghent and the industrial villages of the Westkwartier, caused the local authorities considerable problems.[26] But inevitably the scale of such a return, stealthy and unannounced, is impossible to quantify, and it is hard to know how many members of the churches would have been accounted for in this way. There is, on the other hand, sufficient evidence that a considerable proportion of the foreigners settled in England at the beginning of Mary's reign remained in the country. Unfortunately the London return for the only subsidy of the reign has not survived, but it is still possible to get some idea of the extent of this phenomenon by comparing the last Edwardian subsidy return with the first of Elizabeth's reign. Where both survive, as for instance in Southwark, this comparison confirms that the foreign population was considerably reduced during Mary's reign: 40 per cent fewer names were recorded in 1559 than were listed in 1552, and as strangers continued to come into England during 1552–3 the actual reduction in the population during Mary's reign was probably rather greater.[27] But by the same token, these subsidy lists provide concrete evidence that a considerable proportion of the foreigners settled in the capital did remain, and this is confirmed by the comprehensive surveys of the alien population of 1568 and 1571, which recorded a large number of foreign residents who had been in

[25] Bauer, *Poullain*, pp. 172–84. On the Wesel community see Perussel to Du Val, 29 Sept. 1554 in van Schelven, *Vluchtelingenkerken*, p. 425: 'Les estrangiers de Wesel ne sont pas ceux de Londres, car lors nous nestions que trois hommes de Londres, et maintenant que j'en suis hors il ny a nul (car les deux sont partis)'. The largest group of former members of the London French church was to be found in Emden, although this small French community never numbered more than forty members. See French church at Emden to Perussel, 12 Dec. 1555. *CO*, xv. 885.

[26] Decavele, *Dageraad*, i. 342, 392–3. For Antwerp see below, p. 176.

[27] *Returns*, i. 234–46, 260–7.

England for the last twenty years or more.[28] Whatever the effect of the change of religion of 1553 and the measures of the following year, they clearly did not result in a general exodus of foreigners settled in the capital.

An important category of strangers, those who had taken out letters of denization, were not included in the expulsion order of February 1554.[29] The purchase of denizen status was expensive, and many strangers would have been reluctant to give up hard-won economic advantages in England for the uncertain prospects of a new life abroad. There was also no certainty in the spring of 1554 that those who made this sacrifice would find religious freedom any more easily on the Continent. Such reports as filtered back to England of the tribulation of Lasco and his colleagues would not have encouraged others to take the same course. The asylum for which the ministers had hoped in Denmark sadly failed to materialize. Arriving at the Danish capital after a long and perilous voyage Lasco and his troop presented their petition for a refuge, only to be confronted with a demand that they conform to the local Lutheran rite. When their reply signalled their reluctance to do so, they were promptly ordered out of Denmark. The peregrinations of the community through a cold and hostile winter were later painstakingly chronicled by Utenhove.[30] Utenhove and Lasco took ship to Emden, but the members of the church were dispersed in smaller vessels to Rostock, Wismar, and Lübeck, from which they were successively expelled by the local Lutheran authorities. At the beginning of March 1554 Micron led the re-united bands on to Hamburg, only to meet the same suspicion and intolerance. Ready as ever to dispute doctrine with the local minister (in this case the distinguished and implacable Lutheran, Joachim Westphal), Micron succeeded only in hastening the familiar order to depart.[31] Only

---

[28] *Returns*, i. 402–79, ii. 1–154, iii. 330–439.

[29] *Tudor Royal Proclamations*, ii. 31–2. Renard at one point thought that patents issued during Edward's reign would be repudiated and only those made denizens before 1547 allowed to remain, but if such a step was ever contemplated the plan was allowed to lapse. *Cal. S. P. Span.*, xii. 107, 109.

[30] In his *Simplex et Fidelis Narratio*, printed *BRN*, ix. 1–151. See also F. A. Norwood, 'The London Dutch Refugees in Search of a Home, 1553–1554', *American Historical Review*, 58 (1952–3), 64–72.

[31] Ibid. See also Rudolf Kayser, 'Johannes a Lasco und die Londoner

at the end of a final weary journey to Emden did the community find a secure refuge.

Similar problems attended the newly established French exile communities in both Wesel and Frankfurt. In Wesel the application of the newcomers to use their own rites and ceremonies met with a peremptory refusal, and although Poullain at Frankfurt was initially more successful in securing toleration for his small community, relations with the local Lutheran ministers were soon embittered to a dangerous point.[32] It was the misfortune of the London community to be seeking a new refuge at the time when disagreement between the Reformed and Lutheran confessions over sacramental doctrine had reached a peak of acrimony, and a narrow Lutheran orthodoxy was currently being imposed in many cities which had previously offered a generous welcome to Reformed communities.[33] The tribulation of the exile communities, which resulted in their expulsion from both Wesel and Frankfurt in the course of the next few years, was widely reported, and would hardly have encouraged those who hesitated in London to trust to the generosity of their reception abroad.

If the difficulties of the church abroad were a powerful disincentive to precipitate action, those who remained in London were by no means devoid of protection from the hostility of the ecclesiastical authorities. Interesting in this respect is the evidence of Jean des Forges, who in 1560 complained to the French consistory that he had been refused membership of the church on the grounds that he had informed on his fellow church-members to Bonner.[34] Des Forges claimed that, on the

Flüchtlingsgemeinde in Hamburg', *Zeitschrift des Vereins für hamburgische Geschichte*, 37 (1938), pp. 1–15.

[32] On Wesel see Neuser, 'Aufnahme der Flüchtlinge'; Walter Hollweg, 'Calvins Beziehungen zu den Rheinlanden', in J. Bohatec (ed.), *Calvinstudien* (Leipzig, 1909), pp. 152–67. On Frankfurt see Bauer, *Poullain*; F. C. Ebrard, *Die französisch-reformierte Gemeinde in Frankfurt am Main, 1554–1904* (Frankfurt, 1906).

[33] The wider context of these events is explored in my article, 'The London Exile Community and the Second Sacramentarian Controversy', forthcoming in *Archiv für Reformationsgeschichte*. See also Schilling, *Niederländische Exulanten*, pp. 22–3; E. Bizer, *Studien zur Geschichte des Abendmahlsstreits im 16. Jahrhundert* (Gütersloh, 1940), pp. 275–84.

[34] *Actes I*, p. 22.

contrary, he had been one of those highest on Bonner's list, and that an impressive array of English patrons with Reformed sympathies had helped him elude the bishop's search. In a highly circumstantial account des Forges described how he had been hidden over the course of eighteen months by Sir John Romford, Sir Arthur Darcy, and the son of Lord Paget. It is unlikely that des Forges's story was a complete fabrication, though suspicion of his conduct in London had resulted in his rejection by Poullain's community in Frankfurt. The French consistory in 1560 was more inclined to believe the testimony of Francis Bertie, the stranger merchant who had played an important role in the establishment of the church in 1550, and who now gave evidence against des Forges.[35] After being denounced to Bonner, Bertie was briefly imprisoned, and his release was secured through the intercession of one of the Lord Chancellor's gentlemen and two merchant strangers who had the ear of Renard, the Spanish ambassador. Bertie's influential friends, Jacques van Hove and Jacques Ballin, were both Catholic members of the merchant community, and their intercession on his behalf is suggestive of a strong feeling of solidarity amongst the merchants that cut across confessional lines, and must have helped protect the heretic merchants.[36]

It was not, however, powerful international merchants only who could expect protection as a result of their business connections. There were many in London who had no wish to see the more humble alien artisans, threatened by the proclamation of February 1554, forced to leave the kingdom. The rigid enforcement of this proclamation would in any case have caused many English employers severe economic difficulties. In some crafts non-denizen foreign workers made up a high proportion of the skilled work-force, and English employers had no wish suddenly to be deprived of their services. Within three days of the publication of the proclamation the brewers had petitioned the Common Council for help in an appeal to

[35] Ibid., p. 23.

[36] This community feeling seems to have extended across national boundaries. Rose Throckmorton would later record that her husband Simon was released in similar circumstances after his imprisonment in Mary's reign through the intercession of a visiting nobleman from the Low Countries. See Joy Shakespeare and Maria Dowling, 'Religion and Politics in mid-Tudor England through the eyes of an English Protestant Woman', *Bulletin of the Institute of Historical Research*, 55 (1982), 100.

the Lord Chancellor for clarification of the proclamation as it affected their workmen.[37] The proclamation was particularly alarming to them as their brewhouses were often large-scale operations employing many foreigners, few of whom were denizens.

If government hostility failed to dislodge a large proportion of the foreigners settled in London during Edward VI's reign, the explanation lies partly in the fact that the rigid enforcement of its policy would have offended too many vested interests. In 1556 the Mayor and Commonalty ordered that no foreigners should be employed in the City, but they made several important exceptions: not only brewers but foreign felt-makers and cap-thickers were allowed to continue to work, as were carders, spinners, and knitters in the textile industry.[38] The interests of Londoners reluctant to deprive themselves of the skills which foreigners possessed in these crafts here triumphed over government concern at their potential for sedition. The City of London gave the Council little help in its drive against seditious aliens. In July 1554 two stranger shoemakers were arrested by the constables of Faringdon Ward Without for loitering during the night watch. They were in serious trouble, as they were soon discovered to be non-denizens who had remained in England in defiance of the Queen's proclamation. They were committed to prison, but nine days later the Mayor was authorized to release them, and it seems that no further action was taken.[39]

The government could not rely on the co-operation of the City when its policy cut across vested economic interests, and this provided the strangers with a substantial degree of protection against government hostility. The matter was put very clearly in the case of two alien dyers, Henry van Tynen and Leonard Basshe. In the wake of the order of Common Council forbidding the employment of foreign workmen the Wardens of the Dyers' Company petitioned that these two 'very honest and obedient persons' should be allowed to work, as they were 'very excellent experts and conning men in the art and

---

[37] Above, p. 107.
[38] Corporation of London, Letter Book S, fo. 93ᵛ.
[39] Rep. 13 i, fos. 179, 183.

occupation of dying of woollen cloths and other things so that the want of theyme should be a wondrous great loss and hindrance to all the whole fellowship of Dyers'. The petition was granted.[40]

With such a widespread unwillingness to take part in any harrying of the alien population, it is not surprising that a large proportion of the aliens resident in London at Mary's accession chose to remain. There is even evidence that some strangers continued to come into the country. In September 1554 the Common Council instructed the aldermen to survey their wards to see how many of the aliens in them had come in in the last ten days.[41] The change of regime made little impact on large sections of the alien population. The coopers discussed in the previous chapter are a case in point. Few had joined the stranger churches and almost all the householder denizens in the trade, secure both economically and legally, worked on unaffected by the change of regime. For this group, the only effect of the advent of a regime less favourably disposed towards strangers seems to have been to encourage more of the non-denizen journeymen to join the Company.[42]

The greater number of the strangers who remained in England through Mary's reign were undoubtedly those who, like the coopers, had had little interest in the stranger churches in any case. But some former church members also chose to remain in England. How many it is impossible to say, but quite possibly they presented a significant proportion of the Edwardian congregations. The ministers of the exile churches abroad seem to have been aware that a substantial number of church members had been left behind. Both Pierre du Val, minister of the French church at Emden and John a Lasco published tracts intended for them, du Val dedicating his *Petit Dialogue d'un consolateur* to the French community in London, urging them to remain constant under persecution.[43] Lasco, typically more direct, had his opinion on whether a true Christian might attend Mass reprinted in Dutch, and declared

---

[40] Rep. 13 ii, fo. 432.
[41] Corporation of London, Letter Book R, fo. 310.
[42] See above, pp. 105–7.
[43] *Le Petit dialogue d'un consolateur consolant l'Église en ses afflictions.* See Schickler, *Églises du Refuge,* i. 73–5.

strongly against such attendance.[44] Lasco's anticipation of the result of remaining in England was probably the shrewder: those church members who stayed may have hoped to avoid the need to attend Mass by living in retired obscurity, but not all were proof against pressure to conform to the new state religion. The conduct of those who attended Mass during Mary's reign was sharply condemned by those who returned to England from exile in 1559, and both communities insisted they perform a public act of penitence before they were re-admitted to the community. The experience seems to have been much more general in the French church, and at least fifty church members publicly confessed acts of 'idolatry' in the first months after the refoundation of the churches.

As luck would have it, the names of thirty-four of these lapsed Protestants are recorded in the French consistory minutes.[45] As a group they repay careful attention, for by piecing together what can be discovered of their histories and personal circumstances from surveys of the alien population, subsidy returns, and church records, it is possible to develop a revealing profile of those among the foreign community sufficiently committed to Protestantism to join the stranger churches, yet reluctant to face exile on their dissolution in 1553.[46] Significantly, a high proportion of this French group first settled in London many years before the stranger churches were established. The joiner Jacques Bontemps had been in London since 1528; the buttonmaker Hugh Bertrand settled in Holborn around 1536.[47] At least ten of the thirty-four were veterans of the Henrician era. Inevitably, having lived in London before the foundation of the foreign churches, they were less likely to be strongly affected by their dissolution than later arrivals. Equally pertinent is the fact that most of this group (twenty of the thirty-four) had also taken out patents of

---

[44] *Het ghevoelen Joannis a Lasco . . . Of het den Christenen, ha dien zy het word Godes ende de godlooszheit des Pauwstdoms bekent hebben . . . dat zy zick in den Pauwstlichen godsdiensten . . . vinden laten* (Emden, 1557).

[45] *Actes I*, pp. 5, 13, 15, 37, 39, 52.

[46] See Table 3, below. The information has been compiled from *Returns* and *Denizations*.

[47] *Returns*, i. 351 (James Bowntayne), ii. 9 (Higat Bartram).

denization.[48] As denizens they were exempt from the provisions of the proclamation of 1554 expelling seditious aliens. Since the foundation of the stranger churches in 1550 had been accompanied by a mass enrolment of denizens, a high proportion of the members of the foreign Protestant congregations would have fallen into this category, suggesting that from the point of view of the government the proclamation of 1554 was a rather clumsy instrument for ensuring the departure of the committed Protestants amongst the foreigners. From the point of view of the foreigners concerned, having gone through the expensive and time-consuming business of securing denizen status would certainly have increased their reluctance to throw up these hard-won advantages and leave England.

This reluctance would have been particularly marked if, as was the case with many of these Frenchmen, church members had built themselves a comfortable economic position in London. An assessment for the subsidy of 1549–50 survives for only seven of this French group, but five of them were assessed at between £5 and £10; in other words they were in the same class of comfortable householder as the coopers discussed earlier. Interestingly, four of these five were smiths of one sort or another, and if one adds to these a further two metalworkers (a typefounder and a crossbowmaker) and another two goldsmiths in this group which stayed in England, then a substantial proportion of them worked in trades where their tools and stock would not have been easily transportable. The ownership of substantial capital, stock, or equipment in London would have been a powerful disincentive to withdrawal abroad.

Such practical considerations might be overborne if a church member was particularly committed to the faith. Simon Percy, a French coppersmith working in Southwark, had every reason to wish to remain in England in 1553. He had been in England since at least 1530, had built up a prosperous business, and since 1541 had been a member of the Founders' Company.[49]

---

[48] Mostly in the mass enrolments of 1544 and 1550. Six were listed as denizens in a French petition of 1561 although no enrolled patents survive. *Returns*, i. 287–92.

[49] *Returns*, i. 146 (assessed for subsidy at £6), 351, 472; *Wardens' Accounts of the Worshipful Company of Founders of the City of London, 1497–1681*, ed. C. G. Parsloe (1964), p. 95.

Yet his payments to the Company ceased abruptly in 1553 to resume in 1559, revealing that in Percy's case commitment to the church had outweighed all economic considerations. Percy, in fact, had retired to Emden, where he was granted citizenship with a group of other French refugees in 1555.[50] As has already been shown in the case of the leading alien printers, some church members were prepared to dismantle a very substantial business if need be.[51] For the less committed, however, economic considerations must have loomed very large. They may initially have hoped, as Burnet expressed it, to 'follow their consciences in matters of religion in private', and it is significant in this respect that most of this French group had their homes either in the suburbs or in the liberties of St Martin's and Blackfriars, areas which the authorities found difficult to regulate and where the foreigners may have felt comparatively safe.[52] Yet most ultimately succumbed to the growing pressures to conform. Compromise with Catholicism was probably a matter of slow degrees, but ultimately a general enough experience to cause the churches considerable problems on their refoundation in 1559.

The minutes of the Dutch church record no wholesale acts of penitence in 1560, but this does not necessarily mean that no Dutch church members remained in England and attended Catholic services. The hard line taken by the Dutch community from the outset in 1559 may have persuaded former members who had remained in England to continue attending the English parish churches rather than make the humiliating public penance necessary to rejoin the community. None of the four members of the Coopers' Company who had joined the Dutch congregation left England, and none rejoined the church in 1559.[53] Nevertheless, it may well be that fewer members of the Dutch community had remained in England than their French colleagues; the fact that the influence of Lasco was stronger in the Dutch congregation would account for the difference.

---

[50] *Wardens' Accounts*, pp. 126, 153; Emden Bürgerbücher, ii. fo. 6.

[51] See above, pp. 88–92.

[52] Gilbert Burnet, *The History of the Reformation of the Church of England* (1679–1715), ii. 250.

[53] See above, p. 106.

It is clear from the above that those who remained in England were generally the less committed members of the Edwardian congregations. Those who had given evidence of a zealous commitment to the Reformed church, in England or on the Continent, are mostly known to have followed the ministers into exile. Of the elders and deacons of the Dutch community only one, the cooper Roland Boghaert, is known to have remained in England, and many of his colleagues can be traced in the records of exile communities abroad.[54] The partial list of those who took ship with Lasco also includes the names of a high proportion of those who had fled to England to escape prosecution for heresy in Flanders. One might indeed have expected those who had already once embraced exile for the faith to do so again, and those who left with Lasco made the decision to do so very rapidly.[55] That those left behind were mostly of a different mettle is further indicated by the almost total absence of foreign names amongst those who were prosecuted, or martyred, by the Marian regime. In June 1556 a young Flemish merchant then living in London, Lyon Cawch, was arrested and subsequently executed with a group of thirteen English Protestants at Stratford-le-Bowe, but he apparently was the only foreign victim of the persecution.[56] Otherwise, foreigners make only the most fleeting appearance in the pages of Foxe's annals of the Marian persecution. The German student and servant of Latimer, Augustine Bernher, lingered in London long enough to earn a reputation as a 'diligent attendant upon the Lord's prisoners', and Master Bartley, a stranger, offered Edwin Sandys a temporary refuge when he was on the run from Gardiner.[57] Bartley himself had been briefly imprisoned, as had two Frenchmen, Berard and Lion: Lion was imprisoned in the Lollard's Tower with Thomas Green and comforted his fellow prisoners by singing psalms in French.[58] Perhaps the most interesting reference is

[54] Ten are known to have been in Emden (5 elders and 5 deacons). Emden Kirchenarchiv, Kerkeraadsprotokollen.

[55] Fifteen of the twenty-four Dutch church members mentioned in the Flanders heresy proceedings are known to have left London in 1553. See *BRN*, ix. 89–90, Decavele, *Dageraad*, ii (index).

[56] John Foxe, *Acts and Monuments* (1839), viii. 151–6.

[57] Ibid., vii. 262, viii. 596.

[58] Ibid., vii. 744, viii. 523.

to a Dutch shoemaker by the name of Frog who attended the clandestine Protestant congregation led by John Rough. The meetings apparently took place on occasions in Frog's house, which was conveniently situated in the Liberty of St Katherine's outside the city wall.[59]

This reference to Frog, who is not known as a former member of Lasco's community, is almost the only indication that foreigners played a role in the secret Protestant communities of Mary's reign. In 1558 the landlady of a tavern in Stepney, Alice Warner, informed the authorities that a group of young French, Dutch, and English merchants had met twice in a back room in her house, she suspected for some form of Protestant worship. But as on the second occasion she had warned them not to return, nothing further is known of this company.[60] It is possible that groups of foreigners in the liberties and Southwark conducted services in their own houses. Returning to England in 1559 to assist the re-establishment of the stranger communities, Anthony Ashe made a cryptic reference to those who had met together in Mary's reign, and now formed the core of the group that had already gathered by the time of his arrival. It is not, however, clear from the context whether he is referring to a group of Dutch Protestants meeting separately, or joining English congregations. He was in any case clear that they included no one of sufficient stature to take a leading role in the reconstituted church.[61] All in all it cannot be claimed that the foreigners who remained in England made a very distinguished contribution to clandestine Protestant activity during Mary's reign. The work of former church members abroad in providing vernacular Protestant literature to sustain the faithful in England was probably of much greater significance.[62] Those who chose not to withdraw to one of the established continental exile centres were more likely to have conformed, however reluctantly, with the re-established Catholic rite.

Even for those foreign residents who conformed willingly to the policies of the Marian regime life became progressively

[59] Ibid., viii. 458, 459.
[60] Ibid., viii. 460.
[61] Van Schelven, *Vluchtelingenkerken*, p. 342.
[62] See above, p. 89.

more uncomfortable as the reign wore on. From June 1557 England and France were at war, and early in 1558 the government seemed set to take drastic measures against those Frenchmen still in the country. In January a proclamation authorized any citizen to arrest non-denizen Frenchmen who remained in England in defiance of the proclamation of 1554.[63] This, however, did not allay fears that Frenchmen in the country were a security risk, and when Parliament met in February a bill was introduced to repeal the Letters Patent of all French denizens. After the fall of Calais the Speaker assured the Queen that the French 'be now so odiouse to the Comens that they will now hede by a speciall law at this parlyament (if hir Majestie will condesiend therunto) to banysshie them all as well denyzens as not denyzens out of this Realme'.[64]

Other punitive measures included a ban on the import of French wines,[65] large increases in the impost on French commodities with the introduction of a new Book of Rates,[66] and a plan to make Frenchmen pay a yearly tax for the defence of the realm.[67] Feeling was obviously running high, but when the bill to render letters of denization void came to a third reading, it was defeated in a division by 111 votes to 106.[68] Divisions were unusual in Parliament at this time and defeats extremely rare; the bill had run into substantial opposition during the second reading, and in the end the government had to be content with a substitute bill which allowed it to revoke letters of denization in individual cases, but only after a commission of inquiry had discovered specific breaches of

[63] *Tudor Royal Proclamations*, ii. 83. The order that all Frenchmen should leave the realm was reiterated in the declaration of war in June 1557. Ibid., ii. 79.

[64] PRO, SP 11/12/31, fo. 67ᵛ, quoted by Jennifer Loach, 'Opposition to the Crown in Parliament, 1553–1558' (Oxford Univ. D. Phil. thesis 1974), p. 193; *Journals of the House of Commons* (1803), i. 48.

[65] This measure was discussed in Parliament, but eventually promulgated by proclamation. *Commons Journal*, i. 49–50; *Tudor Royal Proclamations*, ii. 85–6.

[66] Loach, op. cit., p. 223.

[67] This appears under various guises as a bill for the defence of Melcombe Regis in Dorset and as a more general measure. It passed the Commons but was defeated in the Lords. *Commons Journal*, i. 48–50; *Journals of the House of Lords*, i. 531.

[68] *Commons Journal*, i. 49.

the law.[69] Concern at the arbitrary removal of privileges from a whole class of citizens may have accounted in part for the Commons' reluctance to see the first measure pass, but Frenchmen also owed their escape to economic considerations. Their importance in the London economy made the peremptory expulsion of the French denizens a proposition unwelcome to many influential citizens. The economic self-interest of their hosts was the strangers' most significant support through the difficult years of Mary's reign. It would be so again when the leaders of the stranger churches petitioned for their re-establishment on Elizabeth's accession.

[69] Ibid. Thurs. 17 Feb.: 'Arguments upon the bill to avoid the Letters Patents, made to Frenchmen to be Denizens'. 4 & 5 Philip & Mary c. 6.

Table 3. Members of the French Church who admitted attending Mass during the reign of Mary

	Profession	Place of Residence	First in England[1]	Deni-zation[2]	Subsidy 1549 or 1551	1559
William Maubert	currier	Southwark	1531	1541	£5	£8
Estienne Gras	hosier	Langb.	1538	1544		£5
William Lurier	goldsmith	St Mart.		1544	£7	£1
William Berger	coppersmith	Far. Wo.	1533	1550	£10	
Lambert de la Mare						
Noe Hare						
John Guillot	crossbow -maker	Temple B.		1544		
John Sab						
Peter Pavenard		St Kath.		d.		
Glaude Peintre	post	Langb.		1544		
Nicholas le Blond						
Richard Vaillant	tailor	Blanch A.		d.		
Jacques Bontemps	joiner	Southwark	1529	1541	40s.	
John des Champs		Blanch A.		d.		
John Nevel						
Henry Boisseau						
John Besier						
Nicholas Goselin	sadler	BlackF.		1544		20s.
Robert le Maistre	goldsmith	BlackF.	1541	d.		£3
Giles Godet	printer	BlackF.	1547	1551		20s.
Hubert d'Anvillier	typefounder	BlackF.	1551	1553		

continued overleaf

Table 3. (*cont.*).

	Profession	Place of Residence	First in England[1]	Deni- zation[2]	Subsidy 1549 or 1551	1559
Peter Bonneval	feather- dresser	BlackF.	1551			£10
John Petiot	button- maker	Far. Wo.		1550		20s.
Oliver Bidaert						
Hugh Bertrand	button- maker	Holborn	1535	1550		
Robert Riques	school -master					
Simon Chevalier	coppersmith	Far. Wo.	1541	1550	£8	20s.
William de la Mare	hosier	Aldgate	1549			
Robert le Clercq	broker	Langb.	1551			
Leonard du Tertre	smith	Southwark	1541	d.	£10	£4
Thomas de Lille	goldsmith	St Mart.		1544	40s.	
Peter Fouquant	silkweaver		1547	d.		
Paulin Beauvais						
Peter Becke						

Source:
Actes I, p. 15, except Maubert (p. 5), Gras (p. 13), De Lille (p. 37), Fouquant, Beauvais (p. 39), Becke (p. 52).

Abbreviations:
Langb. = Langborne; BlackF. = Blackfriars; Blanch A. = Blanchappleton; Temple B. = Temple Bar; St Kath. = St Katherine's; Far. Wo. = Faringdon Ward Without; St Mart. = St Martin-le-Grande.

Notes:
1. An entry has been made in this column only when it is known that a stranger was in London before he became a denizen.
2. A d. indicates that a stranger was known to be a denizen from a later survey, but that no patent has been found.

VI

The Churches Restored

I. NEGOTIATIONS AND RECOVERY

THE hostility exhibited towards the French in the Parliament of 1558 was, as far as the strangers were concerned, the last throw of a failing regime. In November 1558 Queen Mary died, and with the accession of her half-sister Elizabeth the restoration of Protestantism was widely anticipated. Hopeful signs of the new Queen's sympathy for the new religion were keenly observed both in the leading Continental Reformed churches and by the exiled Protestant divines eager to return to their native land. In December Edwin Sandys could report from Strasburg that there was great hope in London of the promotion of the gospel, and John Jewel on his return to England was able to confirm that the Queen 'openly favours our cause'.[1] The Church at Zurich was quickly aware of developments and hastened to offer the Queen congratulations and a pious exhortation to courage and determination in the service of Reformed religion, and by January 1559, Calvin at Geneva was also confident that Elizabeth 'had entered upon the right path'.[2]

The former leaders of London's foreign community also followed events in England with interest, and as the Reformed sympathies of the new regime became clear the ministers in exile began to hope for the speedy re-establishment of the London stranger churches. Foreign Protestants had been returning to England from the first months of Elizabeth's reign, and in March 1559 the consistory of the exile church in Emden made the decision to send two of its leading members to

[1] Sandys to Bullinger, 20 Dec. 1558; Jewel to Martyr, 20 Mar. 1559; *Zurich Letters*, ed. H. Robinson (Parker Society, 1842–1845), i. 5, 10.
[2] *Zurich Letters*, ii. 3–8; Calvin to Cecil, Feb. 1559, *CO*, xvii. 419–20. Other Protestant powers also hastened to offer their congratultions to the new Queen. *Cal. S. P. For.*, 1558–9, nos. 226, 232, 319, 397.

London to negotiate for the restoration of the privileges of the stranger community. The French (Walloon) community was represented by the doctor Jean Dumas, whilst the Dutch chose Anthony Ashe, a former elder of the Dutch church and a man well-known in English business circles; his command of the English language and English law made him an ideal choice for the task of re-establishing contact with the English court. There was some debate in the Emden consistory as to whether it was in fact safe for Dumas to proceed to England, as the position of French refugees in England was once again complicated by the state of war that existed between England and France. It was decided that the two representatives should proceed to Antwerp and assess the situation from there; if Dumas found it too dangerous to go on to England he might send someone else with Ashe.[3] By the time the delegates arrived in Antwerp, however, the peace of Cateau-Cambrésis had removed this complication. So both men continued on their way, arriving in England whilst Parliament, called to settle the religion of the country, was still in session. The Reformed church at Antwerp also showed a lively concern for the interests of London's foreign Protestant communities, and during the course of 1559 members of the consistories of both the Dutch and Walloon churches found their way to England.[4]

The strangers' representatives did not, however, have the favourable reception for which they had hoped, and Ashe and Dumas were soon reporting unexpected difficulties. On 28 April Ashe reported to the Emden consistory that matters of religion made little progress, and that the time did not yet seem propitious to make any petition on the strangers' behalf.[5] Dumas and Ashe finally presented their petition on 4 June, by which time Parliament had broken up, but the outcome of their interview with Cecil was not a happy one: it was quickly made clear that the foreign churches could not hope to recover the privileges they had enjoyed under Edward VI.[6]

---

[3] Van Schelven, *Vluchtelingenkerken*, p. 132; A. J. Jelsma, *Adriaan van Haemstede en zijn Martelaarsboek* (The Hague, 1970), p. 112 n. 3, quoting Emden consistory minutes.

[4] See below, pp. 158, 176.

[5] Van Schelven, *Vluchtelingenkerken*, p. 342. Van Schelven prints three of Ashe's letters to the consistory.

[6] Ibid., p. 344 (letter of 11 June).

The disappointment of the strangers was keen, as they had expected much better of the English authorities. In order to understand the reluctance of the English government to re-establish the stranger churches after the Edwardian model it is necessary to consider the context of the tense early months of 1559 as Elizabeth's government moved cautiously to institutionalize a change in religion. Interpretation of the events of 1559 has recently undergone something of a re-orientation. Until recently the orthodox view had been that Elizabeth's government was forced by a vociferous Protestant minority within the House of Commons to accept a religious settlement more radical than was originally intended or to the Queen's taste.[7] Recently several studies have suggested that the Elizabethan settlement in fact took very much the shape that the Queen intended and, in the absence of any vociferous Puritan lobby, the most determined opposition came, as might be expected, from the Catholic bishops in the House of Lords.[8] The observations of the strangers tend to support this view. At no point do they hint at any suspicion that the Queen's own inclinations were anything less than definitely Protestant, and they also noted the resilience or 'pride' of the Catholic faction in the spring of 1559.[9]

At the same time the exiles had obviously observed that too close an association with the leading Continental Reformed Church of the day, Calvin's Geneva, would be damaging to their cause. This was not on account of any differences over doctrine, but because the Queen had taken violent exception to John Knox's recent book condemning the government of women which he had published at Geneva, and with which the Queen imagined Calvin was associated. Calvin himself was brought to realize how badly this book had damaged him with the Queen when she received the dedication of his commentaries on Isaiah with scant respect, and he hurried to dissociate himself from Knox in a letter to Cecil.[10] In the

[7] J. E. Neale, 'The Elizabethan Acts of Supremacy and Uniformity', *English Historical Review*, 65 (1950), 304–32.

[8] Norman L. Jones, *Faith by Statute: Parliament and the Settlement of Religion, 1559* (1982); W. S. Hudson, *The Cambridge Connection and the Elizabethan Settlement of 1559* (Durham, North Carolina, 1980).

[9] Ashe to Emden consistory, 28 Apr. 1559. Van Schelven, *Vluchtelingenkerken*, p. 342.

[10] *CO*, xvii. 400–402; *Zurich Letters*, ii. 34.

meantime, however, the 'zealots of predestination' were in bad odour in London, and the strangers were endangered by any association with Geneva. Ashe reported in April that three had been imprisoned as a result of a house-to-house search for Knox's book, and the Queen's resentment was slow to die: over a year later dissident elements in the French church would suggest that des Gallars's appointment as minister should be referred to the Queen for confirmation, aware (as des Gallars explained to the consistory) that his association with Geneva would make him unacceptable to the Queen.[11]

Elizabeth's personal antipathy towards Calvin, now pre-eminent as the leading figure of the Continental Reformation, offers a partial explanation for the difficulties the strangers encountered in re-establishing their communities. Whilst the new government was committed to a whole-hearted Protestant Reformation Elizabeth had no intention of bowing to pressure to conform to Continental models; there would not therefore be the same interest in establishing a model Protestant community which had benefited Lasco in 1550. The short and turbulent life of Lasco's community, and Lasco's own persistent willingness to interfere in the affairs of his English hosts may, too, have made many, otherwise well-disposed to the Reformed faith, reluctant to repeat the experiment of a church with so large a measure of independence.

As a result the strangers' representatives experienced something of a rude awakening at their interview with Cecil in June.[12] Ashe and Dumas had received a sympathetic reception from several members of the Council including Knollys, the Queen's cousin and Vice-Chamberlain (and a Marian exile), and the Earl of Bedford, but all had advised that nothing could be done without Cecil's consent. Cecil, however, refused to consider the re-establishment of the churches as an independent *corpus corporatum et politicum*. This he said was against the wishes both of himself and of the Archbishop of Canterbury, and they would rather that the strangers should be forced to leave England once more than that they should have such a church. The re-establishment of the stranger churches was to be allowed only under much less favourable conditions. The

---

[11] Van Schelven, loc. cit.; Gallars to Calvin, 1 July 1560, *CO*, xviii. 136–7.

[12] Van Schelven, *Vluchtelingenkerken*, p. 344.

strangers were no longer to have their own foreign superintendent, but were now to be placed firmly under the authority
of the Bishop of London. There was even some suggestion that
they might be required to conform to the English rites and
ceremonies; the letter of February 1560 which finally required
the Marquis of Winchester to restore the church of Austin
Friars to the use of the Dutch ordered him to hand it over to
the Bishop of London (so that *he* might appoint suitable ministers to preach there), and noted ominously that no rite nor
use should be observed there 'contrary or derogatory to our
laws'.[13]

This rebuff must have come as a keen disappointment to
the strangers, who might have expected a more sympathetic
reaction from Cecil. During the Edwardian period the strangers had regarded Cecil as a firm friend, and had been quick
to turn to him for help at moments of difficulty. The petition
on behalf of poor French Protestants made by Bucer and other
leading foreign theologians in 1549 was addressed to Cecil,
and in 1551 Poullain sought Cecil's help when his community
at Glastonbury was troubled by an unhelpful English steward.
Lasco had himself enlisted Cecil's help on behalf of the London
community when English officials were attempting to force
strangers to attend the local parish churches; both this matter,
and a further petition in the same year on behalf of the French
printer, Thomas Gualtier, were speedily dealt with to the
strangers' satisfaction.[14]

It is difficult to know whether Cecil's firm reaction to the
strangers' petition in 1559 reflected his own opinion or whether
he was speaking as a representative of the Queen and Council;
in any event, after this initial disappointment, the strangers
could take some satisfaction from what had been secured from
the Secretary. The provision of suitable buildings in which
the foreign churches might gather once more was promised,
and the appointment of Edmund Grindal as Bishop of London
in June neutralized any ill effects the churches might have
expected from the imposition of an English bishop as superintendent. As a former Marian exile Grindal was eager to repay
the hospitality he had received on the Continent, and his

---

[13] PRO, SP 12/11/24.
[14] Strype, *Cranmer*, ii. apps. li, liv, lv, iii. app. cv.

sympathy towards the strangers' institutions and theology was such that Calvin, writing to des Gallars, had no hesitation in urging the strangers to accept his appointment with gratitude.[15] Under his indulgent protection the strangers came in fact to enjoy a wide measure of independence and were allowed to establish their own rites and institutions largely after the Edwardian model.

If the strangers were quickly made aware that there was no longer any intention of establishing a model Reformed community as in 1550, it remains to be explained why, in the changed climate of 1559, the re-establishment of the foreign churches was conceded at all. There were those who favoured absorbing the foreigners into the English parish churches, and the strangers were sporadically troubled by men of this spirit in the Elizabethan period. Sympathy for religious refugees was probably not a negligible factor, particularly in ensuring the advocacy of men like Grindal who had themselves personally experienced the miseries of exile and felt a debt of hospitality and kindness to be repaid. The influence of Grindal and other exiles would hardly, however, have been sufficient to secure the restoration of the church had the government not had its own interest in the alien community. For the government the control of anabaptism was no doubt again a consideration: as in the Edwardian period it was hoped that the stranger churches might be a powerful weapon in controlling the unorthodox amongst the foreign immigrants. At the beginning of Elizabeth's reign considerable alarm was felt at the number of such sectaries coming into England, and in September 1560 a worried government issued a proclamation unceremoniously banning all anabaptists from the kingdom.[16]

The control of anabaptism, however, by no means offered an unambiguous motive *for* the restoration of the official stranger churches. In 1559 there were those who wondered if the foreign churches would not in fact prove dangerous cradles of heterodoxy, and misgivings as to the real religious commitment of many of the new arrivals were expressed even by some, like Grindal, who were otherwise good friends of the

---

[15] *CO*, xviii. 116–17.
[16] *Tudor Royal Proclamations*, ii. 148–9. See also *Cal. S. P. For.*, 1558–9, no. 1025.

foreigners.[17] Such counter-arguments might well have prevailed in 1559, had not those in positions of power and influence found a further motive for encouraging the exile movement. By 1559 it was becoming increasingly clear that the refugees were a potent economic as well as a religious force. In the particular case of William Cecil, 'the Queen's right-hand man in matters of religion', one may demonstrate both a clear recognition of the important role foreigners might play in projects for the introduction of new industries into England, and an awareness of a specific role for the stranger churches in harnessing and directing this economic potential.

Cecil had long recognized the contribution that new industries could make to the economy, both in reducing a dangerous dependence on foreign powers and in preserving stocks of coin in the realm. Lane in his pamphlet on the decay of the exchanges which he delivered to Cecil in 1551 had referred to the costliness of foreign commodities 'a great part not needful' as the 'grandfather of many enormities'.[18] The *Discourse of the Commonweal*, a copy of which is amongst Cecil's papers at Hatfield, stressed how many of the imports brought in in return for English staples and bullion were mere trifles of no more value than the labour employed in the making of them. The example of Venice was cited, where 'they were rewarded and cherished, every man that brings in any new art or mystery whereby the people might be set awork'.[19] The part foreign expertise could play in stimulating these new industries was spelled out in a pamphlet addressed to the King in 1553 by William Cholmely, who advocated keeping the finishing of English broadcloths in England, to which end it would be necessary to bring workmen to England to teach the art of finishing as it was performed in Flanders. Cholmely himself had successfully introduced Continental techniques of dyeing into a dyehouse that he had set up in Southwark in 1551 with the aid of an expert workman from Antwerp.[20]

[17] Grindal to Cecil, 8 Sept. 1562. PRO, SP 12/24/24.
[18] *Tudor Economic Documents*, ed. R. H. Tawney and E. Power (1924), ii. 184. This general argument follows Thirsk, *Policy and Projects*.
[19] *A Discourse of the Common Weal of this Realm of England*, ed. E. Lamond (Cambridge, 1929), pp. 44, 89.
[20] *Tudor Economic Documents*, iii. 132–3.

Cecil's own interest in projects was almost certainly stimulated during the Edwardian period, and as Somerset's secretary from 1547 he would have had the opportunity to observe closely the Protector's project for establishing the weaving of Continental-style worsteds at Glastonbury.[21] His appointment as Elizabeth's principal minister gave him an opportunity to follow up these early experiments at a time when interest in the problems posed by imports was particularly acute. The *Considerations Delivered to Parliament* of 1559 inveighed against the 'false and deceitful wares', for which 'trifles' the foreigners 'filch from us the chief and substantial staples of the realm, where the people might be better employed in making them'.[22] In 1559, too, Cecil received a comprehensive list of the necessary and unnecessary goods brought into the Port of London, 'the overquantity whereof most lamentably spoileth the realm yearly'. This included such sums as £3,000 for pins, £10,000 for satin and silk, £2,500 for gloves, and £8,000 for hats.[23] The *Considerations Delivered to Parliament* advocated a total ban on the import of such products, but Cecil's attention was evidently turning to less drastic ideas for reducing England's dependence on imports. During the early years of the reign he received several proposals for the introduction of new manufactures into England in return for the grant of a monopoly. One such proposal concerned a group of Italian silk-weavers; it was suggested to Cecil that they might be persuaded to journey from Geneva to London to set up their looms if they were allowed to enjoy freedom from custom on their goods and protection from competition for ten years. They were also to be provided with a house and allowed a church in which the Gospel might be preached to them in Italian.[24]

In the early years of Elizabeth's reign such projects almost invariably involved foreign projectors. A stranger was concerned in the first petition to Cecil for a patent, for a new type of dredging machine, and two patents granted in 1561 were both issued to foreigners: to two Frenchmen for the making of hard white soap, and to a Dutchman for making saltpetre

[21] Above, p. 43.
[22] *Tudor Economic Documents*, i. 327.
[23] PRO, SP 12/8/31.
[24] PRO, SP 12/8/32–5.

(an essential raw material in the dyeing process).[25] In 1559 Cecil was also presented with a learned exposition of the theory of patents by the distinguished Italian mathematician and engineer, Jacobo Acontius. Although Acontius was not rewarded with the patent he sought until 1565 he was highly regarded in government circles and received a pension soon after his arrival in England in 1559.[26]

The flurry of interest in projects and monopolies at the beginning of Elizabeth's reign indicates how lively was Cecil's interest in economic innovation, but he was also aware that it was possible to stimulate new industries without the necessity of a formal monopoly. The unnecessary goods carefully listed in the return made to Cecil in 1559—hats, pins, gloves, satins and silks—were all products closely associated with foreign expertise and Englishmen were not slow to see the advantages of encouraging foreign workmen to make these goods in England. It was soon clear that with the intensification of persecution in the cloth-manufacturing towns of the Low Countries such skilled artisans, particularly weavers of the popular 'New Draperies', would be prominent amongst the Elizabethan refugees.

Cecil also appreciated the role that the stranger churches might play in regulating the economic activity of the stranger community in England. The petition for the Italian silk-weavers had already explicitly coupled the introduction of a new technique with the grant of a church, and the ministers of the Dutch church were soon involved in an ambitious project to revive the flagging economic prosperity of Sandwich by the introduction of Dutch workmen. The town council was readily granted permission by the Privy Council to invite a group of Dutch families skilled in the making of bays and says and other cloths new to England to settle in Sandwich. But such craftsmen were not to be recruited direct from the Continent; rather, a draft of the patent authorizing the settlement in July 1561 specified that the Dutchmen should be 'strangers now residing in our city of London . . . belonging to the Church

[25] PRO, SP 12/1/56; Thirsk, *Policy and Projects*, pp. 53–4.
[26] D. S. Davies, 'Acontius, Champion of Toleration and the Patent System', *Economic History Review*, 7 (1936–7), 63–6.

of Strangers'.[27] The first twenty-five households to go to Sandwich were to be approved by the Archbishop of Canterbury and the Bishop of London, and seem to have been selected by the ministers of the London Dutch church who were careful to recommend only workmen possessing the required skills. The Dutch ministers had previously assisted in the negotiations with the Sandwich town council over conditions for the establishment of the community, and the minister Peter Delenus made a brief trip to assist in the setting-up of a church for the community in September.[28]

There is even a hint that Cecil was anxious to extend the benefits received by Sandwich from its Dutch settlers to his own home town of Stamford. Cecil appears to have raised the possibility of a similar settlement at Stamford at the time that the Sandwich negotiation was reaching its successful conclusion.[29] In the event nothing further seems to have been done until six years later, when Cecil was successful in introducing a Dutch congregation to the town.[30]

It was envisaged that the stranger churches would also play a central role in the economic regulation of the alien community in London itself. The idea first mooted in 1553, that no stranger should be eligible for a patent of denization unless he was a member of the stranger churches was speedily revived, and the major enrolment of new denizens in 1562 took place after lists of candidates had been compiled by the strangers' ministers.[31] To use the stranger churches as guarantors of good conduct and orthodoxy before denizen status would be granted had the advantage to the government of exercising some control over the flow of refugees 'not truly religious', and the churches themselves were not averse to such a powerful incentive to foreigners to join the community.[32] The ministers of the foreign churches seem indeed to have hoped initially that church membership might *replace* denizenship as a means of

---

[27] *Tudor Economic Documents*, i. 297.

[28] *KP I*, pp. 192–3, 215, 220–1, 224, 244.

[29] Ibid., p. 224.

[30] Thirsk, *Policy and Projects*, p. 47.

[31] Below, pp. 146–9.

[32] In August 1561 one Peter Becke rather guilelessly confessed to the French consistory that he was applying to join the church only in order to obtain a letter of denization. *Actes I*, p. 52. See also ibid., p. 38 (Anthony le May).

securing economic privileges: their petition of June 1560 asked that all those who joined the churches and submitted themselves to ecclesiastical discipline should be allowed to live freely and exercise their trade without fear of interference.[33]

This, however, proved an over-ambitious request, and if the economic considerations detailed above were arguably important in securing renewed goodwill for the stranger communities, the government dragged its feet when the strangers pressed for the economic protection necessary if their renewed privileges were to be of real value. Cecil's reaction to the petition of the Italian silk-weavers shows him more eager to secure maximum economic benefit from their presence than to gratify their requests for privileges: the term of years for which their manufacture would be protected was carefully pruned, and in place of a church using the Genevan rite Cecil's marginal note allows only a church 'according to the form of the Church of England'.[34] The French and Dutch communities both experienced ominous difficulties before they were re-established in their own former buildings. During the Marian interim the church of Austin Friars had been turned over to the Marquis of Winchester, and seems to have been used as a government storehouse, although a room was made available for the Italian merchants to hear Mass.[35] The Lord Treasurer, who had made his home in the part of the former monastic property granted to him after its dissolution, was reluctant to hand back the body of the church to the Dutch, so that although Cecil had promised the provison of suitable buildings in June 1559, for the remainder of that year the Dutch had to be content with the loan of an English parish church, obtained on their behalf by the minister Haemstede.[36] The return of Utenhove and Delenus in December brought men of sufficient stature for a new appeal to be made to the Court for the return of Austin Friars, and in February 1560 Winchester was finally ordered to make the church over to its former occupants. Even so, the Dutch did not recover all the property they had enjoyed

[33] Hessels, ii. 124.
[34] PRO, SP 12/8/35.
[35] Lindeboom, *Austin Friars*, p. 30; *The Diary of Henry Machyn*, ed. J. G. Nichols (Camden Soc., xlii, 1848), p. 140; *APC*, v. 68.
[36] Jelsma, *Van Haemstede*, p. 117.

in the Edwardian period; the letter makes no mention of the two houses previously provided for the use of the ministers, and in deference to Winchester the community did not press for the return of the churchyard.[37] It was some months still before the church was restored to a fit condition for use, and only in June 1560 do the Dutch consistory minutes record the first baptism after the restoration of the church, fittingly of the son of Anthony Ashe, Samuel.[38] The French, too, experienced considerable difficulties in recovering their church in Threadneedle Street, and were grateful for the intercession of Cranmer's former client, Peter Alexander, who seems to have made a successful petition for its return in April 1560.[39]

With the arrival of Nicholas des Gallars in June 1560 both communities were at last restored to their own premises under capable ministers, and could set about the restoration of their discipline and community life. The problems which the communities encountered in this endeavour will be examined below, but economic security proved just as elusive as domestic peace. In the face of mounting hostility from native Londoners, securing a measure of economic protection for church members became an urgent priority.

The flow of foreign workmen into England, stimulated by Elizabeth's accession, provoked a sharp reaction amongst London's artisans and small tradesmen.[40] They not unreasonably viewed the foreigners not as innovators and purveyors of new and superior techniques but as a threat to their livelihoods, and the members of the stranger communities were soon feeling the effects of their hostility. Although English craftsmen made frequent appeals over the years for changes in the law to control the competition of the strangers, existing statutes provided plentiful opportunities for harrying the foreign artisans, as those newcomers who had as yet had no time or opportunity to secure patents of denization quickly discovered. Refugees who were not aware that non-denizens were forbidden to keep open shops or employ other strangers had a rude awakening,

---

[37] PRO, SP 12/11/24; Hessels, iii. 1213.
[38] *KP I*, p. 495.
[39] See below, p. 153.
[40] Economic tensions between the foreign and English communities are discussed in more detail in Ch. IX, below.

and the ministers of the churches were soon hearing complaints from members of their congregations, threatened with fines or imprisonment by English neighbours or professional informers ('promoters').[41] The restriction on their business activity was dangerous enough, but the newcomers were also finding it increasingly difficult to find lodgings. The statute of 1540 forbade the leasing of property to non-denizens, and English residents who did so in defiance of the law were themselves liable to fines. There seems in consequence to have been considerable reluctance to rent property to foreigners, and it is clear from a rash of cases relating to leases in the French consistory minutes that suitable lodgings were hard to find.[42]

The strangers soon recognized that unless the members of their churches were protected from such vexations the privilege of free worship would be empty indeed. In July 1560 it was agreed in the consistories of both churches to petition the Council to allow church members the quiet exercise of their trades in private houses until a grant of letters of denization could be prepared. The petition hinted that without such protection many of the strangers might be driven to return to their native lands.[43] The petition, delivered by Utenhove and Alexander, produced no immediate response, and at the end of the year the churches faced the problem anew. This time the matter was raised by the French consistory, for whom the problems of their non-denizen members had been highlighted by the case of Philip Bosquiel, a buttonmaker who proposed to withdraw to Reading to find work as he was prevented from working freely in London.[44] The ministers presented their petition once again on New Year's Day 1561, and on this occasion backed their appeal by lobbying influential figures at Court who were known to be sympathetic, namely Sir Robert Dudley and Sir Francis Knollys.[45] On 28 January Utenhove reported a rather more hopeful response: the Queen seemed well dis-

---

[41] On the legal position of the strangers see above, pp. 14–16. 21 Henry VIII c. 16.

[42] 32 Henry VIII c. 16. *Actes I*, pp. 19, 40, 57.

[43] *KP I*, p. 15; Hessels, ii. 124, 134. From the entry in *KP I* it is clear that July is the correct date (the Latin and Dutch copies of the petition in Hessels have different dates).

[44] *Actes I*, p. 16.

[45] *KP I*, pp. 95–6.

posed towards the exiles, and held out some hopes of the grant of the required letters of denization.[46]

In fact, little further progress was made for some months; the Dutch in particular were in any case preoccupied with internal problems.[47] By June 1561, however, affairs had begun to look more hopeful, particularly as Grindal had now taken an active role on the strangers' behalf. After consulting Bacon, the Lord Keeper, Grindal advised a supplication to the Queen coupled with a direct approach to Cecil. Grindal suggested that the churches should forward to Cecil lists of all those who sought denization together with their trades; a note should indicate on the petition which of the supplicants were young men, and whether any worked for Englishmen. Grindal would then add his own voice to that of the strangers to ensure the petition's success.[48]

The churches were quick to compile the required lists and forward them to the Secretary. The French community prefaced their list with a summary of their grievances. They stressed that they were prosecuted under laws of which they had previously been ignorant, prohibiting foreigners from owning houses and placing limitations on their gathering together. Not only were the foreigners themselves pursued for violations of the law, but even the Englishmen who rented them houses were also being prosecuted. The petition asked once more for citizenship rights, or, if that were not possible, at least for protection from the laws which prevented them exercising their trades.[49]

The lists submitted by the French and Dutch consistories both survive, and are most interesting documents.[50] In most cases the petitioners' occupations are recorded, and these make a particularly instructive contrast with the occupations of the members of Lasco's community in 1550. In 1550 the largest occupational groups in the Dutch church were all in trades

[46] Ibid., p. 110.
[47] See below, pp. 169 ff.
[48] *KP I*, p. 211.
[49] PRO, SP 12/48/47, printed in *Returns*, i. 287–8.
[50] *Returns*, i. 273–8, 287–92. The French petition is misdated 1562/3 by Kirk and Kirk and 1564 by Schickler, but can reliably be identified as the French return of June 1561 from internal evidence.

traditionally performed by English artisans in which the competition of foreign workmen was particularly burdensome and resented. There were 50 shoemakers and cobblers, 45 tailors, and 37 assorted woodworkers (mainly joiners and chestmakers).[51] By 1561, if the lists submitted by the consistories are to be believed, there had been a marked shift away from these occupations towards the new skills and luxury crafts that Cecil was keen to see introduced to England. There were now only 12 shoemakers in the Dutch list, and only 6 woodworkers; on the other hand, there were no less than thirty weavers, of which at least nine were silk-weavers, and others, refugees from the industrial towns of Flanders, were doubtless workers in the fashionable New Draperies. No less than 28 of the 34 weavers in the French list were silk-weavers, and the French list also boasted 41 hatters, glovers, and cappers, makers of those 'superfluous goods' whose import was so much resented. Cecil may have been struck by the presence in the Dutch list of both dyers and munitions workers (he was concerned to stimulate domestic production in both areas as the early grants of monopolies show), and three of the Dutch church members listed were employed in the Queen's works in the Tower, presumably as munitions or Mint workers.

It is unlikely that these royal employees would have been troubled by the authorities in carrying on their trades, and their presence on the list encourages the suggestion that this was more than simply a petition from those seeking protection: the communities were also taking the opportunity to show Cecil their most attractive face. In addition to those applying for denizenship those already denizens were also listed. The French community presented 101 candidates for denization and with them were listed 133 members who were already denizens, many of them substantial and prosperous citizens with an established position in the city, some of whom had been in London up to thirty years. Many had English wives, and of sixty-two of these French denizens who can be traced in the surveys of aliens ten years later almost all were still living in the same place, and many had substantial households and servants.[52] The presence of these denizens on the petition

[51] See above, p. 82.
[52] Names traced in *Returns*, i. 402–79, ii. 1–154 (Returns of Aliens 1571).

had the effect of stressing the substance and stability of the whole community. These were men with capital to invest, and both they and the more recent arrivals possessed the skills in which the government was particularly interested. Here were men, the petition seemed to suggest, who ought to be supported and not driven out of the country by discouraging or disabling conditions of work.

The petitions presented in June 1561 produced a more encouraging reaction, as the Secretary undertook to write to the Justices and instruct them to allow the strangers to occupy their trades undisturbed.[53] The next few months saw little further activity, possibly because des Gallars was absent at the Colloquy of Poissy, but it now finally became clear that the goodwill of Cecil was not enough to protect the strangers from harassment. On 19 August the consistories of the two churches conferred over the case of Martin Noel, a Frenchman, who had been reported to the Lord Mayor by a promoter [informer] for keeping a house as a non-denizen and fined £6. He had insufficient funds to pay this considerable sum, and the consistories could at first only suggest that he be left in prison, for, if the informer was paid, the churches feared that others would be encouraged to persecute the poor strangers. A week later the churches sought the Bishop's help and Grindal, summoning the English informer to him, made a strong plea for Noel's release, saying that it was not the Queen's pleasure that poor strangers should be persecuted. The informer, however, refused to release his captive and the law was on his side; Grindal was powerless to act further.[54]

This case may have convinced the strangers, who had previously always petitioned for protection by denization or other means, that nothing less than the full protection of a patent of denization would suffice. They lobbied the Court one more time, and finally achieved success. On 29 December 1561 Lord Keeper Bacon was granted powers to enrol denizens at pleasure for suitable fees, and a major enrolment was soon under way. Representatives of both churches went to Court to hear the good news, and prayers of thanks were said on their

[53] *KP I*, p. 216.
[54] *Actes I*, p. 54.

return.[55] The new denizens were enrolled over a period of six months and the churches remained fully involved during that time. Those seeking a patent in the Dutch church were first subjected to a series of questions (of what nature is not specified) and examined to see how much they were worth; the church borrowed £40 from two of its members to help poorer brethren who could not meet the considerable expense of obtaining a patent from their own resources.[56] Some church members expressed anger at the end of February at the slow pace of the enrolment, but by June at least 50 per cent of those presented by the two churches had achieved a grant of denization.[57]

The mass enrolment of non-denizen members of the stranger churches brought to an end a two-year campaign to achieve economic security for the members of the stranger churches in London. Without such security the re-establishment of the churches would have been of very dubious value, and many exiles might have made a speedy return to the Continent. As we have seen, the government dragged its feet over the grants, and was understandably reluctant to extend rights of citizenship to so many and risk the anger of native workmen. That it eventually complied with the ministers' urgings owed much to a growing recognition of the strangers' economic potential. The desire to exploit the new techniques and skills brought by the foreign refugees was a persistent theme of the relationship between the government and the foreign community during the Elizabethan period. Enthusiasm for a model Protestant community from which Lasco had benefited in 1550 had waned by 1559. In the new circumstances the ministers of the foreign churches were not slow to recognize that the economic argument constituted their best defence.

2. INTERNAL DISPUTES

All in all, the first years of Elizabeth's reign proved extremely difficult for the restored foreign communities, the more so as

---

[55] *Cal. Pat. Rolls Eliz.*, ii. 396, 450–61; *KP I*, p. 278.

[56] Ibid., pp. 280, 282, 297, 318.

[57] Ibid., p. 293. Comparing names from the Patent Roll with the petitions, *Returns*, i. 273–8, 287–92.

their attention was often diverted from the long struggle for
economic security by serious internal problems. Disagreements
amongst the foreigners were not new, and Lasco had faced
several challenges to his authority in the short years of his
superintendency, but these early difficulties were by no means
as damaging as the protracted and bitter wrangles which
erupted in the French and Dutch congregations in 1560. In
both cases the disputes resolved themselves into a trial of
strength between the two ministers; des Gallars and Alexander
in the French community, and Delenus and Haemstede in the
Dutch. A detailed narrative of these events will not be attempted here: the story has been well told by earlier historians
of the churches, and succinctly summarized in a recent biography of their long-suffering superintendent, Edmund Grindal,
the Bishop of London.[58] Yet the quarrels which divided and
disrupted both communities at such an important juncture do
bear further examination, particularly if seen from the rather
different perspective of the ordinary members of the community who became involved, often very reluctantly, in the
controversies between their ministers. In particular, an examination of the role of the consistory in both churches makes
clear that the two disputes, despite superficial similarities, were
in fact very different. Whereas in the French church the clash
between des Gallars and Alexander was essentially personal
and ephemeral, in the Dutch church the dispute between
Delenus and Haemstede turned on an important point of
theological principle, and ultimately proved much more
damaging.

When a French congregation first gathered together once
more in 1559 a suitable minister was not immediately to hand.
Of the Edwardian ministers Vauville was dead and Perussel
occupied at Frankfurt. Jean Dumas, dispatched with Anthony
Ashe from Emden to petition on the strangers' behalf, had no
pretensions to the ministry. The vacuum was filled, quite unofficially, by Ebrard Evrail, a minister who had come to London from Antwerp soon after Elizabeth's accession.[59] By

[58] Schickler, *Églises du Refuge*, i. 91–103, 115–36; Lindeboom, *Austin Friars*, pp.
41–5; Van Schelven, *Vluchtelingenkerken*, pp. 144–52; Patrick Collinson, *Archbishop Grindal*, 1519–1583 (1979), pp. 125–52.
[59] Schickler, *Églises du Refuge*, i. 89–91.

December 1559 Evrail was preaching to the French in London, but the difficulties which faced the fledgeling community quickly brought him to recognize that he could not shoulder the burdens of the ministry alone. Early in 1560 he wrote to his church at Antwerp asking them to furnish another minister. The ministers at Antwerp advised that he should write to Geneva, which Evrail was reluctant to do; by now, however, the French church in London had elected a group of elders who were prepared to take matters into their own hands. In March 1560 ten elders and deacons signed a letter to Calvin which described the difficulties facing the community, and asked for the provision of a minister of calibre. The appeal was endorsed by the Dutch ministers and the superintendent Grindal.[60]

Calvin was quick to respond to this petition, dispatching within two months one of his most experienced ministers, Nicholas des Gallars.[61] Unfortunately for the church, while its messenger was on his way to Geneva another distinguished French minister, Peter Alexander, had arrived in London, and when he offered his services to the community in recovering their former property, the consistory accepted with gratitude. It was probably through Alexander's intercession at Court that the Church of St Anthony was restored to the French on 7 April, and during the next two months Alexander, although not elected minister, was acting as such and preaching to the community.[62] The arrival of des Gallars in June therefore placed the elders of the church in an embarrassing position, as the man who had filled the breach so capably while des Gallars was *en route* from Geneva showed no inclination to lay down his charge.

The stage was set for a clash between two proud and strong-minded men which would cause both the community and its superintendent many difficulties over the next two years. It was the church's tragedy that, despite Grindal's best endeavours, they could not be reconciled, because des Gallars

---

[60] Printed by Schickler, op. cit., iii. 44–7.
[61] The Genevan assembly of ministers elected des Gallars on 20 Apr. Schickler, op. cit., i. 91 n. 2.
[62] Oswald Michotte, *Un Réformateur, Pierre Alexandre* (Nessonvaux, 1913), p. 108.

and Alexander were both distinguished reformers who made a considerable contribution to the church both in England and on the Continent. Nicholas des Gallars was perhaps the fourth-ranking pastor in Geneva at the time of his departure for England; in relinquishing him to serve the London church Calvin gave a sure indication of the importance he attached to the situation in England at the beginning of Elizabeth's reign.[63] A native of Paris, born about 1520, des Gallars was one of the many Reformed ministers of noble stock. He became a minister in Geneva in 1544 and was one of Calvin's closest friends; a capable theologian, he translated several of Calvin's works for publication between periods away from Geneva as minister in Jussy and Paris. Des Gallars was forced to leave this last post by the violence of the persecution in January 1558, but he enjoyed only a brief respite before turning his steps somewhat reluctantly towards London.[64] Des Gallars was sufficiently prominent in the Reformed church to be summoned personally by Coligny to the Colloquy of Poissy in 1561,[65] and after his return to the Continent in 1563 he was quickly appointed minister of the church in Orléans. In 1571 he would serve as secretary to the Reformed synod at La Rochelle.

The London church was honoured by the presence of des Gallars yet, in truth, it might have been equally well served by Peter Alexander had he not so unluckily arrived shortly after the dispatch of the church's letter to Geneva.[66] Some twenty years older than des Gallars, Alexander had been preacher at the court of Mary of Hungary, sister of Charles V and governor of the Low Countries, before his conversion to Protestantism brought his investigation for heresy and pre-

---

[63] On des Gallars see Haag, *La France Protestante* (2nd ed., Paris, 1877–88), v. 298–305; E. Doumergue, *Jean Calvin, Les Hommes et les choses de son temps* (Lausanne, 1899–1917), iii. 597–605. There is an excellent biographical note, with bibliography, in R. Peter and J. Rott, *Les Lettres à Jean Calvin de la Collection Sarrau* (Paris, 1972), p. 81.

[64] Des Gallars received his appointment 'à contre-cœur et vaincu par les objurgations de ses collègues'. Schickler, op. cit., i. 92.

[65] *Actes I*, p. 51.

[66] On Alexander see Michotte, *Alexandre*; J. F. Gilmont, 'Un pseudonyme de Pierre Alexandre: Simon Alexius', *Bulletin de la Société d'Histoire du Protestantisme Belge*, v, 6 (1970–1), 179–88; *Dictionnaire de Théologie Catholique* (Paris, 1903–50), xii, ii. 1800–2. Also the biographical note in the work by Peter and Rott cited in n. 63, above.

cipitate flight.[67] Alexander took refuge at Strasburg before moving to Heidelberg and thence, in 1547, to England where he quickly became an intimate of Cranmer at Canterbury. Cranmer procured for Alexander a prebend at Canterbury and Alexander in return helped the archbishop with his patristic research; several small theological works from his hand survive from this period.[68] Alexander was able to use his position of influence with Cranmer to ensure that the interests of the French community were not forgotten at the time of the establishment of the stranger churches in 1550, and he was sufficiently prominent to earn Gardiner's special attention after the accession of Mary.[69] Summoned before the Ecclesiastical Commission, Alexander wisely fled once more, and in 1555 he took up a position as minister of the French refugee church at Strasburg. His sudden re-appearance in London in 1560 followed his dismissal from this position the previous year,[70] and although his ostensible purpose in returning to England was to recover his prebend at Canterbury, Alexander's contacts at Court made his offer of help to the French church in London especially welcome in the spring of 1560. Alexander would later remind the consistory, to their embarrassment, of the expense to which he had been put in petitioning for the church's restoration.[71] By the time of des Gallars's arrival his service to the church in two reigns put the community under a debt of gratitude which could not easily be set aside.

The embarrassment of the community's leaders, all too successful in their quest for a suitable minister for the community, quickly communicated itself to des Gallars who thought the

---

[67] Jean de Savignac, *Les Mémorables de Francisco de Enzinas* (Brussels, 1963), pp. 282–93.

[68] Now in the Bodleian Library, Oxford, and Corpus Christi College Library, Cambridge: listed in Peter and Rott, op. cit. Michotte prints abridged French versions of the Bodleian works, discourses on Purgatory and Excommunication. Michotte, *Alexandre*, pp. 134–89.

[69] See above, pp. 36–7, 116.

[70] Michotte, *Alexandre*, pp. 84–105; Jean Rott, 'L'Église des réfugiés de langue française à Strasbourg au XVI⁰ siècle', *Bulletin de la Société de l'histoire du protestantisme français*, 122 (1976), 533–5.

[71] *Actes I*, p. 19.

greater part of the community viewed his arrival with displeasure.[72] Opposition was soon expressed to the imposition of a new minister, as it seemed, from outside, and the insistence that there should be a proper election was supported by the disappointed Alexander. This suggestion however was rejected by Grindal, whose welcome to des Gallars had been warm and heartfelt. The superintendent decreed that since des Gallars had been invited by the most substantial element of the community (meaning, no doubt, the consistory) a new election was unnecessary, and nothing remained but to confirm him in office.[73] On 24 June Grindal came to the church and, with Alexander acting as his interpreter, exhorted the church's members to accept des Gallars as minister. The community signified its consent by silence.[74]

This was by no means the end of the community's troubles. Alexander nursed his sense of grievance for two weeks before coming to the consistory to complain that he was no longer invited to preach.[75] The deposed minister Evrail was also busy fomenting trouble for des Gallars, who remained deeply suspicious of the community's loyalties; one of his first acts after his election was to insist that the whole consistory should submit themselves for re-election.[76] Des Gallars seems to have been convinced that his supporters were an embattled minority in the community. In his first letter to Calvin he suggested that a party amongst the elders was opposed to him, and he subsequently singled out some of the most affluent and respected members of the community, including Jean Dumas, as partisans of Alexander.[77]

Des Gallars's reference to the hostility of some of the more substantial members of the community has encouraged the suggestion that the resistance to the Genevan minister revealed

---

[72] Des Gallars to Calvin, 30 June 1560, *CO*, xiii. 134. Des Gallars's letters to Calvin are one of the two principal sources for the dispute in the French church, and their inevitable partiality should be kept in mind.

[73] *CO*, xviii. 135; Schickler, *Églises du Refuge*, i. 94.

[74] *CO*, xviii. 139; *Actes I*, p. 4.

[75] *Actes I*, p. 5.

[76] *CO*, xviii. 162–3; *Actes I*, p. 4.

[77] *CO*, xviii. 134, 143, 164.

some fundamental division within the community.[78] The church's more well-to-do members might indeed have been expected to resent the imposition of a narrow doctrinal orthodoxy, and clashes with those in full sympathy with the discipline were a distinct possibility. However, although the French church did face serious internal problems in the years after its restoration, one may doubt whether their roots were social or economic in any narrow sense. By far the most divisive issue at this time was the question of how those who had remained in England during Mary's reign should be dealt with on the church's re-establishment. As we have seen, at least fifty former members of the Edwardian French church who had remained in London were forced to make public acts of penitence before being re-admitted.[79] Many of them were substantial and well-established citizens who had probably conformed only reluctantly in Mary's reign, and they were certainly unwilling to undergo public humiliation in order to rejoin the congregation in 1559. They found an ally in Ebrard Evrail, who was inclined to look indulgently upon their offence and forget the past. According to des Gallars, Evrail had built a party within the church by advancing former apostates to positions of responsibility, particularly in the diaconate.[80]

The French community certainly experienced considerable tension between those who had remained in London and those who now returned to England after the privations of exile. Yet the treatment of the Marian apostates was not the root cause of the opposition to des Gallars, nor of the tension between des Gallars and Alexander. Even at the height of the personal bitterness between them des Gallars was prepared to recognize that Alexander was doctrinally orthodox, and Alexander was as resolute as himself in condemning those who had compromised with Catholicism. Alexander made no secret of his views on the matter and had as a result earned the resentment of Evrail, who took advantage of Alexander's temporary absence from London in June 1560 to attempt to incite the

[78] Collinson, *Grindal*, p. 131.
[79] Above, p. 125.
[80] Schickler, *Églises du Refuge*, i. 98; *CO*, xviii. 163.

community against him.[81] In any case it is clear that, even before the arrival of either minister, those who advocated a firm line against the apostates were firmly in control of the community. The election of a group of elders hostile to Evrail in December 1559 demonstrated that his supporters were already in a distinct minority, and after his removal from the ministry the consistory treated Evrail with barely concealed contempt. A petition from him concerning a business dispute received scant sympathy, and when he presumed to sit on the bench reserved for the consistory in the church he was peremptorily ejected by Jean Dumas.[82] Evrail had to content himself with work as a schoolmaster, and by the spring of 1561 he had decided to leave the inhospitable church to which he had once ministered. He departed in March, furnished with a conciliatory letter of recommendation.[83]

By this time Evrail's influence in the church was negligible. The elders who had insisted on his replacement had all been confirmed in office in the election held at des Gallars's insistence, and the election to the diaconate (considered Evrail's stronghold) produced only one nominee who had to be rejected as a result of Marian apostasy.[84] The elections demonstrated that amongst the more substantial members of the community the orthodox were in a dominant position, and by the end of the year those who had attended Mass and wished to remain members of the community had undergone the required act of public penance.[85] Although the issue of the treatment of the Marian apostates was potentially very damaging for the French community, serious long-term consequences were avoided, partly because the consistory had taken firm action, and partly because on this issue at least, des Gallars and Alexander were at one.

[81] *CO*, xviii. 137. Alexander had gone to Canterbury to take possession of his prebend. Des Gallars to Calvin, 13 Sept. 1560: 'Unum me solatur, quod Alexander purae est doctrinae . . .'. *CO*, xviii. 180. In his *Epistre aux frères de l'Église de Jesus Christ . . . qui sont maintenant en dispersion* (1556), Alexander had argued strongly for exile as against attendance at Mass: see Gilmont, 'Alexandre'. There is a copy of this rare tract in the library of Clare College, Cambridge.

[82] *Actes I*, pp. 10, 27.

[83] Ibid., p. 33.

[84] Ibid., pp. 4, 5.

[85] Ibid., pp. 14, 15, 20. A few more trickled back into the church during 1561. Ibid., pp. 32, 33, 37, 39, 52.

Support for Alexander within the community was, then, not based on any perceived differences between the ministers over fundamental issues, though it is hardly surprising that des Gallars, perplexed and injured by a reception less enthusiastic than he justifiably expected, should have misunderstood the restraint initially exhibited by some of the elders and more substantial members of the community. The truth of the matter may simply have been that the elders had been placed in an impossible position by the arrival of the two ministers, and their subsequent behaviour. Des Gallars clearly came to London with a settled prejudice against his rival. Passing through Strasburg *en route* to London he had been made acquainted with the circumstances of Alexander's dismissal from the church there, and in London he flatly refused Grindal's suggestion that he should accept Alexander as a colleague, threatening that if this were insisted upon he would be forced to reveal what he knew of Alexander's recent conduct. Grindal strenuously opposed this provocative course and when Calvin too urged des Gallars to let the matter drop he somewhat grudgingly concurred.[86] Alexander seems initially to have behaved in a more conciliatory manner and during the summer of 1560 he took an active role in the ministry. But des Gallars's request in November that the consistory settle his salary and the expenses of his wife's journey to England was enough to spark another outburst of jealous resentment.[87] Notwithstanding his initial undertaking to serve the church unpaid (Alexander had the income from his prebend at Canterbury to live on), Alexander now requested a salary for himself. The consistory offered an annual twenty marks, and although Alexander was not satisfied with this the quarrel was for the moment patched up by Grindal, who invited both men to dinner and effected a fragile reconciliation.[88] But it was clear that resentment was simmering beneath the surface and new quarrels in the summer of 1561 brought matters to a head.

By this time Alexander had succeeded in uniting the consistory against him but this had not always been the case: only

---

[86] *CO*, xviii. 138, 213.
[87] *Actes I*, pp. 8, 12, 17.
[88] Ibid., pp. 18, 19, 21.

three of the eight elders seem to have been enthusiastic parti-
sans of des Gallars from the time of his arrival. One of these,
Anthony Capell, had taken the leading role in securing des
Gallars's appointment, carrying the consistory's letter to
Geneva and accompanying the minister back to London.
Capell also provided the initial capital for the printing of des
Gallars's new Form of Discipline, and his forceful and abrasive
character soon brought him into conflict with Alexander.[89]
Alexander would later claim that Capell and his colleague
Peter Castelain had mocked him because he had formerly been
a monk; Castelain had already been involved in another
exchange of insults with the minister at the beginning of the
year, although on this occasion the quarrel was made up on
the instructions of the consistory.[90] The third of des Gallars's
partisans, Jean Hette, was less prominent, though he was
quick to report a slander on des Gallars by another who fell
foul of the consistory.[91] All three of these elders were men of
substance, and all three were new arrivals in England in
Elizabeth's reign. Capell and Castelain were silk-weavers, and
both had been members of the consistory of the Reformed
church at Antwerp.[92] The arrival of two important members
of the Antwerp community in London by the end of 1559
suggests conscious planning, and it seems probable that they
took the lead in seeking a more suitable minister than Evrail,
whom they would have known from his time at Antwerp. Hette
too was a silk-weaver, though he came from Normandy.[93]

These new residents were des Gallars's most zealous advocates, but the reaction of the four elders who were longer-term
residents would be of equal importance. It seems to have been
this group who felt some initial reservations towards des Gallars, a reserve which he was inclined to interpret as opposition.
Two, Anthony du Ponchel and Jacques le Chalon, had first

[89] Ibid., pp. 34, 39, 50. For this Form of Discipline (a revised version of the church order) see below, n. 117.

[90] Ibid., pp. 27, 50.

[91] Ibid., p. 36.

[92] *Returns*, i. 451 (Peter Shattelan), iii. 417 (Capell). *Actes I*, p. 53 (reference to case brought before consistory at Antwerp while Capell and Castelain were both members).

[93] *Returns*, i. 290 (Johannes Haitie, *fimbriarius*). Castelain, Capell and Hette all received their patents of denization on the same day, along with other new arrivals in 1559. *Cal. Pat. Rolls Eliz.*, ii. 451, 461.

arrived in England during the reign of Edward,[94] whereas Simon Percy and Jacques Marabut were both survivors from the Henrician era. Percy had first come to London some thirty years previously and settled in Southwark, whilst Marabut, a locksmith, had built up a substantial business in the Temple Bar district.[95] All four of these prosperous and influential figures seem to have been of unimpeachable orthodoxy. Ponchel, Marabut, and le Chalon all signed the appeal to Geneva which brought des Gallars to England, and whilst Percy did not do so this was probably because he had not yet returned to England from Emden, where he had settled after the dissolution of the Edwardian church in 1553.[96] There is no hint that any of the other three remained in England during Mary's reign. It would have been a comparatively easy matter for Ponchel, a merchant with considerable property in Antwerp,[97] to slip across the Channel, and Marabut could probably have removed his tools more easily than Percy. Le Chalon, a typesetter, was a rather younger man who would presumably have had no difficulty finding work abroad. All these well-respected men played a conscientious role in the running of the community. The English-speaking Ponchel was secretary to the consistory, and frequently took part in negotiations with both the superintendent and the Dutch community.[98] The senior figures of Percy and Marabut were much in demand as arbitrators in business disputes, and Jacques le Chalon took the leading role in the consistory's process against the persistent troublemaker Nicholas Wilpin.[99]

The initial coolness towards des Gallars of this group amongst the elders cannot be put down to any lack of zeal in the community's affairs. Ponchel, in fact, was sufficiently well disposed towards the Genevan minister to lend the paper for the printing of his Form of Discipline.[100] More likely these

[94] *Returns*, i. 164 (Pounsell), 420 (Jacob de la Forest). *Denizations*, p. 74 (de Pouthell).
[95] *Returns*, i. 27, 150 (Marabotte, Marybottes), 289. *Denizations*, p. 161 (Marabrit). He is also described as comb-maker and gunsmith. On Percy see above, pp. 126–7.
[96] Schickler, *Églises du Refuge*, iii. 46.
[97] See his will, PCC 1582 (39 Tirwhite).
[98] *Actes I*, pp. 30, 54.
[99] Ibid., pp. 10, 11, 14, 30, 33, 36.
[100] Ibid., p. 39.

survivors from the Edwardian church were especially conscious of the church's debt to Peter Alexander, and felt acutely the embarrassment of their position, having accepted the services of two distinguished but quite incompatible ministers. The elders made a valiant attempt to preserve the peace between the rival ministers. When Alexander was ill in the summer of 1560 they visited him in a body to suggest terms on which he should continue to serve, and in December met his demands for a salary.[101] The consistory conveyed its answer to this request through Jean Dumas, the eighth elder and Alexander's closest associate on the consistory, and although they would not accept his claim for a further four marks the elders made a final gesture of reconciliation in February 1561 by offering him a gift of two marks.[102] By now, however, those formerly sympathetic to Alexander were beginning to lose patience, as may be seen from the changing attitude of the influential Anthony du Ponchel. Ponchel had initially shown Alexander a great deal of sympathy, presenting his request for a salary to the consistory and offering a loan to cover the cost if the church did not have the money. Alexander's refusal to be satisfied, however, ultimately alienated Ponchel, and in the spring of 1561 he told the minister he ought to leave the church and go back to Canterbury.[103]

By this time Alexander had in fact succeeded in uniting the whole consistory against him. Matters came to a head when the annual election to the consistory came round again in July 1561. Alexander had favoured a new election, but when this confirmed all the existing elders in office, he denounced the process in a long outburst of frustration from the pulpit.[104] The support of the present elders for des Gallars was by now clear, and with the return of Jean Dumas to the Continent in April Alexander had lost his firmest friend in the consistory.[105] His place was taken by Jacques Fichet, a signatory of the original letter to Geneva and a firm supporter of des Gallars. Alexander's isolation was now complete. The elders responded

---

[101] Michotte, *Alexandre*, p. 120; *Actes I*, p. 18.
[102] *Actes I*, pp. 20, 28.
[103] Ibid., pp. 18, 50.
[104] Ibid., p. 48.
[105] Ibid., p. 39.

to Alexander's public attack by suspending him from office, and although Grindal was able to contrive a new reconciliation at the beginning of August, necessity rather than conviction seems to have governed this latest suspension of hostilities: des Gallars had been summoned to the Colloquy of Poissy and there was no alternative but to leave the church under Alexander's temporary care.[106]

The settlement did not restore confidence between Alexander and the elders, who had at one point threatened to resign if he were not removed, and during the three months that des Gallars was absent there seems to have been no celebration of Holy Communion in the church.[107] By October Alexander and the consistory were once more in dispute, this time over the conduct of ecclesiastical discipline. In the absence of des Gallars the consistory declined to argue the question, and the matter was suspended until his return.[108] Des Gallars returned from France in December, and summoned Alexander to submit his objections to the discipline in writing to the consistory, which according to des Gallars, Alexander refused to do.[109] Des Gallars's account of events is, in fact, rather less than candid, for Alexander did at some point set down his arguments on paper, and des Gallars's annotations on the document demonstrate that he was aware of its existence.[110] Theologically Alexander seems to have had rather the better of the argument, but although Grindal made one last attempt to obtain a compromise there was no longer any real prospect that the ministers could be reconciled. Any residual sympathy for Alexander within the community was forfeited when he made a wild accusation against the deacons of having misused church funds.[111] A commission of inquiry vindicated the

[106] Ibid., pp. 49, 50.
[107] *KP I*, pp. 258–9. The minutes of the French consistory for this period have not survived, partly because Ponchel gave up writing in the original minute-book whilst des Gallars was away.
[108] *KP I*, pp. 253–4, 259.
[109] Schickler, *Églises du Refuge*, i. 132; *CO*, xix. 338–43.
[110] P. Denis, 'Pierre Alexandre et la Discipline Ecclésiastique', *BHR*, 39 (1977), 551–60.
[111] Michotte, *Alexandre*, pp. 129–30; *CO*, xix. 341–2. A similar accusation had marked the final stage of Alexander's dispute with the church at Strasburg. Rott, 'Église des réfugiés', 534.

deacons, encouraging des Gallars to push matters to a conclusion. Informing the church that he and Alexander could no longer serve together, des Gallars demanded that the congregation choose between them. There was no doubt that he would be victor in such a struggle. To the confirmed support of the consistory he now added the prestige of his successful participation at the Colloquy of Poissy. Des Gallars returned with a letter of recommendation to the Queen signed by Anthony of Navarre and the grateful thanks of the English ambassador in Paris, Nicholas Throckmorton, for whom des Gallars had provided regular briefings during the Colloquy.[112] Throckmorton recommended that des Gallars be rewarded with a gift of £20, and that his colleagues in London should be informed how much his services had been valued.[113]

Even Alexander could now see that his position was hopeless, and without waiting for the popular election which des Gallars had called he left England (around the New Year 1562).[114] Within a few months he was dead. Des Gallars did not linger long to enjoy his triumph; exhausted by the controversy and shaken by the death of his wife and two children, he hankered after a return to Geneva. In June 1563 he departed, taking with him the now sincere regard of his congregation and an effusive letter of thanks from Bishop Grindal.[115] Grindal wrote that des Gallars had found the church in a very disturbed condition on his arrival, but now left it 'in a state of quietness and good order'. There was a great deal of truth in this; the problems which faced the community on its restoration had been successfully overcome, and with Alexander's departure the last source of opposition to the authority of the minister and consistory had been removed. The clash between des Gallars and Alexander was essentially a personal one. Those sympathetic towards Alexander were not doctrinally hostile towards des Gallars, but simply more conscious of the debt the church owed the older minister. No point of principle was involved, and in consequence the dispute left no lasting division within the community. Of the sixty-three

---

[112] *Cal. S̄. P. For. Eliz.*, 1561–2, 458, 485, 492, 511, 569, 583, 611, 677.
[113] Ibid., 518.
[114] Schickler, *Églises du Refuge*, i. 133.
[115] *Zurich Letters*, ii. 96–7.

church members named in the French petition of 1561 who can be traced in the surveys of the foreign population a decade later, fifty-eight were still attending the French church, a striking measure of continuity.[116] Even the resolute pursuit of Marian apostates in 1560–1 left no enduring hard feelings. The case was very different in the Dutch church, where the dispute between Delenus and Haemstede left a much deeper scar.

The legacy of which Grindal spoke was not confined to des Gallars's role in presiding over the restoration of economic security and internal peace. His short ministry also saw significant changes in the institutions and practice of the community which, though their import was not immediately clear, were indicative of longer-term trends within the exile movement. On his arrival in London des Gallars had produced a new version of the church order for the use of the French congregation and in 1561 this was published both in the original Latin and in a French translation.[117] This *Forme de Police* was essentially a shortened version of Lasco's *Forma ac Ratio* marginally amended, but the changes, though subtle, were of some significance.[118] More precise regulations were laid down for the conduct of the congregational prophesy, an institution which never achieved the popularity in the French church that it enjoyed in the Dutch: des Gallars had already persuaded the consistory that it should be held only on feast days, the regular midweek exercise being replaced by a sermon.[119] In contrast rather greater emphasis was given to the Censure, the regular (in des Gallars's order quarterly) meeting of ministers and elders for mutual reproof and admonition. In the case of elections to the consistory universal suffrage was maintained 'for the present', but the order anticipated a greater degree of consistorial control over the community's choice.[120]

---

[116] *Returns*, i. 287–92, 402–79; ii. 1–154.

[117] *Forma politiae ecclesiasticae*, STC 6774.5; *Forme de police ecclesiastique*, STC 6775. The revised *STC* gives 'France?' as the place of publication of the French edition, though there is no hint of this in the consistory minutes when arrangements were made for its publication. *Actes I*, p. 39.

[118] Schickler, *Églises du Refuge*, i. 103–5. The relationship between the two orders is discussed at much greater length in Denis, 'Les Églises d'étrangers à Londres'.

[119] *Actes I*, pp. 11–12.

[120] Schickler, *Églises du Refuge*, i. 107.

All these changes were consistent with des Gallars's purpose in overhauling the institutions of the church, to bring the London French community into greater conformity with the practice of the church at Geneva. Some passages of des Gallars's *Forme de Police* follow the Genevan church order verbatim, and where differences were preserved (as in the case of the duties allocated to the deacons) des Gallars was at pains to explain why the peculiar circumstances of the community in London made this necessary.[121] In other respects des Gallars's alterations anticipated the developments of the following decades as for instance with the abandonment of communal participation in elections to the consistory (a change institutionalized by the new church order of 1578 but probably made some years before).[122] During the Elizabethan period the French church developed into an orthodox Calvinist community. Its ministers maintained a stringent doctrinal orthodoxy, epitomized by their pursuit of the Spaniards Casiodoro and Corro in the 1560s, and by their refusal to accept the distinguished French professor Baro as their minister in 1579.[123] In this respect as in others the French church diverged from the Dutch during the Elizabethan period, for the Dutch never developed the close relationship with Geneva that characterized the French, and could never have been regarded as a pillar of Calvinist orthodoxy. And here the different experience of the two communities at the beginning of the reign was of some importance. For whereas the French accepted apparently uncomplainingly the imposition of doctrinal orthodoxy, similar pressures in the Dutch community provoked a very different reaction.

Events in the Dutch church seem at first sight to have followed a tragically similar path to what was taking place in the French community at much the same time. In both cases a distinguished minister who had offered himself to the community was involved in a bitter dispute with an officially established competitor, and in both cases the result was the displacement of the first-comer. But the differences were as important as

---

[121] Ibid., i. 110.
[122] Ibid., i. 167, 230.
[123] Collinson, *Grindal*, pp. 143–52; Schickler, *Églises du Refuge*, i. 235.

the apparent similarities: Delenus and Haemstede initially co-operated quite happily together, which des Gallars and Alexander found impossible from the first, and no difficulty attended the foundation of the Dutch church comparable with the division in the French community over the question of the Marian apostates. The Dutch community seems not to have been faced with this problem on anything like the same scale: only a very few acts of repentance were recorded in the consistory minutes before the first communion.[124] Although several hundred Dutchmen had taken out letters of denization during Edward's reign, those who were members of the Dutch church seem generally to have followed Lasco abroad in 1553: the Dutch petition of June 1561 listed only twenty-three members of the Dutch church who were already denizens (in contrast to the 133 in the French church) and many of these were leading members of the church known to have been abroad in the interim.[125] Some Dutch members who had remained in England did not attempt to rejoin the church in 1560,[126] suggesting that the small number of denizens may partly reflect the Dutch church's harder line on apostates from the first. (The French might initially have hoped, with Evrail as minister, to avoid a humiliating public act of repentance.) In all probability, however, there were fewer members of Lasco's Dutch community in London: he had made his view of their obligation perfectly clear, and the Dutch were more likely to have followed his lead in large numbers than the French. Many former members of the London Dutch church were now comfortably established abroad and showed no inclination to return after Elizabeth's accession.[127]

There was in consequence no substantial Dutch resident in London capable of negotiating for the re-establishment of the church before the arrival of Ashe from Emden in March 1559. As a community gathered once more it was clearly desirable that a minister of stature should return to England as soon as possible, particularly in view of the difficulties that Ashe was encountering in his negotiations. There was little prospect that

---

[124] Only nine in all: *KP I*, pp. 32, 96, 123, 142, 196.
[125] *Returns*, i. 273–7.
[126] For example Walter Lynn and the coopers discussed in Ch. III.
[127] Few of those who settled in Emden returned to London in 1560.

John a Lasco would be induced to abandon the new field he had discovered for his energies in his native Poland.[128] Martin Micron was an obvious candidate, but although his return was canvassed by the Emden consistory he was now established at Norden and in any case fell victim to the plague before the end of the year.[129] His colleague Gualter Delenus did return to England during the summer of 1559, but he was now an old man and was understandably reluctant to take up the burdens of office once again. His influence, however, was by no means negligible, and it may have been at his suggestion that the leaders of the Dutch community decided to urge his son Peter to take on the ministry of the London church.

Peter Delenus was an apt choice for the task of re-establishing the London community.[130] As a young man in London during Edward's reign he had followed his father into the ministry of the Dutch church, and was evidently serving in some capacity before its dissolution in 1553. Delenus and his father had remained to minister to the scattered remnant of their church until they were forced to leave London in 1554, after which both settled with the other leading members of the Dutch church in Emden.[131] During the period of exile Delenus had grown steadily in stature. He was highly thought of both by Utenhove, for whom he undertook translation of a portion of the ill-fated Dutch New Testament, and by the Emden consistory, who dispatched him on a mission to West Friesland and ignored difficulties with the Emden authorities caused by Delenus's brave if indiscreet denunciation of the vices of local notables in his preaching.[132] Delenus was subsequently invited to serve as minister at Groningen and the consistory also considered establishing him at Aachen, but these plans came to nothing when Delenus's current employer, the Baron Tydo van Knipphus, refused to release him. It was

---

[128] Although he dispatched with Utenhove a letter to the new Queen exhorting her to forward the true religion. *Cal. S. P. For., Eliz.*, 1558–9, 130.

[129] A. A. van Schelven, 'Karakter en Stand van Van Haemstede', *NAK*, 8 (1911), 353–4.

[130] On Peter Delenus see *BWPG*, ii. 427–9.

[131] See above, pp. 117–18.

[132] Hessels, ii. 40 n. 1; *BWPG*, ii. 428.

because of this employment that the London community hesitated to press Delenus to come to England when his appointment was first mooted in the summer of 1559, but by November it was known that he had left the Baron's service. An urgent letter was dispatched to Emden, urging the consistory to persuade Delenus to take up his ministry in London once more.[133] Delenus paused only to meet up with Jan Utenhove, who was then at Frankfurt, before setting out for London, and before the end of the year he was re-established as minister in the Dutch congregation.

During the six months since Delenus's appointment was first discussed the community had not been entirely without a minister and preaching. The vacuum had been at least partially filled, albeit unofficially, by Adrian van Haemstede.[134] Haemstede's arrival in England was unexpected and largely unplanned, but as a preacher of considerable international reputation Haemstede was able to secure permission to preach in several English parish churches, and the Dutch community gratefully availed themselves of his services. 'A learned and eloquent man', according to Ruytinck, the first historian of the Dutch church, at the time of his arrival in England Haemstede had just completed the martyrology for which he is principally remembered.[135] A native of Zeeland, and like so many reformers, of noble stock, Haemstede had received an orthodox and thorough education at the University of Louvain before his conversion to the Reformation in the early 1550s. It has been suggested that he was briefly in England during the reign of Edward VI but evidence for this is entirely circumstantial.[136] In any event, by 1556 he was serving the Reformed community at Antwerp where he immediately became a controversial figure. The Reformed community, under the leadership of Gaspar van der Heyden, had reacted to the threat of persecution by meeting in closed groups in

[133] E. Meiners, *Oostvrieschlandts kerkelijke Geschiedenisse* (Groningen, 1738–9), ii. 28–30.
[134] On Haemstede see Jelsma, *Van Haemstede; BWPG*, iii. 439–46; W. G. Goeters, ' Dokumenten van Adriaan van Haemstede', *NAK*, 5 (1908), 1–67.
[135] Ruytinck, *Gheschiedenissen*, p. 31; *De Geschiedenisse ende den doodt der vromer Martelaren* (Emden, 1559).
[136] *BWPG*, iii. 440.

great secrecy, and Haemstede's refusal to confine his ministry to this tightly organized congregation seemed to threaten their security.[137] A first dispute was settled through the intercession of the Emden church, but in 1558 Haemstede began to preach to large crowds in public, and a severe persecution resulted. Early in 1559 Haemstede was forced to leave the city with a price of 800 guilders on his head, and after a short period ministering to a group who had left Antwerp to settle in Aachen, he turned his steps towards London.[138]

The Emden consistory, already made aware of Haemstede's turbulent independence by their involvement in the Antwerp troubles, received this news with alarm. They had a high regard for Haemstede's capabilities (early in 1559 consideration was being given to appointing Haemstede minister in Groningen), but felt that in view of the sensitivity of the situation in London, Haemstede was not the best man to promote the interests of the Reformed refugees. In May 1559 they briefed their representative in London, Anthony Ashe, that Haemstede came of his own initiative and that if he seemed likely to cause trouble then Ashe should remind him that he was not an official representative of the church.[139] Haemstede's conduct in London, however, proved such fears to be groundless. He played a constructive role in the community's affairs, presiding in June over a meeting at his house to elect deacons to take care of the poor,[140] and at the end of July Ashe was prepared to leave the community in Haemstede's hands while he returned to Emden. Although Haemstede was prepared to assist in the re-establishment of the church, he seems to have had no pretensions to a permanent position at its head: a letter to the Elector Palatine in September suggests that he envisaged staying in London only until the brethren had had an opportunity to elect a minister for themselves.[141] His attitude explains how it was that he and Peter Delenus were initially able to co-operate so easily after the arrival of the latter in December

[137] Jelsma, *Van Haemstede*, pp. 18–42.
[138] Ibid., pp. 42–110.
[139] Ibid., pp. 111–14.
[140] Ashe to Emden consistory, 11 June 1559, Van Schelven, *Vluchtelingenkerken*, p. 344.
[141] Goeters, 'Dokumenten van Haemstede', 63.

1559. In contrast to Peter Alexander, Haemstede seems to have been content to play second fiddle to the minister summoned by the consistory. The spring of 1560 saw him playing a full part in the life of the church, preaching and endorsing as minister the French petition to Geneva.[142] The recognition that he was performing valuable work caused him to abandon his plans for a speedy departure, and in February he brought his child forward for baptism in the church.[143]

The signs are, therefore, that the troubles that broke out in the Dutch church in July 1560 arose suddenly and unexpectedly. On 3 July 1560 the consistory met at the house of the elder Jacob Nicholaes to discuss the report of a meeting between Haemstede and certain anabaptists.[144] It was alleged that the minister had extended to them the hand of brotherhood, and Haemstede, appearing in person the next day, acknowledged this to be the case: he explained that he had made the approach not because he agreed with their teaching but in the hope of *rapprochement*. The consistory could hardly be satisfied with this explanation, and, declaring that Haemstede had erred, they demanded that he openly confess and repudiate his fault. Haemstede stalked indignantly from the consistory.[145]

A prolonged period of negotiation between Haemstede and his colleagues now ensued. It was immediately clear that Haemstede himself was no anabaptist. A succession of church members would give evidence on his behalf that he had preached in London against anabaptist teaching, and Haemstede had opposed the anabaptists fiercely in Antwerp: anabaptist martyrs were deliberately excluded from his Martyrology.[146] Haemstede was simply not prepared to condemn those who were in error on certain points of doctrine which he regarded as non-fundamental, particularly as the anabaptists with whom he had come into contact in London were law-abiding and peaceable. He hoped, it was reported to the consistory, to make clear to the lay authorities that these were

[142] Schickler, *Églises du Refuge*, iii. 46.
[143] *KP I*, p. 494.
[144] Ibid., p. 6.
[145] Ibid., pp. 9–11.
[146] *KP I*, pp. 60, 127–8; Jelsma, *Van Haemstede*, p. 127.

not anabaptists of the Münster type, advocating community of women and goods, and that toleration of their error offered no threat to the temporal power.[147]

Haemstede's defence of this group gained, then as now, a great deal of sympathy, and the relentless obduracy of the consistory caused much resentment. The consistory must not, however, be too lightly condemned. Haemstede's own doctrine was not always as unimpeachably orthodox as he would have had the ministers and bishop believe: there are hints of a connection with free-thinkers such as Castellio and Franck, and with the Family of Love.[148] Perhaps, though, more important than the doctrinal points at issue between Haemstede and the consistory was the fact of his defiance. A comparison with the earlier dispute with the minister Gualter Delenus in the Edwardian period is illuminating here.[149] The charges against Delenus had been, if anything, more serious; not merely that he had condoned error in others but that he held erroneous doctrine himself. Delenus, however, had admitted his error and the matter was closed; he remained a respected figure both in exile in Emden and back in London in 1559. Haemstede, on the other hand, met the criticism of his colleagues with truculent defiance. First he walked out of the consistory. When articles were put to him condemning anabaptists, which would have settled the quarrel within the first fortnight, he agreed to sign but only after adding marginal qualifications which were unacceptable to the consistory. Reproached with having missed many consistory meetings he scornfully threw a handful of money on the table (fines for non-attendance had recently been introduced).[150] After a month of futile negotiation, the church, having taken advice from the French community, decided to remove Haemstede from office. Haemstede greeted this decision with light-hearted contempt, comparing his colleagues with the elders and Pharisees who persecuted Christ.[151]

---

[147] KP I, p. 7; Jelsma, Van Haemstede, pp. 123 ff.

[148] CO. xviii. 366–8; Hessels, ii. 205. Haemstede had on previous occasions expressed distinctly unorthodox views on infant baptism. KP I, p. 45; Jelsma, Van Haemstede, p. 95.

[149] Above, pp. 64–5.

[150] KP I, pp. 450–2, 457.

[151] Ibid., p. 28.

In the face of Haemstede's truculent defiance the Dutch consistory had little choice but to proceed reluctantly to disciplinary action. At each stage the consistory sought the advice of their French colleagues, and des Gallars, in particular, took as unyielding a line as he did against Alexander's opposition in his own church.[152] On 2 September, with Haemstede still refusing to compromise, the case was reluctantly made over to Grindal.[153] Grindal, too, had little sympathy for anabaptist error. On 9 September he called the protagonists before him and lectured Haemstede on the dangers of suspect doctrine. A compromise seemed possible as Haemstede was prepared to sign seven articles on the doctrine of the Incarnation now presented to him, but Delenus and des Gallars pointed out how much his previous writings and utterances disagreed with this confession, and set about collecting examples.[154] The bishop referred the case to his chancellor and a protracted series of hearings ensued, but the final resolution of the dispute was hastened by Haemstede's challenge to the consistory to a public disputation. This Delenus and Utenhove were not prepared to contemplate until Haemstede had definitely been condemned, and the bishop was brought to comply. On 14 November formal sentence of excommunication was proclaimed against Haemstede, to be repeated in the Dutch church on 17 November.[155]

If Haemstede's defiance made such an outcome inevitable, his attempts to popularize his cause met with a large measure of success. Conciliatory in the presence of the bishop or other witnesses, Haemstede did not hesitate to denounce the consistory in public, and made frequent attempts to appeal over its head to the community at large. The consistory was understandably nervous about support for the deposed minister within the community, particularly after the experience of 22 August when a great crowd sympathetic to Haemstede turned up when he came to the church to defend himself.[156] But further

---

[152] *KP I*, pp. 457–8. Des Gallars wrote to Calvin that he regarded Haemstede as a greater danger to the church than Alexander. *CO*, xviii. 174–5.
[153] *KP I*, p. 460.
[154] *KP I*, pp. 461–3.
[155] *KP I*, pp. 66, 71, 73.
[156] *KP I*, pp. 3, 456–7.

manifestations of support from church members during September and October did not persuade the consistory to relax its persecution of Haemstede. On the contrary, once the bishop had been brought to excommunicate the minister himself, it turned its attention to his sympathizers. All those who had given evidence on Haemstede's behalf were examined, and in December the consistory began a thorough investigation of the whole church to identify critics of their policy.[157]

All in all, the consistory minutes record the names of some thirty-one church members (twenty-six men and five women) who at some point expressed support for Haemstede or criticized the consistory's handling of his case. Few of them made a clear expression of support for his doctrine: most objected to the speed or the manner of the consistory's proceedings. But a number were sufficiently disenchanted to make a public protest by occupying the consistory and submitting to excommunication rather than recant their objections.[158] Obviously their support for Haemstede went deeper than a mere question of procedure. These thirty-one repay close attention if one is to analyse the division which this damaging dispute revealed in the community. As with the dispute between the French ministers, a prima-facie case can be made that Haemstede's stand against rigid doctrinal orthodoxy struck a chord principally amongst the more prosperous members of the community, who were likely to feel uncomfortable inside a narrowly defined community, and be unwilling to submit to the oppressive moral and doctrinal controls of the consistory. Certainly one of the more substantial charges against Haemstede in Antwerp had been his willingness to preach to the so-called 'salon-meetings'. These were frequented by the more prosperous citizens who were well-disposed to the Reformed religion but unwilling to subject themselves to the control of the consistory of the official Reformed church.[159]

Haemstede did indeed receive the support of several respected and established members of the community, and a significant number of his supporters were professional men or

---

[157] *KP I*, pp. 84, 85, 88.
[158] *KP I*, pp. 107, 158–9, 186–8.
[159] Jelsma, *Van Haemstede*, pp. 49–50.

engaged in occupations of high status.[160] The surgeon William Moelens accompanied Haemstede to his last dispute with Delenus, and the merchant and searcher Henry Lievens was one of those who testified to Haemstede's orthodoxy.[161] Two goldsmiths, William Sadler, one of the few survivors from the Edwardian church, and Moses Focking (probably his apprentice) were revealed as sympathizers by the survey of December 1560.[162] Neither pressed his opposition to the point of excommunication, and the clothmaker Peter Trion also made his peace after initially supporting Haemstede.[163] Embarrassing as was the criticism of such men to the consistory, Haemstede's most powerful support undoubtedly came from the merchant-historian, Emanuel van Meteren, and the Italian theologian and engineer, Jacobo Acontius. Acontius, a gifted and enterprising thinker whose writing on the theory of patents had already brought him to the attention of Cecil, seems to have been the driving force behind Haemstede's stubborn resistance.[164] As a pensioner of the Queen, Acontius could oppose the ministers of the stranger churches with impunity, and des Gallars, for one, regarded him as more dangerous than Haemstede himself. Acontius's experiences in London would later inspire him to write the work for which he is now principally remembered, *Stratagemata Satanae (Satan's Stratagems)*, a systematic defence of the principle of religious toleration, and his theological gifts were also employed on Haemstede's behalf: two days after Haemstede's final confrontation with the consistory (to which Acontius accompanied him), the Italian dispatched a long and subtle defence of Haemstede's position to des Gallars, and he seems at some point also to have petitioned Grindal.[165] The merchant Emanuel van Meteren, himself no inconsiderable scholar, also offered Haemstede sturdy support.

---

[160] Unfortunately it is seldom possible to glean any information about their wealth from the very scanty surviving subsidy returns of the early 1560s.

[161] *KP I*, pp. 38, 60; *Returns*, i. 274, 277. Moelens had been a deacon of the Dutch church during the Edwardian period. *Returns*, i. 202.

[162] *KP I*, pp. 109, 130, 136; *Returns*, i. 209, 276, 277.

[163] *KP I*, pp. 106, 130, 149–50; *Returns*, i. 276.

[164] See above, p. 141. On Acontius see E. R. Briggs, 'An Apostle of the Incomplete Reformation: Jacopo Aconcio (1500–1567)', *HS*, 22 (1970–6), 481–95.

[165] *KP I*, pp. 38, 68; P. Denis, 'Un Combat aux frontières de l'orthodoxie', *BHR*, 38 (1976), 55–72. For *Stratagemata Satanae* (Basle, 1565) see Briggs, 'Apostle of the Incomplete Reformation', 487–94.

The son of an Antwerp printer who had made a distinguished contribution to the early history of Protestantism, van Meteren's connections with the leading scholars and artists of the Anglo-Dutch community made his support for Haemstede a particular embarrassment to the consistory.[166] Van Meteren was a man not easily cowed, and was one of those who pressed his opposition to the point of excommunication in the spring of 1561.

Such support was of great weight, but this should not disguise the fact that many of those who disapproved of the consistory's handling of Haemstede were very ordinary church members. The four who carried Haemstede's offer of a debate to the consistory before his excommunication were a joiner, a sawyer, a weaver, and a tapestry-maker;[167] amongst those later identified as his supporters were two shoemakers, a collarmaker, and a silk-weaver.[168] As a group Haemstede's supporters do not have a markedly different social profile from that of the church as a whole, or of those whose activity identified them as supporters of the consistory. This group, who testified to Haemstede's involvement with the anabaptists or to the unorthodoxy of his doctrine, followed a similarly varied group of trades, and were mostly, as were Haemstede's supporters, recent arrivals in England. Interestingly, no less than half of these supporters of the consistory were refugees from heresy proceedings, as opposed to only four of Haemstede's supporters (none of whom pressed his opposition to the point of excommunication).[169] These refugees, at least, seem likely to have been amongst the most zealous and orthodox members of the church. This apart, Haemstede's stand seems to have split the

[166] W. D. Verduyn, *Emanuel van Meteren* (The Hague, 1926); J. L. Nevinson, 'Emanuel van Meteren, 1535–1612', *HS*, 19 (1952–8), 128–45. Van Meteren's *Album Amicorum* (Bodleian Library, MS Douce 68) contains entries by the artists Joris Hoefnagel and Lucas de Heere and the eminent cartographer Abraham Ortelius, van Meteren's cousin. Van Meteren's father, Jacob, printed Coverdale's New Testament. Nevinson, art. cit., 129.

[167] Henry Moreels, Peter de More, James Marcellis, John Latron. *KP I*, p. 66; *Returns*, i. 274–6.

[168] Peter de Vischer, Herman van Gogh, Simon Verwaest and Peter de Moll. *KP I*, pp. 86, 110, 111. *Returns*, i. 275–7.

[169] Seven of the fourteen named as witnesses against Haemstede can be found in Decavele's list of Flanders heretics. *KP I*, pp. 9, 45, 55, 463; Decavele, *Dageraad*, ii. *passim*.

church on all social levels. This is perhaps no more than one
would expect, as doubts as to the rightness of the consistory's
proceedings were expressed far beyond the borders of the community itself. A letter from Antwerp asking for less haste in
condemning Haemstede was received shortly after his excommunication, and the church there was sufficiently concerned
to send over one of its deacons to investigate what was going
on in London.[170] The excommunication of Haemstede's most
obdurate supporters brought further expressions of concern
from both Antwerp and Emden, the latter church dispatching
a letter of enquiry to London containing eight questions relating to Haemstede's case.[171]

The consistory, although concerned to convince the leading foreign churches of the justice of its proceedings, was
unmoved by all representations on behalf of Haemstede and
his supporters. Haemstede's sympathizers were repeatedly
examined by the consistory and urged to recant, and those
who could not be brought to a humiliating act of repentance
were finally, in April 1561, excommunicated.[172] It is unlikely
that Delenus and Utenhove could have accomplished such a
thorough purge of the community without the full-hearted
support of the elders and deacons. In contrast to the French
church, where a proportion of the consistory had a great deal
of sympathy for Peter Alexander, the Dutch consistory presented a united face from the start. Two days after first hearing
of Haemstede's negotiations with the anabaptists the consistory declared him to be in error, and thereafter its members
were active in prosecuting the erring minister.[173]

The individuals who made up the first Dutch consistory in
the Elizabethan period were as distinguished as their Edwardian predecessors, and their activity in support of Delenus
should be stressed as a counter-weight to the support given
to Haemstede by such influential figures as van Meteren. The
first full list of elders and deacons appears in the consistory
minutes only at the time of their re-election in May 1561, but
almost all of those listed had previously been prominent in

[170] *KP I*, pp. 81–2, 158.
[171] *KP I*, p. 227.
[172] *KP I*, p. 188.
[173] *KP I*, p. 10.

consistory business. Of the six elders confirmed in office at this election four had been acting as elders since at least November 1559, when they signed the letter to Emden asking for the dispatch of Peter Delenus as minister.[174] All four took part in the proceedings against Haemstede, and two, Jacob Nicholaes and Jan Engelram, were particularly active. Nicholaes, a doctor, was the host of the consistory that first heard of Haemstede's meeting with the anabaptists, and he was one of the delegation sent to inform the minister of his suspension.[175] Engelram, an apothecary and the consistory's secretary for part of this period, was dispatched to inform the bishop of Haemstede's offence and subsequently delegated to present the consistory's version of events to the church at Antwerp. Engelram was an acerbic character, and one of Haemstede's supporters would later accuse him of acting out of partiality.[176] The other original elders, Francis Marquino and Lewis Tyry, played a less prominent role, but Marquino was punctilious in reporting a slander on Delenus, and Tyry was active in summoning Haemstede's supporters for questioning by the consistory.[177] A prosperous skinner, Tyry had been a member of the Edwardian church and spent the reign of Mary in Antwerp. As a member of the consistory Tyry had entertained the ministers of the church at his house there, but Haemstede for some reason had been reluctant to accept his hospitality and the hostility may well have continued after both men had fled to England.[178] Several of those prominent in proceedings against Haemstede had a connection with Antwerp, including another elder, Jan Beaugrand, and their presence in London ensured that Haemstede's turbulent record as minister there would not be forgotten. Tyry and Beaugrand were both forced to flee Antwerp during the persecution which followed Haemstede's public preaching.[179]

The four original elders were reinforced by several others during the course of 1560, most notably Jan Utenhove and

[174] *KP I*, pp. 201–2. Above, n. 133.
[175] *KP I*, pp. 6, 28, 32, 55, 74; *Returns*, i. 275 (Claesson).
[176] *KP I*, pp. 44, 48–9, 60, 190; *Returns*, i. 275.
[177] *KP I*, pp. 106, 132.
[178] *Returns*, i. 207, 276; Jelsma, *Van Haemstede*, p. 45.
[179] Jelsma, *Van Haemstede*, p. 75. Decavele, *Dageraad*, ii. 70, 184.

Anthony Ashe. Utenhove was in all respects an equal partner with Delenus in the proceedings against Haemstede, and the return of Ashe was a further addition of strength for the consistory. After his initial sortie as the representative of the Emden consistory Ashe returned briefly to the Continent in the summer of 1559, but was soon back in London once more and acting as an elder of the church. His command of English made him invaluable to the consistory when Haemstede's case was transferred to the bishop's chancellor, and Ashe also busied himself collecting Haemstede's heretical writings on the consistory's behalf.[180] Ashe was the target of more than one hostile accusation from Haemstede's supporters, and it was alleged that he had said in Emden that he would stop Haemstede preaching when he came to London.[181]

Several other elders and deacons were active against Haemstede. Jan Camphin and Jan Lamoot reported having heard Haemstede slander the consistory, and though it was originally intended to send one of them to Flushing in September 1560 they were both instructed to remain in London to give evidence against Haemstede. Both were zealous opponents of anabaptism, and had attempted to debate with the group with which Haemstede was associated before the controversy broke out.[182] The other deacons played a more sporadic role, but Cornelis Stephens, Martin Janson, and Henry Marshall were all active at some point in the conflict, and with no member of the consistory was there ever a suggestion of dissent from the firm line being taken.[183]

This firm line extended to any that had expressed the slightest criticism of the consistory's actions. When Walter Helstmeer expressed the opinion that those who objected to the consistory's methods of dealing with Haemstede should not be excommunicated, he was told that he must retract this opinion or himself be excommunicated.[184] It was little wonder that in the face of this severity many of Haemstede's supporters capitulated, particularly as from an early stage they were deprived of Haemstede's sustaining presence. Less than a month

[180] *KP I*, pp. 57, 61, 64, 67, 71.
[181] *KP I*, p. 136.
[182] *KP I*, pp. 8, 33, 41.
[183] *KP I*, pp. 67, 71, 74, 76, 89, 128.
[184] *KP I*, pp. 145–6.

after his condemnation Haemstede abandoned his hopes of a disputation and left London, arriving in Emden after a shipwreck and perilous cross-country journey.[185] The consistory's powers of persuasion were also augmented by a further formidable weapon in bringing recalcitrants to obedience. In the spring of 1561, when the consistory was pursuing its enquiries into the orthodoxy of the membership, both communities were also compiling petitions for the granting of letters patent of denization to their members; the petitions were submitted in June, shortly after Haemstede's most resolute supporters had been excommunicated.[186] None of the excommunicates benefited from the church's negotiation, as they were excluded from the petition: on the other hand, almost all those who had recanted were recommended by the church. Just how powerful a pressure this was is illustrated by the case of Peter de More. More made a reluctant recantation only days before his excommunication was to be pronounced, but he did not cease speaking ill of the ministers. Examined again, he admitted that he had only submitted so as not to lose the chance of becoming a denizen.[187]

Having dealt so ruthlessly with dissent in the community, it was not to be expected that the consistory would act with any less decision when Haemstede suddenly reappeared in London in July 1562, and came to the church at the time of the service.[188] On the following day a warrant was obtained for his arrest, and when Haemstede refused a new and humiliating form of recantation submitted to him by the bishop, sentence of excommunication was pronounced for the second time. On this occasion, however, Haemstede was summarily deported back to East Friesland.[189] Haemstede's intention in returning to London is not entirely clear. Most probably he hoped to patch up his quarrel with the London church in order to seek a new place to exercise his ministry on the Continent, and with this in mind he had extracted a letter from the Emden consistory asking the London church to retract his

[185] *KP I*, p. 90. Hessels, ii. 144.
[186] Above, p. 146.
[187] *KP I*, pp. 177. 193, 284.
[188] *KP I*, p. 331.
[189] *KP I*, pp. 334, 343, 351; Jelsma, *Van Haemstede*, pp. 198–202; Hessels, ii. 202–4.

excommunication.[190] In London, however, Haemstede's demeanour was once again less conciliatory than his purpose. While still at liberty he hawked the letter from Emden around the streets, delivered a copy to the bishop before the consistory had seen it, and had it translated into Dutch: once again, he was appealing to the community over the heads of the consistory. The consistory were careful to compile a summary of these events in Dutch for the community's benefit, and inform the Emden church of the use to which their recommendation had been put.[191]

The Emden consistory were by no means pleased at this, and on Haemstede's return to the Continent declined to help him further. By the end of the year, deprived of any useful function, Haemstede was dead.[192] The conflict left the Dutch church deeply scarred. For this was not, as in the French church, primarily a clash of personalities, but a clash of principle on two levels. Most of the consistory's critics objected to the way the ecclesiastical discipline had been exercised, with too much severity or too great haste; behind this criticism was the more fundamental issue of how narrowly the community should be drawn, and whether doctrinal deviation on a single point put men outside the church. The consistory's stand for a narrowly circumscribed orthodoxy was successful in that the number of excommunications was kept down to ten, but the legacy of bitterness was considerable. Peter de More finally left London, declaring that he would rather deal with Turks and heathens than the ministers of the Dutch church.[193] Many of those who recanted probably did so with doubtful sincerity, and manifestations of sympathy for the excommunicates occur at intervals through the consistory minutes. In July 1562 Jan Kuytman was forbidden the communion for having invited one of the excommunicates to a marriage feast, and two other church members were soon in trouble for having attended Emanuel van Meteren's marriage celebrations. (One of them was also alleged to have said that he regarded the excommunicates as being as pious as any members of the community.)[194]

Those excommunicated did not submit passively to their fate, petitioning a representative of the Antwerp church visiting London in 1562.[195] Yet few seem to have swallowed their pride and rejoined the community; indeed it is striking how few of those involved with Haemstede at any point are subsequently found in the Dutch church records. Peter de More attempted to make his peace on his death-bed and Emanuel van Meteren was reconciled in 1571,[196] but none of his other erstwhile supporters (even those who were reconciled) are found in church records after 1564. Four of the ostensibly reconciled supporters of Haemstede may be traced in the 1568 list of those who went sometimes to an English church and sometimes to the Dutch, further evidence that their reconciliation in 1561 was only skin-deep.[197]

The dispute with Haemstede revealed deep divisions within the Dutch community. The determined action of the consistory silenced criticism for a time, but within three years of Haemstede's departure new troubles had arisen to disturb the peace of the troubled church. The implications of this new dispute will be considered in a later chapter, but important points of comparison with the earlier confrontation with Haemstede are immediately apparent: once again, a minister and the consistory, in attempting to enforce the discipline found that they had lost the confidence of a substantial section of their congregation.[198] The contrast between the success of the French consistory in establishing doctrinal orthodoxy and the continuing turbulence within the Dutch congregation is stark, and to explain the difference one must look outside the narrow contours of the London communities. To some extent, the divergent experiences of the two churches reflect the different patterns of development of the French and Dutch Reformed churches in the same decade. Whereas the pattern of Geneva quickly established its pre-eminent influence over the Reformed communities in France, Dutch Calvinism always retained a certain independence. The survival of a strong indigenous tradition of essentially non-doctrinal evangelism, and

[195] *KP I*, p. 319.
[196] *KP II*, p. 222; Verduyn, *Emanuel van Meteren*, pp. 91–7.
[197] *Returns*, i. 386. The four were Henry Moreels, Peter de Moll, Peter Trion, and Herman van Gogh.
[198] Below, pp. 243 ff.

particularly the resilience of a numerically powerful anabaptist community gave the Dutch Reformed movement a pluriformity which marked it out from the more closely controlled French church.[199] The foreign churches in London could never be insulated from the repercussions of the issues which moulded and divided the Reformed churches on the Continent, and the Haemstede affair was a graphic illustration of this. Those who spoke up for Haemstede did not necessarily share his sometimes idiosyncratic doctrinal views, but many sympathized with his refusal to condemn those whose beliefs did not square in all particulars with those of the community, and others found the lengths to which the church hierarchy would go to enforce its will repugnant. The implications of their defiance would return to trouble the community long after the departure and death of their discredited champion.

Whatever their differences, in the case of both the French and Dutch churches in London it was unambiguously clear that they had returned in 1559 to a changed world. The rising star of Calvin and Geneva now promised to transform the international Reformed movement: in England, moreover, a different climate of opinion obliged the leaders of the foreign community to couch their appeal for protection and support in very different terms. The success of the community in adapting themselves to the altered priorities of their hosts whilst fulfilling a continuing and profoundly felt obligation to their homelands will be considered shortly (in Chapters VIII and IX). But it would be misleading to suggest that strategic considerations of this sort were uppermost in the ministers' minds, or that the internal problems described above absorbed all their energies. From day to day the consistories' most pressing concern was undoubtedly the maintenance of discipline within the community, and the task of caring for members in need. The scope of this pastoral role will be examined next.

[199] R. M. Kingdon, *Geneva and the Coming of the Wars of Religion in France 1555–1563* (Geneva, 1956). W. Nijenhuis, 'Variants within Dutch Calvinism in the sixteenth century', *Low Countries History Yearbook*, 12 (1979), 48–64. L. Knappert, *Het Ontstaen en de Vestiging van het Protestantisme in de Nederlanden* (Utrecht, 1924). Alastair Duke, 'The Ambivalent Face of Calvinism in the Netherlands 1561–1618', in M. Prestwich (ed.), *International Calvinism* (Oxford, 1985). I am most grateful to Mr Duke for allowing me to see a copy of his article before it had gone to press.

VII

Social Concern and Social Control

BOTH the French and Dutch churches grew swiftly in the years after their restoration in 1559. By 1561 the Dutch church had registered almost 700 communicant members (429 men and 257 women), and the influx of refugees during the course of the decade increased the size of the community to a peak of nearly 2,000 men, women, and children in 1568.[1] No registers survive for the French church (beyond the 234 adult males listed in the petition of 1561), but by 1568 their community was 1,800 strong, according to the return of the alien population of that year, and apparently still growing.[2] One must bear in mind, too, that these bare figures conceal a great deal of coming and going between England and the Continent, so that the number who at some time passed through the London community was far greater.

The regulation and control of such a community posed formidable problems. Many of the newcomers were penniless refugees, and the churches had to address themselves both to their immediate needs, and to the wider implications of broken homes, divided families, and a floating population. The constant movement between England and the Continent also made it considerably more difficult to enforce social discipline within the community. The community's response to these two parallel problems, the maintenance of social control and the provision of help for members in need, will be the principal concern of this chapter, though it will also become clear that the consistory did not feel obliged to limit its attention exclusively to enrolled members of the church. In a very real sense, the churches were the focal point of the whole foreign community.

---

[1] *Returns*, i. 278–87, 393.
[2] *Returns*, i. 393, ii. 139, 154.

Any survey of the churches' pastoral role within the foreign community must be heavily dependent on the churches' own records, and here the years after their refoundation offer a much more encouraging picture. Any intervention by the ministers and elders in the community's affairs was first discussed at their weekly meetings in the consistory. In both churches detailed minutes were taken of their deliberations. Many of these minute books have been preserved: not an unbroken sequence in either church, but enough to give a clear impression of the range and scope of the consistory's activities.[3] The consistory minutes are by far the most important source for what is known about the day to day running of the churches, and they will form the basis of what follows. First, however, two important qualifications must be made about the way in which they have been exploited for the purposes of this chapter. As will be clear, cases before the French consistory are cited rather more frequently than similar cases in the Dutch community. This is simply because the French minutes tend to be more detailed and circumstantial and consequently more revealing, but as both communities faced very much the same problems, and adopted (broadly speaking) the same solutions, this concentration on French examples should have no distorting effect.[4] Secondly, the scope and nature of the consistories' activity will be illustrated by describing particular cases rather than by offering any sort of statistical analysis. To say that 12 per cent of cases dealt with in the French consistory had to do with drunkenness and 12 per cent with sexual incontinence may be helpful, though the technical problems encountered in the course of such classification have not always been recognized by historians who have used the consistory minutes in this way.[5] But only by a treatment of actual cases can one

---

[3] The Dutch consistory minutes (Kerkeraads-protocollen) for 1560–63 and 1569–71 have been published (cited here as *KP I* and *KP II*) and further manuscript minute-books for the periods 1571–5 and 1578–85 are preserved in the church archive now deposited in the Guildhall Library, London (MS. 7397). The Huguenot Society of London has published the first two surviving minute-books of the French church covering the period 1560–61 and 1564–5 (cited here as *Actes I*) and 1571–7 (*Actes II*). A third volume for the years 1578–89 is currently being prepared for publication.

[4] Small differences in the application of the discipline are noted below, p. 191.

[5] Various attempts to classify the business of the London consistories for different periods are to be found in Denis, 'Les Églises d'étrangers'; Benedict, *Rouen during the*

get a sense of the very human concern and understanding shown by the consistories in dealing with their erring brethren.

That the consistory approached disciplinary cases in a positive and humane manner may come as something of a surprise, and certainly accords ill with the customary picture of a severe and implacable Calvinist discipline. Yet, whilst the consistory did often manifest an immovable determination to enforce its will, the minutes also reveal many instances of a sympathy and insight into the frailties of the human condition which suggest that our mental picture of the Calvinist system may require substantial modification. Indeed, whilst historians have tended to view the consistory as a repressive institution, it is very possible that members of the churches were themselves more conscious of the positive aspects of a community which manifested such evident concern for their moral and physical well-being, and offered such an impressive level of support for the sick and the poor. The consistory minutes reveal how far the ministers and elders were prepared to step beyond a narrow disciplinary role to advise, conciliate, or provide help for members in need. For the members of the community at least, the advantages of the church's social concern must be set against any resentment they might have felt at the element of social control.

Wars of Religion, p. 108; A. Kuyper, 'De Hollandsche gemeente te Londen in 1570–71', in *Voor driehondert jaren* (Bronsveld, 1870), p. 156. The first-fruits of a major comparative study of three Continental consistories are revealed in an article by Heinz Schilling, 'Reformierte Kirchenzucht als Sozialdisziplinierung? Die Tätigkeit des Emder Presbyteriums in den Jahren 1557–1562', in Wilfried Ehbrecht and Heinz Schilling (eds.), *Niederlande und Nordwestdeutschland* (Cologne, 1983). The above works tend to adopt different categories for consistory business making comparison hazardous, but more serious problems concern basic methodology. How, for instance, should one deal with cases which are discussed more than once by the consistory? To count a quarrel discussed on six occasions as the equivalent of six different cases of drunkenness settled at once would have an obvious distorting effect, yet to enumerate each case only once, regardless of how often it came before the consistory, would be equally misleading in the opposite direction. The Haemstede affair accounts for 20% of entries in the Dutch consistory minutes for 1561, yet it is essentially one case. It would be ludicrous to suggest that 'doctrinal disputes' were as common as drunkenness (which accounts for a similar proportion of entries) on the strength of it, yet clearly the case occupied as much of the consistory's attention. A second problem is posed by cases which involved several different types of offence. How, for instance, should one classify a quarrel leading to a fight after a drinking bout? (*Actes I*, p. 33). Cases of this sort are far from infrequent given the human tendency to bring new allegations against a neighbour already revealed as a bad character, and for one thing to lead to another.

The range and sympathy of the churches' concern is well illustrated by their involvement in members' marital affairs. The Marian exile had left its mark on the community in many ways, not least in the disruption of family life. As a result many marital cases and domestic scandals had to be dealt with in the first months after the churches' refoundation, and the regulation of marriage continued to be a major preoccupation thereafter.[6] Faced with the problem of a community which had in many instances been uprooted from the normal social constraints of family and home environment, the churches struggled valiantly to reimpose a measure of control on personal relations. The French consistory insisted that any who wished to marry in the church must first be betrothed in good order in the presence of a minister or elder.[7] In 1564 it was decided that such ceremonies should henceforth take place in the consistory, as going to the houses of church members was putting the ministers to too much expense.[8] The purpose of such public engagements was to ensure that both parties had the consent of their parents, and that both were free to enter into marriage. Friends could usually be found to testify to previous good conduct, but the first condition was not always so easy to fulfil, particularly when young church members were separated from their families abroad. Even so the churches would insist on evidence of parental consent before allowing the banns to be read, and those who came to the consistory without a letter from their parents were told to write for one: one young Frenchman was even forced to go to Metz in person to secure the consent of his parents for his marriage.[9] That the consistories were justified in such a stipulation is suggested by the fact that some parents, thus prompted, wrote refusing permission.[10] Church members who attempted to circumvent this provision by claiming their parents were dead might be asked to provide proof.[11]

[6] *Actes I*, pp. 7–8, 12, 13.
[7] Ibid., p. 10.
[8] Ibid., p. 94.
[9] Ibid., p. 85; *KP I*, pp. 207, 286.
[10] *Actes I*, p. 71; *KP I*, pp. 51, 58.
[11] *Actes I*, p. 94.

Members wishing to marry who sought to conceal inconvenient details of their past lives were unwise to presume upon the ignorance of the consistory. Even those recently arrived in London often found a former neighbour there prepared to inform the consistory of the true facts of the case.[12] In the circumstances it is hardly surprising that an increasing number of church members, impatient of delay or fearful of rejection by their own consistory, opted for marriage in an English parish church where fewer questions were asked.[13] By 1571 the practice was sufficiently prevalent in both churches to require firm action, and in August the French consistory warned members that any who contracted such marriages would be forbidden the communion and required to make a public act of repentance. Those who ignored this warning found that it was no idle threat.[14]

The stringent conditions attached to marriage in the church did not always produce happy results. The case of Anne de la Haye was particularly tragic. When she and her fiancé Jean Ronville came to the French consistory they were told that he must have the consent of his parents for marriage, and as this was impossible to obtain the two lived together unmarried. When Anne became pregnant Ronville abandoned her, and although she followed him to Arras, he disowned her and she was forced to return to England alone.[15] But it would be misleading to give too much attention to the occasional case of this sort, where the firm control exercised by the consistory proved counter-productive. The migratory nature of the community made stringent checks necessary; otherwise the occasional case where a wife was abandoned abroad and a new one taken in England might have been endlessly repeated.[16] And although, inevitably, the consistory minutes cases highlight cases where controls had failed or the discipline was defied, other members of the community clearly had reason to be grateful for the consistory's painstaking regulation of marriage and betrothal. One young Frenchman, for instance,

---

[12] See below, p. 219.
[13] *Actes II*, pp. 8, 70, 76; *KP II*, pp. 69, 117.
[14] *Actes II*, pp. 8, 102.
[15] Ibid., pp. 36–7.
[16] See below, p. 226.

who became engaged to a woman known to the consistory as a bad character, was perfectly happy to be released from his engagement when the circumstances were explained to him.[17]

The consistory's involvement in members' domestic affairs was by no means limited to preventing unsuitable marriages. A good deal of time and energy was devoted to repairing existing relationships, and here the ministers and elders went to considerable pains to reconcile husbands and wives even after an act of adultery had violated marital trust. Jean Soloe was permitted to take back his penitent wife, and an elder was deputed to attempt to reconcile Jean le Clercq and his wife after he had admitted adultery.[18] The consistory even sought to persuade the wife of Nicholas le Chemin, a man excommunicated by another French church, to return to him.[19] Humble domestic quarrels were not beneath the churches' attention. The French church required Louis Creton and his wife to repent their errors in the consistory in the presence of neighbours who had been scandalized by their quarrelling, and ordered Martin le Picquart's wife not to nag him for working late at night.[20] The Dutch church, too, recorded several successful reconciliations between husband and wife, and did not shrink from forbidding one husband from the communion table until he had made up his quarrel.[21] An apparently harmless quarrel between Jean Coterel and his wife became one of the longest-running sagas in the French consistory minutes. Returning late one evening Coterel found supper on the table and an enraged and suspicious wife. They quarrelled, and when Coterel raised his fist to silence her his wife fled to neighbours. The two were frequently admonished to behave better over the next year or more, though with notable lack of success.[22] The pains taken by the consistory in this regard are not without significance: marriage was regarded as a sacred bond, and if it could not be undertaken without the strictest regard for propriety, its preservation was the proper concern of the community.

---

[17] *Actes II*, pp. 79–82, 84.
[18] *Actes I*, p. 12; *Actes II*, p. 66.
[19] *Actes II*, pp. 125–6.
[20] *Actes I*, pp. 88, 93.
[21] *KP I*, pp. 275, 276; *KP II*, pp. 61–2, 253.
[22] *Actes II*, pp. 9, 10, 52, 58, 72, 95.

Naturally enough, cases of casual fornication were dealt with with much less sympathy. Terms of abuse such as *putain* and *paillard* were flung around very liberally when disputants were roused to anger, and members were frequently called upon to make up a quarrel where such an exchange of insults had given the matter a much more serious aspect than circumstances warranted. But it is none the less remarkable that the consistory was very often able to establish the truth of a charge of sexual incontinence from the reports of witnesses: at once an indication of how little privacy most church members can have enjoyed in the crowded houses and tenements of the city, and a monument to a timeless and indefatigable curiosity. Jean de Quief, accused of violating the wife of a church member as they journeyed back from the Continent, made a plausible defence, but was finally brought to confess after the consistory had heard damning evidence from the companions of his journey.[23] Guillaume Clottebouse and his future wife ignored an instruction from the consistory not to see each other so frequently and paid the penalty when their neighbours revealed how scandalously they had behaved.[24] Gabriel Haymon and Barbe le Challeur might think themselves unlucky to be seen by no less than four people who knew them when they arranged a clandestine afternoon rendezvous at a tavern in St Katherine's, particularly as one, Susanne Roger, had the time to linger at her door for an hour to see if they came out again (they didn't).[25] Such eager tale-bearing not unnaturally sometimes left a legacy of bitterness between witnesses and their guilty friends. Denis Boningham, having denied fathering the child of Christian Marissal, was understandably angry that the friends to whom he had confided his guilt revealed this to the consistory. Boningham confessed, but later had to be summoned back to the consistory and admonished for insulting those who had witnessed against him.[26]

While much of the consistory's energies were absorbed in combating sexual licence in the alien community, it also waged

---

[23] *Actes II*, pp. 41, 43–4, 45–6, 50.
[24] Ibid., pp. 66–7.
[25] Ibid., pp. 97–8.
[26] Ibid., pp. 10, 20, 26, 42, 47.

an unrelenting battle against those other classic objects of Calvinist disapproval: drunkenness, gaming, and dancing. All were regarded as serious infringements of the discipline, and particularly heinous if committed on a religious festival. Drinking and cards often went together, and the French consistory was especially shocked by a report that a group of hatmakers had spent six shillings on drink over a game in a Southwark tavern on the first day of Lent.[27] On this, as on so many other occasions, the evening ended in a fight. The consistory was no more sympathetic when the subject of one of these tavern brawls was theological, as when Robert Questel and Robert du Worke became embroiled with the landlord of the Ball; the discussion became so lively that the constable was called and all three ended up in custody.[28] On one occasion the consistory required one of those present at such a brawl to repair to the deacon of his district for religious instruction; probably he was a young man, and the consistory certainly regarded the corruption of youth as one of the most serious risks of these moral vices.[29] The feeble excuse of John le Gallois, when accused of gambling, that he had been led on was brushed aside on the grounds that as the older man he should have known better. He was further enjoined to remember his duty towards the young in future.[30]

The punishments meted out to erring brethren suggest that the consistory made no clear distinction between the seriousness of sexual and social dissipation. The ministers and elders were very conscious that immoderate revelling and brawling might damage the reputation of the community as a whole, and reacted particularly sharply to any misdemeanour which had come to the attention of the English authorities. Members who found themselves arrested by the guard and hauled before the magistrate as a result of a drinking bout could expect an extremely cool reception from the consistory.[31] The consistory expected the conduct of its own members to be exemplary, and an elder or deacon guilty of any lapse could expect no

---

[27] *Actes I.*, p. 33.
[28] Ibid., p. 29.
[29] Ibid., p. 41.
[30] Ibid., p. 10.
[31] Actes II, p. 13. See below, p. 3.

special favour. When the wife of the French elder Jacques Marabut was reported to have danced at a wedding, he was ordered to bring her to the consistory for admonition, in order, as the minutes put it, that the consistory might begin by reforming itself before reforming others.[32] None was spared, even the by now aged and irascible Anthony de Ponchel, who shortly after his retirement from the consistory came to blows with another member outside the church. For this he was suspended from the communion.[33] When a deacon of the Dutch church, Gilles Brothers, was reported for drunkenness and fighting, he was removed from office and had to do public penance,[34] and a similar case in the French church proved one of the most enduring sources of rancour. In July 1560 one of the newly elected deacons, Nicholas Wilpin, was barred from office on the grounds that he had been seen drunk on the street. Wilpin insisted that the reason for his deposition should be made known to the community, but even when this was done he refused to be reconciled and continuously slandered his former colleagues in the streets. After several attempts to bring him to obedience the community was forced to take action, and Wilpin was finally excommunicated.[35] Even after this the consistory continued their efforts to reconcile him, even involving the Dutch in this endeavour. The affair rumbled on for some years, and as late as 1571 it was held against a former member who wished to return to the community that he had supported Wilpin a decade before, although Wilpin himself was by this time long dead.[36]

The case of Wilpin illustrates one of the most evident characteristics of the consistories in their maintenance of the discipline; their sheer dogged persistence in pursuing cases to a conclusion. In this respect the churches often added to their problems by their unbending conscientiousness, for whilst members were often prepared to admit a fault, many baulked at the public humiliation of a recantation in open church which was the penalty for any offence which was widely known. For

---

[32] *Actes I*, p. 34.
[33] *Actes II*, p. 129.
[34] *KP I*, pp. 122–3, 124, 125, 126–7, 131–2, 133.
[35] *Actes I*, pp. 6, 9, 12, 33, etc.
[36] *Actes II*, p. 99. Wilpin died in 1564. See his will, Archd. London 1564 (3, fo. 130).

all their swaggering defiance when confronted with their sins in the consistory, few could contemplate public degradation with equanimity, and some would go to almost any lengths to avoid or mitigate this penalty. Didier Bonnair offered a sum of money to the poor if he could be excused: he knew, he said, how people would laugh and mock.[37] This was refused, as was Jean Dehors's last desperate request that, if he must do penance in open church, it might be on a weekday rather than at the main Sunday service.[38] A delegation of friends appealed on behalf of Nicholas Bizeau, threatening that he would not be prepared to undergo a public humiliation. On this occasion too, however, the consistory proved unbending, and Bizeau was forced to submit.[39]

Many of these repentant sinners might have envied Nicholas Ourseau, permitted on account of his age and infirmity to make his profession of guilt privately to an elder and deacon (presumably he was too weak to come to church).[40] For the most part, however, the most mitigation that would be permitted in the severity of punishment was that practised in the Dutch church, where on occasion, after confession in the consistory, an account of the offence was published in church but with the name of the offender suppressed. The consistory was moved to such an indulgence only in occasional circumstances, as when a certain Matthew Verhaege took an Englishwoman out drinking and the two became intoxicated and were arrested. Verhaege appealed for moderation of the severity of his punishment on the ground that the woman's husband would give a crown to know who had been out with his wife, and, perhaps to avoid further violence, the consistory concurred.[41]

This suppression of names, which seems to have been practised only in the Dutch church, was a prerogative of mercy, but the decision whether an act of repentance should be in front of the whole church or in the consistory depended on the nature of the offence. If the sin was known only to a few,

---

[37] *Actes I*, p. 77.
[38] Ibid., pp. 85–6.
[39] Ibid., pp. 106, 107.
[40] *Actes II*, p. 98.
[41] *KP II*, p. 180.

repentance might be expressed in front of those who were offended in the consistory, but any transgression that had become a public scandal required atonement in front of the whole community.[42] The decision whether a sin was private or public was often a difficult one, and gave rise to frequent controversy. One of the charges made against the consistory by Haemstede's supporters was that the consistory made his case public before having attempted private admonition, and Alexander's final dispute with the French consistory also concerned the issue of whether the degrees of discipline were being properly applied.[43] One of the elders who opposed Alexander on this occasion, Anthony Capell, later found himself out of step with his colleagues when he argued that the offence of one Claude Brizquet did not demand public repentance, and Capell even threatened to resign when his colleagues required him to defer to the majority view.[44]

The determination of erring members to avoid a public humiliation made the role of the consistory a very difficult one, for it was easy to resent being forced to make an act of repentance for a comparatively trivial offence. The severe punishment of public denunciation could, indeed, be counter-productive, as to many it was a greater ordeal than the churches' further sanction of refusing communion. When Robert le Maistre was informed that the consistory required of him a public act of repentance, he told them he would rather die than submit; the last that is heard of him is a threat to go off and join an English church.[45] The ease with which members could carry out such a threat might seriously have undermined the discipline, and the ministers were very conscious of this danger. As it was, many who had been forbidden the communion remained outside the community for many years rather than face a public ordeal on their return. The Dutch church archive also includes several letters from former members who had left to join another community rather than submit to the discipline in London.[46]

---

[42] Micron, *Ordinancien*, pp. 107–11.
[43] *KP I*, p. 107; Denis, 'Pierre Alexandre', 552–3.
[44] *Actes I*, pp. 60–3.
[45] *Actes II*, pp. 107, 185.
[46] Hessels, iii. 288, 554.

The inexorable application of the discipline had another potentially serious distorting effect, for whilst very serious offences could be expiated by an expression of repentance, members who refused to submit faced severe penalties, however trivial the original offence. Thus Jean le Merchant was understandably taken aback when, after a dispute had been decided in his favour, he was required to repent his part in the exchange of insults that had taken place. Merchant refused in some indignation, and it was only after three months and an appeal to the assembly of the three stranger churches (the *coetus*) that the consistory had its way.[47] It is worthy of remark how very serious were some of the offences that the churches were prepared to deal with without involving civil justice. In 1561 the French church considered the case of a member who had battered his wife so severely that she had miscarried. The guilty man was advised that in English law this was regarded as murder, but even so the church was prepared to give him a chance to mend his ways.[48] On three occasions the French church dealt with brawls that had ended with one party being wounded with a knife, on one occasion seriously, but the punishment was no more severe than for much more trivial offences.[49]

So far this survey of the activity of the church has dealt exclusively with cases brought to the attention of the consistory by church members, but the ministers and elders were quite capable of seeking out erring brethren to admonish and reprove on their own initiative. Members of the community who absented themselves from the communion for a prolonged period could expect a visit from a minister or elder, and be required to furnish an explanation for their absence; it was sometimes not enough to plead illness.[50] From the first days of the church, members of the consistory had each taken responsibility for a particular district of the city, and they were expected to keep themselves well-informed about what church members in their *quartiers* were about. Both churches reorganized the districts into which they had divided the city

[47] *Actes II*, pp. 80, 82, 84, etc., 143.
[48] *Actes I*, p. 41.
[49] Ibid., p. 117; *Actes II*, pp. 3, 130.
[50] *Actes II*, pp. 11, 130, 131; *KP II*, p. 40.

during the early Elizabethan period. The Dutch church had soon increased the four elders and deacons elected in 1550 to ten of each, and although at the beginning of Elizabeth's reign eight elders seem to have been thought sufficient in both churches, the arrival of many more strangers during the 1560s made further adjustments necessary. By 1571 both churches had twelve elders, the French having by this time appointed elders for the outlying districts of St Helen's and St Martin-in-the-Fields.[51]

Elders were expected to visit all church members in their districts at least once a year, and any negligence earned them a speedy reproof from their colleagues: Jacques Marabut, when he reported a rather vague rumour of some ill-behaviour in his district was sharply ordered to go and find out what precisely had occurred.[52] The elders, bearing as they so frequently did messages of rebuke and admonition, were subjected to many insults and counter-accusations. For the most part they received solid support from their colleagues, but occasionally the elder himself was taken to task for the inflammatory way in which he had conducted his duties.[53] The consistory, subjected so often to defiant abuse, was not without a certain sympathetic understanding for the frailties of the human condition. On one occasion, having heard a torrent of insults from Denis Balingham (who compared appearing in the consistory unfavourably with being strung up on a gibbet), the French consistory decided to send him away until another occasion without taking much notice, as he was so obviously drunk.[54] A Dutchman who compared his consistory to the Spanish Inquisition was soon back to plead his case anew, with no apparent hard feelings on either side.[55]

The disciplinary control exercised by the churches was wide-ranging and far-reaching, but it would be wrong to stress this disciplinary role to the exclusion of the more positive aspects of the churches' concern. The constructive and sympathetic role the consistory might play has been suggested in the case

---

[51] *Actes II*, pp. 65–6; *KP II*, p. 3.

[52] *Actes I*, p. 27.

[53] *Actes II*, p. 22; *Actes I*, pp. 68–9, 75 (Castelain).

[54] *Actes II*, p. 23.

[55] *KP II*, pp. 189, 195, 196, etc.

of marital conflict and domestic quarrels, and the church also
provided a wide range of services which reached into every
aspect of the community's need, and, it will be suggested,
extended far beyond the narrow confines of the communicant
members of the church. The churches took an active role in
regulating the business practice of members of the foreign
community, and dealt with a steady stream of cases concerning
debt, breach of contract, and apprenticeship agreements.
When a young man was apprenticed to a craftsman a formal
contract or bond was usually drawn up, and the consistory
was frequently invited to arbitrate when a violation was alleged
on either side. The consistory was clearly expected to protect
the servant from unfair treatment, and could not be accused
of looking after the interests of the master at the apprentice's
expense: complaints were heard from relatives that apprentices
were being ill-treated or that the master was not giving the
promised training, and the French church on one occasion
stepped in to prevent an apprentice being made to work on
Sunday.[56] When an irrevocable breakdown occurred between
master and servant, the church helped to arrange compen-
sation, and on occasion the terms of an apprenticeship
agreement might be ratified in the consistory.[57] With skilled
workmen at a premium, considerable bitterness arose from
masters poaching each other's servants, and in 1561 the French
church attempted to stamp out the practice. It was ordered
that no master should employ a servant unless he had a letter
of discharge from his last master, and any who failed to obey
this order were to be disciplined.[58]

The churches often attempted to settle disputes of this sort
by referring them to arbitrators appointed to act on the consistory's behalf.[59] The system had the advantage that disputes
might be settled with the authority of the consistory without
all its members having to grapple with the full complexities
of a case. The custom in the French church was that each of
the parties to the dispute would appoint one arbitrator, and
the consistory would add a third. Sometimes men working in

---

[56] *Actes I*, pp. 47, 73; *KP I*, p. 404.
[57] *Actes I*, pp. 20, 40.
[58] Ibid., p. 43.
[59] *Actes I*, pp. 27, 36.

the disputants' own trade would be appointed, but members of the consistory, as respected senior members of the church, also found their services much in demand. Once both parties had agreed to accept arbitration they had to abide by their decision on pain of a forfeit to the poor-chest; entries in the French deacons' accounts for 1572–3 testify that such forfeits were on occasions being paid.[60] The poor-chest might also provide a convenient way out when neither party was prepared to give way, as when Nicholas Avril and Pierre Boulle agreed to hand over a sum disputed between them to the poor (if the other did not benefit it seemed that each was content).[61] Church members, even when they had agreed to accept arbitration, did not always meekly accept a decision that had gone against them. The tempestuous Didier Bonnair had previously accepted the church's arbitrators as God's elect, but when he heard their decision he denounced them as traitors. Nicholas Ourseau was reported to the consistory for having said of his arbitrators that they had robbed him to give his goods to a villain.[62] Such a response was regarded as a serious offence, and both Bonnair and Ourseau were required to make a public retraction of their allegations of partiality.

Where the business affairs of members were concerned, disputes with which the churches had to deal most frequently related to contested payments or debt, although the early 1560s saw a number of disputes over leases. At this time, with landlords apparently reluctant to rent houses to foreigners for fear of legal sanction, property was in short supply, and there were several cases where two members claimed the right to occupy the same house. The consistory was generally able to resolve these problems, even if, on occasion, it had to recommend that tenancy should be shared for a period.[63] Disputes over money were rather more difficult as the disputants' accounts of the facts of the case might be completely at variance, as when the wife of Gabriel Haymont claimed that she had taken £4 to Nicholas Binet's wife for safekeeping, which the latter flatly

---

[60] London, French Church Soho Square, MS 194 (Deacons' Account Book, 1572–3), fos. 3^v, 72^v.
[61] *Actes I*, p. 113.
[62] *Actes II*, pp. 1, 79.
[63] *Actes I*, pp. 19, 40, 57, 94.

denied: how this problem was resolved is not recorded.[64] Many of the sums involved in such cases were comparatively trivial. Jan du Lond and Jan de Dehors had to seek arbitration over the division of 28s. between them, and an alleged debt of 23s. 4d. caused hard words to be spoken between Jean de Vick and Jacques de la Fosse. Renault le Perdrix was reproved by the consistory for repeatedly insulting François du Rosier and even appearing in front of him and his wife totally naked, all to recover a debt of four shillings.[65] The consistory was fully aware that disagreements over money could breed bitterness and even violence, as was the case when an argument between Denis Balingham and Jean Merquignon over some spoiled material ended with the latter drawing a pistol.[66] On another occasion two old and respected members of the French church had to be sharply reproved when a dispute over money caused them to come to blows as they left the church.[67] Where possible, arbitration was intended to defuse such tensions, and the churches' view of debt proceeded from the same principle. Debtors were encouraged to pay up before serious dissension arose, and the consistory was quite capable of refusing to admit a member to communion until he satisfied his creditors.[68] On the other hand, the churches disapproved equally of members who flouted the churches' procedures and arrested other members for debt before bringing the case to arbitration. The offence was regarded as particularly heinous if the arrest took place as the victim left church: in 1573 it was ordered that the wife of Jean Chamberlain should be suspended from the communion if a report that she had offended in this way proved correct, and later in the same year Loys le Seigneur did penance for a similar offence.[69]

The variety of economic cases treated in the consistory simply reflects the variety of the members' own economic interests,

[64] *Actes II*, pp. 62–3.
[65] Ibid., pp. 33, 52, 129.
[66] Ibid., p. 43.
[67] Ibid., pp. 129–30.
[68] Ibid., pp. 47, 110.
[69] Ibid., pp. 119, 129. See also *KP I*, p. 311, *KP II*, p. 195. The church apparently had no objection to lending at interest. Indeed, the French consistory on one occasion decided to lend out the surplus from the poor-chest for the profit of the church. *Actes I*, p. 121.

for whenever two or more members were involved in a co-operative venture problems might arise. The consistory was used to hammer out an agreement between the widow Typre and Jan Caillon whereby she undertook to set him up in business and pay for his denization.[70] The church became involved when a Frenchman laid out a great deal of money on a dubious project for an ever-running fountain, and seems to have been swindled.[71] At times members presumed a little too much on the willingness of the church to act as a centre for their commercial transactions: a woman of the Dutch community had to be told to look elsewhere when she wanted to use Austin Friars for the sale of the goods of a deceased friend, and asked permission to advertise the sale from the pulpit.[72]

Regulating the business affairs of members occupied a great deal of the consistory's attention, but the essence of the churches' social concern lay in their care for the poor, the sick, and the dying. The churches' concern for foreigners dying in London is evident from the surviving wills of the period. These are an important source of information in any survey of the churches' role in the stranger community. Approximately 250 wills proved in London courts during the period 1550–80 may be definitely identified as those of foreigners, and of these more than 100 name a minister, elder, or deacon of the stranger churches (often several) as witness, executor, or overseer. Wills were usually drawn up very close to death, and the frequency with which ministers were named as witnesses is eloquent testimony to their attendance on the dying. Delenus, Carineus, Winghen, Regius, and Wybo all appear in Dutch wills, and Cousin is named by several Frenchmen; none, however, seems to have rivalled Peter Oliver, named on no fewer than twenty-nine occasions, for assiduous attendance at the sick-bed.[73] Elders and deacons were also frequent witnesses, those named usually having responsibility for the district in which the

---

[70] *Actes I*, pp. 71–2.

[71] Ibid., pp. 98–9.

[72] *KP II*, p. 60.

[73] Little is known of Oliver, who is not included in lists of ministers of the church. It is possible that he was employed to assist Cousin during the plague epidemic of 1563–4, and stayed on as visitor of the sick. In April 1564 he asked to be paid the balance of his wages so that he could return to France (*Actes I*, p. 58), but he must have decided to remain as he continued to witness wills until at least 1578.

testator lived. Wills were not usually drawn up by the representatives of the church attending a sick man; the foreign
community had its own notaries who performed this task, but
on occasions death came too quickly for a notary to be called
to draw up a formal document. On these occasions the minister
might be amongst those who testified that the dead man had
expressed his wishes for the disposal of his goods verbally
before expiring, and a nuncupative will might be drawn up.[74]

Representatives of the church were frequently required by
testators to undertake more burdensome tasks than simply
acting as witnesses to their will. Elders and deacons were often
named as executors, charged with the responsibility of carrying
out the testator's instructions. If the dying man followed the
more usual practice and named his principal beneficiary as
executor (frequently his wife), then an elder or deacon might
be asked to exercise a more general supervisory role by acting
as overseer. A dying man would usually name overseers if he
left young children, so that their interests might be protected
if his wife died or married again, and the members of the
consistory who undertook these duties must often have been
called upon as friends of the family rather than always acting
in an official capacity.[75] Not every stranger, however, had
friends on whom he could rely to perform these offices, and
in such cases the elders and deacons might well be appointed.
The executor's task, in particular, was often a troublesome
burden, and at least one testator was refused by two of his
friends before he found one prepared to accept the charge.[76]
Some testators got round this problem by neglecting to inform
beforehand those they intended to name to act for them.[77]

Executors usually received a small legacy for their trouble,
and most of the wills in which church officials were named as
witnesses or executors also included a legacy for the poor of
the church. Usually, but not always: the fact that some 25 per
cent of the wills witnessed by ministers and elders included
no such legacy should absolve them from any suspicion of

[74] Wills of Victor van den Berghe, London Comm. 1575 (16, fo. 211); James Soest, PCC 1575 (36 Pyckering); Bernard Cocquet, PCC 1578 (40 Langley).
[75] Harvie Paroz named Jacques Marabut as an overseer in 1571. Marabut had been an elder, but had retired by this date. PCC 1575 (36 Pyckering).
[76] Stephen Mulicum, London Comm. 1563 (15, fo. 141).
[77] Renier Cuenellis, PCC 1575 (37 Pyckering).

having abused their position at the sick-bed.[78] Such legacies
were extremely welcome to the church, but often carried with
them considerable administrative burdens for those charged
with receiving them. The churches were left sums in foreign
currency, for which exchange had to be arranged, and clothing,
household goods, and books. On occasion the church had to
undertake the substantial labour of disposing of all a man's
property, as in 1571 with Jacques Pranger, who left the French
church 'the small portion of temporal goods it pleased God to
grant me'. Pranger was a tailor who arrived in England in
1568 and put down no real roots; it is no surprise that he
appointed Nicholas Fontaine, an elder of the French church,
his executor.[79] Clare van Tiell left a will which was just an
inventory of her household goods and clothing, all of which
she left to be sold to the profit of the poor of the Dutch church.[80]
More work still was required to carry out the last wishes of
Nicholas Provancher, a French goldsmith who died in 1571.[81]
Provancher left the church £10 but the long-suffering ministers
whom he appointed his executors had first to liquidate his
stock; this involved returning gold to customers who had provided it to be made up into bracelets, and searching out
craftsmen who were owed for their work. Provancher was also
owed money for goods supplied and for rent. The residue was
to go to a brother and sister, probably not in England. The
French ministers Cousin and des Roches would have fully
earned the £3 they were granted for their pains.

The church was often left the residue of a testator's goods
after all debts and legacies had been paid, or in the event of
his heirs predeceasing him. The French church was to have
all Provancher's goods if his brother and sister were no longer
alive. Jacques Sarrhe's goods were to go to the poor-chest of
the French church after his wife's death, and the widow of
John le Duc, Margaret Nolier, left all her goods to the French

---

[78] Of 103 wills where a representative of the church acted as overseer, executor,
or witness, there is no legacy to the poor of the church in 27.

[79] London Comm. 1571 (16, fo. 50ᵛ). Pranger was living in the house of the widow
Hollertot, which seems to have been a sort of boarding house. *Returns*, iii. 348.

[80] Archd. London 1571 (4, fo. 3).

[81] London Comm. 1571 (16, fo. 64ᵛ). Provancher was another recent arrival in
England. *Returns*, iii. 408.

church if her son were no longer living.[82] Derick Everwyn, a
painter who arrived in England in 1568 and died seven years
later, left all his goods to his wife, but if she died also their
goods were to be sold, and, after several small legacies had
been paid, the residue was to go to the poor of the Dutch
church.[83] When legacies were contingent on the death of one
or several relatives the church usually did not benefit; such a
deposition was often just a comforting catch-all clause for the
testator wishing to leave nothing to chance. Occasionally, however, the circumstances against which provision had been
made did come about. In May 1564 the French church heard
that the heir of the late Rioll de Carre had died in the fighting
in France and set about collecting the residue of Rioll's estate,
which was to revert to the poor of the church.[84] A legacy of
any remaining property after other obligations had been
fulfilled could bring them substantial benefit. Nicholas de la
Salle had no surviving relatives, and so left the French ten
crowns and the residue of his estate after certain stated legacies
had been paid. From the deacons' accounts, which survive for
the year of de la Salle's death, it emerges that this legacy
brought in a total of over £30.[85]

Such substantial legacies were extremely welcome in helping
to meet the mounting burden of caring for the community's
poor. The French church received £20 from the will of the
prosperous merchant Peter Boullen and £15 from the widow
of John Cousin, and the Dutch church was left £20 by its
former elder Thomas Coenen.[86] It is, however, of no less significance that a legacy of some sort was the rule rather than
the exception in these strangers' wills. The poor were remembered in 154 of those discovered, over 60 per cent of the total,
and in the vast majority of these cases the poor of their churches
were specifically mentioned. Usually these legacies ranged
from 5s to £5, but it was not unknown to leave the church a
purely nominal one shilling.[87] Gifts of such tiny amounts

[82] Both London Comm. 1577 (16, fos. 316, 338ᵛ.).

[83] London Comm. 1575 (16, fo. 219ᵛ.); *Returns*, i. 422.

[84] London Comm. 1564 (15, fo. 187), 'Redulle Decarry'; *Actes I*, pp. 60–1.

[85] London Comm. 1572 (16, fo. 109); French Church MS 194, fos. 30ᵛ., 72ᵛ., 96ᵛ.

[86] PCC 1575 (7 Pyckering); London Comm. 1578 (16, fo. 409); PCC 1573 (2 Martyn).

[87] Baldwin de Keyser, Jacques de Navarre, both London Comm. 1574 (16, fos. 166ᵛ., 167ᵛ.).

suggest that testators recognized a social responsibility however humble their means: the fact that so many left to the poor
of the foreign churches suggests that their central role in the
provision of care was generally recognized in London's
stranger community.

Caring for the poor was, indeed, an important aspect of the
churches' community life. The collection and disbursement of
the community's charity was entrusted under John a Lasco's
church order to a separate group of officers, the deacons, who
were established in office by a ceremony of laying-on of hands
as were other ministers of the community.[88] The symbolism
was significant, for the care of the poor was to be regarded as
as sacred a charge as the ministry of the Word or the government of the community. Lasco's instructions laid down that
the deacons should make a regular collection for the poor at
the door of the church at the end of each service, and it was
their responsibility to keep the common chest and present a
regular monthly account to the consistory. In both churches
the responsibility was delegated to one, and later two, deacons
on a rotating basis. At the beginning of the Elizabethan period
no distinction was made between funds donated for the poor
and for the general needs of the church, and so the poor-chest
of the French church contributed towards the cost of printing
des Gallars's Form of Discipline; later, however, the functions
were divided.[89] Ministers' salaries were from the beginning
paid from a separate fund, which seems to have been raised
by a levy on all the members.[90] During the Edwardian period
the collections at the church door may have been sufficient to
meet the needs of the poor, but as the numbers of refugees
increased in the years after 1559 it was found necessary to
augment the income of the poor-chest in other ways. Even so
the resources of the church were subjected to considerable
strain in times of crisis.[91]

The responsibilities of the deacons were by no means limited
to disbursing aid to those who sought their help. The deacons
were expected to know the church members living in their

[88] Micron, *Ordinancien*, pp. 55–8; *Lasco Opera*, ii. 79; *Toute la Forme*, p. 35.
[89] *Actes I*, pp. 14, 39; *KP II*, p. 249.
[90] *KP I*, p. 249; *Actes I*, p. 14.
[91] See below, pp. 206 ff.

districts, and to visit the sick and indigent in their houses. In 1561 the French consistory respectfully asked des Gallars to tell the deacons the address of any member he recommended for help, to facilitate finding them. (Des Gallars agreed, whilst remarking that this had not been necessary in Geneva, which was a much smaller town.)[92] The bulk of the churches' help took the form of outdoor relief for those who had fallen upon hard times, but both churches in addition maintained a poor-house with one of the deacons (in the case of the Dutch, at least) as overseer.[93] A poor-house was necessary, not least because many of those who took refuge in England were already old or chronically sick and had little chance of making their own living.[94] The ministers and elders shared the responsibility of providing them with spiritual and bodily comfort, but the rent and upkeep of the poor-house must have been a major drain on the churches' resources. Residents were expected to be of exemplary conduct, and one Dutchman who fell foul of the consistory was peremptorily expelled.[95] By 1572, though, supervision in the French house seems to have been rather lax: in this year one of the inmates was delivered of a bastard without its having previously being realized that she was pregnant.[96]

The consistory minutes do not enable us to discover in what style the residents of the poor-houses were maintained, but the communities' response to need was on occasion generous. The loans provided by the Dutch church to help poorer members purchase letters of denization have already been mentioned,[97] and both consistories responded to a wide variety of appeals for financial assistance. Michael Blanc was awarded ten shillings from the common chest to help with the expenses of a journey to the Continent to fetch his wife, and Paulin Beauvais was lent £2 to help him out of prison (presumably he was there for debt). The French church also heard with

---

[92] *Actes I*, p. 21.

[93] *KP I*, p. 50; Ruytinck, *Gheschiedenissen*, p. 43.

[94] In 1572 the Emden church recommended to London a blind man who wished to try to earn his living in London. In all likelihood, though, he would have become an extra burden on the community's resources. Hessels, iii. 161.

[95] *KP I*, p. 225.

[96] *Actes II*, pp. 69–70.

[97] Above, p. 149.

sympathy an appeal on behalf of a family imprisoned by the Turks.[98] The churches looked sympathetically on poor members who wished to work but lacked the wherewithal to set themselves up in business. The French church lent £2 to one Robert Somaner, a vine grower, and twenty shillings to Pierre Wallet to help him out of temporary embarrassment whilst he waited for his money to reach him from the Continent. A poor buttonmaker, newly arrived from France, was given some silver leaf so that he could start to earn his living.[99] The consistories would on occasion refuse help to those whose need was not so great. The printer Urban van Coelen was told to look to his friends for assistance as he was sufficiently well-known in England.[100] Such judgements could, of course, cause considerable bitterness and ill-feeling, and, to protect themselves from charges of favouritism, the deacons made all decisions as to who should be assisted together. On one occasion Arnold de Boulogne threatened, as keeper of the chest for the month, to make a disbursement on his own initiative if it was not agreed to help one case he thought worthy, but his threat was reported to the consistory and it is unlikely that it was ever carried out.[101]

The deacons' activities, then, were not limited by a narrow view of their own responsibilities; nor, it seems, was the churches' concern narrowly limited to their own communicant members. It has been pointed out in an earlier chapter that by no means all of London's foreign residents joined the new churches in the Edwardian period, and this continued to be the case in the latter part of the century. The surveys of the alien population in 1568 and 1571 revealed that something under half the foreign population either attended parish churches or no church at all, but they were not for that reason entirely excluded from the foreign churches' social net.[102] A concern for the wider community is particularly evident in the churches' care for the sick and the dying. In only just over half the cases where a representative of the stranger churches

---

[98] *Actes I*, pp. 17, 82, 101.
[99] Ibid., pp. 94, 121.
[100] *KP I*, p. 47.
[101] *Actes I*, p. 123.
[102] *Returns*, i. 393, ii. 139, 154.

is named in a will is the testator known to have been a member of the church. An absence of full membership lists would account for some of the others, but it seems clear that the churches did not confine their ministry to foreigners *in extremis* to their own members. Such evident concern also evoked a response from the community as a whole. These same wills reveal that many strangers who were not members of the stranger churches remembered the poor of the communities in their wills. A significant group in this respect were the foreign merchants who, whilst not permanently settled in London, happened to die in England. Most left the bulk of their property abroad, but a majority also remembered their poor brethren in London. John Lestuy of Valenciennes left the French church £3, and John Adam, a merchant from Mons, left £2.[103] Jacques des Bourdes, a merchant of Bordeaux, appointed executors from his home town to wind up his estate, but still remembered the French and Italian churches in London.[104] Hercules Freemantle, a merchant from Flanders trading to the Low Countries, left £1 to the Dutch church.[105] These merchants possibly attended the services of the stranger churches when in the city, but none were enrolled as members, and their legacies indicate that the churches acted as a focus for the charitable giving of a much wider circle than merely their own members. Those strangers who made other charitable legacies usually left small sums to their parish churches or unspecified 'poor'; hardly ever does one find examples of legacies to the English institutions which absorbed much of the charitable interest of native Londoners, such as the London hospitals. The concern of the ministers to succour any fellow countrymen in evident need, taken with the generous response of foreigners to this endeavour, argues strongly for a sense of community which went beyond the frontiers of the gathered church community. The stranger churches had for the foreign community a social role which for many was as important as their spiritual function. Or even more so: many were tempted to attend the church for such reasons who had no wish to

---

[103] PCC 1569 (12 Sheffield), PCC 1572 (2 Daper).
[104] London Comm. 1577 (16, fo. 350).
[105] London Comm. 1575 (16, fo. 216v.).

subject themselves to the strict discipline imposed on communicant members. From time to time the consistories considered whether to take action to force these fellow-travellers to a greater measure of commitment. For the most part, however, they wisely decided to leave well alone.[106]

The churches' greatest response to the community is evident in times of crisis, when their resources were also subjected to their severest test. It is worth, finally, taking a closer look at two such crises, which forced the churches to adapt their practices and institutions to cope with sudden extra burdens. Sources exist which make possible an examination of the Dutch church's response to the mortality crisis of 1563–4, and the French church's handling of the flood of refugees which followed the massacre of St Bartholomew's Day in 1572. In each case a heroic effort was required to maintain the social provision of the community at an adequate level.

The plague epidemic which swept across Europe in 1563 was claiming its first victims in London by the late spring, and during the hot summer months it took root as soldiers, returning from the garrison at Newhaven, spread the bacillus through the capital. The epidemic decimated the population of the city and the foreign artisans, crowded into insanitary accommodation in the poorer quarters, had little chance of avoiding the full severity of the visitation.[107] Something of the havoc wrought by the plague is evident from surviving wills; of the eighty-five foreign wills identified proved in the three main London courts during the 1560s, over half date from the two years 1563 and 1564.

By the beginning of July the plague was rife in the Dutch community, and a special meeting of the ministers, elders, and deacons was convened to discuss emergency measures.[108] A commendable priority was given to the relief of poor victims, and a surgeon, Rembart, was appointed to do what was possible for them. The deacons decided to offer him a salary of

[106] *Actes I*, p. 43.
[107] Ramsay, *City of London*, p. 33. See Grindal to Cecil, 30 July 1563, *Remains of Archbishop Grindal* (Parker Society, 1843), p. 259. Paul Slack, *The Impact of Plague in Tudor and Stuart England* (1985), pp. 144–69.
[108] *KP I*, p. 429.

sixteen shillings (a generous gesture as he had asked only for twelve) and an additional five shillings a week whilst he was caring for the poor; the surgeon was invited to extract a fee from his richer patients himself. In the same week the community appointed two deacons as visitors of the sick to take the place of the overburdened ministers.[109] They, too, were generously remunerated, and it is perhaps characteristic of the Dutch community that even in this emergency the appointment was accompanied by a hard-headed business contract. The visitors were given a choice between a payment of seven shillings a week, with the understanding that they might keep any fees proffered for their services, or they might compound for 10s. on condition that they surrendered half their fees to the community. They chose the latter.

The visitors were charged with appointing watchers to remain with the afflicted and with drawing up their wills, a task performed since the beginning of the emergency by the ministers as no notary would willingly enter the house of a plague victim. The visitors were to bring the wills to the ministers who would sign them in the presence of witnesses, but as the plague raged ever more fiercely the visitors seem quickly to have been overwhelmed by their tasks and by mid-August two other members of the community had been appointed simply to look after wills.[110] Testamentary business became the overriding concern of the community as the summer progressed. Jan Utenhove was asked to translate wills from Dutch to Latin, presumably for the purpose of proving them in the English courts; he agreed to do this, and several of the surviving registered copies bear his signature.[111] In September the community decided to keep a reckoning of the wills in both a rough book and fair copy, and the bookseller Bartholomew Huysman was approached for the necessary materials. At this time too Anthony Ashe agreed to help Lewis Tyry scrutinize the wills (presumably to ensure that they complied with English legal practice).[112] The activity of the consistory in ensuring that

---

[109] *KP I*, pp. 431–2.

[110] Ibid., p. 488.

[111] *KP I*, p. 487. Peter Delenus, London Comm. 1563, Walter a Maddau, Francis Buscodensis, London Comm. 1564 (15, fos. 186ᵛ., 195, 199), Hubert Uyghen, Stephen van der Muelen, PCC 1564 (1, 2 Stephenson).

[112] *KP I*, p. 490.

dying plague victims drew up a will in due order was important if the church were not to be swamped by a flood of litigation in its aftermath. Many of the victims would have been comparatively new arrivals in England, very often with heirs still abroad; without such care over the drawing up of testaments the task of tracing those with a legitimate claim to property would have been wellnigh impossible.[113]

Those charged solely with responsibility for wills were much less generously paid than the visitors and surgeon, a measure perhaps of the risks these latter ran in performing their duties. The churches held an inconclusive debate at the beginning of July as to whether the plague was contagious, but they must soon have been convinced, for by the end of the month it was ordered that those charged with the care of the sick should sit apart in church (though in places of honour).[114] Victims were charged not to come back amongst the community until they had been certified fully fit by the surgeon. The appointment of visitors was probably intended as much to protect the ministers from infection as to relieve them of the burden of work, but if so this proved a vain precaution as by September both the ministers were dead. The minutes for 2 September note that an approach had been made to Sandwich to provide a helper for Carineus after the death of Delenus; three days later the minutes break off abruptly as the writer, Carineus, had himself succumbed.[115] The response of the church at Sandwich was commendably prompt and by 9 November their minister Godfrey van Winghen was in London, but the loss of two experienced ministers in the course of a few weeks was a severe blow to a community already under heavy strain.

The break in the minutes on the death of Carineus makes it impossible to know what further emergency measures were necessitated by the plague. Probably those instituted at the outset proved sufficient, but the burden of care for the poorer victims placed considerable strain on the community's financial resources. Property left to the church by plague victims was a help, realizing over £100 during the time of the mortality,

---

[113] Even so the property of at least one plague victim had not reached his heirs six years later. Hessels. iii. 103–4.

[114] *KP I*, pp. 430, 435.

[115] *KP I*, pp. 490, 491.

but this money was disbursed as quickly as sale of the property could be made.[116] The consistory was obliged to order a weekly collection in all the districts to help meet the extra costs, but even so the plague seems to have set off a prolonged crisis of liquidity. In May 1565 the Dutch were forced to borrow £10 from their French colleagues to help meet their obligations, and five years later claims for payments due for service rendered during the plague had still not been met.[117] In 1571 the community was still in financial difficulties, and the accounts of the receipts and disbursements of the keepers of the plague-house were yet to be finally settled. In 1573 the church hit upon the idea of asking the City to institute a levy of a halfpenny per cloth on all the bays brought by foreign merchants to Blackwell Hall. The city authorities proved amenable, and this measure may well have been responsible for restoring the poor-chest to solvency.[118] The plague of 1563–4 had a permanent influence on the institutions of the church, as the office of visitor of the sick was continued after the mortality had subsided.[119] All in all, the response of the Dutch to the crisis of the plague was impressive. Bold and imaginative measures were taken as they became necessary, and the community made no attempt to limit its obligation in line with its limited resources. An effort of similar proportions would be required in the early 1570s, particularly in the French community in 1572.

The plague of 1563–4 was sudden and dramatic in its impact, whereas the difficulties faced by the communities at the end of the decade arose from the mounting pressure on their resouces caused by the steady deterioration of the position of their co-religionists on the Continent. Hostilities were resumed in France in 1568 and an edict banning Reformed ministers in September brought many to England, but already Alva's repression in the Low Counties had provoked a sharp increase in the number of more humble Protestant refugees in London. A list presented by the ministers of the French church to the

---

[116] *KP II*, p. 319.
[117] *KP I*, p. 432; *Actes I*, p. 112; *KP II*, p. 59; Hessels, iii. 101, 128.
[118] Rep. 18, fo. 22; Corporation of London, Letter Book X, fo. 218ᵛ.
[119] *KP II*, p. 118. Will witnessed by visitor of the sick (Melchior Laet), PCC 1570 (10 Lyon).

Privy Council in January 1569, listing over 400 members of the church who hailed from the dominions of the King of Spain, is a reminder that the Council of Troubles included many French-speaking Netherlanders amongst its victims.[120] By 1571 the problem of caring for these refugees, many of whom had fled almost penniless, was placing a severe burden on the resources of the French church. On 21 October the consistory was informed by the deacons that the poor-chest had fallen £30 into arrears over the last two months, and it was decided to re-institute the weekly house-to-house collection which had been discontinued three months before.[121] This, however, was unlikely to bring in large sums of money, so in December it was decided to call together a group of the most substantial members of the community and make a direct appeal to their generosity. This proved a great success. After listening to an oration from the minister des Roches, those summoned volunteered £82.[122]

This considerable sum seems to have enabled the community to keep its head above water through the early months of 1572. The situation was completely transformed, however, by the St Bartholomew's Day massacre of 24 August and the wave of imitative massacres that followed through September. The massacre itself goes curiously unremarked in the consistory minutes, but its effect was almost immediately apparent. As boatloads of refugees from the Huguenot congregations of northern France crowded into the ports of south-eastern England, it seemed for a moment as if the London church might be overwhelmed by the sheer weight of numbers. At the main service on Sunday morning the church was filled to overflowing, and it was necessary to institute an extra service at seven in the morning to deal with the crush.[123] The French hoped that the Dutch might help, and appealed for the use of the much larger church of Austin Friars at this earlier time so that they might all worship at one service once again. The Dutch, though, proved remarkably unhelpful, answering

---

[120] *Returns*, i. 394–9.
[121] *Actes II*, p. 28.
[122] Ibid., p. 47.
[123] *Actes II*, p. 89.

rather disingenuously that they too had been thinking of holding of early Sunday morning service.[124]

The extra burden placed by these new arrivals on the community's financial resources was an equally intractable problem. The survival of a single volume of deacons' accounts for
the fourteen months from November 1572 to December 1573
makes possible a close scrutiny of how the French consistory
met the challenge posed by the massacre and its aftermath.[125]
The scale of the problem is immediately clear. In November
1565 the poor-chest had disbursed £10 in ordinary and extraordinary payments.[126] By 1573 the community's ordinary
expenditure (comprising regular weekly payments to the community's own needy members) was on its own rather more
than this total, whilst extraordinary payments had shot up to
over £70 a month.[127] In 1573 some fifty poor were regularly
in receipt of charity. Many were widows and orphans, and
the men on the list were most likely disabled or too old to
work: they all received weekly doles of between 8*d.* and 2*s.*,
amounting to around £15 in all. The bulk of the church's
resources, however, was being consumed by the new arrivals:
by February 1573 the deacons were making some 460 disbursements in the course of a month.[128] In addition to the many
poor artisans some sixty Reformed ministers had fled to London, and the community attempted, as far as was possible, to
maintain them in rather better style. From July 1573 payments
to the ministers were recorded separately, and up to £20 per
month was distributed to them.[129]

Finding such enormous sums was a formidable task. Exhortation and a sense of the urgency of the problem produced a
modest increase in the regular collections at the church door,
but this on its own was hardly sufficient. The deacons could
expect £2 or £3 from the Sunday morning service, and a further
10*s.* in the evening. The weekday services usually brought in
rather smaller sums, and rarely more than £1. The largest

[124] Ibid., p. 93.
[125] French Church, MS 194.
[126] *Actes I*, p. 124.
[127] French Church, MS 194, fo. 3 ff., fo. 17 ff.
[128] Ibid., fo. 45 ff.
[129] Ibid., fo. 107.

sum, sometimes £6 or £8, was collected at the monthly communion.[130] There was little room for manœuvre here, even
with a special fast and service of prayer which might bring in
a few pounds extra, and the church could not expect income
from the collections after services to go much above £25 per
month. The weekly collection through the districts of the city
made only a modest, if regular, contribution to the needs of
the community.[131] Deacons often presented less than 5*s.* as the
fruits of four weeks' collecting, and the total raised monthly
averaged about £10. An enormous gap remained to be filled
between the community's expenditure and its regular income.
Wills brought in a useful £60 during the course of the year,
but such income was necessarily sporadic and unreliable. The
vast proportion of the sum outstanding was met by individual
donations. Richer members of the community were amongst
the contributors, and some of the better-off exiles remembered
their poorer brethren,[132] but the large proportion of these donations was from sympathetic Englishmen. In 1572 the French
refugees were clearly a cause of national interest: collections
on their behalf were made in several counties, and many of
the most distinguished figures of the Protestant establishment
were amongst those who contributed.[133] The church, however,
owed its continued solvency very largely to the massive sum
of £320 provided by the Bishop of London in December 1572.[134]
This money was delivered to two elders, who seem to have
disbursed as much monthly as was necessary to keep the
deacons' accounts in credit. This system apparently worked
well until October 1573, when once again the account slipped
back into deficit.[135]

As a result of the bishop's generosity the deacons were able
to distribute an enormous amount of charity during these
months. If the refugees brought the church considerable extra
problems, the consistory was understandably not averse to

---

[130] Ibid., fos. 3, 17, etc.
[131] Ibid., fos. 4, 18, etc.
[132] The Vicomte de Chartres, himself in receipt of a pension from the English
government, gave £3 in October 1573. French Church, MS 194, f. 131ᵛ.
[133] See below, pp. 271–2.
[134] *Actes II*, p. 100.
[135] French Church, MS 194, fos. 52, 72ᵛ. The money was in the hands of Biscop
and Bisquet.

taking advantage of any compensating benefits. The refugee ministers were on occasion asked for their advice, and when it was decided to institute a series of lectures in theology and doctrine for the benefit of the refugees one of their number was asked to undertake them. Two refugee ministers were also given responsibility for the catechismal training of the youth of the church.[136] Relations between the deacons and the refugee ministers were not always easy. The latter resented having to claim relief (like beggars, they said), and complained that the deacons had made the insulting suggestion that they go out and learn a trade. An acrimonious exchange resulted, and the decision to list the support given to the ministers separately may have been a means of patching up this quarrel.[137]

The deacons' accounts are missing after December 1573, but it is clear that the crisis was by no means past by that time. In the first days of 1574 it was decided to visit the houses of those who did not contribute to the poor, and on 30 March it was necessary to borrow £50 from Jacques Hagoubart to top up the poor-chest.[138] In April it was decided to repeat the experiment of calling together the more substantial members of the community to ask for a special donation as the poor-chest was so much in arrears; on this occasion, however, the man-œuvre failed, as most of those summoned, no doubt forewarned, failed to turn up. Instead it was resolved to make a roll at the next Sunday service and encourage all on it to promise a weekly subscription for the support of the poor.[139]

This hint that the crisis was finally overcome by the institu-tion of a poor-rate within the community is tantalizingly unconfirmed, but over the next few years the pressure on resources seems to have subsided. The arrival of so many exiles in these years produced in the French church, as had the plague in the Dutch, a response which was remarkable, if not always remarkably successful. Both communities faced unprecedented problems, the French in the scale, the Dutch in the nature of the demands upon them, and neither attempted to shirk or limit their responsibility even if the generosity of

[136] *Actes II*, pp. 99, 101, 123, 135.
[137] Ibid., pp. 106, 110–3.
[138] Ibid., pp. 130, 133.
[139] Ibid., pp. 135–6.

their response stored up problems for the future. The diligence of the consistories and deacons in the face of these difficulties epitomizes the concern for the community which marked the churches' conception of their responsibilities. Members of the churches might expect the control of the consistory to reach into all areas of their communal and even domestic life, but in return the church's support was equally wide-ranging. Times of crisis made explicit what was, in fact, always the case: that the ministers and elders recognized a responsibility to maintain the community in distress or hardship, and that their concern extended far beyond those who formally submitted themselves to the discipline of the church; indeed, it embraced the whole foreign community.

VIII

The Churches and the Continent

THE provision of charity for foreign refugees on their arrival in England was only one aspect of the foreign churches' continued involvement with their former homelands. It goes without saying that the foreigners who came to England did not abandon their concern for their own countries; indeed, many of the exiles saw their time in England only as a necessary but temporary respite before they returned to continue the struggle for religious freedom. For this reason, and because of the sheer scale of the exile movement, events in France, and to a still greater extent in the Netherlands, had an immediate and far-reaching impact on the exile communities in England. The London churches, as the largest and most powerful of the English communities, could never take a detached view of events abroad, and the issues raised by the bitter struggles of their brethren in the 'churches under the cross' could have serious repercussions for the exile communities. Indeed, on occasion disagreements, which in the constrained circumstances of the Reformed communities abroad remained fairly amicable, were to prove deeply divisive in London.[1]

At the same time the relative freedom enjoyed by the exile communities in England gave them an invaluable opportunity to advance the cause of the Reformation in the lands of their birth. From the time of the first gathering of Reformed communities in the towns of Flanders and Brabant to the establishment of a public church in the independent United Provinces, the exile churches played a crucial role in the survival and eventual triumph of the Reformed faith in the Netherlands. In France too, the contribution of the exile communities was far from negligible, although as a result of the close direction of the movement from Geneva the French-speaking churches in England played a much less important role. The bulk of

[1] See below, pp. 240 ff.

this chapter will be devoted to an assessment of the exiles'
influence on the wider Reformed movement; but first it is
worth looking in rather more detail at the means by which
the refugee communities maintained their links with their
former homes. The more closely one examines this intricate
web of connections, the more one is struck by the sophistication
of communications, not only between the exile churches and
the Reformed communities on the Continent, but also between
ordinary members of the churches and their friends and relatives at home. It was the strength of these close and enduring
ties which made it possible for the exile churches to exercise
such a potent and immediate influence on events.

Attention in this work has so far largely been directed towards
the more stable elements of the stranger population, those
who, like the long-term residents prominent in the Edwardian
church, came and remained. But it must be held in mind that
for a large part of the stranger population residence in London
was never intended to be permanent. Merchant strangers
travelled freely back and forth across the Channel and 'lived'
where convenient, and at a more humble level many artisans
came speculatively in search of work, in much the same way
that young Englishmen flocked to London in the hope of
finding fortune. Some would settle, marry, and put down roots,
but others would drift away to be replaced by new arrivals.
The foreign population of the city was thus constantly changing
even in normal times, and this tendency was greatly exacer-
bated by the arrival of great numbers of religious refugees
during the 1560s and 1570s. Whilst many refugees remained
in London for an extended period, others returned as soon as
possible, with the result that successive influxes were often
quickly followed by large-scale movements back to the Continent.

The accession of Elizabeth opened England to a quickening
tide of foreign arrivals from both France and the Netherlands,
but when the French minister des Gallars returned to France
for the Colloquy of Poissy in 1561 many of the more optimistic
of his fellow-nationals also apparently departed for home.[2]
Their hopes for peace were dashed by the outbreak of hostilities

---

[2] Schickler, *Églises du Refuge*, i. 131.

in 1562, but many who fled to England during the first religious war seem to have returned home after the Pacification of Amboise, particularly as the volte-face of the Huguenot leader Condé, which fatally undermined the English expedition to Newhaven, outraged English opinion against the French.[3] The pattern was repeated with the renewal of hostilities in 1568 and the peace of 1570, and with the massacre of St Bartholomew's Day in 1572 the successive waves of refugees became a torrent. A similar pattern may be discerned for the Netherlands. As persecution intensified in the years after 1558 many sought refuge across the Channel, but the apparent success of the opposition to Granvelle in 1563 encouraged some bolder spirits to return.[4] The concession of a measure of religious toleration with the Moderation of April 1566 brought the return of some hundreds of exiles and many others followed during the course of the summer, but with the collapse of the reform movement in 1567 and the systematic repression instituted by Alva, many thousands of new refugees sought safety abroad.[5] When the descent of the Sea Beggars on the coast of Holland in 1572 raised the standard of revolt once more there was an immediate response from the exile communities in England, and a steady interchange of men and resources continued through the decade. A final major influx occurred with the fall of Antwerp in 1585, with the result that there were still large numbers of refugees in London into the 1590s.[6] It is worth reminding ourselves that these events in the Netherlands had almost as great an impact on the French as on the Dutch church in London. A fluctuating but always considerable proportion of the members of the French church were from the Netherlands rather than metropolitan France, and in consequence the numerical impact of French events on the size of the London French community was not always as marked as one might expect: during 1568–70, for instance, the drift of Huguenot ministers back to France was more than compensated by a vast influx of new refugees from the French-speaking Reformed strongholds of Valenciennes, Tournai, and

[3] See below, pp. 285–6. Schickler, *Églises du Refuge*, i. 139–41.
[4] KL, iii. 307, 360.
[5] Parker, *Dutch Revolt*, pp. 70–4, 118–20.
[6] See below, pp. 258–9.

Lille during the time of the Council of Blood.[7] These major movements of refugees caused significant fluctuations in the number of foreigners in London, but there was also a steady movement back and forth between foreign communities in England and the Low Countries which appeared to take little account of high politics. One reformer settled in England who was captured by the authorities on a return trip to Flanders confessed that his behaviour was by no means exceptional: many refugees, apparently, regularly crossed the Channel to buy in the markets of Hazebrouck and Tournai. Others came across for similarly mundane purposes, to visit an aged parent or secure their portion of a deceased father's goods.[8] The ease of movement between England and the Netherlands was equally well attested by the activities of Reformed ministers in the early 1560s, many of whom interspersed periods of service in Flanders and Brabant with visits to their colleagues in the English exile communities.[9]

Such freedom of movement was essential to the continuation of close contact between the exiles and their homelands, but it also brought with it considerable problems for the London churches. Quite apart from the scale of relief demanded by sudden increases in the flow of refugees, there was the perennial problem of deciding which of the newcomers were genuinely religious. This was a highly pertinent question, given the sensitivity of the government and city authorities to the charge frequently made against the foreigners coming into the capital, that most of them were either criminals seeking a refuge or anabaptists and sectaries.[10] In truth, it was all too tempting for tradesmen and craftsmen harassed by debt or domestic difficulties to attempt to leave such problems behind by crossing the Channel, and the churches had no wish to encourage dereliction of this sort. The examination of new arrivals who applied for membership of the churches was therefore necessarily rigorous, both to protect the doctrinal orthodoxy of the community, and to ensure that it did not become an asylum for miscreants and malefactors.

---

[7] *Returns*, i. 394–9. See also below, p. 255.

[8] Coussemaker, i. 346–54, ii. 235.

[9] P. M. Crew, *Calvinist Preaching and Iconoclasm in the Netherlands, 1554–1569* (Cambridge, 1978), p. 99. See also p. 243 below for Winghen's movements.

[10] See below, pp. 287–8.

The churches' handling of the problems posed by a constantly shifting membership provides impressive evidence of the sophistication of their contacts with Reformed communities abroad. The easiest way to secure speedy acceptance into the church was to produce a letter of recommendation from another Reformed community.[11] But inevitably many arrived in London without such a letter, either because they had not been members of a community abroad or because they had recently been constantly on the move. In this case they might expect careful examination to determine if they understood the fundamental doctrinal tenets of the church, and they would also be expected to produce witnesses who could testify to the sobriety of their lives abroad. Those who hoped that some inconvenient fact of their past life might remain concealed often found they had underestimated the resources of the church. On occasion new arrivals were pursued by a letter from the last church of which they had been a member testifying to their evil conduct, and the London churches would similarly warn brother churches against their own recalcitrant members.[12] Generally, however, a man had more to fear from his fellow church members, for it was the nature of the London community to have some other member who could throw light on events which the new arrival would rather had remained in the shadow. Hugh Serieu was refused permission to marry by the French consistory as they knew of his previous engagement to a girl in Antwerp, and the Dutchman Peter van Uden was frustrated in his attempt to escape from marriage with a servant-girl who had borne his child when witnesses appeared to testify to his relationship with her in the same town.[13] Faced with cases in which allegations of ill-conduct abroad were strenuously denied, the churches could often piece together the true facts of the case in a quite remarkable way. In 1571 Abel Conroyeur asked the French consistory to release him from his engagement with Catherine de la Deulle, whom he had discovered had been responsible for the death of a man in Antwerp. But witnesses were able to testify that the wound

[11] *Actes I*, pp. 42, 43, 46, 90, etc. An example of such a letter is preserved in the Dutch church archives. See Hessels, iii. 204–5.

[12] *KP I*, p. 276.

[13] *Actes I*, p. 35; *KP II*, pp. 53, 89, 92, 99, 137.

Catherine had inflicted had not been mortal, and that, in any case, Abel had known of the incident at the time of his engagement. The consistory decided that he should be held to his promise.[14]

When no witnesses came forward the church made its own enquiries, and took considerable pains to secure accurate information. Usually a request for information would be made to the minister of the local Reformed church, and from these and other references in the consistory minutes to communication with Reformed communities abroad, one can gain a fair impression of the range of the London churches' Continental contacts. The French church was most regularly in contact with the churches of the Low Countries, of which Antwerp and Valenciennes were pre-eminent. The church also had links with Lille and Tournai in the French-speaking region of Flanders, and after 1570 with the churches of Flushing and Middelburg in Zeeland. The influence of Geneva, though strong, is not very evident from the consistory minutes, but they do record the receipt of occasional letters from the principal French exile churches in Germany, at Emden, Frankfurt, and Wesel. Of the Huguenot churches in France, only Rouen and Orléans (the latter because of the presence of their former minister des Gallars) enjoyed regular contact with London.[15] The Dutch church had particularly strong links with Antwerp and Emden, and the consistory minutes also mention communication with Ghent, Brussels, Middelburg, Veere, Kortrijk, and Hondschoote in the Low Countries and the exile towns of Aachen and Frankfurt. From letters in the Dutch church archive it is clear that they were also in contact with Geneva and the refugee churches at Norden, Wesel, and Frankenthal, whilst their involvement in the troubles in the Low Countries brought exchanges of letters with Flushing, Dordrecht, Enkhuizen, Zierikzee, Schiedam, and Brill in addition to the communities listed above.[16]

It was only in very exceptional cases that the London churches dispatched a letter by special emissary. This was

---

[14] *Actes I*, pp. 16–20.
[15] *Actes I* and *Actes II*, passim. For the French ministers' contacts with Geneva see below, p. 273.
[16] *KP I* and *KP II*, Hessels, *passim*.

extremely expensive, and even if the church wanted to make urgent contact with a foreign community it was more likely to make use of one of its merchant members going in the right direction.[17] Yet it is clear from the consistory minutes that opportunities to communicate with the Continent by letter were frequent, and by no means confined to the consistory acting in an official capacity; indeed, the range and frequency of such contacts suggests the existence of something approaching a reliable postal network. When young couples came to the consistory to ask permission to marry it was usual to require them to present written authorization from their parents if they were still abroad. If they had not brought such authorization with them, they were told to write for it.[18] The frequent repetition of such an order suggests that it was both practical and economic for ordinary members of the London stranger community to communicate with their relatives abroad.[19] Much such mail was no doubt carried by friends and acquaintances amongst the merchant community who crossed the Channel regularly in the course of their normal business activities, but by the 1560s other more formal mechanisms had been developed. A remarkable collection of letters discovered in the archive of the Council of Troubles offers revealing evidence as to how communications were maintained even at a time of sustained persecution of the Reformed communities.

In February 1570 a boat travelling between St Omer and Calais was stopped and a young man on board apprehended. A search of his person and baggage revealed seventy-nine letters from residents of the French-speaking Netherlands, all addressed to co-religionists in England.[20] Through their chance survival these letters provide an invaluable record of the correspondence of ordinary members of the London foreign community with their friends and relatives on the Continent. The

---

[17] *Actes I*, p. 63. A messenger to the Prince of Orange in 1572 cost the Dutch church £12. Hessels, ii. 441.

[18] *KP I*, pp. 207, 286.

[19] On occasion young people did bring to the consistory letters they had received from their parents giving permission for their marriage. *KP I*, pp. 239, 264, 265.

[20] A. L. E. Verheyden, 'Une correspondance inédite adressée par des familles protestantes des Pays-bas à leurs coreligionnaires d'Angleterre (11 novembre 1569–25 février 1570)', *Bulletin de la Commission Royale d'Histoire*, 120 (1955), 95–257.

courier had gathered them up over a period of three weeks in the vicinity of Valenciennes and Lille. As he moved from town to town word of his destination was passed around, and many of the letters were written in haste to avoid missing him, one at five in the morning.[21] Anxious though these correspondents were to avail themselves of this chance of getting a letter to England, there are indications in the letters that many of them were in fairly regular communication: fifteen mention a letter received by the writer, many within the last month.[22] Contact between these inland towns in Flanders and England was not only fairly simple, it was evidently comparatively rapid. In one case a reply was written on 6 January to a letter dated 26 December,[23] and it was not exceptional for a letter to arrive within three or four weeks of dispatch.

These letters were written at the height of the persecution of the Council of Troubles, and the sophisticated lines of communication they reveal between England and Flanders must be seen against the background of strenuous efforts on the part of the authorities to limit contact between religious refugees and their friends and relatives at home. The archives of state and local authorities record their occasional success. In 1568 one Raes Pieters was condemned to be whipped and confined to his home parish for three years for carrying letters to England; another courier, Jean Pollet, was first examined under torture and then whipped and banished for ten years for transporting letters and goods destined for England to Calais.[24] The magistrates of Nieuwpoort apprehended Jean Bertheloos with forty letters for England,[25] but these isolated successes suggest rather the density of the traffic than the effectiveness of the authorities' attempts at interception. The government was aware that much more was getting through, and the frequent mentions of letters received in the Verheyden collection tend to bear out their suspicions.

The traffic across the Channel was by no means confined to letters: many of the exiles found the means to receive or

---

[21] Ibid., 128. 23 other letters are marked 'in haste'.

[22] Ibid., nos. 3, 4, 10, 12, 16, 18, 19, 25, 26, 27, 34, 36, 37, 45, 54.

[23] Ibid., no. 3.

[24] Coussemaker, iii. 260, iv. 126, 210.

[25] A. L. E. Verheyden, 'Le Protestantisme à Nieuport au XVIᵉ siècle', *Bulletin de la Commission Royale d'Histoire*, 116 (1951), 6–7.

send not only news but money and goods as well. Several of
the letters in this bundle mention money dispatched or given
to the courier to deliver, and other correspondents responded
to requests for clothes or essential papers.[26] Some who wrote
were unwilling to entrust sums of money to the road, but had
a private arrangement to enable money received in London
to be paid back at home. François Guilmart was promised
that anything he disbursed to the son of a friend (probably
his apprentice) would be repaid, and the wife of one recent
exile wrote that she had repaid the money her husband had
borrowed in London.[27] It is clear from this correspondence
that the Antwerp mart played an essential role in arrangements
for the transfer of resources between London and the Continent. The wife of Thomas le Clercq wrote that she had dispatched the stuff he wanted and thence onward as he asked,
and several other correspondents mentioned a recent visit or
a letter received via the metropolis.[28]

It might come as something of a surprise that such a large
proportion of these letters, all written to religious refugees,
should have contained references to business transactions. Yet
although the recipients of these letters had themselves been
forced to flee, many chose to leave behind members of their
families to carry on their business operations.[29] By maintaining
legitimate trading connections, these families certainly greatly
facilitated the dispatch of news and other goods for the sus-
tenance of the exile community. An instruction sent to the
magistrates of the Channel ports by the Governor in 1567 is
revealing in this respect. It had been reported that many were
leaving for England with their goods and furniture; the officers
of Nieuwpoort and Dunkirk were therefore instructed to
examine those taking ship, and whilst those who went to trade
were to be allowed to pass they were not to take with them
their furniture and utensils. A similar protest had previously
been made to the town magistrates of Ypres that many of the
bourgeois of the town were leaving and taking all their goods

[26] Verheyden, 'Correspondance inédite', nos. 35, 40, 46, 57, 65.
[27] Ibid., nos. 3, 9.
[28] Ibid., nos. 19, 30, 35, 41, 62.
[29] Ibid., nos. 15, 22, 24.

with them.[30] But more stringent controls at the ports did not prevent many exiles transferring property and resources to England. If they could not always carry goods with them, the value could frequently be realized by relatives left behind for the purpose. Some care had to be exercised, because the goods of those who had left their homes were liable to confiscation: the wife of one exile wrote that she had not yet made a sale because the King would take the profit.[31] Yet the relatives of other exiles had obviously succeeded in quietly selling property, or else were in the process of doing so. The sister of Guillaume le Mieux had raised over one thousand pounds from the sale of his goods, and had succeeded in paying less than thirty to the King's receiver in tax, whilst the wife of Jacques le Puys had remained behind to sell up their more humble stock of furniture.[32] The wife of Jean Dambrune wrote to ask whether she should sell up and follow him, or put their goods in the hands of friends.[33] Ruses of this sort were evidently widely practised: Eloy Bacler's goods were saved from confiscation, for instance, by being transferred to the nominal ownership of his children.[34]

The question of how much property exiles brought with them to England is of some importance. To the English authorities such prosperous newcomers were obviously much more attractive than penniless (albeit skilled) refugees; but from English sources it is often impossible to determine whether those immigrants who prospered did so with the advantage of imported wealth or purely on the strength of their energies in London. The evidence from these letters tends to support indications from other sources that many foreign immigrants did successfully transfer their resources with them. Philip Benedict suggests that in Rouen many departing Huguenots managed to circumvent decrees confiscating the goods of those that had left their homes, and cites a fascinating document from Montpellier, recording the efforts of city officials to levy a special tax on the Huguenots: few who had fled

[30] Coussemaker, iv. 320, 352.
[31] Verheyden, 'Correspondance inédite', 174–5.
[32] Ibid., 144–5.
[33] Ibid., 152.
[34] Ibid., 194.

were found to have left much property behind to be seized.[35] Some years earlier it has been noted that the Antwerp printer Stephen Mierdman was able to bring with him to England not only money but his printing type as well, and Jan Utenhove had been able to preserve much of his fortune (despite the confiscation of his goods by the Council of Flanders) by the device of a contract with his brother, ceding his share of their inheritance in return for a cash sum.[36] Peter Heuzeck, a former member of the London church, captured and interrogated by the authorities, claimed that Francis Bolle had arrived in London with eight hundred rix-dollars, and that Clays van der Scaert brought one hundred rix-dollars with him for a brother. It was Heuzeck who revealed that many exiles were returning with apparent impunity to buy in the markets of Flanders, a revelation which underlines the impossible task the authorities faced in limiting the flow of men, money, and goods.[37] With such large quantities of goods and capital travelling between England and Flanders in the normal run of trade it was almost impossible to prevent the wholesale movement of resources between the exile community and the Continent. If greater efforts of control made it more difficult to emulate Mierdman and remove all one's equipment and household goods, it was evidently by no means impossible, proceeding with due caution, to transfer much of the value of one's property with or after one into exile.

The comprehensive web of contacts between the refugees in London and their home communities, as revealed by the letters in the Verheyden collection, should not, of course, obscure the fact that, for many, exile involved considerable pain and hardship. There are frequent and poignant reminders of this in their correspondence. Several of the letters cited above are from parents separated from their children, and no fewer than twelve are to husbands from their wives.[38] Often the husband had gone on ahead of his family to find work and this seems to have been a characteristic experience in the London foreign

---

[35] Benedict, *Rouen during the Wars of Religion*, p. 144.

[36] Decavele, *Dageraad*, i. 80. Above, p. 91.

[37] Coussemaker, i. 346–54.

[38] Verheyden, 'Correspondance inédite', nos. 13, 21, 23; Ibid., nos. 3, 12, 15, 19, 26, 28, 31, 42, 45, 46, 73, 76.

community. Their wives coped valiantly with the responsibility of caring for their children alone, or even stoutly carried on their husband's business, but many clearly felt acutely the pain of separation: in several letters the wife asks whether the husband will soon return, or whether she should follow. One, Jacqueline Laurent, lamented that she had not heard from her husband for two years.[39] She feared that he had abandoned her, and although, happily, her fears proved groundless in this case,[40] there was a danger that some who left wife or family behind them would be tempted to separate themselves from former responsibilities and make, quite literally, a new life. In 1573 the French church in London refused communion to Jean le Clercq who had married here although he still had a wife in the Netherlands, and four years later Nicholas de Marchene was reported for taking a second wife while his first was still living abroad (he claimed she had deserted him).[41] The Dutchman Jan Holborn, his conscience awakened by an attack of the plague, admitted having abandoned his wife and three children in Ghent.[42]

The London churches were fully aware that without the utmost vigilance the number of such cases of bigamy and abandonment might be endlessly multiplied, and their strictest control was exercised over those who sought marriage in the church. Although circumstances often demanded that a man should come on ahead of his family to find work, the churches were careful to ensure that separation did not become permanent. In 1577 the Frenchman Jean Provost was sharply reminded of his duty to his wife, reported to be living in great poverty in Rouen. Barbe Cornelle, who had left her husband in Middelburg against his wishes, was ordered to return to him, notwithstanding her plea that she had suffered great want there, whereas in London she earned enough to keep herself and her children.[43]

[39] Ibid., nos. 12, 26, 28, 31.

[40] According to the return of aliens for November 1571, Jacqueline was by then living with her husband, Jean Dambrune, in the Blackfriars. *Returns*, ii. 16; see also *Actes II*, p. 13.

[41] *Actes II*, pp. 115, 203–4.

[42] *KP II*, p. 247.

[43] *Actes II*, pp. 171, 201. See Hessels, iii. 924, 932 for similar cases in the Dutch church in the 1590s.

It should be borne in mind, too, that although several letters speak of regular correspondence, the package cited so frequently above did go astray: contact between England and the Continent was never entirely reliable. The churches took account of this in their official correspondence to the extent that if the first copy of a letter had not arrived within a reasonable time a second was dispatched. But even with their privileged channels of communication the time letters took to travel between the churches might be extremely erratic.[44] After 1568, in view of the disruption caused to communications by the Troubles, the Dutch church was sometimes forced to waive the requirement that young people should have written permission to marry from their parents when it was proved that a genuine effort to obtain such permission had proved unavailing.[45]

Separation from home and family was one of the hardships of exile, but religious persecution could also on occasions result in considerable material sacrifice. Something of this is evident from wills left by members of the London foreign community. Whilst many refugees were able to bring the bulk of their property with them to England, others clearly suffered substantial losses as a result of their flight. Saint Demeurs was able to bequeath only small sums to her sister and to the French church, with the provision that a further £11 was to be distributed by her children 'if it pleased God to set them again in possession of their goods in the Low Countries'. Demeurs had fled from the Netherlands six years previously in 1568, and she and her children had been forced to lodge in the house of her sister and brother-in-law; she expressed her gratitude for this hospitality with a legacy of £3 per annum.[46] William Coppin had lost possessions on a much greater scale. The will he had previously made in Valenciennes was declared void as a result of his losses, and his wife, who had previously been left 2,700 *livres tournois*, had now to be satisfied with the remains

---

[44] Letters could reach the Dutch church in three days from Antwerp, but might take up to ten weeks. Hessels, iii. 149, 476. Fastest and slowest journeys from other places include Dordrecht: 5 days, 4 months; Enkhuizen: 10 days, 9 weeks; Emden 12 days, 5 months. Hessels, ii. 324, 420; iii. 177, 186, 216, 239.

[45] *KP II*, pp. 26, 60, 146.

[46] London Comm. 1574 (16, fo. 187). *Returns*, iii. 402.

of his goods. His son, who was to have had 1,400 *livres*, would now get three hundred, with another 400 'when liberty should be in the Low Countries and the profit and sale of my goods which are at Valenciennes may be made and my testament may be effected'.[47] Anthony de Keyser seems to have saved his own property but left an income to a cousin of £3 per annum 'until such time as it may please the Lord to grant her again and have that which she hath lost in the Low Countries for Religion's sake'.[48]

Wills occasionally provide a glimpse of the personal tragedy of a family divided by religious conflict. Jacques Sarrhe disinherited his kin in France 'because they knew God and had forsaken him'. Instead he wished his wife after her death to give half of all his goods to the poor of the French church.[49] John Merchant, in the event of his wife and children predeceasing him, gave one half of his goods to the poor of the French church and the other half to his kinsmen, but only 'if they be of our religion protestants'. If they were papists it was all to go to the French church.[50] Monica, the widow of Richard Mongie, left the arrears of rents due to her in Utrecht to her friends there, 'those which are in the monasteries only excepted'. These three nuns were to receive only one guilder apiece, but if they chose to leave their monasteries, 'forsake the papistry and follow the right religion according to God's word', then they might take their equal shares of the Continental property.[51]

These wills are a timely reminder that exile entailed considerable suffering and sacrifice for some who left property or prosperity behind them. The temptations to abandon Protestantism in favour of a return home must often have been strong. In 1571 the Dutch church considered the case of Hans Driesche, one of the newly elected elders. Driesche had served the Reformed community at Oudenaarde but after its dispersal had apparently written a letter to a local nobleman offering to abandon the Gospel if he would help him recover his land.

---

[47] PCC 1573 (26 Peter).
[48] PCC 1573 (2 Martin).
[49] London Comm. 1577 (16, fo. 316).
[50] London Comm. 1576 (16, fo. 259).
[51] PCC 1570 (12 Lyon).

Driesche did not deny having written the letter, but had not in the end sent it, preferring to suffer exile in England. The London church, not unsympathetic, decided that as he had ultimately resisted temptation he might take up the office to which he had been elected.[52]

Many refugees, then, faced separation and hardship as the price of their convictions, but the wills of those strangers who died in London also provide further impressive evidence for the continuity of contact between England and the Continent. A remarkable proportion of strangers whose wills have been traced, over 25 per cent, left goods or property abroad. Many of these, as one might expect, were merchants trading between England and the Continent. Glaude Sohier, a merchant of Valenciennes, left to his wife and children his interest and stock in his partnership there; he also left lands and rents in Tournai and Lille. John Lestuy left his wife 'all the rents of my marsh lands lying in the parish of Tree in Henego [Hainault]'.[53] Alexander Mynntley left goods at Liège, the town from which he traded, and Jacques de Boordes at Bordeaux and La Rochelle; his property was considerable, and he appointed executors in both London and La Rochelle.[54] John Adams's liquid capital seems mostly to have been in London, but he also left his children a rent of twenty-five guilders on property in the Low Countries, whilst the disposition of the lands of Hercules Freemantle at Watervliet in Flanders was covered by letters of inheritance registered there.[55]

Merchants who divided their time between London and the Continent had no reason to dispose of lands or goods abroad, although they might die with considerable stock in London. The need for a working capital abroad applied equally to foreign residents who, whilst permanently settled in London, were engaged in international trade, and several such men left instructions for the disposal of Continental property. Peter Boullen settled in England before 1568 and became an elder of the French church, but at his death in 1575 he bequeathed

[52] *KP II*, pp. 322, 324–6.
[53] PCC 1568 (18 Babington); PCC 1569 (12 Sheffield).
[54] London Comm. 1571 (16, fo. 84ᵛ.); London Comm. 1577 (16, fo. 350).
[55] PCC 1572 (2 Daper); London Comm. 1575 (16, fo. 216ᵛ.).

to his wife £1,000 and 'such lands as she hath at Breda'.[56]
Anthony de Keyser, a merchant from Tournai, was also in
England by 1568, but at his death, five years later, still had
his castle at Havynes to bequeath to a cousin.[57] Harmon Pottey
was one of the first Elizabethan influx and set up house on a
substantial scale at Billingsgate; his executors were instructed
to take all his keys and books and make an inventory of what
he had left abroad, for the profit of his wife and children.[58]

Such merchants might have been expected to leave goods
abroad, though Boullen and de Keyser were possibly exiles
who had not made an entirely free choice. More significant,
perhaps, is the number of non-merchant foreigners who left
goods or property abroad. Francis Derickson, a shoemaker
with considerable property in England, left his wife one
hundred pounds flemish to be raised on goods in Delft; the
rest of his property there was to go to his mother.[59] James
Matheenson, a painter who died in 1570, left his property at
Breda to be divided between his wife and children, and
appointed executors in Breda, Enghen, and London to carry
out his instructions (each was to have a picture as a keepsake).[60]
Renier Cuenilis, a tailor, had considerable property in England
but also rents through his wife on property in Antwerp, which
were to return to his wife's kinsfolk. James Isacke, another
tailor, left his goods in Brabant to his wife, who might sell
them if she wished.[61] Some of these strangers had, we know,
been in England a considerable time. Jasper van Dalem, a
surgeon, arrived in England about 1558 (not apparently having
any religious motive for coming). When he died in 1570 he
still had a house 'and appurtenances' in Delft which were to
be divided amongst his children.[62] Garrett Cook was apparently part of the first Edwardian wave of immigrants; he
arrived in 1547, and was made denizen in 1548. A cobbler by
trade, at his death in 1570 he had over £100 worth of property

[56] PCC 1575 (7 Pyckering).
[57] PCC 1573 (2 Martin).
[58] PCC 1574 (6 Pyckering).
[59] London Comm. 1564 (15, fo. 181ᵛ.). See *Returns*, i. 300.
[60] PCC 1570 (27 Lyon).
[61] PCC 1575 (37 Pyckering); Archd. London 1564 (3, fo. 52).
[62] London Comm. 1570 (16, fo. 6); see *Returns*, i. 310, 353, iii. 345.

in Gelderland in the hands of his father.[63] Another Edwardian arrival, Adam Effler, left to his eldest son fifty dollars in the hands of a friend living at 'Shatteleron' in the dominions of the Bishop of Cologne.[64]

At least four strangers who had settled in England in the reign of Henry VIII still had property abroad when they died many years later. Mark Adams, a cooper long established in East Smithfield, left lands in Liège to his wife when he died in 1566,[65] and the goldsmith Cornelis Bristow mentioned goods abroad when he died in 1567.[66] The longest-term residents in this group were Nicolas Dering and Matthew Tiseman. By the time of his death in 1574 Dering had been in England almost fifty years. A goldsmith, Dering seemed fully assimilated into the English community: he was a citizen of London, he left money to the poor of his parish church, and his daughters had married Englishmen. But he also remembered kinsmen in 'Hanibrowe', and amongst the considerable properties that he left to his wife and children were rents in Antwerp.[67] Matthew Tiseman had settled in London by 1535, but at his death in 1570 he still had property abroad and left the income to his daughter.[68] Tiseman had obviously been able to enjoy the income from his property abroad while in England, and had no doubt that his daughter would continue to do so: he left clear instructions that she was not to sell her inheritance.

Many of those who arrived in England during the Troubles seem also to have preferred to leave property abroad. Jacques Fourre, a schoolmaster first recorded in England in 1569, left his daughter a modest income through a part share in her mother's property in Landas.[69] Gratien de Roy seems to have arrived at about the same time; his will in 1574 revealed one

---

[63] London Comm. 1570 (16, fo. 10ᵛ.); *Returns*, i. 323; *Denizations*, p. 52.

[64] Archd. London 1575 (3, fo. 150); *Returns*, i. 461 (Efflewes).

[65] Archd. London 1566 (3, fo. 176); *Returns*, i. 22, 253; Guildhall Library, MS 5606 (Coopers Company Wardens' Accounts), fo. 83 *et seq.*

[66] Archd. London 1567 (3, fo. 207); *Returns*, i. 11, 334; *Denizations*, p. 32.

[67] PCC 1574 (38 Martin); *Returns*, i. 93, 411; Corporation of London, Letter Book Q, fo. 183.

[68] PCC 1570 (1 Lyon); *Denizations*, p. 232; *Returns*, i. 313, 327 (Tyse Tyseman).

[69] London Comm. 1574 (16, fo. 174ᵛ.); *Returns*, i. 396.

hundred guilders in ready money and two houses in Valenciennes amongst his assets.[70] James Soest, a surgeon who fled
for religion in 1571, left goods in Leiden to be divided equally
between his kin there and his wife in London when he died
four years later.[71] Given that those who wished to transfer
their capital to England seem, on the whole, to have been able
to do so, the fact that so many London residents left property
in their former homes at their death is highly significant. Several reasons may be advanced for their doing so. Many no
doubt came to England without having made any decision to
remain permanently, and if they hoped one day to return, the
laborious effort of selling-up was pointless. Even whilst they
were grateful for England as a refuge, the experience of Mary's
reign was fresh in the memory of many foreign residents, and
it may have seemed politic to maintain foreign property as a
form of insurance. In addition, when persecution in the Netherlands and France was intense, any large-scale sale of property
had to be conducted with some stealth for fear of confiscation
and, probably, as a result it would have been difficult to realize
the full value at short notice.[72] Many did sell up despite this,
but for others the most important consideration may simply
have been an unwillingness to cut links with their homeland,
particularly as it seems to have been possible to continue to
enjoy income from abroad. Helpful relatives might manage
the property, and the transfer of money and goods between
England and the Continent seems to have been perfectly feasible for many foreign craftsmen and traders.

Examples of the casual dispatch of money and household
goods have been cited from the Verheyden letter collection;
that such transactions were commonplace is the clear inference
to be made from the numerous examples of foreigners who
left legacies to friends and relatives abroad. Noe Pora left his
goods to a brother in Douai; in the absence of relatives in
England, his executors were members of the French church.[73]
Katherine Rouen left the bulk of her goods to a brother in
Valenciennes.[74] It was probably less troublesome for executors

[70] London Comm. 1574 (16, fo. 184); *Returns*, i. 395 (Gherart de Roy)?
[71] PCC 1575 (36 Pyckering); *Returns*, ii. 67.
[72] See Benedict, *Rouen during the Wars of Religion*, p. 144.
[73] London Comm. 1574 (16, fo. 172).
[74] London Comm. 1578 (16, fo. 419).

to advise relatives of a substantial inheritance than to see that numerous small legacies reached their destination. If Derick Everwyn's wife and children predeceased him, £3 were to go to each of his six brothers and sisters in Antwerp.[75] The merchant Herman Holman left his brother in Antwerp £1, and the beer-brewer John Adrians also gave instructions for a legacy of five crowns to be delivered to a brother there.[76] Adrians also left £3 to his mother in Julich, and another beer-brewer, John Mongoyen, left twenty crowns to a brother in the same town.[77] Stephen Pasman left £18 to his brethren, in unspecified places beyond the seas.[78] Hercules Freemantle left a bequest to Mistress Cuypers at Kortrijk, 'if she do live', and Gregory Wise may have puzzled his executors by leaving a quarter of his goods 'to the old maid at Hendrick . . . called Jane'.[79] Nicholas Sarasino requested his executors to send a letter to one Lawrence at Brussels concerning certain pictures he owned: if Lawrence sent word he might have them; otherwise they were to be sold to the profit of the poor.[80] While one must no doubt spare a thought for the unfortunate executors, on occasion charged with delivering legacies to persons only dimly remembered, the fact that wills so frequently included instructions for the disposal of goods to friends and relatives abroad suggests that it would generally have been possible for the executors to fulfil their obligations.

It should perhaps be of little surprise that between communities such as London and the towns of Flanders and northern France with long-established commercial ties, an apparently easy flow of information, goods, money, and people should continue, notwithstanding political and religious difficulties between the nations. The weight of commercial traffic made the flow of what were deemed less desirable commodities almost impossible to regulate, no matter how hard the authorities tried to keep a check on the journeyings of religious

---

[75] London Comm. 1575 (16, fo. 219ᵛ.).
[76] Archd. London 1578 (4, fo. 142ᵛ.); Archd. London 1567 (3, fo. 191ᵛ.).
[77] Archd. London 1563 (3, fo. 30).
[78] Archd. London 1569 (3, fo. 225ᵛ.).
[79] London Comm. 1575 (16, fo. 216ᵛ.); Archd. London 1575 (4, fo. 70).
[80] London Comm. 1577 (16, fo. 347).

dissidents and their means of comfort and support. By exploiting the network of merchants trading across the Channel, not
only the churches but comparatively humble foreigners were
able to keep in close contact with friends and events abroad.
In consequence, and because many foreigners came to England
for a comparatively short period, the foreign community in
London remained very much an open one, closely attuned to
events elsewhere. This openness caused the consistories certain
problems, but equally it enabled the London churches to have
an important influence on events on the Continent, to a consideration of which it is now necessary to turn.

From the time of the stranger churches' first foundation in
1550 it was envisaged that they might play an important role
in the promotion of the Reformation on the Continent. In his
letter reporting the establishment of the church to Henry Bullinger, Martin Micron expressed the hope that if the church
were granted a few years prosperity, great consequence in the
Low Countries might result. 'We shall attack our Flanders
with fiery darts', he eulogized, 'and, I hope, take it by storm'.[81]
The short life of the Edwardian churches ensured that Micron's
ambitious plans remained largely unfulfilled, but there is evidence that even in these early years Reformers in the Low
Countries appreciated the value of England as a refuge and
source of help. As early as 1549 Jan Sheerlambrecht of Bruges
was in contact with the future minister Karel de Koninck in
London. Sheerlambrecht was an important figure in the local
Reformed community, acting as a middleman between them
and London, and helping to spirit across the Channel monks
who wished to leave the religious life. He now asked de
Koninck's advice on doctrinal questions and received from
him according to the authorities 'diverse little books full of
abusive heresy and mistaken teaching, by diverse disapproved
authors'.[82] By 1558 several of the liturgical and polemical works
printed for the use of the Dutch church in London had been
included on the Index of forbidden books, a sure sign that

[81] *OL*, ii. 571.
[82] Decavele, *Dageraad*, i. 336.

they were circulating widely amongst the Reformed communities of the Netherlands.[83] The Antwerp martyr Jan van
Ostade also looked to the London community for comfort in
adversity, exchanging letters with Martin Micron in London
from his prison cell in the short interval between his arrest
and execution in 1551.[84]

The death of Edward VI in 1553 abruptly terminated these
early contacts, but even in this short time the main lines of
the exiles' contribution to the preservation and propagation
of the Reformed faith at home had been established. This
contribution was essentially fourfold: the provision of financial
help and advice for the clandestine congregations, and the
printing of Reformed literature and propaganda for their use;
the training of ministers and, most fundamentally, the provision of a secure refuge for reformers forced to flee from persecution. In all four respects the churches established during
Edward's reign were beginning to make an important impact.
That is not to say that, when the London churches were
restored in 1559, they automatically resumed their directing
role. In the interim of their enforced closure during Mary's
reign other exile communities had emerged to carry on their
work, notably at Emden and Wesel in Germany, and they
continued to exercise an important influence on the Reformed
movement in the Netherlands.[85] This was particularly evident
in the case of printing. The printers who were members of the
London Dutch church had in 1553 transferred their presses
to Emden, and they showed no inclination to shift their well-
established businesses back to England. Instead they kept up
a steady production of bibles, catechisms, and works of
Reformed propaganda for their co-religionists at home from
their base in East Friesland. These printed works included

[83] F. Heinrich Reusch, *Die Indices librorum prohibitorum des sechzehnten Jahrhunderts*
(Tübingen, 1886), pp. 68–70 (including the London catechism, the *Korte ondersoeckinghe
des gheloofs*, and the *Kort begrijp der leeringhe*).

[84] Jelsma, *Haemstede*, p. 21.

[85] Van Schelven, *Vluchtelingenkerken*, pp. 114–30, 281–301; D. Nauta, 'Emden, Toe-
vluchtsoord van Ballingen', in D. Nauta and J. P. van Dooren (eds.), *De Synode van
Emden Oktober 1571* (Kampen, 1971), 7–21; Philippe Denis, *Les Églises D'Étrangers en
Pays Rhénans, 1538–1564* (Paris, 1984), pp. 161–236; G. Moreau, *Histoire du Protestantisme
à Tournai, jusqu'à la veille de la Révolution des Pays-Bas* (Paris, 1962), pp. 127–32, 140–1,
298, 330, 387.

numerous editions of the catechisms and service books of
Lasco's London community, which enjoyed in consequence a
continued influence in the Netherlands throughout the 1560s.[86]
New editions were also printed in London but these were
primarily for the use of the exiles in England. The primacy
established by Emden in the printing trade was never seriously
challenged by the restoration of the London churches.

Nevertheless, the speed with which Continental reformers
reacted to the accession of Elizabeth and the subsequent re-
opening of the London churches suggests that the enormous
value of a secure refuge across the Channel was widely
appreciated. As early as June 1559 Philip's special envoy in
London, Aquila, was reporting the movement of large numbers
of people from the Low Countries to England; three years later
a survey conducted by the Lord Mayor of London found that
15 per cent of the foreigners in the capital were recently arrived
religious refugees.[87] In Flanders networks were established to
hurry those who fell foul of the authorities to safety: the Nieuw-
kerke reformer David Cambier had a servant whose special
responsibility it was to bring those who wished to escape to
the port, where they waited for a favourable opportunity to
cross the Channel.[88] It is as well to remember that by no means
all those who came to England were convinced Calvinists. In
many cases the experience of exile, and membership of the
stranger churches, turned a vague Reformed sympathy into a
deep and informed commitment to the faith. Several of those
who became committed reformers in exile returned to the
Continent as ministers, and the role of the London churches
in training ministers for service in the homeland was one of
their most significant contributions to the Reformation in the
Netherlands. Some twenty-five of the ministers active in Flanders and Brabant during the disturbances of 1566–8 had at
some point been in England; five came to England during the
Troubles before returning to preach, and fourteen made a

[86] Wijnman, 'Emigrantendrukkerijen', *Het Boek*, 36 (1963–4), 140–68. Paul Heinz
Vogel, 'Der Niederländische Bibeldruck in Emden, 1556–1568', *Gutenberg Jahrbuch*,
1961; Micron, *Ordinancien*, pp. 4–5; M. Nijhoff, 'Nederlandsche boeken in het buiten-
land gedrukt', *Bibliographische adversaria*, 1st series, V (1883–6), 243–61.

[87] KL, i. 541; *Returns*, i. 293.

[88] Decavele, *Dageraad*, i. 407.

more extended stay.[89] Almost all of those who had lived in
England came as newly converted reformers, and many were
from a humble artisan background. Erasmus Top and Jan
Lamoot were weavers, Peter Bert and Sebastian Matte were
both hatmakers.[90] Men of this sort were the principal benefi-
ciaries of the institutions established by the far-sighted founders of the community in 1550: the catechisms, examination of
doctrine, and in particular the mid-week exposition of scripture, all designed to improve the biblical and doctrinal knowledge of the congregation. After 1559, in addition, the London
churches instituted a separate examination for those who
wished to be advanced to the ministry. Candidates were
required to expound a chapter of scripture in a trial sermon
before the whole community, and the Dutch consistory minutes
for 1562 record that at least one candidate, Erasmus Top, had
successfully completed such an examination.[91]

Men who returned to minister in the Low Countries did
not necessarily go back to their home provinces. The exile
communities were quick to recognize an obligation to the whole
Netherlands. It has tentatively been suggested that the experience of exile was an important contributory factor in the
development of a sense of national unity in the Netherlands
during this period.[92] Exiles from different provinces would
meet together in a congregation abroad, and the regional par-
ticularism which so inhibited common action in the Netherlands might be eroded. The extent to which the London French
church contributed to the support of Reformed communities
well north of the language line is worthy of comment in this
connection.[93] The London communities certainly played an
important role in the developing unity amongst the churches
of the Low Countries. The congregations 'under the cross'
looked to London for advice in determining points of doctrine
and discipline, and the London churches played an important

[89] Crew, *Calvinist Preaching*, p. 98.
[90] *Returns*, i. 274, 275; Crew, *Calvinist Preaching*, pp. 186–7.
[91] *KP I*, pp. 69, 71, 74, 78.
[92] A. Duke, 'From King and Country to King or Country? Loyalty and Treason
in the Revolt of the Netherlands', *Transactions of the Royal Historical Society*, 5th series,
32 (1982), 125–6.
[93] Below, p. 255.

part in the discussions leading to the establishment of a common corpus of doctrine. On several occasions in 1560 and 1561, for instance, the church at Antwerp appealed to London for advice, with questions about marriage, baptism, and whether those who came to services but were not full members of the church should be subject to the discipline.[94] Similar enquiries continued even after formally constituted synods had begun to lay down clearer guidelines on these tricky issues in the 1570s and 1580s.[95]

The importance of London as a refuge, training centre, and source of comfort and advice for the Reformed movement in the Low Countries was not lost on the authorities there. From early in Elizabeth's reign determined efforts were being made to stem the flow of exiles through Flushing, and in 1562 officials at St Omer were instructed to prevent people making their way to England across the Flanders border and through Calais.[96] Any who had been to England and returned were immediately suspect: the royal agent Jacques Hessels was ordered to make a tour of the villages around Armentières to examine any who had returned from England, and even the testimony of the local *curé* that a man was perfectly orthodox was treated with scepticism.[97] In 1560, in an incident which sent shockwaves through the entire exile fraternity, three members of the London Dutch church who had returned to Veurne to visit their families were arrested and subsequently executed despite a plea for their lives by Bishop Grindal.[98] Yet in view of the stranger churches' record of turning men of little religious commitment into convinced Calvinists the authorities were right to be extremely wary of returning exiles, particularly in the light of mounting evidence that the exile communities were beginning to play a much more sinister role in the disorders at home. As religious dissent turned to open resistance it was increasingly apparent that many of the reformers' more aggres-

---

[94] *KP I*, pp. 42, 51, 104. The Dutch church referred the last of these questions to the *coetus. Actes I*, p. 25.

[95] Hessels, ii. 573, iii. 412.

[96] KL, i. 552–3; Coussemaker, ii. 69.

[97] Coussemaker, ii. 232–3. See also Titelmans' report, ibid., ii. 62.

[98] *Correspondance de Marguerite D'Autriche*, ed. M. Gachard, I (Brussels, 1867), pp. 250–4; *KP I*, p. 22; Decavele, *Dageraad*, i. 411.

sive initiatives originated in the exile communities in England.

In the years which followed the restoration of the exile churches in London the Reformed communities in the Netherlands enjoyed a phase of rapid if cautious expansion.[99] The authorities struck back, but frequent searches and arrests, and less frequent executions, could hardly check the progress of the new religion. As the Reformed grew in confidence there were those who argued that the faithful were not obliged to accept the ill-treatment meted out by their persecutors with docile resignation. The example of the Huguenots in France proved infectious, and from 1561 an increasing number of incidents occurred which manifested a new spirit of militancy. In many of these incidents the exile communities in England were heavily implicated. In November 1561 an armed crowd freed a Nieuwpoort reformer, Jean Hacke (a colporteur of Reformed books), from the prison at Mesen. This was the first of a number of similar raids, in the most famous of which the minister William Damman was freed from the prison at Ypres by a band which had come from England specifically to do the deed.[100] Two months later, in an equally dramatic gesture of defiance, the Reformed held a public service in the village of Boeschepe. The sermon, timed to coincide with the Mass, was preached in the cemetery to a congregation estimated at 150–200, many of whom carried weapons. The audacity of the act startled the authorities into a severe repression, and seventy-eight who were found to have attended the sermon were subsequently convicted and punished. Marcel Backhouse, who has investigated the events and aftermath of the preaching, has found no evidence that the local consistories of the Westkwartier were in any way involved in its organization.[101] On the other hand, there is evidence to suggest that the event may have been carefully planned in advance from England. The minister who preached, Ghilein Damman, had

---

[99] M. F. Backhouse, 'De verspreiding van het Calvinisme in Vlaanderen in de XVIe eeuw', *De Franse Nederlanden*, 1982, 62–79; Decavele, *Dageraad*, i. 322–434.

[100] Coussemaker, i. 348, iii. 74–5; A. A. van Schelven, 'Het begin van het gewapend verzet tegen Spanje in de 16e-eeuwsche Nederlanden', *Handelingen en Mededeelingen van de Maatschappij der Nederlandsche Letterkunde te Leiden*, 1914–15, 128–9.

[101] M. F. Backhouse, 'The Official Start of Armed Resistance in the Low Countries: Boeschepe 12 July 1562', *Archiv für Reformationsgeschichte*, 71 (1980), 198–224.

come from England for the sermon, and afterwards returned to Sandwich. Another who came specially from England was an elder of the Dutch church in London, Jan Lamoot; of these known to have been present no less than fourteen were registered as members of the London church in 1561, or of the community at Sandwich in 1562.

This progressive radicalization of the Reformed movement was not universally applauded. Indeed, the violent incidents of 1561 and 1562 set off a lively debate in which the exile communities were soon embroiled. The London ministers held resolutely to a pacific line and found themselves increasingly out of step not only with the leading Continental churches, but also with a substantial part of their own community. The thorny question of how far true believers might legitimately oppose the authorities seems first to have been raised in London with the receipt of a letter from the minister Godfrey van Winghen, then serving the churches in Flanders.[102] The consistory minutes for April 1561 record that the letter raised three principal issues: whether the faithful might defend themselves with weapons against the papists, whether clerics acting as inquisitors should be regarded as representatives of the authorities, and whether it was permissible to break open prisons to free arrested Reformers. The Dutch referred these questions to their monthly consultation with the French church, which returned an answer effectively ruling out armed resistance.[103] The question of prison-breaking was raised anew before the end of the year, after the release of Jean Hacke at Mesen. The freed man fled to Sandwich, and held a noisy and highly public party to celebrate his release, prompting an elder of the church to refer the matter to the consistory.[104] A conference was convened at the house of Jacob de Buzère, the minister of the community, attended by amongst others Peter Hazaert, one of the leading ministers in the Netherlands who condoned radical action. Hazaert and de Buzère were, however, opposed by a party amongst the elders, and the verdict

---

[102] *KP I*, p. 166. Winghen's letter is probably that printed in Hessels, ii. 334–7, misdated 1570 by the editor. See van Schelven, 'Het Begin', 135–6.

[103] *Actes I*, p. 38; *KP I*, p. 167.

[104] Van Schelven, 'Het Begin', 129, 134–5; Coussemaker, i. 348.

went against them. Hazaert returned to the Continent after the conclusion of the discussion somewhat disenchanted.[105]

These early discussions in England by no means settled the question of prison-breaking. The issue was raised once again at a conference of Reformed ministers held in Antwerp early in 1562. The synod, chaired by George Wybo (another minister who would play an important role in the later troubles in England) and attended by Hazaert and Herman Moded, decided that in certain circumstances prison-breaking might be justified, though they stopped short of actually condoning the use of armed force.[106] This qualification was not enough to satisfy the ministers of the London churches. Indeed, the letter dispatched to inform London of the synod's decisions produced such an intemperate reaction from Peter Delenus that it was resolved to send Moded and Hazaert to remonstrate with him in person. A conference in the London consistory in June effected some sort of reconciliation.[107] Delenus agreed that he had been wrong to allude to Thomas Müntzer and the anabaptists in his protest against the synod's decisions, and Hazaert and Moded both performed the conciliatory office of preaching to the congregation of Austin Friars before they returned to the Continent. But the ministers were unable to agree whether the Dean of Ronse, Titelmans, the chief inquisitor and most energetic persecutor of reformers, was protected from reprisals as a representative of the authorities, and a report of hard words spoken against Delenus by the Antwerp ministers on their return home broke the fragile peace. By the end of the year relations between London and the Antwerp ministers were effectively ruptured, with Moded refusing to sign letters of recommendation for persons coming to London.[108]

The first dispute foreshadowed difficulties of the same kind later in the decade. The divergence of opinion between London and a leading church of the Netherlands, in this case Antwerp,

---

[105] J. Decavele, 'Jan Hendrickx en het Calvinisme in Vlaanderen 1560–4', *Handelingen van het Genootschap voor Geschiedenis gesticht onder de Benaming Société D'Émulation te Brugge*, 106 (1969), 20–1; Coussemaker, i. 347.

[106] Van Schelven, Het Begin, 136–7; *KP II*, pp. 261, 268.

[107] *KP I*, pp. 320–2.

[108] *KP I*, pp. 322, 349, 397.

was already marked, as it would be at several points in the protracted debate, and there was always a certain amount of resentment to the rigorous line taken by London on such questions from the safe haven across the Channel. It is clear, too, that even at this early stage, the views advanced by the London consistory were by no means universally shared in the refugee community in the city. News of escapes from prison was eagerly received in England, and when William Damman was freed in May 1562 there was widespread rejoicing amongst the brethren, whatever the consistory might think.[109] Even in the London consistory it is by no means certain that Delenus enjoyed unanimous support for his point of view. In April 1562 the elder Jan Lamoot raised the question of resistance to the magistrate, and although it was not at this time discussed, one month later he was present at the armed preaching at Boeschepe.[110] The following April a member of the London church was forced to undergo a public penance for criticizing Delenus's preaching in Antwerp.[111] Thus far, at least, the London consistory was evidently able to impose its view on the community, but this became increasingly difficult as the events of the 1560s brought many new refugees to England. This movement seems to have effected a significant change in the nature of the membership of the London community, a change with an important bearing on subsequent events.[112] For the body of permanent, settled, long-term residents, concerned above all to preserve good relations with the English authorities, became a diminishing proportion of the community, whilst a growing number had personal experience of persecution and a firm commitment to the homeland. The established group, at first firmly in control of the consistory, increasingly found themselves imposing their views on members with grave misgivings as to the course of action dictated. It was this autocratic tendency which was, as much as anything, at the root of the troubles which focused on the turbulent figure of Godfrey van Winghen.[113]

[109] Hessels, ii. 165; Coussemaker, i. 348.
[110] *KP I*, p. 307; Backhouse, 'Boeschepe', 218.
[111] *KP I*, p. 399.
[112] Van Schelven, *Vluchtelingenkerken*, p. 143.
[113] On Winghen see *NNBW*, iii. 1433–7; Hessels, ii. 50 n. 2.

The London community was at first extremely grateful to have a minister of experience to whom it could turn when the plague epidemic of 1563 carried off both Peter Delenus and Nicholas Carineus within a month. Winghen had been in England during the first years of the church's life, when he had been employed as tutor to John a Lasco's children.[114] He moved with the ministers to Emden in 1553, and there assisted Utenhove with his translation of the New Testament into Dutch. After Utenhove left Emden for Poland the wearisome responsibility for the publication of the Testament seems to have fallen largely on Winghen, who was bitterly disappointed at its poor reception.[115] In May 1559 Winghen was invited by the Emden consistory to serve as a minister in Flanders, where his periods of service were interspersed with two brief sorties to England, to London with Utenhove at the end of 1559, and to Sandwich in 1561.[116] Towards the end of 1561 Winghen travelled to Frankfurt at the request of the Dutch refugee church there to attempt to mediate their quarrel with the Lutheran town authorities, but despite being furnished with a letter of recommendation from Grindal, Winghen was unable to achieve the desired reconciliation, and by May 1562 he was back in England and established as minister in Sandwich.[117] When the London church found itself without a minister Winghen was quick to offer his services, and by the end of 1563 he was serving as sole minister to the London church.[118]

One of Winghen's first acts as minister in London was to issue a decree that any father seeking baptism for his child had first to submit a declaration by two persons willing to act as witnesses.[119] It is not immediately clear why this order should have been so controversial, although the apologetic tone in which it was presented suggests that opposition was expected. The decree pointed out that such an order was not

---

[114] Though he is not recorded in the first register of the Dutch church. See Utenhove, *Simplex et Fidelis Narratio, BRN,* ix. 114, 127.

[115] Hessels, ii. 50, 63.

[116] *NNBW, iii.* 1434. See also Hessels, ii. 75–6.

[117] Grindal to the magistrates of Frankfurt, 12 Nov. 1561, Grindal, *Remains,* pp. 247–52; Hessels, ii. 195.

[118] Hessels, ii. 217, 221.

[119] The best account of the controversies raised by Winghen is in van Schelven, *Vluchtelingenkerken,* pp. 152–78. See also Lindeboom, *Austin Friars,* pp. 46–51.

in conflict with holy scripture, nor was it an outright innovation, as Lasco had made a similar provision in his *Forma ac
Ratio*.[120] It is perhaps only possible to understand the strong
feelings that the order provoked in terms of the Continental
situation. For the consistory the order must have seemed a
reasonable extension of the controls necessitated by the pace
of new arrivals from overseas. When new arrivals requested
marriage in the church, it was often the case that little was
known of their background. The witnesses at baptism were
intended to guarantee that a child had been born of parents
who were entitled to membership of the church; in other words,
the child was a true offspring of the community. Against this
opponents of the order might argue that the matter was one
of church order rather than of divine prescription, and that
in such an indifferent thing members should not be forced to
accept an institution against their consciences; behind such
an argument, however, there seems to have been a deeper
uneasiness about the institution of godparents. The issue had
been briefly controversial in Lasco's day, when Gualter
Delenus had mentioned godparents amongst his objections to
the church order, and there may have been resonances from
the Haemstede affair of the previous year.[121] As in that case,
the real objection of the consistory's opponents may have been
an unwillingness to see the community too narrowly drawn
by an insistence on proof of the doctrinal orthodoxy of newcomers. With a constant stream of new arrivals from the Continent,
by no means all the church shared the consistory's wish to
limit membership to those wholly orthodox, and there was a
deep seam of sympathy within the community for the sectaries
and radicals persecuted along with the Reformers in the
Netherlands.[122]

An appreciation of such deeper resonances may be necessary
to understand the widespread sympathy for the deacons in
their objection to the new ordinance. The objectors initially
numbered six, and in the case of their spokesman, Bartholomew Huysman, resentment may have been fuelled by an
old feud with Winghen dating from the time of their association

<hr>

[120] *Lasco Opera*, ii. 106; *Toute la Forme*, p. 67ᵛ.
[121] See above, pp. 64, 170 ff.
[122] For a remarkable instance of such fellow feeling see Decavele, *Dageraad*, i. 335.

in Emden over the publication of Utenhove's New Testament.[123] The intransigence of the consistory, however, soon
united the deacons in opposition, and by June the dispute was
serious enough to require the arbitration of Sandwich.[124] The
ministers were at this point prepared to concede that none
who objected to godparents should be forced to accept them,
but a subsequent insistence that any who had opposed the
consistory should recognize this as a fault was in clear breach
of the spirit of the compromise, and the angry deacons
threatened resignation. The consistory was inclined to accept
these resignations and fill their places by co-option, doubtless
with reliable supporters, so the deacons withdrew their offer
until such time as they were promised a free election to replace
them.

The resignation threat gave the dispute a new aspect, raising
the issue of whether authority for the election of office-holders
lay with the consistory or with the whole community. Deadlock
appeared total, and so the matter was referred to Grindal.
The superintendent heard submissions from both sides, and
then, predictably enough, issued a judgement which substantially backed the minister.[125] The deacons and their supports
had by now set their sights on a new election for all office-
holders, and during the summer they referred their case both
to a group of English preachers and to the churches of Antwerp
and Emden for arbitration. Here they could expect a more
sympathetic reception. Antwerp, perhaps still smarting from
the criticisms of the London consistory over prison-breaking,
returned a letter sharply critical of the consistory, and Emden
too was by no means unsympathetic towards the deacons.[126]
The Emden church, however, was not prepared to condemn
Winghen unheard, and in a response to their request for further
information the London consistory dispatched a comprehensive account of its proceedings.[127] Meanwhile the deacons had
provided impressive evidence of the extent of the support for

---

[123] Huysman was the bookseller charged with selling the ill-fated edition. Hessels,
ii. 63.
[124] Van Schelven, *Vluchtelingenkerken*, pp. 158 ff.
[125] Hessels, iii. 36–7.
[126] Van Schelven, *Vluchtelingenkerken*, pp. 160–1.
[127] Printed by van Schelven, op. cit., pp. 345–64.

their point of view within the community. A letter in the Emden church archive, dated 16 October, was signed by a total of 120 supporters of the deacons' party, sixty-eight men and fifty-two women.[128]

With the arrival of the consistory's submission the Emden church was prepared to give judgement, but at this point news arrived from England of a new reconciliation. This was effected by the bishop and a group of English arbitrators, together with Jean Cousin, the minister of the French church. Although the deacons made the most substantial concessions the consistory did not have all things all its own way.[129] The deacons agreed to accept godparents and expressed their readiness to obey those in authority in the church, acknowledging the competence of the minister in matters of faith and doctrine. But they had the comfort of Grindal's opinion that to refuse to take godparents was not a mortal sin, a view expressed on his behalf by the English minister Calfhill when he announced the settlement from the pulpit of the Dutch church.[130] On the question of elections the competence of the whole church was re-asserted; this was a crucial point as the consistory had accepted that a new election would be held when the church was once again in a state of calm. With these important concessions the deacons were prepared to ask forgiveness for their conduct, and the minister and elders in return confessed that they had acted over-hastily. The reconciliation was sealed at a meeting of all parties in Grindal's house, where the bishop provided his customary balm of hand-shaking and communal drinking.[131]

This was not an outcome to satisfy a man of Winghen's disposition, and the fragile peace did not last beyond the spring of 1565. The consistory proved reluctant to proceed with the promised new election, and caused great offence by refusing to accept a minister whom they had requested from Emden

---

[128] Emden, Kirchenarchiv, MS 320 A 58/1–2. The list appears to be longer because the second folio repeats many of the names of the first. I am most grateful to Mr Alastair Duke for providing me with a photocopy of this document.

[129] Hessels, iii. 38–40.

[130] Ibid. *Actes I*, p. 88.

[131] *Actes I*, p. 87.

to share Winghen's duties, apparently on the grounds of over-much familiarity with the deacons.[132] The dissidents seem now to have believed that only Winghen's resignation would heal the breach, and although Grindal reaffirmed his support for the minister in a new Formula of Pacification in July,[133] it proved once again necessary to turn to Emden for help. In September the respected minister Cornelius Cooltuyn and a colleague arrived in London to arbitrate, and in spite of the coolness of the consistory, who refused to join the superintendent and deacons in giving the arbitrators full powers, over the next six months a new settlement was arrived at.[134] Once again it was the deacons who made most concessions, accepting the institution of godparents and finally abandoning their demands for a new election. They secured only the concession that those who could not accept the settlement might withdraw to an English parish church, and it is a measure of the disenchantment with the consistory's autocratic demeanour that many did so. On a list, submitted by the church in 1568 of former members who now frequented English churches, no less than twenty-four of the thirty-five named are identifiable as members of the deacons' party from the petition presented to Emden.[135] At some point the deacons withdrew from the church in a body, and a portion of the community began meeting separately; the consistory minutes from these years are lost, but a letter in the Dutch church archive refers to a time when the deacons had separated from the community, and taken their account-book with them.[136] An apparently small dispute over the institutions of the church had taken a heavy toll amongst its most committed and conscientious members.

Nor were the church's troubles yet at an end. Within a few months of the settlement negotiated by the arbitrators from Emden the hedge-preaching had broken out in Flanders, to be followed later in the year by a wave of iconoclastic attacks

---

[132] Van Schelven, *Vluchtelingenkerken*, pp. 162–3.

[133] Ibid., pp. 374–5.

[134] Cooltuyn's dispatches to Emden are printed by van Schelven, ibid., pp. 375–82.

[135] *Returns*, i. 386. Collated with the document cited in n. 128.

[136] Hessels, ii. 210–12. See also the letter of the deacons' party, van Schelven, *Vluchtelingenkerken*, pp. 385–90, and Cousin's letter to the church at Geneva, 1 May 1568, Schickler, *Églises du Refuge*, iii. 69–73.

on churches and monasteries. The iconoclasm evoked a sympathetic response amongst the exiles, and indeed was initiated
by two ministers who had recently crossed the Channel from
England, so when Winghen in the summer of 1566 reasserted
the former position of the London church condemning such
violence, renewed dissension was the inevitable result.[137] Winghen's outburst brought a renaissance of the deacons' party,
and the battle with the consistory was rejoined. The fires of
controversy were fuelled by the publication of a pamphlet by
one of the elders, Jan Engelram, sharply criticizing the violence
and denouncing the deacons.[138]

An attempt to secure mediation from Norwich proved unsuc-
cessful, as the minister there, perhaps wisely, refused to become
involved, and a further reassertion of support for Winghen by
the bishop in a decree of December 1567 similarly failed to
heal the breach.[139] This latest order, in fact, rather deepened
the rift, as Grindal ordered that all who had separated themselves from the Dutch church should now return, on pain of
being judged contumacious. Five of the consistory's opponents
were imprisoned at this time.[140] Some of the deacons' party,
however, preferred not to wait for the bishop's judgement, but
instead withdrew to Norwich, where they were welcomed by
a church much more sympathetic towards direct action on the
Continent. The consistory in London was by no means pleased
by the action of its sister church in welcoming the rebels, and
the dispute now took on the extra aspect of a conflict between
the two churches.

The London church decided on decisive action, and drew
up twenty-seven articles which it insisted its opponents should
sign.[141] These articles effectively asserted the right of the consistory to impose an autocratic discipline. The limits of Christian freedom were severely circumscribed, as were the rights
of individuals to scruples on matters of conscience. Those who
disobeyed officers of the church were roundly condemned, and
in a reference to Norwich, so too were churches which accepted

---

[137] Parker, *Dutch Revolt*, pp. 74–5; Van Schelven, *Vluchtelingenkerken*, pp. 166 ff.
[138] Van Schelven, 'Johannes Engelram', *Stemmen des tijds*, V (1916), 179–86.
[139] Hessels, ii. 276, iii. 55–6.
[140] *Cal. S. P. Span. Eliz.*, 1558–67, p. 690.
[141] Van Schelven, *Vluchtelingenkerken*, pp. 168–9.

members who had been excommunicated elsewhere. The articles took the trouble to defend the institution of witnesses in baptism, demonstrating that the issues which divided the church were connected in the eyes of the consistory as well as of their opponents. (The Spanish Ambassador, in fact, believed that the issue of godparents was still central in the dispute.[142]) A final section contained an uncompromising rejection of any right of resistance to the authorities.

These articles were immediately submitted for comment to leading Continental churches. The Emden church, twice prompted, returned only a very lukewarm response, but the London church's major effort was on this occasion directed towards Geneva. The choice of Geneva was significant, as the consistory may well have realized that it had by now little hope of a favourable judgement from the churches of the Netherlands: given Calvin's former strictures on resistance to lawful authority the Swiss church must have offered a much better prospect of securing agreement to the London church's viewpoint.[143] The two emissaries of the London consistory, Jan Engelram and William Mayard, reached Geneva in June 1568, three weeks after a deputation from Norwich sent to put their point of view (a deputation led by the minister Herman Moded, who had already crossed swords with London over the issue of resistance and was now serving a term as minister there).[144] The judgement of the Venerable Company was broadly favourable to the London consistory. Although the tone of the London articles was criticized, there was little quibbling at the substance, and the Bishop and Winghen were sufficiently satisfied with the reply to have it printed in three languages (Dutch, English and Latin) on the emissaries' return.[145] Engelram and Mayard, though, had also canvassed the opinions of other leading Swiss churches before their return, and from these the response was much less favourable. Berne and Zurich limited

---

[142] *Cal. S. P. Span. Eliz.*, 1558–67, p. 690.

[143] Van Schelven, 'Het Begin', 141–56.

[144] *Registre de la Compagnie des Pasteurs, III, 1565–1576*, ed. O. Fatio (Geneva, 1969), p. 19. On Moded see above, p. 241.

[145] Van Schelven, *Vluchtelingenkerken*, pp. 171–4. The judgement of the Genevan ministers is printed in *Correspondance de Théodore de Bèza*, 9, ed. H. Aubert (Geneva, 1978), pp. 220–30. The Dutch version is in Ruytinck, *Gheschiedenissen*, pp. 67–77, and the English in Strype, *Grindal*, App. 28.

their reaction to a general exhortation to reconciliation, and it may have been the softening impact of these letters which encouraged the church to embark on a further effort to make up its differences through the winter.[146] A conference with Norwich was arranged, and after this a putative agreement was reached. Crucial to this was the ministers' concession that the long-sought fresh elections should now take place.

It is hard to know how Winghen was finally moved to make this vital concession. Possibly the fact that he was no longer the sole minister of the church was of some importance. After two abortive efforts to find Winghen a colleague in his ministry to a congregation which was probably growing rapidly at this time, the consistory had, by March 1568, called George Wybo from Emden.[147] By the end of the year Wybo, after some initial reluctance, accepted the post, and his arrival made an immediate impact. As a highly respected and senior figure in the Reformed church Wybo was able early in 1569 to make suggestions designed to settle difficulties over authority and disputes in the church,[148] and it was probably he who steered the warring parties towards the agreement of April. Equally important was the fact that Wybo held views on the question of resistance very different from those of Winghen. He had taken the chair at the Antwerp synod of 1562, and Winghen's supporters would later accuse him of several attacks on the minister in London.[149] By the proposed form of pacification those who had separated themselves from the church agreed to accept any penance imposed by the French ministers, acting as arbitrators.[150] In return the minister recognized that he had exceeded the limits of forbearance, but the real concession was in the matter of the election. It had been suggested in a letter to Emden that Winghen had lost the confidence of the majority of the community as early as 1565,[151] but now, certainly, the elections were an unmitigated disaster for him and his supporters. The new consistory and deacons were solidly from that

[146] Van Schelven, *Vluchtelingenkerken*, pp. 173–5. The Genevan ministers also made clear their reservations about the way in which the consistory had conducted themselves in a private letter. *Registre de la Compagnie des Pasteurs*, iii. 250–3.

[147] Van Schelven, *Vluchtelingenkerken*, p. 176; Hessels, ii. 291.

[148] Hessels, ii. 311.

[149] Ibid., ii. 362–3.

[150] Ibid., ii. 315.

[151] Van Schelven, *Vluchtelingenkerken*, p. 175, n. 6.

part of the community hostile to his views, and included some who had been in opposition as early as 1565.[152]

The old consistory, used as they were to the exercise of authority, did not take their removal lightly. The minutes of the new consistory are full of cases brought by their predecessors, mostly claims for money owing to them, as if to emphasize how they had served the community with their time and substance over the previous decade. Five former elders made some sort of financial claim, and when these were not met, they promptly seized the books and papers of the community still in their hands, and refused to hand them over to their successors.[153] Demonstrations of this sort could not, however, alter the new realities of the church's government, and Winghen could expect no sympathy when, frustrated and isolated, he repeated his strictures on the image-breakers in June 1570. Examined by the consistory, Winghen refused to retract his view, and on 16 July he was suspended from the ministry.[154]

Winghen's former colleagues now rallied to his defence, while the minister himself refused to attend the consistory and ostentatiously sat in the body of the church during services.[155] Some of the deacons also expressed misgivings over his suspension, and after Winghen had secured a mandate from the bishop reserving the case to his judgement, his supporters presented a comprehensive indictment of the proceedings of their opponents, going back to the synod of Antwerp in 1562, and not neglecting to associate the opinions of those who condoned resistance with the anabaptist error which tainted their nation: once again the case for authority was being made in terms of the safeguarding of doctrinal orthodoxy.[156] But now it was Winghen and his supporters who were the dissidents, and the decision of the bishop (now Sandys) was by no means entirely favourable to him.[157] The consistory was reproved for suspending the minister without consultation and Winghen was restored, but the judgement equally criticized Winghen

[152] For instance Hubrecht Elinck and Melchior van As. *KP II*, p. 3. Van Schelven, *Vluchtelingenkerken*, p. 390.
[153] *KP II*, pp. 13, 35, 36.
[154] Ibid., pp. 160, 165–71, 179.
[155] Ibid., pp. 179, 182.
[156] Ibid., pp. 183, 193–4. Hessels, ii. 357, 361.
[157] *KP II*, pp. 257–9.

for his indiscriminate condemnation of those who resisted authority in the Low Countries.

With that, the matter seems finally to have been laid to rest. With the revolt of 1572 and the support of the States of Holland, which rendered it legitimate even in the eyes of Winghen, the minister was one of those who returned to the homeland to serve the new Reformed communities; his reappointment to the ministry in London in 1574 proved that there were no enduring hard feelings there. By 1576, the appointment of godparents, no longer a controversial issue, was left to the conscience of the individual.[158] If the storms that afflicted the London Dutch community in the 1560s may seem to the observer bewilderingly disproportionate to the importance of the point at issue, the final outcome was of considerable significance for the future character of the community. For the election of the new consistory in 1569 represented to a large extent the triumph of those determined not to be separated from the events and concerns of the homeland, and a repudiation of those who sought the protection of a narrow orthodoxy in comfortable isolation and security. In the following decades London was once again an important source of support for the Reformed communities in the Netherlands. In the meantime, however, the protracted dispute had taken its toll, not least where London's influence on the wider reformed movement was concerned. In the Netherlands leading Reformed communities such as Antwerp found themselves increasingly disenchanted with the views of the London hierarchy, and inclined to look elsewhere for direction and assistance.[159] Even in England the initiative passed increasingly to the exile communities in Norwich and Sandwich which made no secret of their sympathy for radical initiatives. It was no coincidence that one of those who began the image-breaking in August 1566 was Jacob de Buzère, minister of the Dutch church at Sandwich, and after the collapse of the Revolt in the spring of 1567 resistance was continued by a band of marauders recruited in Norwich and Sandwich, who carried out a series

---

[158] Lindeboom, *Austin Friars*, p. 51.

[159] To Emden, for instance. In 1563 Herman Moded went to Emden in person to put to the consistory there questions on church discipline of the sort previously referred to London. Emden Kirchenarchiv, Kerkeraadsprotocollen, 5 Apr. 1563.

of brutal attacks in Flanders before being rounded up early the following year.[160] The organization of the first synod of the Dutch Reformed church (which met in Emden in 1571) went ahead in the years after 1569 almost without reference to London.[161] This was a measure of the extent to which London's directing role had been forfeited as a result of a decade of internal strife.

Nevertheless the London churches still had an important role to play and the following years saw them emerging once again to a position commensurate with their status as the biggest and richest of the exile communities. The election of a more sympathetic consistory was followed in 1572 by the revolt of Holland, an event which brought a complete transformation in the prospects of the rebellion, and evoked an immediate and enthusiastic response from the London communities. The London churches had provided William of Orange with a certain amount of rather cautious financial assistance for his campaign in 1568, and again in 1570,[162] but when the Sea Beggars landed at Flushing and Brill in April 1572 their support was on an altogether different scale. Alva's agents reported the recruitment of over 500 troops from amongst the refugees within a fortnight, and by the end of the month the London congregations had raised £500 to buy arms.[163] This prompt aid by no means satisfied the rebels, and over the next months the Dutch community was bombarded with appeals for help, coming direct from the beleagured towns as well as from the consistory of Antwerp and William of Orange himself.[164] Flushing and Enkhuizen appealed for men, victuals, artillery, and ammunition, and although the Dutch consistory sent an emissary to collect contributions from the East Anglian communities, the main burden of support fell

---

[160] On de Buzère see *NNBW*, iii. 179; Crew, *Calvinist Preaching*, pp. 11, 41, 98, 99. After 1567 de Buzère was joined in the ministry of the Sandwich church by two ministers, William Damman and Isbrand Balck, who were themselves no strangers to radical action. See Crew, op. cit., pp. 45, 49; M. F. Backhouse, 'Guerilla War and Banditry in the Sixteenth Century: The Wood Beggars in the Westkwartier of Flanders (1567–1568), *Archiv für Reformationsgeschichte*, 74 (1983), 232–55.

[161] J. P. van Dooren, 'Voorbereiding en deelnemers', in *De Synode van Emden*, 75–81.

[162] Hessels, ii. 293, 302. *Cal. S. P. Span. Eliz.*, 1568–79, p. 55.

[163] KL, vi. 384–5, 395.

[164] Hessels, ii. 397, 400, 412, 420, 423.

on London. By the end of the year some £1,400, had been
raised for Flushing, and the money used to equip 200 soldiers.
In addition some of the richer members had fitted out fifty
men on their own account, and others had acted as sureties
for the ammunition purchased on behalf of Flushing and dispatched thence with an elder of the church, Lieven de Herde.[165]
The support of the London community did not stop at men
and munitions for the military effort. In the towns which had
declared their support for the Beggars the insurgents wasted
no time in setting up Reformed communities, but they were
hampered by an acute shortage of ministers. The London
church was quick to respond to their urgent appeals for assistance, and by the end of the year two of the three London
ministers, Winghen and Bartoldi Willhelmsoen, had departed
for Holland.[166] In the spring of 1573 two new ministers were
appointed to fill their places; Johan Cubus, a learned young
man who had acted as secretary to the important synod held
in Antwerp in 1567, and Jacob Regius, who at the time of his
appointment was ministering to a small Dutch congregation
at Coventry.[167] These new ministers were soon themselves the
object of renewed appeals for help, but the London community
understandably declined to release them.[168] Notwithstanding
their undoubted commitment to the cause, the London communities were soon finding it increasingly difficult to meet the
repeated demands of Orange and their embattled co-
religionists. Orange appealed to the London churches a further
four times, with varying degrees of civility, during the course
of 1573, and although they did manage to find a further £100
at the end of the year, the churches' resources were not endless,
and several of Orange's demands went unheeded.[169] But in
these, the most desperate years of the Revolt, Orange had
little option but to continue to extract what help he could from
the London exiles. In 1575 a new embassy was dispatched,
led by the former London elder Lieven de Herde to seek the
exiles' help in rearming his ships and fortresses, though it was

[165] Ibid., ii. 403–9, 437–42. See also *Cal. S. P. Span. Eliz.*, 1568–79, pp. 390–4, 401.
[166] Hessels, iii. 173, 192.
[167] Hessels, iii. 205, 206; *NNBW*, iv. 1130–2.
[168] See Hessels, iii. 217.
[169] Hessels, ii. 445, 454, 471, 490; Ruytinck, *Gheschiedenissen*, p. 99.

extremely unlikely that the London churches could have provided the hundred iron cannon which Orange suggested as their contribution.[170]

In the face of these unremitting demands for more men, munitions, and financial help, it was extremely important that the French community was prepared to play a full part in shouldering the common burdens. In April 1572 the French had provided a large proportion of the money and troops raised for the Flushing campaign, and the bilingual Saravia (a former minister of the Walloon church in Antwerp) was one of the first to answer the call for ministers to serve there.[171] The French contribution in the spring of 1572 is a timely reminder that events in the Netherlands had as great an impact on the French church in London as did events in France. This became increasingly evident as the refugees who had fled to England after the St Bartholomew's Day massacre returned to the Continent. Immigration from France tended to be of short duration; a sudden influx would be followed, after the promulgation of one of the numerous edicts of toleration during the French Wars of Religion, by an equally prompt return.[172] French immigrants caught the eye in London, partly because they numbered amongst them a high proportion of ministers and gentlemen who were able to make their presence felt at Court. But it was the victims of the sustained persecution in the Netherlands who made up the greater proportions of the membership of the church.[173] As a result the French church in London had a curiously hybrid character, with a largely Walloon membership and consistory presided over by a succession of distinguished French ministers from leading French Reformed communities, who maintained close ties with Geneva and a continued interest in events in France. There

[170] Hessels, ii. 513, 520.

[171] KL, vi. 395, 412; *Actes II*, p. 96; Willem Nijenhuis, *Adrianus Saravia* (Leiden, 1980), pp. 15, 22–3.

[172] Schickler, *Églises du Refuge*, i. 153–6, 185–97, 223–5.

[173] In the late 1560s as many as two-thirds of the church's members came from the Low Countries. The Return of Aliens of 1568 recorded only twelve hundred Frenchmen in the city, at a time when the membership of the French church was over eighteen hundred. Since half these Frenchmen probably attended parish churches, the balance of the church's members (twelve hundred) must have been Netherlanders. Returns, iii. 439. For the French ministers and nobles in London see Schickler, *Églises du Refuge*, i. 148–53, 198–200.

was no sign, however, that this dichotomy was ever the cause of any strain within the community, perhaps because the French church was so quick to recognize its obligations in the Netherlands. The French church was included in the invitation to the Synod of Emden, and would clearly have participated as an equal partner had the churches been permitted to send delegates: a meeting in the French consistory had nominated Cousin and Winghen as joint representatives of the churches in England.[174] After 1572 Orange was able to address his appeals to both churches equally, and even at one point claimed that the French had been more generous to him. (Possibly this was a ploy to extract further contributions from the Dutch.)[175] When in 1576 Orange and the Queen were briefly at loggerheads the churches deputed the French minister de Villiers to try to mediate an agreement between them, and two years later he took up permanent service with Orange.[176]

By 1576 the rebels' prospects of success were much improved, but the strain imposed on the exile communities by their enormous efforts on behalf of the insurgents was increasingly evident. Their difficulties were compounded by the fact that the burden of meeting these obligations was falling on a rapidly diminishing membership. As the rebels' hold on Holland was consolidated many exiles returned to the Netherlands, and this included many of the more prosperous members of the exile churches. The smaller communities in Kent and East Anglia were the first to feel the effects of this return. Already in 1576 the churches at Yarmouth and Dover appeared to be on the point of collapse, and by the following year the community at Maidstone was also beginning to break up. Even the largest provincial community at Norwich was reporting serious problems by 1578, with eight of their twelve elders either having returned to the Netherlands or on the point of doing so.[177] The London churches were forced to take increasing responsibility for maintaining these smaller communities either with financial support or with the loan of one of their own ministers.[178] But the London communities were also seriously depleted during these years. In November 1576 the church at Sandwich sent an urgent plea that the many members of the London church passing through the town should be provided with sufficient travelling money. The following year the Prince of Orange lent his support to a scheme to resettle members of the London churches at Haarlem and Leiden.[179] The promulgation of the religious peace at Antwerp and elsewhere in 1578 produced another substantial movement back to the Low Countries from both French and Dutch communities.[180]

It was a measure of the London churches' resilience that they could continue, despite these reductions, to play an important role in supporting the churches in the Netherlands. In the wake of the Pacification of Ghent in November 1576 the demands, if anything, increased as the Reformed strained to take advantage of new opportunities to spread the Gospel in the southern provinces. Many of the new Reformed communities were too small to support themselves and the London churches gave what financial assistance was possible.[181] But the most pressing need was once again for ministers. In 1577 Johan Cubus left London to take up a post in Antwerp, and in the following year the London church also reluctantly released Jacob Regius to serve at Ghent.[182] For a time the Dutch church was reduced to one minister, but they hoped soon to benefit from the training scheme established some years previously in response to the evident need for new candidates for the ministry. From 1576 the London community sponsored a number of promising young men to study in Geneva, the expenses being paid by a collection raised amongst the most prosperous members of the church.[183] The scheme was a great success, and the students were soon much in demand. Already in 1579 the church at Antwerp was attempting to establish its prior claim to the services of Assuerus

---

[178] Ibid., 371, 380, 398, 454, 548, 613.
[179] Ibid., ii. 583, iii. 405.
[180] Ibid., iii. 486; Schickler, *Églises du Refuge*, i. 227.
[181] Hessels, ii. 577, 609, iii. 490, 499, 537, 555, 591.
[182] Ibid., iii. 457, 501, 505, 509.
[183] The subscription list is printed in *Returns*, ii. 202–12. In 1579–80 the students moved from Geneva to Neustadt and Heidelberg. Hessels, ii. 631, 664.

Reghenmortel when the London consistory was satisfied that his studies were complete, and the churches in the Netherlands did not scruple to enter into direct negotiations with students in order to pre-empt their neighbours.[184] A new note of exasperation is evident in the London consistory's responses to these persistent appeals, particularly as the consistory was finding it increasingly difficult to meet its own obligations. A reply to a request for help from the *classis* of Brabant in 1580 admitted frankly that so many of the church's own members were returning to the Continent that the assistance they could offer was now very limited.[185]

The problems of the exile communities received scant sympathy, it must be said, from their co-religionists in the Netherlands. In 1583 the London consistory wrote to the church at Brussels to ask that Daniel de Dieu, a student educated at their expense and subsequently granted to Brussels be returned to them. The consistory explained that the ministry of the London church was now reduced to the aged Winghen, and Jan Selot, who spoke no English. But the request was met with a flat refusal: the Brussels church, came the reply, had only six ministers, and de Dieu could not be spared.[186] The attitude of the Reformed communities in the Netherlands was neatly encapsulated in a letter from Antwerp in 1581. Given the size of the potential harvest in the Low Countries, they wrote, two ministers in London would be a greater luxury than twenty in Antwerp. In the following year the London consistory seemed to concede the point, as they finally allowed Assuerus Reghenmortel to take up the position in Antwerp he had first been offered three years previously.[187]

Reghenmortel's service in Antwerp was to prove tragically short-lived. Within a few years the principal churches in Flanders and Brabant had all fallen victim to the inexorable progress of Parma's campaign of reconquest, and with the capitulation of Antwerp in August 1585 the total collapse of the church in the southern provinces became inevitable. The destruction of the Reformed churches in Ghent, Brussels, and

184 Hessels, ii. 659, 664, 476, iii. 550.
185 Ibid., iii. 598.
186 Ibid., iii. 710, 713.
187 Ibid., iii. 632, 669.

above all Antwerp, was a bitter blow to their brethren in exile, but the immediate consequence, paradoxically, was to give the London communities a new lease of life. Many members of the expelled Reformed communities resettled in Holland but a considerable number chose to take the familiar route across the Channel. For the Dutch church in London one welcome consequence was the return of their ministers Regius from Ghent and Reghenmortel from Antwerp.[188] The events of 1585 ensured that there would be a substantial foreign population in London well into the 1590s, particularly as the fall of Antwerp coincided with the promulgation of a new edict banning the exercise of the Reformed religion in France. A new survey of the stranger population in 1593 registered over 7,000 foreigners in the capital, not far short of the peak totals of 1568–71.[189]

Nevertheless, this apparent continuity was in some ways deceptive, for 1585 was to prove a watershed in the foreign churches' relationship with the Continent. By the end of the century the character of the London communities had quite perceptibly changed. With the fall of Antwerp in 1585 any realistic hope for the recovery of the southern provinces was gone, and many Reformed exiles from Flanders and Brabant had finally to face the prospect that they would never return to their homelands. A high proportion chose to settle instead in Holland and Zeeland; those who remained in London were increasingly those who saw their residence in London as permanent. The French church, too, particularly after the return of a number of Huguenot ministers to France after the death of Henry III in 1589,[190] was increasingly a community of settled residents, most Walloons for whom a return home was impossible. This growing stability was evident in the ministry of the two churches. After the bewildering changes of the 1570s, with ministers repeatedly being called away to serve in Holland, the 1590s saw a reassuring measure of continuity. Reghenmortel and Regius both served the Dutch church unchanged from 1585 until Regius's death in 1601, reinforced by younger men

---

[188] Ibid., iii. 807, 817, 861.

[189] *Return of Strangers, 1593 etc*, ed. Scouloudi, p. 90. The 7,113 foreigners registered included some 2,443 children born in England of foreign parents, who were not technically foreigners (though clearly still regarded as such). See also below, p. 289.

[190] Schickler, *Églises du Refuge*, i. 245.

appointed to fill the vacancy left by the death of the veteran Winghen in 1590. The French ministers Fontaine and Castol also served from 1585 until the end of the century, with occasional assistance from junior probationary ministers. Fontaine died in 1611, after thirty-seven years in the ministry of the French church.[191]

Inevitably, too, the relationship of the London churches with their brethren abroad underwent a perceptible change. After 1588 the United Provinces were never in serious (or at least imminent) danger of military defeat, and this growing security, together with the accession of vast new resources brought by the refugees from the southern provinces, meant that the church in Holland was increasingly able to shoulder alone the burdens of governance and support for the Dutch Reformed church. In the 1590s the urgent pleas for assistance and intellectual dependence of earlier decades were replaced by a fraternal interchange of resources and opinions. The London ministers and their colleagues in Holland continued to co-operate to enforce the discipline on erring brethren who sought refuge across the Channel, and exchanged testimonials for members who wished to move between the communities.[192] The students educated at the expense of the London church were still very much in demand, but by this time the consistory had taken to sending them to the new university in Leiden rather than to Geneva or Heidelberg as had been customary.[193] In this way the relationship between London and the Continental churches settled into a happy equilibrium, though the ties which bound the foreigners to their homelands were never broken. In 1601 the Norwich community suggested a general day of fasting to pray for the Queen and the prosperity of the country: but also for Maurice of Nassau's forthcoming campaign.[194] This continued sense of involvement with events across the Channel is hardly surprising. Many of those who chose to remain in England had relatives abroad, mostly now

---

[191] Hessels, iii. 908; Schickler, *Églises du Refuge*, i. 270–7, 402–3; Lindeboom, *Austin Friars*, p. 204.

[192] Hessels, iii. 932, 942, 947, 954, 971, 984.

[193] Ibid., 912, 924, 940, 968; *Album Studiosorum Academiae Lugduno Batavae* (The Hague, 1875), cols. 31 (Joannes Marcuinas), 33 (Samuel Montanus).

[194] Hessels, iii. 1061.

in Holland rather than in Flanders. For well-established members of the exile community it was perfectly natural to continue their business operations from an English base, but they and other members of the community moved back and forth as interest and preference dictated, and their trading interests remained firmly centred on the land of their birth.

The continuing vitality of these business connections was a fitting monument to four decades of exile involvement in Continental affairs, during which time the London exile community had made a significant contribution to the survival of the Reformed church in the Netherlands. Well-established trade routes facilitated the movement of refugees back and forth across the channel, and made possible the steady flow of books, letters, financial contributions, and advice which sustained the 'churches under the cross'. The authorities in the Netherlands were well aware of what was going on, but the weight of legitimate trade was such that they could not hope to intercept more than a small proportion of this clandestine traffic. The London churches were themselves not always fully in control of events and their ministers for many years held out against radical initiatives. But their status and influence as the largest of the exile communities was such that they could not be ignored, and ensured that they would play a vital role in ensuring the eventual triumph of the Reformed religion in their homelands.

IX

The Churches and the English

THE relationship between the foreign community and their English hosts posed two distinct problems for the strangers. On the one hand, they were conscious of the need to conciliate the governors of church and state, whose indulgence had brought the churches into being, and on whose continued goodwill they relied for their existence. On the other, the strangers' leaders faced mounting problems in protecting their members from hostility from sections of the London population, particularly the poorer artisans and craftsmen who associated their own economic problems with the coming of the strangers. The strangers relied heavily for protection on their patrons amongst the Privy Council and the governors of the City of London, and much effort was expended by the ministers of the churches to ensure that this protection was not withdrawn. The English authorities, for their part, were aware both of the benefits to be derived from the stranger population and of the strong feelings they excited; their continued sympathy may be said to have depended very largely on the strangers' utility outweighing any threat they seemed to pose to the stability of the capital. The strangers' position thus inevitably became more perilous at times of high domestic or international tension, but in periods of calm the city authorities offered them steady protection, in return for the ministers' co-operation in exploiting the foreigners' skills to the benefit of their adopted home.

It has already been suggested that the stranger churches owed the renewal of their privilege of separate worship under Elizabeth largely to an appreciation on the part of leading members of the Privy Council of the economic advantages to be gained by encouraging the stranger communities.[1] When the Council sought to extend these advantages to other towns

---

[1] See Ch. VI above.

it had no hesitation in calling on the resources of the London churches to help establish these settlements. The example of Sandwich, supplied with makers of bays and says and other skilled craftsmen from amongst the strangers in London under the direction of the Dutch ministers, has already been cited, and this operation established a pattern which was to be repeated later in the decade. In 1565 the Mayor and Corporation of Norwich considered the distress of the local cloth industry after a particularly severe winter, and put the problem to the Duke of Norfolk in an interview at his palace.[2] The Duke had already been in contact with Jan Utenhove, the dominant figure in the London stranger community after Elizabeth's accession, and the Corporation now resolved 'to invite divers strangers of the Low Countries, which were now come to London and Sandwich for refuge, which Strangers had obtained licence from the Queen to exercise the making of Flanders commodities of wool in her Majesty's dominions'. The Privy Council soon approved the request, and whilst the necessary Letters Patent were being prepared the consistory of the London Dutch church was entrusted with the organization of the movement, largely from Sandwich, of the thirty households permitted under the terms of the agreement. The London churches were involved again two years later when the town of Maidstone petitioned for licence to receive sixty families of strangers active in specified trades.[3] Cecil quickly gave the desired permission, and it was decided that the representatives of the town and the leading aliens wishing to go there should wait in London whilst the Letters Patent were being drawn up. These declared that the petition had been granted for the repair of Maidstone and the 'relief and convenient placing of certain Dutchmen aliens now residing within our citie of London and ellswhere, within our realme of England, being very skilful in divers arts . . .'.[4]

[2] W. J. C. Moens, *The Walloons and their Church at Norwich* (Huguenot Society Publications, 1, 1887–8), pp. 17–18.

[3] Valerie Morant, 'The Settlement of Protestant Refugees in Maidstone during the Sixteenth Century', *Economic History Review*, 2nd series, 4 (1951–2), 210–14. PRO, SP 12/43/19.

[4] PRO, SP 12/43/28. *Cal. Pat. Rolls. Eliz.*, iv. 39–40.

In the same year negotiations were successfully concluded for a settlement of twenty families of Walloon refugees in Southampton, and for a group of Dutch weavers to move to Stamford.[5] The London churches were happy to give assistance as required in setting up these separate colonies of foreign workmen, and kept in close contact with them. The provision of a church in which the foreigners might worship was almost invariably a part of the original contract, and these smaller churches frequently turned to London for help and advice in the years that followed.[6] The close co-operation between the London churches and the Privy Council broke down only under the pressure of increasing numbers of refugees in the early 1570s, when the Council resorted to arbitrary measures to encourage new arrivals to move on from London to the stranger communities in other towns.[7] Even so the Privy Council still felt able to call on the assistance of the foreign ministers when, towards the end of the century, it was felt necessary to move members of some of the larger provincial communities to less crowded towns.[8]

The role of the London churches in assisting the establishment of these new foreign artisan communities was by far the most significant way in which their position at the focal point of the foreign community was exploited. But the government was by no means blind to other incidental advantages in the presence of eminent foreigners in the capital, as was demonstrated by the role sporadically played by the leaders of the stranger churches in foreign diplomacy. The way had been pointed by John a Lasco, who came to England not only to assist the establishment of a Protestant Reformation, but also to conduct diplomatic negotiations for setting up a general league in defence of Protestantism. Initial negotiations on his first visit proved abortive, but Lasco returned in 1550 with new letters of credence to act for the German Protestant princes. When in December 1551 an envoy from the Duke of Mecklenburg was reluctant to risk the perils of a winter Channel crossing he was content to send his instructions to Lasco

[5] PRO, SP 12/43/11 (Stamford); 12/42/71, 43/16, 44/8, 15/13/80–2.
[6] Hessels, iii. 189, 207, 262, 314, etc.
[7] *Actes II*, pp. 42, 54–5; Hessels, ii. 499–501.
[8] *APC*, 1589–90, p. 413; Hessels, iii. 907.

instead.[9] The dispatch to London in 1560 of so eminent a representative of the French Reformed church as Nicholas des Gallars presented the English government with new diplomatic opportunities which it was not slow to exploit. When des Gallars was summoned to the Colloquy of Poissy in 1561 Cecil was insistent that he should attend, and des Gallars regularly provided the English government with information during the course of the Colloquy through the English representative in Paris, Throckmorton.[10] Having thus earned the trust of the English government it is not surprising that des Gallars should have been involved once more when negotiations were opened with the French Huguenots in 1562. The outcome of these negotiations was the Treaty of Hampton Court, by which the Huguenots were to be assisted in their struggle against the Crown in return for the restoration of Calais to England. Although the precise role played by des Gallars in the negotiations remains shadowy, it is of interest that in the months before the conclusion of the treaty Throckmorton should recommend that des Gallars be kept fully briefed, 'as one in great credit with the Prince [Condé] and such as profess the religion', and able thereby to guarantee their good faith.[11]

The international contacts of the stranger community were even more significant during the negotiations of 1563–4 which resulted in the moving of the English cloth staple from Antwerp to Emden.[12] The crucial role here was played by Jan Utenhove, a familiar figure at the English Court, but also a close friend of the dowager Countess of East Friesland, who had received the refugees from England with such generosity in 1554. The English government had no agent in north-west Germany after the autumn of 1560 and so Utenhove was soon acting as a sort of unofficial ambassador.[13] These, at first routine, diplomatic contacts took on a new significance when in December 1563 the Regent of the Netherlands, Margaret of Parma, placed

[9] *Cal. S. P. For. Edward VI*, nos. 216, 253, 517; Dalton, *Lasco*, pp. 365–75.

[10] Grindal to Cecil, 11 Aug. 1561, PRO, SP 12/19/18, Grindal, *Remains*, p. 244; *Cal. S. P. For. Eliz.*, 1561–2, nos. 458, 492, 511, 569, 583, 611, 684.

[11] *Cal. S. P. For. Eliz.*, 1561–2, no. 1060.

[12] A detailed account of these negotiations is in Ramsay, *City of London*, pp. 229–44.

[13] Ramsay, op. cit., p. 231; Utenhove to Cecil, 22 Mar. 1562, BL, MS Lansdowne 6/3; Utenhove to Grindal, Grindal to Cecil, 6 Aug. 1562, PRO, SP 12/24/3.

an embargo on all English goods. The ostensible reason for this was the plague in London, but it gradually became apparent that the embargo was a hostile act intended to cause the English government maximum embarrassment by closing the Antwerp mart to English cloths. The idea of moving the cloth mart to Emden as an emergency measure was soon receiving serious attention, and Utenhove was immediately deeply involved in the affair. Within days of the embargo Cecil had enquired of Utenhove, through Grindal, about the practicalities of the Emden scheme.[14] By February 1564 the Merchant Adventurers in London were prepared to grasp the nettle and enter into negotiations with the Countess in Emden, and before setting out they turned once more to Utenhove for advice.[15] Unfortunately Utenhove had been struck down with one of his frequent bouts of illness and the commissioners had to go off without having seen him, but on his recovery he busied himself with the task of securing the new ties of interests and policy between England and the family of the Countess.[16] After the successful conclusion of an agreement between the Merchant Adventurers and three commissioners from the Countess in March the Emden mart went ahead in the summer of 1564.

With the arrival of a number of distinguished French ministers in England after the St Bartholomew's Day massacre of 1572, the London churches were once again able to play a significant diplomatic role. In 1574, at a time when the Queen and her advisers were seriously considering a policy of active intervention on behalf of the Huguenots in France, the French ministers were frequently summoned to Court to confer with sympathetic counsellors and emissaries of the Protestant powers. De Villiers in particular seems almost to have been acting as a permanent diplomatic representative for the Huguenot nobles at this time, and with his contacts at Court he ensured that messengers from Orange and his allies had speedy access

---

[14] Cecil's letter does not survive, but its sense may be deduced from Grindal's reply of 21 Dec., printed in Grindal, *Remains*, p. 266. Utenhove to Cecil, KL, iii. 577–8, for Utenhove's initially cautious response.

[15] Grindal to Utenhove, 10 Feb. 1564, Hessels, ii. 210–13.

[16] Utenhove to Cecil, 17 Mar. 1564, Hessels, ii. 213–17.

to the leading English exponents of a forward foreign policy.[17] But de Villiers and his colleagues still had to exercise some discretion, lest their enthusiastic advocacy of the Protestant cause should compromise their hosts. In March 1575 the French ambassador, Fénélon, was able to report with some satisfaction that the French ministers' public celebration of Damville's victory over the King's forces in Languedoc had earned them a stinging rebuke from the Queen.[18]

This incident provides a neat illustration of the government's attitude towards the foreign communities and their contacts with their co-religionists abroad. Whilst it was prepared to make full use of the diplomatic opportunities afforded by the presence in London of distinguished refugees, it was not prepared to be led by the foreigners' enthusiasms into dangerous foreign policy initiatives. The control exercised by the council over the churches' activities in this sphere was both close and finely calculated. When in 1568 Orange dispatched an agent to the London churches to appeal for financial assistance for his forthcoming campaigns the foreign ministers were careful to consult Cecil before making any decision. Cecil sent word that the collection could go ahead, so long as its true purpose remained concealed.[19] The insistence on secrecy is understandable, given that Cecil was at the same time denying any knowledge of warlike preparations amongst the refugees in England to the Spanish ambassador, and even went as far as to agree that measures should be taken to prevent any assistance being sent. After two months of insistent pressure from de Silva a proclamation was eventually issued to carry this resolution into effect, though the sceptical ambassador believed that by this time any of the exiles who intended to leave would have done so.[20]

In the unsettled and threatening international climate of 1568 the government's cautious and watchful attitude was entirely comprehensible, but by the time the revolt in the

[17] Fénélon, Bertrand de Salignac, Seigneur de la Mothe, *Correspondance diplomatique* (Paris, 1838–40), vi. 81, 167, 219, 248, 282, 301; Wallace T. MacCaffrey, *Queen Elizabeth and the Making of Policy, 1572–1588* (Princeton, 1981), pp. 181–90.

[18] Fénélon, *Correspondance*, vi. 394.

[19] Hessels, ii. 293.

[20] *Cal. S. P. Span.*, 1568–79, pp. 27–8, 52–60, 62–3; *Tudor Royal Proclamations*, ii. 296–7.

Netherlands flared into life once more in 1572 with the Sea
Beggars' descent on Flushing and Brill the foreign policy
perspective had changed considerably. The Dutch and French
communities in London were now positively encouraged to
provide help for the rebels. The churches were urged to make
collections for the purchase of arms and the equipment of
troops, and arms and munitions were sold to them from the
royal stockpile in the Tower.[21] It is fair to say that Elizabeth
hereafter never wished the Dutch to be completely defeated,
but her commitment to William of Orange, after this encouraging beginning, was erratic to say the least, and it was not
always easy for the foreign communities in London to keep in
step. An example of the difficulties under which they laboured
occurred in 1576, when a complicated wrangle between
Elizabeth and the Prince resulted in mutual seizures of ships
in the ports of Zeeland and England. The Privy Council dispatched brusque instructions to the Dutch church to have no
further dealings with the Prince of Orange until the affair was
settled.[22] The letter contained a scarcely veiled threat of the
withdrawal of government protection if its wishes were not
complied with, urging as it did that the foreigners should
proceed very cautiously in view of their unpopularity with the
commons, particularly since the latest dispute. Similar instructions were sent to the other foreign communities in England,
which were in effect being invited to choose between their
support for the Prince and their loyalty to their adopted home.
The correspondence of the churches suggests that, whilst they
were deeply unhappy about the rift between Orange and the
Queen, they regarded the latter obligation as paramount. The
churches at Sandwich, Norwich, and Maidstone all expressed
the hope that they would not be compromised by Orange's
action, in which they denied all complicity.[23] The French
church at Canterbury put the point most directly, arguing
that they should not support the Prince if he proceeded unjustly
against his enemies, still less against the Queen.[24] These reactions suggest that there was some truth in Orange's sometimes

---

[21] KL, vi. 395; *Cal. S. P. Span.*, 1568–79, pp. 391–4, 396.
[22] Hessels, ii. 561–4; MacCaffrey, *Queen Elizabeth and the Making of Policy*, pp. 206–7.
[23] Hessels, iii. 381, 383, 385.
[24] Ibid., iii. 384.

bitterly expressed view that the security of their exile was more
important to many in England than their homeland. At the
very least the exile communities recognized that their obligation to their adopted home put considerable restraint on their
freedom of action.

The stranger churches were also forced to submit to the
English government on the issue of attendance at Continental
synods of the Reformed church, though again they did so with
evident reluctance. In 1571 the Dutch Reformed communities
were generally agreed on the desirability of a General Synod
to discuss and settle points of doctrine and discipline, as a
step towards more uniform worship amongst the exile churches
and the communities in the Netherlands itself. The English
exile churches, regarded as a separate province of the church,
were invited to meet and elect delegates to attend the first
General Synod to be held at Emden. Clearly the English
churches hoped to comply with this request, but although they
met together in London and elected Cousin and Winghen to
represent them, the synod was eventually forced to proceed
without them.[25] The government had in fact forbidden their
participation, and in March of the following year the Dutch
church was forced to write that it would not be possible for
the churches in England to take part in such synods.[26] It was
even in doubt whether the stranger churches would be allowed
to meet together for discussion in England. The meeting of
the stranger churches called to subscribe to the decrees of the
Synod of Emden had clearly displeased the English authorities,
and permission to form a *classis*, as the Emden synod had
recommended, was initially refused.[27]

The relationship of the stranger churches with the Reformed
church abroad was a sensitive issue for the English authorities.
By conforming to the decrees of a General Synod of the Dutch
Reformed church the stranger churches would in effect be
recognizing a higher authority abroad, whereas they were now
under the authority of the English Church. Although they
enjoyed remarkable freedom in fact, the government's action
in 1571 was a reminder that they had to tread carefully. The

[25] *Actes II*, p. 17; Hessels, iii. 150.
[26] Hessels, ii. 391.
[27] Ibid., ii. 410.

foreign churches in England were forced to limit their participation to a commitment to do whatever possible to
demonstrate agreement with synodal decisions, without promising formal submission to decrees, and this solution was reluctantly accepted by the churches of the Netherlands. The Synod
of Dordrecht in 1578 accepted that the English churches should
adopt decrees only in so far as they had the goodwill of their
superintendent and such action was consistent with the peace
of the community in the country.[28] In due course, too, the
churches were allowed to meet together as a *classis* (called in
England the *colloquia*), but here again discretion was necessary:
in 1575 the church at Sandwich advised against too frequent
and unnecessary meetings which might attract the hostile
attention of the English authorities.[29]

The strangers were well advised to tread warily as such
classes, the distinctive feature of a presbyterian church order,
had unfortunate resonances for a government about to move
to the suppression of such conferences of ministers in the Anglican Church.[30] The tensions within the English church certainly left their mark on relations between the strangers and
the English authorities, and the strangers' contacts with
English churchmen of a more radical persuasion was one of
the points of most acute sensitivity.[31] But before turning to a
consideration of these tensions, it is worth dwelling upon the
contacts between the foreign churches and their English
neighbours in the religious sphere that were altogether less
controversial. Many of the first generation of Elizabethan
church leaders had enjoyed the hospitality of Continental
churches during the Marian exile, and the foreign churches
benefited from several manifestations of a sympathetic concern
on their re-establishment. An English merchant, Thomas
Heton, was present at the first election of elders for the French
church on its re-formation, and the English minister Young

---

[28] Ibid., ii. 392, 510, iii. 525.

[29] Hessels, iii. 319; *Acten van de Colloquia der Nederlandsche gemeenten in Engeland, 1575–1609*, ed. J. J. van Toorenenbergen (Marnix Society, series 2, part 1, 1872).

[30] Patrick Collinson, *The Elizabethan Puritan Movement* (1967), pp. 177–9, 191 ff.

[31] See especially Patrick Collinson, 'The Elizabethan Puritans and the Foreign Reformed Churches in London, *HS*, 20 (1958–64), 528–55.

helped supervise the casting of ballots a year later, a circumstance which attracted the unfavourable comment of Peter Alexander, thereby excluded from the supervisory role.[32] The struggling communities were grateful in these early years for gifts from English sympathizers, amongst them the courtier Killigrew, the minister William Whittingham, and the merchant Thomas Hotson.[33] The generous concern of their superintendent the Bishop of London was amply demonstrated in his painstaking and invariably unavailing efforts to reconcile the protagonists in the disputes surrounding the turbulent Haemstede, Alexander, and Winghen, and other sympathetic ministers were on occasions called in by the warring parties. The mediators who helped bring a temporary end to the dispute between the Dutch consistory and the deacons were three distinguished English churchmen, Calfhill, Philpott, and Colman, and the martyrologist John Foxe.[34]

The greatest opportunity to show solidarity with the strangers came with the St Bartholomew's Day massacre in 1572. The outrage of the massacre inspired a wave of sympathy for the penniless refugees who were soon arriving in boatloads on the English coast. The problems these refugees posed the French church have been described,[35] but their difficulties were at least partly eased by generous donations from English sources. The Bishop of London provided a considerable lumpsum, but other English ministers also contributed: the Bishop of Durham sent £4, whilst the strangers were not forgotten by their old friends William Whittingham, now Dean of Durham, and Grindal, who collected £50 in the archdiocese of York.[36] More humble ministers sent their own modest contributions,[37] and donations were no less welcome from friendly laymen such as the merchant Henry King and Alderman Richard Martin. A certain Edward Bennet sent frequent gifts of a shilling, sometimes twice monthly.[38] News of the massacre obviously

[32] *Actes I*, pp. 4, 48.
[33] Ibid., pp. 22, 28, 99.
[34] Hessels, iii. 39.
[35] Above, pp. 210–14.
[36] French Church, MS 194, fos. 3, 41ᵛ, 84ᵛ.
[37] A Mr Clerk sent 6s. 8d., and Lefy, the Bishop of London's chaplain, half as much. Ibid., fos. 96ᵛ., 108.
[38] Ibid., fos. 3, 145, 163, etc.

spread rapidly, and collections for the strangers were made in Bedford, Leicester, and amongst the gentlemen of both countries. Gray's Inn and the Company of Merchant Taylors in London made similar collections.[39] The strangers would have been particularly grateful for gestures of support from the rich and powerful, and from leading members of the Council: Lord Berkeley and the Countess of Sussex both sent contributions, as did Sir Francis Walsingham and the Earl of Bedford.[40]

The strangers, then, had many friends who might be depended upon to rally in times of difficulty, but their sympathizers in government circles were generally much less enthusiastic about the influence of the stranger churches on the English Church. At the time of the churches' re-establishment there had been no wish to repeat the experiment of the model church of Lasco's day, although under Grindal's indulgent supervision the strangers had been permitted to institute a form of government and rites significantly more in tune with Reformed practice on the Continent than was the English Church. Those ministers critical of the compromises of the Elizabethan settlement made little secret of the fact that they saw the stranger churches as a more congenial model. The Parliament of 1572 saw a remarkable attempt to empower bishops to license clergy to omit parts of the Prayer Book in their services: specifically they might consent to 'such forme of prayers and mynistracion of the woorde and sacraments, and other godlie exercises of religion as the right godlie reformed churches now do use in the ffrenche and Douche congregation, within the City of London or elswheare in the Quenes maiesties dominions and is extent in printe'.[41]

The events in Parliament illustrate the point that, although English Puritans often looked abroad for the models of correct Reformed practice, they were also aware that such models were available closer to hand. One Puritan writer acknowledged the churches in Geneva, France, Germany, and Scotland as parts of the Church Universal, but also 'in London the Italian church, the Dutch, and the French'.[42] In the debate of

1572 it was emphasized that the strangers' church order was freely available in print, so that members had little excuse for not being familiar with it, and English reformers obviously studied the strangers' form of worship with some care. John Field owned a copy of des Gallars's *Forma politiae ecclesiasticae*,[43] and the publication of Lasco's *Forma ac Ratio* in an English version was evidently being considered by some godly Englishmen, to judge by a complete manuscript translation discovered in the Bodleian Library.[44]

If the stranger churches offered a model of proper Reformed practice close to home, they also provided an essential channel of communication between the leading Reformed churches of the Continent and their English admirers. Des Gallars and Cousin were in close touch with Calvin, and after his death Beza, in Geneva, and it was evidently customary for Geneva to use the French ministers to pass messages or letters to English friends. In 1565 the French consistory minutes record Cousin journeying to Court to deliver a great bundle of letters sent with greetings to the Queen by Beza, and two years later Percival Wiburn recommended that if Henry Bullinger had any reply to make to his letter he should send it to Beza at Geneva, 'by whom it may be afterwards forwarded to the minister of the French church in London (a thing they do very frequently). Your letter will by this means safely reach me, if it is directed to me by name'.[45] Writing to Cousin in 1572 Beza asked that greetings be passed on to Cartwright, Wiburn, Sampson, Whittingham, and Gilpin, suggesting not only that the Genevan reformer was able to use this channel to keep in contact, but that Cousin was sufficiently intimate with these prominent ecclesiastics to pass on such good wishes orally.[46]

The government was fully aware that the stranger churches could be a channel for unwelcome Reformed influence, but had no intention that they should be a focal point for dissidence. The French consistory was sailing very close to the

[43] BL, MS Add. 48096; see Collinson, 'Elizabethan Puritans', 533, 548.

[44] Bodleian Library, MS Barlow 19. The manuscript is in a standard secretary hand, and the translator unknown. There are, however, several pages of notes unconnected with the translation (fos. 165–7) in a hand which Professor Collinson suggested is similar to Grindal's.

[45] *Actes I*, pp. 115; *Zurich Letters*, i. 190.

[46] Hessels, ii. 427–8.

wind in 1565 when it agreed to lend the church for a baptism to be performed by one of the English ministers who refused to wear the surplice. The Queen was to have been a godmother, but having heard who was to perform the ceremony she angrily dispatched another minister properly arrayed.[47] Possible problems with the foreign churches offering a haven to discontented Englishmen had been anticipated early in the reign by Grindal, who asked the churches to show discretion in whom they received.[48] The churches agreed, but the French community received English visitors frequently in the early years. In April 1561 the presence of the minister Whittingham and many other Englishmen at the monthly communion was recorded, and as a similar group were noted at the communion of March 1564 it seems probable that they attended intermittently in between.[49] The French admitted the occasional Englishman to membership of the community: the English gentleman Robert Askew, for instance, in August 1564, and a servant of Sir Nicholas Throckmorton, John Roger, two months later. In 1571 an Englishman, John Bodley, was even elected an elder of the French community.[50]

The number of Englishmen attracted to the services of the stranger churches probably climbed steadily as pressure on non-conformists mounted through the first decades of Elizabeth's reign. By February 1573 the Privy Council had decided that it was time to call a halt, and on 22 October a sharp letter was dispatched to both French and Dutch communities warning them not to meddle in the affairs of the English Church. In particular the foreign communities were warned to refuse to accept dissident Englishmen as members.[51] The Dutch church returned a prompt reply promising obedience. The letter noted that the church had in fact only four English members, two of whom had joined the community on their return from exile at the beginning of the reign, whilst the other two both had Dutch wives.[52] The French reply is

[47] *Actes I*, p. 109.
[48] Ibid., p. 25.
[49] Ibid., pp. 38, 105.
[50] *Actes I*, pp. 72, 83; *Actes II*, p. 65, 'Jehan Baudele, Anglois'. Bodley was the father of the founder of the Bodleian Library. See Collinson, 'Elizabethan Puritans', 550–1.
[51] Hessels, ii. 456–9; *Actes II*, p. 127.
[52] Hessels, ii. 482–5.

not known, but it is unlikely that they could have been so sanguine. English radicals seem to have favoured attendance at the French rather than the Dutch church at this time, possibly because of the closer links between the French church and Geneva, possibly for linguistic reasons. In any case it was necessary for the French consistory to instruct the elders to visit the English members resident in their districts and warn them not to come to communion for the time being.[53] The following February the French church decided that it would admit no more Englishmen unless they came with an attestation from their parish priest that they had not separated themselves from the English Church out of contempt for the English ceremonies.[54] How strictly this order was enforced may be open to doubt as it proved necessary, at the bishop's prompting, to instruct the elders to remind any English members of this requirement three years later in 1577.[55] The problem was still apparently a source of rancour in 1581 when Convocation heard a petition from the London clergy against the many citizens who deserted to the French and Dutch churches.[56]

The somewhat half-hearted efforts of the stranger churches to fall in with the government's wishes respecting the reception of Englishmen in their congregations did not succeed in removing suspicion of the role of the churches in the religious sphere. How important this source of irritation to the English authorities might have become is well illustrated by a letter addressed by the London Dutch community to Antwerp in 1577, explaining why it was impossible to release the minister Regius for service in the Low Countries.[57] The church, it was argued, had already stretched its resources to the very limit in order to assist the Netherlands with ministers, and if Regius was released, services in London might have to be suspended. Once given up, it was unlikely that the church would ever be allowed to start up again, on account of the differences in ritual between the strangers and the English Church. Matters did not come to such a head during Elizabeth's reign, but there were obviously many whose sympathy for poor refugees

[53] *Actes II*, p. 127.
[54] Ibid., p. 132.
[55] Ibid., pp. 195, 202.
[56] Collinson, 'Elizabethan Puritans', pp. 547–8.
[57] Hessels, iii. 472.

from foreign persecution was strained to breaking-point by the encouragement which the stranger churches offered, even by their very existence, to dissidents inside the English Church.

The same might also be said of those who saw the strangers less as religious troublemakers than as an economic threat. The strangers' connections with Puritans were probably the greatest source of irritation to the government, but they could not but be aware of the profound hostility felt towards the foreign community by many of their subjects because of the threat which the strangers posed to their livelihoods. How endemic and how widespread this hostility was has been the subject of little detailed examination; it can too lightly be assumed that xenophobia was a national characteristic in the sixteenth century, whereas in fact, as has been shown above, many sixteenth-century Londoners had a clear appreciation of the benefits to be derived from offering hospitality to skilled foreigners, and others felt a genuine sympathy towards suffering co-religionists. The large-scale immigration of the decades after 1540 thus provoked different reactions in the capital, and revealed a genuine conflict both of interests and of attitudes. An examination of the control exercised over the stranger population by the City authorities offers a telling illustration of these conflicting pressures. Generally the governors of London were disposed to offer the strangers protection, even encouragement, but in the face of a marked increase in the flow of immigrants or when the atmosphere at home was particularly highly charged, the City was prepared to act in the face of instructions from above, or particularly clamorous demands from below, to limit or control the strangers.

The City governors' attitude to strangers in stable times may be discerned from the handling of cases relating to foreigners in the reign of Edward VI. In view of the widespread sympathy for the experiment of the strangers' church and an awakening sense of the economic opportunity presented by skilled immigrants one might expect strangers to be treated with indulgence, but in fact the City showed no especial laxity in their direction. The City was as determined as ever to protect its civic rights against encroachment, and was extremely reluctant to welcome strangers into the freedom of the City on special terms even when the request was presented by as powerful a personage as Protector Somerset.[58] The laws against retailing by foreigners were enforced as punctiliously as ever, and there was a steady trickle of prosecutions of strangers who sold illegally to Englishmen or other strangers, and of Englishmen who connived at the process by 'colouring' strangers' goods.[59] There seems, however, to have been no resentment on the strangers' part at the enforcement of these regulations. The privileges of the City were upheld just as rigorously in regard to other 'forrens' (the confusing contemporary term for all non-freemen, whether English or strangers), and the strangers seem to have suspected no special hostility. That they were confident of fair play from the City courts is suggested by the appointment of an interpreter to the court of Common Council for the convenience of such strangers 'as there chance to be arrayned'.[60]

The City's attitude was not radically altered by the change of regime on Edward's death, despite the profound hostility of Mary's government to many of the strangers. No increase occurred during the reign in the number of prosecutions in retailing cases, suggesting that native tradesmen who hoped to take advantage of the changed climate of opinion to settle old scores with alien competitors received no encouragement from the City authorities. The absence of any radical change in official attitudes is not difficult to explain. Whatever the Privy Council's suspicions of the religious sympathies of the strangers, their skills were invaluable in many occupations; to the brewers and others, foreign workmen were essential.[61] Entrepreneurs seeking to introduce new techniques into their crafts still petitioned successfully for dispensation to employ skilled foreign workmen, and in times of emergency the employment of strangers was authorized to supply a want of native craftsmen.[62] There was also in the 1550s a clear feeling that foreign workmen were not only more skilful but also more

---

[58] Rep. 12. fo. 76.
[59] Ibid., fos. 83, 289ᵛ. (strangers retailing), 190ᵛ., 336 ('colouring' strangers' goods).
[60] Ibid., fo. 378.
[61] Above, pp. 122–4.
[62] Rep. 13, fo. 432 (Petition of Dyers' Company), 516 (Armourers authorized to employ strangers).

amenable than natives. In 1551 the Common Council forbade any union of the ale-brewers and beer-brewers after an uncharacteristic display of truculence by the latter. The Council was of the opinion 'that the seid bere bruers being strangers born and not free of this city durste not so stowtely to have proceded . . . without the ayde and help of the said Alebruers being mere Englishmen free and corporate'.[63]

The first decade of Elizabeth's reign saw a smattering of cases in which aliens who had offended the retailing laws were brought to book. In 1566 the chamberlain was ordered to shut up the windows of shops kept open in violation of the City's ordinances.[64] At the same time the City continued to turn to strangers for special expertise, or to teach English workmen new techniques. In 1560 the City employed two Dutch engineers in a project to improve the City water supply, a problem to which the Aldermen returned in 1574 with a new project and a new projector, this time a Frenchman.[65] In 1568 the Company of Tilers received permission to employ two foreign workmen on special work in a building in Mincing Lane.[66] The City made particular use of foreign skills when devising work for the inmates of the City hospitals. In 1568 the Weavers' Company agreed to co-operate in providing two young men to help the stranger who had been engaged to set up the manufacture of bed-covers in Bridewell.[67] In the next year an offer from a foreign workman to teach the children of Christ's Hospital was considered. No immediate decision can have been reached in this case as the project was discussed again in 1575 and finally agreed upon; two years later another stranger was engaged to teach the children the art of making tapestry.[68]

Whilst many continued to appreciate the value of foreign expertise, this, on the whole happy, equilibrium of control and encouragement was under increasing pressure from the first decade of Elizabeth's reign. As persecution on the Continent

[63] Corporation of London, Letter Book R, fo. 105.
[64] Rep. 15, fo. 459ᵛ., 16, fos. 16ᵛ., 382ᵛ., 18, fo. 309; Rep. 16, fos. 80ᵛ., 385ᵛ.
[65] Rep. 14, fos. 382, 493, 18, fo. 307 ff.
[66] Rep. 16, fo. 343.
[67] Ibid., fos. 341, 445ᵛ. ('ticks').
[68] Ibid., fos. 430ᵛ., 471, 18, fo. 369ᵛ., 19, fo. 268.

stimulated a greatly increased movement of small tradesmen
and artisans to England, the City faced a rising tide of complaint from Englishmen who feared, with some justice, for
their livelihoods. Their fears were reflected in wild rumours
of the numbers of strangers in the realm. In June 1559 the
envoy of the Emden consistory Anthony Ashe heard a rumour
that there were already ten thousand aliens in the city, and
two years later the Dutch church provided the bishop with a
catalogue of their members, partly to give the lie to a report
that there were now forty thousand strangers in London.[69]
The City's response to such wild talk was to order an official
count to establish the truth of the matter. Surveys of this sort
were nothing new in Elizabeth's reign. In the spring of 1551,
a time of high tension and food shortages in the capital, similar
hostile talk about the number of strangers in the City and
their responsibility for the present crisis had been prevalent.
The Aldermen were therefore required to discover how many
strangers had in fact come in during the last year, how many
were denizens, where they lived, and how much rent they
paid.[70]

The wave of hostility towards the strangers quickly subsided
in 1551, but such surveys were increasingly frequent in
Elizabeth's reign. A first count was made in 1559, and two
years later the Aldermen presented new certificates of the
numbers of strangers in their wards in response to the Lord
Mayor's directions.[71] The Spanish ambassador reported this
listing of foreigners and imagined that it was intended to expel
some; he, however, seems to have picked up some of the wilder
rumours as he had heard that the number of foreigners was
'incredible', whereas in fact a further comprehensive survey
ordered in April 1562 found only 4,500 strangers in London
and its environs, of which 700 were religious refugees who had
arrived in England since the beginning of the reign.[72] Further
general surveys of the alien population were ordered in 1565

[69] Van Schelven, *Vluchtelingenkerken*, p. 345; *KP I*, p. 210. Grindal was persuaded
to have the true state of affairs explained in a sermon at Paul's Cross.
[70] Rep. 12, fo. 313. See above, p. 83.
[71] Van Schelven, *Vluchtelingenkerken*, p. 345; Rep. 14, fo. 520ᵛ.
[72] *Cal. S. P. Span. Eliz.*, 1558–67, p. 211; PRO, SP 12/27/19, 20, printed in *Returns*,
i. 293.

and 1567. But although the strangers were thus fairly constantly monitored by the City authorities, such surveys seem
at this stage to have been largely intended for their protection,
by giving the lie to wild rumours which might stir up hatred
and disorder. In 1567, for instance, having received the results
of the count ordered in February of that year, the Mayor called
together the wardens of the Companies and ordered them to
make known to their members that the number of strangers
in the City and liberties was 'but 3,562 and no more'; the
wardens were further charged to keep a close eye on their
apprentices to see that the strangers were in no way misused.[73]

If the surveys of the early 1560s were intended to defuse a
potentially dangerous situation by providing accurate information, there is evidence that by the end of the decade the government was becoming concerned on its own account by the
continuing flow of strangers into the capital. In July 1568 Cecil
demanded from the Mayor the names and professions of all
the strangers who had arrived in London since the last survey.[74]
It is a tribute to the efficiency of the City's ward organization
that figures of the number of strangers that had arrived within
the last three months were available within ten days, and a
further comprehensive survey was completed during the year.[75]
Walsingham was at this point suggesting that the strangers
arriving in the capital should be certified weekly, and in March
of the following year a further survey of non-denizen strangers
was ordered by the Mayor and Aldermen.[76] 1571 saw two
comprehensive surveys of the alien population. In May, as
part of a general survey of strangers in the whole country,
London aliens were examined as to their nationality, profession, and age; they were also required to say how long they
had been in the country and whether they were denizens.[77]
Even supplied with this mass of information the government
was sufficiently concerned to order a listing of all new arrivals

---

[73] Rep. 15, fos. 487, 488ᵛ, 16, fos. 161ᵛ., 202.

[74] PRO, SP 12/47/19.

[75] PRO, SP 12/47/28, printed in *Returns*, iii. 440–1; BL, MS Lansdowne 202, printed
in *Returns*, iii. 330–439.

[76] PRO, SO 12/47/72; Rep. 16, fo. 449ᵛ.

[77] PRO, SP 12/84, printed in *Returns*, i. 402–79. See SP 12/78 for returns from
other parts of the country.

in October. For London in fact, they received a new comprehensive survey, which in addition to the information provided above also noted the strangers' motives for coming to England and which church they attended.[78]

This flurry of concern about the stranger population partly, no doubt, reflected genuine anxiety at the large numbers arriving in England. This, however, was also a time of high tension in other respects. In the summer of 1571 the government was gradually unravelling the Ridolphi plot, leading to the arrests of Norfolk and his associates in September and October. As the ramifications of the conspiracy were discovered the atmosphere in the capital became increasingly highly charged, and the government took the precaution of strengthening the watch and imposing a curfew.[79] At such times there was an inevitable tendency for the government to become suspicious of aliens in its midst, and abandon the enlightened protection of peacetime. A parallel may be drawn here with the events of 1551, when a regime generally sympathetic towards foreigners gave ear to hostile rumours of their insidious influence only at a moment of acute instability, with widespread distress in the country and the renewal of Somerset's threat to Northumberland's authority in the Council.[80] Now, in 1571, the Privy Council was sufficiently alarmed at the prospect of disorder to forbid the entry of foreigners into the country. Clearly there were doubts as to how far the loyalty of strangers could be relied upon, and the City authorities were ordered to make a search of strangers' houses to see what arms they possessed. If necessary any arms discovered were to be taken off into safe custody.[81]

Thus far, whilst punctiliously carrying out Council mandates, the City authorities had been fairly unwavering in their protection of the strangers. But perhaps under the influence of a threat to national security, or out of concern for the scale of the immigration, the rulers of London seemed by this time to be sharing doubts about the benefits to be derived from the

---

[78] Rep. 17, fo. 220; PRO, SP 12/82, printed in *Returns*, ii. 1–139.

[79] J. B. Black, *The Reign of Elizabeth* (Oxford, 1936), pp. 148–52; Wallace MacCaffrey, *The Shaping of the Elizabethan Regime* (1969), pp. 263–74.

[80] Jordan, *Threshold of Power*, pp. 63–7, 80.

[81] Rep. 17, fos. 220, 220ᵛ., APC, viii. 50.

foreigners' presence. In September 1571 the citizens of London presented a comprehensive catalogue of grievances against foreign merchants and handicraftsmen, specifying the numerous statutes which were flagrantly abused.[82] It is not clear who these 'citizens of London' were, but by 1574 the Court of Aldermen was itself supporting a comprehensive indictment of the strangers. In 1573 a new survey of strangers had been ordered.[83] The City gathered the required information and forwarded it to the Council, adding its own strong call for action against the unprivileged aliens and those who abused their privileges.[84]

With the rulers of London now apparently lending their support to the grievances long expressed by native handicraftsmen, this is perhaps an appropriate moment to consider the nature and depth of the hostility with which foreign residents in London had to contend. An assumption of xenophobia amongst sixteenth-century Englishmen, all too often evidenced by the single example of Evil May Day, does little to elucidate how widely hostility to foreigners was felt, and which grievances were most commonly articulated. In order to gain some sense of the issues which most roused Englishmen against foreigners it is worth looking in some detail at the complaints made by the City authorities on behalf of the citizens in 1574. If these articles are then compared with references to foreigners in the popular literature of the day, it may be possible to suggest whether the grievances articulated by the City authorities reflected short-term economic tensions, or a more general popular antipathy.

Stereotypes of the tricky, untrustworthy foreigner would be expected in contemporary plays and interludes,[85] but it is striking that the dramatists of the day in fact went straight to the heart of the same grievances against foreigners that were most commonly expressed in formal petitions against their activities.

---

[82] PRO, SP 12/81/29, printed in *Tudor Economic Documents*, i. 308–10.

[83] Rep. 18, fo. 30.

[84] Ibid., fos. 148ᵛ. ff.

[85] As for instance in Robert Wilson's *The Three Lords and Ladies of London* (1590), *STC* 25783. 'Dissimulation' is half Italian, half Dutch; 'Fraud' is half French and half Scottish. I am most grateful to Miss Corinne Richards for calling my attention to this reference, and to the article cited in n. 87.

The action of 1573–4 was particularly directed against strangers who lodged with others ('inmates' to contemporaries), and the City's submission of 1574 backed repeated calls from citizens that such inmates should be removed from London.[86] Overcrowding, and the effect it had on rents, was one of the most frequently expressed grievances against foreign residents, and found its echo in popular literature. In Robert Wilson's *The Three Ladies of London* an Italian usurer is advising Lady Lucre how to make her tenements yield greater returns:

Madonna me tell ye vat you shall doe, let dem to straunger
    dat are content
To dwell in a little roome, and to pay muche rent:
For you know da french mans and fleminges in dis countrey be many,
So dat they make shift to dwell ten houses in one very gladly:
And be content a for pay fiftie or three score pounds a yeare,
For dat whiche da English mans say twenty marke is to deare.[87]

George Wapull's morality play, *The Tide Tarrieth No Man*, is even more pointed. 'Neighbour' asks for help in evicting one 'tenant' from a coveted house. An observer comments:

For among us now, such is our countrey zeale,
That we loue best with straungers to deale,
To sell a lease deare, whosoever that will,
At the french, or dutch Church let him set up his bill,
And he shall haue chapmen, I warrent you good store,
Look what an Englishman bids, they will give him as much more.[88]

Strangers without denization were forbidden by law to rent houses, and informers presenting foreigners for this offence were a considerable irritation to the stranger community in the early Elizabethan years.[89] The willingness of the immigrants to live in crowded conditions, however, obviously proved too great a temptation to many landlords, particularly as, according to Stow, a great deal of property in London was vacant at the beginning of the reign as a result of the dissolution

---

[86] Rep. 18, fo. 149.
[87] A. B. Feldman, 'Dutch Exiles and Elizabethan Playwrights', *Notes and Queries*, 196 (1951), 531–2. *STC* 25784, Sig. Ciii^v.
[88] *STC* 25018, Sig. Biv^v. Feldman, 'Dutch Exiles', 531.
[89] Above, pp. 145, 148.

of the religious houses.[90] Within a few years much of this property had been divided into small tenements and occupied, and, as the influx of aliens continued, complaints from natives multiplied that they could hardly find lodging at a reasonable price. In 1564 the Court of Alderman took action, forbidding householders to take in any more strangers as lodgers, but the order seems to have had little effect.[91] The precepts for the survey of non-denizens in 1569, which particularly instructed aldermen to note which houses in their wards were 'pestered' or overcrowded, suggests that further action was being contemplated, and houses where many strangers lived were marked 'pestered' in the return of 1568.[92] The problem of overcrowding was particularly severe down by the waterfront. Stow observed about this time that there were now some 150 families of strangers in Billingsgate Ward where there had previously been few, and that they were prepared to give £20 for a house lately let for four marks.[93] In 1571 the City attempted to tackle the problems caused by strangers concentrating in these riverside wards by ordering that no leases falling vacant in Botolph's Wharf or Somer's Key should be let to aliens. But such attempts at control were apparently unavailing, and in 1574 the City's report drew attention once more to the problem of concentrations of strangers at the waterside.[94]

These Thames-side wards were generally the poorest and least salubrious areas of the city, and the fear that the overcrowding and subdivision of houses was a health risk was a further reason for concern. The Privy Council specifically mentioned the dangers of the spread of plague as a reason for ordering that lodgers should be moved on from crowded houses in September 1573, and although the Privy Council directive referred only to houses which harboured an inconvenient number of inmates, the City was by 1574 prepared to extend this policy to all lodgers.[95] The problem of overcrowding and

---

[90] Stow, *Annales* (1615), p. 868. Quoted by J. F. Bense, *Anglo-Dutch Relations from the earliest Times to the death of William the Third* (Oxford, 1925), p. 100.

[91] Rep. 15, fo. 328.

[92] Rep. 16, fo. 449ᵛ.; *Returns*, iii. 334–6, 359, 361, 365, 375.

[93] Stow, *Survey of London*, p. 208.

[94] Rep. 17, fo. 90ᵛ., 18, fo. 149ᵛ.

[95] *APC*, viii. 135; Rep. 18, fos. 76, 149.

high rents could not so easily be solved, however. Strangers continued to congregate in the riverside wards, and in 1579 the City was still warning landlords who had converted 'mansion houses' into small tenements, this time in Portsoken Ward, another area where strangers were particularly thick on the ground.[96]

If the effect of immigration on rents was a constant source of grievance, so too was the competition of aliens in trades and crafts. The City's survey of the situation in 1574 asked the Privy Council to consider which strangers were living by arts 'to the hurt of freemen', a plea which found its echo in the literature of the day. Wilson's *Pedler's Prophecy*, for instance, made pungent criticism of the aliens in London, under the transparent disguise of setting the play in 'Tyre'. Alien competition in handicrafts was alleged to be the cause of unemployment, even starvation. An artificer commented:

> I would gladly get my living by mine Art,
> But Aliants chop up houses so in the Citie,
> That we poore crafts men must needs depart
> And beg . . .

The 'pedler' himself added 'Three parts in London are already Alians', and followed this with the assurance that some day 'they shall all cut our throates'.[97] The fears of English craftsmen for their livelihoods were in large measure responsible for the anti-stranger rioting in 1517, and there was a similar sudden flare-up of hostility in 1563 following the breakdown of the alliance between Elizabeth and the French Huguenots. The Queen was understandably furious at the perfidy of her allies, and when the French King issued a proclamation ordering general hostilities against English subjects, Elizabeth responded in kind, authorizing inhabitants of the ports to harry French subjects.[98] The proclamation was intended for the Channel ports, but worded as it was with somewhat intemperate imprecision, it was all the excuse Londoners needed to turn on the French in the city. Many were

---

[96] Rep. 19, fo. 501.
[97] *STC* 25782, Sig. Dii. Feldman, 'Dutch Exiles', 532.
[98] *Tudor Royal Proclamations*, ii. 227–8.

seized and imprisoned and the Lord Mayor was forced to act quickly to draw the attention of the Privy Council to the consequent disorder in the capital. The people, he wrote, were 'very fervent, and a great number unquiet and without order in the execution of the same [proclamation]'.[99] The representations of the Lord Mayor were reinforced by a personal plea on the strangers' behalf from Grindal to Cecil, and their combined intervention was sufficient to persuade the Council to issue a new proclamation ordering that denizens and other strangers living peacefully in London should not be molested.[100] The City authorities were required to print the new order and post it prominently all over London, but even with this firm action the violence did not immediately subside, and a further proclamation was apparently required before Frenchmen were completely safe.[101]

The disorders of 1563 had demonstrated how easily grievances could accumulate and well up into violence against the strangers, and although there were no further incidents of this sort, pressure on the City authorities to limit their economic activities mounted steadily. In 1570 a group of English tailors appealed for redress against strangers using their occupation, and, although no action is recorded in this case, in the next year it was decided to give a bill drawn up by the poor handicraftsmen against the stranger artificers the support of the City and recommend it to Parliament. Later in this same year the 'citizens of London' presented their complaint against the stranger handicraftsmen to Cecil, asking that the seven-year apprenticeship be enforced on strangers: a copy of a draft bill to this effect is to be found in the papers of the Dutch church, together with a protest entered by the church against it.[102] Whether or not the stranger churches lobbied effectively against such hostile measures, no bills relating to strangers reached the statute book in this Parliament. But it is clear from a spate of applications for exemptions that

[99] BL, MS Lansdowne 7/19. See also *KP I*, p. 436.
[100] BL, MS Lansdowne 6/65, Grindal, *Remains*, p. 260; *Tudor Royal Proclamations*, ii. 232.
[101] Rep. 15, fo. 279ᵛ.; *Diary of Henry Machyn*, pp. 311–12.
[102] Rep. 17, fos. 14, 144; PRO, SP 12/81/29; Hessels, iii. 125–8.

the order forbidding the employment of foreign workmen was being particularly rigorously enforced from the beginning of 1571, and the City seems to have been successful in maintaining at least some restrictions on the strangers' economic activity for the rest of the decade.[103]

Notwithstanding these harsh measures in the winter of 1571–2, clearly some residual sympathy remained for the religious refugees amongst the poor strangers. Earlier in 1571 the Court of Aldermen agreed that Michael Symonson, a Dutchman 'who is come over for consciens sake' should be allowed to bake bread to sell to his fellow-countrymen despite the regulations to the contrary.[104] Increasingly, however, such claims on the conscience were bypassed by the suggestion that many of the newcomers were not truly religious refugees. Even as firm a friend of the strangers as Grindal had expressed doubts about harbouring all foreign immigrants quite indiscriminately, and the certificate of strangers in London presented to the Council in 1561 had carefully divided the refugees from 'others not come for cause of religion'.[105] Now, ominously for the strangers, the comprehensive enrolment of November 1571 noted whether they attended the foreign churches, parish churches, or no church at all.[106] The French and Dutch churches were at the same time required to furnish the bishop with a catalogue of their members, presumably as a double check, and it must have been clear that some punitive action was intended against those of no church: in 1573 they were ordered to depart the Queen's dominions.[107] The remarks of the City in their submission of 1574 reflect the extremely tough line that was being taken against such strangers (they suggested that it was probably not sufficient to banish them from London), and echoed the commonly held belief that many of them were anabaptists and other dangerous sectaries. Such a view was certainly expressed on the stage. In *The Pedler's Prophecy* a foreign mariner is denounced for bringing in 'Anabaptists, libertines, Epicurians, and Arians'. The mariner

[103] Rep. 17, fos. 91, 99, 114. See also Hessels, iii. 486.
[104] Rep. 17, fos. 113ᵛ., 284.
[105] Grindal to Cecil, 8 Sept. 1562. PRO, SP 12/24/24.
[106] *Returns*, ii. 1–139.
[107] *Actes II*, p. 32; *APC*, viii. 135.

indignantly protests, 'we bring in none but Gospellers', and is dismissed with the cynical reply:

> There is no heresie, no impietie, no sacriledge on sought,
> And all painted out, with the cullour of the Gospell.[108]

The concern of the stranger churches to protect their orthodoxy must be seen in the light of this popular willingness to denounce the foreign community as a breeding-ground for heterodoxy. Their cause was not helped when the government in 1575 rounded up an anabaptist cell, the members of which were all Dutch. Five were condemned to death, and two of the most stubborn eventually executed. The Dutch church in London made a plea for mercy, but it was muted enough for there later to be suspicion that they were implicated in the executions.[109] Other stranger communities in England were certainly more concerned about whether the incident would result in the churches falling into disfavour with the government.[110]

The churches were sorely tried by the need to defend their poorer members against economic harassment and their reputation from the taint of heterodoxy, and by 1574 even their denizen members, whose security had apparently been guaranteed by the resolute petitioning of the first Elizabethan ministers, were under threat. In their submission of 1574 the City authorities invited the Council to consider the position of the denizens: they asked whether there ought to be some restraint on the granting of further patents, and, more ominously whether there ought to be an examination of existing patents to see if any were void in law or rendered void by breaches of their privileges.[111] Previously antipathy had been largely focused on the poorer non-denizen strangers, but clearly now, Elizabethans were beginning to consider the implications of longer-term settlement and here there was a seam of naked

---

[108] Sig. Dii. Feldman, 'Dutch Exiles', 532.

[109] Hessels, iii. 315, 420, 611. The suspicion of complicity arose from the fact that the bishop made use of the Dutch ministers to examine the prisoners, who spoke no English or Latin. See Hessels, ii. 700–2.

[110] Ibid., iii. 319.

[111] Rep. 17, fo. 149ᵛ.

racial prejudice to be tapped. The 'father' of *The Pedler's Prophecy* probably spoke for many when he said:

> I and mine auncestors were English men borne,
> And though I be but a simple man,
> To marry my daughter to an Alian I thinke scorne.

His wife's remarks suggest that this was already a problem:

> Yet either they be Alians, or Aliant sonnes indeed,
> Who through marriage of English women of late,
> Hath altered the true English blood and seed,
> And therewithall English plaine maners and good state.[112]

Parental prejudice does not seem to have prevented young English men and women from associating with young foreigners,[113] but racial hostility must have had much to do with the concerted attack in the late 1570s on the status of strangers' children born in England. By law such childen were English, but clearly there was a widely held opinion that they retained their loyalty to their countries of origin. The Common Council, indeed, asserted as much in justifying an injunction of October 1574 forbidding freemen to take any apprentice whose father was not a native-born Englishman. The following year the city companies were instructed to put this order into effect.[114] This was a significant limitation on the privileges of the denizen, and the stranger churches prepared to fight the order in Parliament. A bill was prepared pointing out that denizen status was procured at great cost and involved giving up all old allegiances: to handicap their children in this way was thus a great injustice.[115] The aggrieved denizens had a certain amount of official support for their bill, but were not able to press matters to a successful conclusion in Parliament.[116] The strangers were, however, able to fend off a new bill which

---

[112] Sig. Bii^v. Feldman, 'Dutch Exiles', 532.
[113] See below, pp. 303–4.
[114] Hessels, iii. 270–2; Rep. 18, fo. 406.
[115] Hessels, iii. 272–3.
[116] PRO, SP 15/24/67. Two 'Bills for Denizens' passed through both Houses of Parliament, but these seem to have been private bills for the naturalization of Englishmen born abroad rather than the bill exhibited by the strangers. *Commons Journal*, i. 107, 108, 110, 112; *Lords Journal*, i. 740, 744–6.

sought to force strangers' children born in England to pay the alien rate of subsidy. The bill was rejected in the House of Commons on a vote at second reading.[117]

The attack on the status of foreigners born in England was renewed in 1579–81. Again this was a time of high tension at home, when two attempts sponsored by the papacy to stir Ireland to revolt added point to popular apprehensions of the Catholic menace abroad. In the summer of 1579 there were fears of a rising in England, and the imposition of a curfew in London was accompanied by a new general survey of aliens.[118] 1580 saw a new protest to the City against the stranger artificers, and a new attempt to legislate against strangers' children followed when Parliament met in the early months of 1581.[119] On this occasion the bill limited its attention to the children of non-denizen strangers, and probably for that reason it made better progress. The bill was one of the first introduced in the session and made steady progress despite substantial alterations in committee. The strangers, though, clearly still had their defenders, as the bill was recommitted after its third reading after a lengthy debate, and finally passed only after further amendments and 'many arguments first had and made'. The bill was sent to the Lords, where it was read twice but then disappeared.[120]

The ultimate failure of this bill suggests that, although there was a considerable groundswell of hostility towards the strangers, they might still, in the last resort, rely on powerful protectors. The 1581 bill ran into a great deal of opposition in the House of Commons. It was argued that the changes proposed were against both the natural law and the law of charity, and there were obviously considerable misgivings about tampering with fundamental property rights in a way which could rebound to the general disadvantage.[121] But most importantly, the government had no wish to make fundamental changes in the law in order to pander to the prejudices of its subjects,

---

[117] *Commons Journal*, i. 107, 108; *Proceedings in the Parliaments of Elizabeth I, 1558–1581*, ed. T. E. Hartley (Leicester, 1981), pp. 481–2, 486.

[118] *Cal. S. P. Span. Eliz.*, 1568–79, p. 686; Rep. 19, fos. 477ᵛ., 485ᵛ.

[119] *Analytical Index to the Remembrancia . . . of the City of London, 1579–1664* (1878), p. 507; *Commons Journal*, i. 118–23.

[120] *Commons Journal*, i. 127; *Lords Journal*, ii. 34, 38.

[121] *Proceedings in the Parliaments of Elizabeth I*, pp. 528, 532, 533, 537.

and although the bill eventually passed the Commons it was safely buried in the Lords. The protection offered to the strangers by the government was particularly important when hostility towards the foreign community reached its peak in the last decade of the century. These were extremely difficult years for the ageing Queen and her counsellors. Whether or not one is justified in talking of a 'crisis of the 1590s' with general European manifestations, certainly the coincidence of endemic plague, poor harvests, high taxation, and political insecurity as a result of the war with Spain put abnormal strains on the fabric of society, and inevitably the problems were most acute in the capital.[122] As in previous periods of high domestic tension, the strangers were an easy scapegoat for society's ills. A rising tide of protest against alien competition in trade and handicrafts issued in a new proposal, backed by the City of London, to prevent strangers selling by retail, and a bill to this effect was debated at some length in the Parliament of 1593.

Once again all the old grievances were aired.[123] It was argued that the strangers impoverished native traders, that they had got the whole trade of England into their hands, that they enjoyed unfair trade advantages. One speaker alleged that foreign residents would buy and sell only from their own countrymen, another raised the fact that strangers were exempt from apprenticeship regulations, a long-standing source of rancour. Yet for each that spoke against the strangers, there was one to raise his voice in their defence. Sir John Woolley pointed out that London had grown rich on the strangers' skills. They should not be made the scapegoats for England's economic ills urged another judicious speaker. Even the old religious sympathy was not completely dead. 'In the days of Queen Mary', it was observed, 'when our cause was as theirs is now, those countries did allow us that liberty which now we seek to deny them. They are strangers now, we may be strangers hereafter. So let us do as we would be done to.' Although the

---

[122] R. B. Outhwaite, 'Dearth, the English Crown and the "Crisis of the 1590s"' and Peter Clark, 'A Crisis Contained? The Condition of English Towns in the 1590s', in Peter Clark (ed.), *The European Crisis of the 1590s* (1985), 23–66.

[123] Sir Simon D'Ewes, *Journals of all the Parliaments during the Reign of Queen Elizabeth* (1682), pp. 505–9.

bill eventually passed the Commons (on a vote, 162 – 82) it once again failed to satisfy the Lords, where it was decisively rejected at the second reading.[124] The failure of the bill was probably due to the continuing benign influence of Lord Burghley. The strangers' first and firmest advocate, he had already made one intervention on their behalf in 1592 to protect a group of Dutch chandlers from prosecution by informers. In the Commons debate his son, Robert, had made a characteristically subtle and judicious speech in the strangers' defence, suggesting to the House that the bill would not have the desired effect, and ensuring that it was referred back for further consideration in committee before finally being passed to the Lords.[125]

The progress and eventual failure of the bill to limit strangers' rights to sell goods by retail in the Parliament of 1593 prompt two further observations about the agitation of this year. In the first place, those who spoke out in defence of the foreign community had shown a certain amount of courage in doing so. In the early months of 1593 feelings were running high, and the publication of a spate of libellous tracts urging attacks on the foreigners gave an added urgency to the Parliamentary agitation. One manifesto, a copy of which was pinned to the wall of the churchyard of the Dutch church warned that unless the strangers had departed by July, 'Apprentices will rise to the number of 2,336. And [they] . . . will down with the Flemings and strangers'.[126] Beset as they were with problems on all sides, it would have been easy for the Council to run with the tide and use the strangers as scapegoats.[127] But it is also the case that the government in resolutely defending the foreigners had logic on its side. It has already been noted that a substantial number of foreigners remained in London in the 1590s, but they were a very much diminished proportion of the total population. If, as seems possible, up to 10,000 foreigners were settled in London by

---

[124] D'Ewes, *Journals*, p. 511; *Lords Journal*, ii. 182, 184.

[125] Hessels, iii. 939–40; D'Ewes, *Journals*, p. 509.

[126] Clark, 'Crisis Contained', 53.

[127] At least one prominent courtier, Sir Walter Raleigh, associated himself with the popular agitation, and spoke out strongly against the strangers in the Commons debate. D'Ewes, *Journals*, pp. 508–9.

the end of Edward VI's reign, then this represented a proportion of the total population of the city and suburbs (about 10 per cent) which was never again attained during Elizabeth's reign, even during the peak immigration of the years 1567–72. The 7,000 foreigners registered in the survey of 1593 were, indeed, a rather smaller proportion of the population than the 3,000 strangers living in London at the beginning of the century (about 3½ per cent as opposed to 6 per cent).[128]

The real problem, as Elizabeth's government was only too aware, was that in the last decade of the reign, London was inundated by a rising tide of newcomers from other parts of England. Returning soldiers, unemployed labourers, 'masterless men and vagabonds', all flocked to the capital in search of food, work, or relief. The city's institutions, the hospitals, markets, and system of poor relief, were extremely hard put to cope with the influx, and to house the newcomers subdivision of tenements (of the sort blamed on the foreigners in the 1570s) was practised on a large scale.[129] The Queen and her counsellors were thus perfectly justified in their resolute refusal to allow blame for London's problems to be focused on the increasingly stable and substantially diminished foreign element in the city population. Energetic measures were put in hand to identify and punish those responsible for the planned attacks on foreigners in 1593. Orders were given that suspects should be rounded up and their houses searched for incriminating evidence. If necessary they were to be examined under torture to force them to reveal their accomplices.[130]

Of course, sound reasons quite apart from considerations of natural equity explain why the Council should have been anxious to protect foreign residents. By this time both France and the United Provinces were allies in the war against Spain, and the English government frequently called upon nationals of both nations settled in the capital for assistance in prosecuting the military struggle. Whereas in earlier decades the foreign

[128] Above, pp. 17, 78. These proportions are based on the assumption that the population of London rose from about 50,000 in 1500 to 90,000 in 1550 and to 200,000 by 1600. Finlay, *Population and Metropolis*, p. 51.

[129] Clark, 'Crisis Contained', 50. Mr Ian Archer of Trinity College, Oxford, is engaged on a study of City government during the 1590s.

[130] *APC*, 1592–3, pp. 187, 200–1, 222.

refugees had organized and dispatched military aid direct to their co-religionists abroad, after 1585 their contributions were invariably channelled through the English Privy Council. In 1586 Walsingham looked to the foreign churches for a substantial loan to finance the raising of new troops for the Low Countries, and when in the following year the government was attempting to raise a force of 10,000 men to defend the country in the Armada campaign the churches were again expected to contribute generously.[131] The churches also co-operated in efforts to raise troops from amongst the foreign community and money to help equip them.[132] On occasion the churches must have felt that the English government, like William of Orange before, had an exaggerated view of their financial resources, but on the whole co-operation remained close and amicable. Towards the end of the reign the government took to recovering money overdue from the United Provinces by forced loans on foreign merchants settled in London. Over £20,000 was raised in this way between 1598 and 1601.[133]

The financial demands of the last decade of the reign, if not always welcome to the prosperous members of the foreign community who bore the brunt, were at least tangible proof that the all-important relationship between the foreign community and their protectors in government had survived the last difficult years of the century intact. In return for their financial services the Council continued to offer the strangers protection. After the crisis of 1593 the Dutch ministers were able to return to the Council in the following year to petition on behalf of certain of their poorer members troubled by informers. On this occasion Burghley intervened to prevent the actions proceeding in the Court of Exchequer, and when in the following year the problem recurred the Council instructed the Lord Mayor to ensure that the strangers were not troubled further. In 1595 an affray in Southwark was defused by prompt action on the part of the Lord Mayor, who was able to prevent

---

[131] Hessels, ii. 803, 826; *APC*, 1587–8, p. 429. A list of foreign contributors to the levy is in *Returns*, ii. 414–15.

[132] Hessels, iii. 809, 888–9; *APC*, 1592–3, p. 138.

[133] PRO, 12/265/86, 275/143, 278/8–15; *APC*, 1598–9, p. 736; *Returns*, iii. 109–110.

a planned attack on the foreigners.[134] With the death of Burghley in 1598 the strangers had lost their firmest friend, but his former colleagues continued his policy of enlightened protection. When in 1599 some of the Dutch workmen were again troubled by informers and the Lord Mayor on this occasion gave his support to the native craftsmen, the church obtained a letter from the Privy Council ordering the City authorities not to proceed further. Two years later the Lord Treasurer, Buckhurst, intervened with the Attorney-General to prevent native candlemakers taking legal action in their long-standing battle against their Dutch competitors.[135]

In this way the foreign communities saw out the sixteenth century, bruised perhaps, but very much still intact. In 1603, after several months of anxious waiting, they were able to present their congratulations to the new King, and received in return a gracious assurance of continued favour and hospitality.[136] The churches' punctilious care in respect of their formal submission to James is one further example of their constant attention to the preservation of good relations with the authorities of the state. For the ministers were well aware that, for as long as a substantial section of the city population regarded the foreigners settled in the capital as a dangerous threat to their livelihoods and an alien presence, the security of their exile would depend on the steady protection they received from the governors of church and state. For their part, the City authorities and, to a still greater extent, the Privy Council retained their dispassionate appreciation of the benefits brought by the foreigners to the towns in which they settled, and for this reason gave them steady protection. The government might on occasion treat the foreigners with scant sympathy, and was not above exploiting their unpopularity to bend them to its will, but it was too conscious of the advantages of their presence to support any punitive action which might encourage them to leave the kingdom. The strangers and the government were, ultimately, tied together by strong ties of mutual interest, and this was to prove the most effective protection of the strangers' privileges.

[134] Hessels, iii. 963–4, 975, 980.
[135] Hessels, ii. 899–906, iii. 1034–8.
[136] Hessels, ii. 922–3.

X

Conclusion

By the end of the sixteenth century London's foreign residents had achieved a certain position in English society. It would be an exaggeration to say that the immigrant population had won universal acceptance. But clearly the official churches had successfully negotiated the strains and conflicts of the Elizabethan era, and as the reign drew to a close their congregations had begun to manifest the characteristics of an increasingly stable community with real economic power. In this respect there had been a significant change since the early years of the reign, when the large numbers of impecunious refugees made up the preponderant element in the church communities. The passage of time was partly responsible for this change, but political circumstances had also played their part. By the end of the century, the original rationale of the churches, as a refuge, had receded. Those who remained in England did so more for reasons of economic convenience and many of them proved extremely successful. Of course, there had always, since the middle ages, been a number of very rich men amongst the foreigners settled in the capital. But whereas in the past the most prosperous amongst them were almost invariably members of international merchant families, by the end of the sixteenth century some of the richest of the foreigners living in the capital were men who had made a fortune in England and considered themselves at home.

To illustrate their growing prosperity one can do no better than sketch the careers of one or two of the foreign residents who were required to contribute to the forced loans and levies to raise troops collected by the Council towards the end of Elizabeth's reign. Peter Trion and Jan Godschalk were two religious exiles who came to London soon after Elizabeth's accession. Both were marked on the Dutch petition of 1561 as clothmakers, but both soon took the opportunity to diversify their businesses, Trion as a merchant, Godschalk by selling cloths made by the Dutch weavers settled in Norwich and Sandwich on the London market.[1] Both men had their difficulties with the rulers of the Dutch church (Trion had initially spoken up in Haemstede's defence, and he and Godschalk both supported the deacons against Winghen),[2] but this did not prevent either of them laying the basis of a formidable personal fortune. By 1576 Trion was a £70-subsidy man; he was required to pay £200 towards the Armada loan, and no less than £2,000 towards the forced loan of 1600. But he could well afford it: at his death in 1611 he left an estate valued at over £25,000.[3] Godschalk also contributed £200 in 1588, and although he died soon after, his son Jacob was expected to find £1,000 for the loan of 1600. No doubt the biggest fortunes were to be made by merchants, but neither Trion nor Godschalk seems to have come to England with wealth on this scale.

Other exiles working in the new trades for which the refugees were justly esteemed could take comfort from the heartening story of Balthazar Sanchez, a Spanish-born member of the French church who had taken refuge in England in Edward's reign. Sanchez was a confectioner, and during forty-five years in England he was able to build a considerable fortune by exploiting the notorious English sweet tooth. In 1582 he was assessed at £100 for the subsidy and in 1588 he was able to contribute a further £100 to the Armada loan. At his death in 1596 Sanchez left £300 to provide an annual income for the French poorhouse.[4] Legacies of this sort were another indication of the growing prosperity amongst the foreign residents of the city. The 1590s saw the beginnings of the very large individual donations to the foreign churches which reached their apogee in the seventeenth century, with benefactors regularly bestowing hundreds (even thousands) of pounds on the churches' poor. Even allowing for inflation this reflected a

---

[1] *Returns*, i. 211, 276, ii. 24 (Trion); ibid., i. 275, 390, ii. 90 (Godschalk).

[2] *KP I*, pp. 92, 149; van Schelven, *Vluchtelingenkerken*, p. 390 (Deacons' party to Emden, June 1566).

[3] *Returns*, i. 167, 414, iii. 109; *Calendar of Wills enrolled in the Court of Hustings, London*, ed. R. R. Sharpe (1889–90), i. 734–5.

[4] *Returns*, i. 336, ii. 231, 415, iii. 380; W. K. Jordan, *The Charities of London, 1480–1660* (1960), p. 145.

quantitative change since the 1560s and 1570s when £10 represented a very substantial legacy.

Happily for the strangers, their growing economic power was matched by an equal durability in the political sphere. In the closing decades of the sixteenth century the churches had been able to protect their poorer members in the face of considerable hostility from powerful sections of London society, and this same resilience was again evident when their privileges and independence came under attack in the following century. The most serious challenge came with the appointment of Laud as Archbishop of Canterbury in 1633.[5] The archbishop, no friend of an exempt jurisdiction in his diocese or of the churches' presbyterian form of government, acted almost immediately to bring the foreign communities under his control. All the foreign churches were instructed to adopt a translation of the English liturgy in place of their own servicebook, and all their members born in England were ordered to transfer to parish churches. The churches were under no illusions as to the seriousness of the threat: by this time as many as one-third of their members were the children of foreigners born in England and the churches were hardly economically viable without them. Laud's order was stubbornly resisted. When petitions and argument proved ineffective the churches resorted to passive resistance, and, in the event, they were able to outlast their antagonist. By 1641 the hapless archbishop was deprived of his authority and under arrest, and the churches were able to take advantage of the new turn of events to petition the Long Parliament for the confirmation of their privileges. Their enterprise was rewarded with an Act of Parliament guaranteeing their freedom from further interference. The foreign churches, in fact, came through the political turbulence of the seventeenth century remarkably unscathed. Their privileges were confirmed by the Commonwealth and the restored monarchy in turn, and, with the renewal of persecution in France under Louis XIV culminating in the Revocation of the Edict of Nantes in 1585, the consequent influx of refugees inspired an enormous effort of charitable giving,

---

[5] On the churches' troubles with Laud see Schickler, *Églises du Refuge*, ii. 3–63; Lindeboom, *Austin Friars*, pp. 136–49; H. R. Trevor-Roper, *Archbishop Laud* (1940), pp. 197–204.

as the dispossessed Huguenots became once more a domestic political issue of some importance.[6]

In both the economic and political spheres, the seventeenth century thus saw the foreign community building on the firm foundations established by the first generation of Protestant refugees. But what was the overall importance of the sixteenth-century immigration, and of the central institutions of the foreign community, the stranger churches? It should by now be clear that the immigration had remarkably wide-ranging implications for English society, and this chapter will conclude with a brief assessment of its impact on the religious, social, and political issues of the day. But first, what of the churches themselves; how important was their role in harnessing and directing the enormous creative energies of the foreign community?

During the three and a half decades between 1550 and 1585 many thousands of foreign refugees came to London, perhaps as many as forty or fifty thousand.[7] Immigration on this scale was potentially disorientating for London society, and the newcomers inevitably aroused a fair degree of resentment. The foreign churches played an important role in defusing this hostility. In the first place, the churches' leaders functioned very effectively as spokesmen for the foreign community. With their contacts at Court and friends amongst the rulers of the English church and state they were able both to represent the interests of their poorer members and, when carrying back Council mandates for the foreign community, to see that they were enforced. In this way the ministers of the church helped smooth the path of the newcomers into English society, and to ensure that no incidents or misunderstandings occurred

---

[6] R. D. Gwynn, 'The Arrival of Huguenot Refugees in England, 1680–1705', *HS*, 21 (1965–70), 366–73; id., 'James II in the light of his Treatment of Huguenot Refugees', *English Historical Review*, 92 (1977), 820–33; *French Protestant Refugees relieved through the Threadneedle Street Church, London, 1681–1687*, ed. A. P. Hands and I. Scoulardi, (Huguenot Society Publications, 49, 1971).

[7] Although there were probably never more than 10,000 foreigners in London at any one time the rate at which they came and went suggests that this estimate of the total is reasonable. Estimates of the total number that fled from the Netherlands vary widely. See Heinz Schilling, 'Innovation through Migration: The Settlement of Calvinistic Netherlanders in Sixteenth- and Seventeenth-Century Central and Western Europe, *Histoire Sociale*, 16 (1983), 9–10. Schilling suggests a total of just under 100,000 emigrants (in England and Germany).

which might sour the crucial relationship between the community and their patrons in government. But in a more subtle way, too, the churches did much to render the immigration acceptable to London residents. For ministers and consistory were careful to ensure that their church communities presented the immigration and its consequences in the best possible light. There can be no doubt that particular efforts were made in this regard. In the disciplinary field the consistories treated with special severity cases where misdemeanours had come to the attention of the English authorities. Their reasoning was obvious; the churches' leaders wished to present their community as peaceable and orderly and in all respects a credit to their adopted home, and were therefore bound to react strongly to anything which damaged this image. In 1569, for instance, the Dutch consistory required two members whose open drunkenness was said to have given offence to English citizens to do public penance.[8] The Dutch were perhaps particularly sensitive about incidents of this sort as they had no wish to give credence to the comic stereotype of the drunken Dutchman frequently met with in the drama of the period. But they also came down hard on a member accused of fighting in the presence of Englishmen, and another whose criticism of the discipline might have caused the English to think ill of the community.[9] The churches' policy of dealing with serious offences within the community was also no doubt a reflection of this same desire to keep incidents which did the strangers little credit away from the public eye.[10]

The churches' efforts to impress their hosts with the good order maintained within the stranger community did not go unrewarded, judging from the high regard shown by the English authorities for their institutions and procedures. The city authorities would on occasion refer strangers who had fallen foul of the law to the churches for correction rather than deal with them in the usual way. In 1571 one Jean Wyart was apprehended drunk by the guard at Whitechapel and brought

---

[8] *KP II*, pp. 27, 78.

[9] *KP II*, pp. 82, 84. Feldman, 'Netherlanders on the Early London Stage', *Notes and Queries*, 196 (1951), 333–5 and 'The Flemings in Shakespeare's Theatre', *Notes and Queries*, 197 (1952), 265–9.

[10] See above, p. 193.

up before the local justice, who dispatched him to the ministers of the French church for correction. Later in the same year two English officers in Southwark referred another drunken Frenchman to the church, which suspended him from the communion. An oblique tribute to the discipline of the church came from one of the masters of Bridewell in 1572: in referring a French inmate to the church's attention the master confessed that he would not have put up with his ill-behaviour so long had he not been 'covered with the mantle of this church'.[11] The churches could feel equally gratified by the confidence shown in their procedures for settling business disputes. Several important cases were sent to the churches for arbitration by the Privy Council in the 1590s, even, in one instance, when not all of the parties concerned were foreign. But the English plaintiff in this case signified his consent that it should be dealt with by representatives of the Dutch church, obviously satisfied that his interests would be dealt with fairly.[12]

The authorities' confidence in the churches' regulation of business relations within the foreign community partly no doubt reflected the widely-felt admiration for the foreigners' skills and industry. Several examples of the use of these skills have been cited, especially when the Privy Council asked for the help of the London community to plant colonies in other towns and the city authorities employed foreign workmen to teach new techniques to apprentices. One might also cite the Governors of Christ's Hospital's practice of apprenticing their boys to foreign masters to learn a trade.[13] Once again the churches did what they could to promote a favourable image of the community. Their efforts bore fruit in the Parliamentary debate of 1593, when grievances against the strangers were being comprehensively aired. One speaker who spoke up in their defence praised the strangers' industry and cited the good example of the church in this regard. No sooner was a child of the church able to walk, he said, than he was taught to serve God and flee idleness.[14]

[11] *Actes II*, pp. 14, 43, 50, 73.
[12] Hessels, iii. 917, 920, 982.
[13] *Christ's Hospital Admissions, 1554–1599*, ed. G. A. T. Allan (1937), pp. 38, 39, 41–5.
[14] D'Ewes, *Journals*, p. 506.

In ensuring that the immigrant community appeared in the most favourable possible light, industrious, well-disciplined, and co-operative, the churches helped to protect newcomers from outbursts of native hostility. This was less tangible perhaps, but no less important than other services they offered to newly-arrived immigrants: financial support in setting up businesses, a sense of community for bewildered newcomers, and, most importantly, a highly effective system of poor relief. The strength of the diaconate enabled the churches to deal with repeated waves of new immigrants without their becoming a charge on domestic institutions. This was no mean achievement, but could it be argued that the strength of the churches' institutions actually retarded the process by which newcomers became assimilated into English society? If the churches represented to many what was the most attractive about the stranger community, they were also a symbol of its separateness. And there was certainly a danger that the very efficiency of the church's organization would obviate the need for newcomers to accommodate themselves to the English way of life. Dutch or French refugees arriving in London could, through the church, be provided with help on arrival, medical assistance and schooling for their children, worship and fellowship, all without the need to learn the language of the country or even consort with Englishmen. And, settling in a district where large numbers of foreigners were already living, they could probably also buy and sell, find recreation and marry, all within the foreign community. English residents were not slow to voice their disquiet at this; the feeling that the foreigners deliberately excluded Englishmen from their business relations was one of the most sensitive grievances behind the agitation of the native craftsmen.[15]

But did the foreign churches deliberately encourage the foreign community to remain separate? This is a difficult question to approach. The process by which an immigrant group is integrated into the host community is not easy to observe, particularly given the limited time-scale of this work and the restricted data available. Nevertheless, many examples may

---

[15] See the petition of London citizens of 1571, PRO, SP 12/81/29. Printed in *Tudor Economic Documents*, i. 308–11.

be cited of foreigners who slipped apparently effortlessly into English society, and to the anxieties expressed in petitions and plays may be opposed frequent instances of progressive assimilation both in trade and in the field of personal and social relations. Where trade was concerned, there is evidence for a great deal of fairly easy business contact between immigrants and Londoners. Indeed, whilst some English craftsmen evidently felt excluded by the foreigners allegedly trading only with one another, a more common complaint was that the foreign workmen competed all too successfully, forcing English workmen out of business with their higher-quality goods and lower costs.[16] In 1593, faced with the allegation that the foreigners jealously guarded the secrets of their trade, and that they would not employ English workmen, the Council ordered that the next survey of the alien population should record how many Englishmen were employed by foreigners. The survey duly found that the 1,500 foreign householders employed between them more than 1,600 English servants. It was a convincing rebuttal of the allegation that the foreigners neglected their generally-accepted obligation to teach English workmen their superior techniques.[17]

Much the same sort of impressionistic evidence may be cited when one considers the mixing of foreigners and English at a personal and social level. The Returns of Aliens indicate that some 25 per cent of the strangers regularly attended the English parish churches, and both the French and Dutch churches had to reckon with a steady seepage of their own members away to English congregations.[18] The minutes of both consistories also record frequent cases of members who married in the parish churches, and although this was clearly arranged on occasion to avoid awkward questioning by their own ministers, in other instances members went to the parish churches because they were taking an English spouse.[19] Neither church looked with particular favour on mixed marriages, possibly because they had no wish to lose members to the laxer parish churches, but, ministerial disapproval notwithstanding, many

[16] Idem.
[17] *Returns of Strangers, 1593 etc*, ed. Scouloudi, p. 90.
[18] *Returns*, i. 393, ii. 139, iii. 439.
[19] Actes II, pp. 8, 70, 74, 91, 102; *KP II*, pp. 69, 117, 182, 224.

members of the stranger community clearly did marry English men and women. The French petition of 1561 noted that most of the long-term residents from the precincts of St Martin's and St Katherine's had English wives,[20] and as foreigners settled into a local community over a course of years they inevitably developed useful contacts with their English neighbours. Foreigners were not exempt from corporate obligations, and the city insisted that they should serve their turn as constables or watchmen, offices which were regarded more as a burdensome obligation than as positions of trust.[21] But besides fulfilling these social duties foreigners often built up for themselves a position of some importance in their local community. Again, wills provide much the best evidence of this. Long-term residents such as Nicholas Dering and Harmon van Collen married their daughters to Englishmen, bought tenements from English citizens, and had their wills witnessed by English neighbours.[22] In addition to his substantial legacy to the French church, Balthazar Sachez, who had married an Englishwoman, left £640 to build an almshouse in Tottenham.[23] It is worth returning briefly to the career of Peter Trion, described above. Trion made up his differences with the Dutch church after 1570, and remained a loyal member until his death in 1611. But then, in addition to generous benefactions to the foreign churches, he also left considerable sums to English institutions (Christ's Hospital and the hospitals) and to the English poor. His two daughters were both married to Englishmen.[24]

The experience of Sanchez and Trion and others like them suggests strongly that a continuing sense of obligation to their own community was not incompatible with building an established position in English society. For a slightly later period one might also cite in this connection the wills of Rachel Campbell and Lady Conway, two women of immigrant stock who married into English families but still generously remembered their Dutch community at the time of their deaths.[25] In

---

[20] *Returns*, i. 288.
[21] Rep. 16, fos. 246ᵛ., 255ᵛ., 257ᵛ., 18, fo. 326.
[22] PCC 1574 (38 Martin); PCC 1570 (27 Lyon).
[23] Jordan, *Charities of London*, p. 145.
[24] *Returns*, ii. 204, 410. *Calendar of Hustings Wills*, i. 735.
[25] Jordan, *Charities of London*, pp. 127, 291, 347, 414.

the same way the development of a sense of loyalty to their adopted home was in no way impeded by sentimental ties to their homeland and a continuing identification with the struggle abroad. When the changing political situation produced a potential clash of loyalties (as when Elizabeth and the Prince of Orange were at loggerheads in 1576)[26] the foreign community in London realistically acknowledged the former obligation as paramount.

The existence of the French and Dutch churches in London did not prevent foreign residents making a real contribution to English society. By assisting newly-arrived refugees, and by defusing possible points of tension with the city and government, they assisted peaceful integration. These activities were more influential than those which served to separate the community from their English hosts. It is worth pointing out that friction between the immigrants and native population never led to violent demonstrations on the part of the newcomers, a fact not without significance in view of the subsequent history of race relations in the capital. The churches must take some of the credit for this. Their institutions provided both the means of control and a forum for grievances at times of tension within the stranger community, and thus helped defuse potentially dangerous situations before rancour turned to unrest.

What finally can be said of the wider impact of the immigration? In the years after the establishment of Lasco's community in 1550, the first ministers of the church set themselves two bold aims: to influence the course of the English Reformation by acting as a spur for a further, more complete reform; and to contribute to the establishment of a Reformed church in their own homelands. As far as the first of these goals was concerned, the foreign churches' eventual influence was extremely modest. The foreign ministers and their English allies, most notably Hooper, signally failed to convince the leaders of the Edwardian church that a complete reform on the Swiss model was feasible or even desirable. Although the 1552 Prayer Book made substantial amendments to the order of service these fell a long way short of what Lasco and his colleagues wished. The strangers' church order and discipline

[26] Above, p. 268.

ultimately found its admirers not amongst the establishment but amongst the free thinkers on the fringes of the Anglican Church; and, after the uncomfortable experience of Lasco's outspoken and persistent lobbying, the ecclesiastical and lay authorities in Elizabeth's reign went to some trouble to ensure that the foreign churches' contacts with English critics of the church were closely controlled. The foreign ministers continued to function to some extent as a conduit for Swiss Reformed influence, at least on a personal level; they had, after all, the only legally-permitted Calvinist churches in England. But in terms of the high expectations expressed in the formative years of the Edwardian Reformation this was a modest achievement.

In contrast, the exile communities' influence on events in their former homelands was much more profound. It is hard to over-estimate the contribution of the London communities to the propagation of the Gospel in the Netherlands, a contribution which earned them the designation 'mother and nursery of all Netherlands Reformed churches'.[27] Here the liturgical and theological labours of Lasco and his colleagues found their true reward. Lasco's church order, spurned as a model by the English Church, found its echo in the forms established in the Netherlands, even to the extent of the incorporation of sections of Micron's *Christlicke Ordinancien* in later indigenous productions. In due course Utenhove's psalms and the London catechism were replaced by the more durable productions of Dathenus and the Heidelberg catechism, but Micron's shorter catechism and the *Korte ondersoeckinghe des gheloofs* both retained their popularity for a remarkably long period: the first synods of the Dutch Reformed church specifically authorized the continued use of the *Korte ondersoeckinghe* as an alternative to the Heidelberg Catechism.[28] In the 1560s, before the Reformed movement in the Netherlands achieved its final regulated form, all of these London works enjoyed a wide currency in the

[27] 'Mater et propagatrix omnium reformatorum ecclesiarum belgicarum' (Festus Hommius). Quoted Lindeboom, *Austin Friars*, p. 89.

[28] *Acta van de Nederlandsche Synoden der zestiende eeuw*, ed. F. L. Rutgers (Marnix Society, series I, part III, 1889), pp. 57–8, 198. Lindeboom, *Austin Friars*, pp. 89–90; Knappert, *Ontstaen*, pp. 329–32; Woudstra, *De Hollandsche Vreemdelingen-gemeente*, pp. 117–22; M. A. Gooszen, *De Heidelberger Catechismus* (Leiden, 1890). On Utenhove's psalms see Hessels, ii. 332; *KP II*, p. 302; H. Slenk, 'Jan Utenhove's Psalms in the Low Countries', *NAK*, 49 (1968–9), 155–68.

Netherlands, often through reprints published in Emden.[29] It was in these earlier decades that the influence of the London exile was most profound. With the enforced interruption of 1553–8, the London refuge played a vital role in the survival of the embryonic Reformed communities in the towns of Flanders and Brabant. As persecution grew less effective and the Reformed movement gathered strength and confidence, London continued to be an important source of ministers, money, comfort, and advice. By the time the Reformed communities were securely established in later years London was one exile community amongst many, but the churches still turned to their earlier friends for help and support, and the London exiles were never slow to respond.

The involvement of the exiles in events abroad did not go unnoticed by the English government. Elizabeth and her ministers made no secret of their refusal to close their doors to those who sought refuge from Continental persecution, but the freedom of action afforded the exiles went far beyond what could decently be explained away on humanitarian grounds. On occasion, as for instance in both 1568 and 1572, the Council clearly connived at the dispatch of assistance for the rebels at a time when official policy was still apparently directed towards good relations with Philip of Spain.[30] The implications of these remarkably bold (or injudicious) initiatives have not fully been grasped in studies of Elizabethan foreign policy. May we identify, many years before England intervened openly in the Netherlands and France, a Protestant lobby which recognized the inevitability of war with Spain, and sought to influence the Queen towards the rebel cause? Given the undoubted risks of such a policy, and since the Spanish ambassadors would inevitably discover what was afoot (as they did), is the traditional stress laid by historians on the caution and restraint of English policy justified? These are questions which await further, more systematic, investigation.

Much less speculative but certainly no less significant, was the profound impact of the refugee movement on the English economy. Again, a comprehensive assessment of the immigrant

---

[29] The London catechisms, Confession of Faith, and *Ordinancien* went through nineteen Emden editions. Knappert, *Ontstaen*, pp. 296–7. Micron, *Ordinancien*, pp. 4–5.
[30] See above, pp. 267–8.

contribution to the development of numerous crafts and industries during the course of the sixteenth and seventeenth centuries has still to be written. It is clear, however, that in several towns during the Elizabethan period settlements of foreign workmen made a crucial contribution to the regeneration of a faltering local economy. In the more robust economic climate of the capital the skills and ingenuity of the strangers were no less in demand, and it was here too that the dissemination of foreign techniques through the dispatch of foreign workmen to provincial towns was planned and executed by the Privy Council with the co-operation of the ministers of the London foreign churches. It is worth dwelling a moment on the Council's initiative in this area. At a time when an English consumer market was only beginning to respond to the rich variety of products and goods made available partly by the exploitation of foreign skills, the Council reacted with great energy and insight to the opportunity presented by the arrival of large numbers of refugees, a development which less far-sighted contemporaries viewed more as a threat to the traditional balance of society. In an age when the potentialities of government action were distinctly limited, it is hard to quarrel with the conclusion of one recent study that the encouragement and management of the refugee influx was probably the most significant act of state in the social or economic sphere.[31] The foreign churches certainly played their part in ensuring that foreign potential was harnessed for the English economy. The churches' founding fathers would, no doubt, have been amazed by the suggestion that this contribution would outweigh their influence on the religious settlement in England. But this seems, indeed, to have been the case.

London's foreign residents made up an infinitely mixed and varied community. The refugee movement of mid-century added a new element and one rich in possibilities, but even before their arrival the stranger community comprised men with an enormous variety of experiences and reasons for leaving their homelands. This continued to be the case after the foreign churches had been established to succour and regulate the refugee population. Many foreigners still came to London

---

[31] D. M. Palliser, *The Age of Elizabeth* (1983), pp. 322–5, 381–2.

in search of work; others came to join members of their families already settled in the city, some no doubt with no clearer end in view than a desire for a change of scene. And whilst some remained to live out a prosperous old age in their adopted home, others quickly returned to the Continent, to be replaced in their turn by other hopeful newcomers. This skilled, diverse, and changing community made up one of the most dynamic elements in the highly mobile population of the rapidly growing capital. And the stranger churches played an essential role, both in meeting their immediate needs and in channelling their talents and energies to such telling effect for English society and for their former homelands.

Bibliography

(A) MANUSCRIPT SOURCES

London, Guildhall Library
 MS 5606 (Coopers' Company Wardens' Accounts).
 MS 7397 (Kerkeraadsprotocollen, 1571–85).
 MS 7402 (Dutch Church Register).
 MS 9051 (Archdeaconry Court of London Wills).
 MS 9171 (Commissary Court of London Wills).
 MS 10055 (Ruytinck's Notes).
——, Public Record Office.
 SP 11, 12 (State Papers Domestic).
 Prerogative Court of Canterbury Wills.
——, British Library.
 Lansdowne Manuscripts.
 MS Add. 48096.
——, Corporation of London Record Office.
 Repertories of the Court of Aldermen.
 Letter Books Q, R, S.
——, Greater London Record Office.
 Consistory Court of London Wills.
 Archdeaconry Court of Surrey Wills.
 DL/C/614.
——, City of Westminster Archives Department.
 Wills of the Peculiar of the Dean and Chapter of Westminster.
——, French Church, Soho Square.
 MS 194 (Deacons' Account Book, 1572–3).

Oxford, Bodleian Library.
 MS Barlow 19.
 MS Douce 68.

Emden, West Germany, Archiv der evangelische reformierte Gemeinde.
 MS 320 a, b (Correspondence).
 Kerkeraadsprotocollen.
——, Stadtarchiv.
 Bürgerbücher.

Frankfurt am Main, Stadtarchiv.
 Bürgerbücher.

(B) PRINTED SOURCES

Place of publication is London unless otherwise stated.

(1) Primary Sources

Acta van de Nederlandsche Synoden der zestiende eeuw, ed. F. L. Rutgers (Marnix Society, series 2, part 3, 1889).

Acten van de Colloquia der Nederlandsche gemeenten in Engeland, 1575–1609, ed. J. J. van Toorenenbergen (Marnix Society, series 2, part 1, 1872).

Les Actes des Colloques des Églises Françaises et des Synodes des Églises Étrangères réfugiées en Angleterre, 1581–1654, ed. A. C. Chamier (Huguenot Society Publications, 2, 1890).

Actes du Consistoire de l'Église Française de Threadneedle Street, Londres, vol. 1, 1560–1565, ed. Elsie Johnson (Huguenot Society Publications, 38, 1937).

Actes du Consistoire de l'Église Française de Threadneedle Street, Londres, vol. 2, 1571–1577, ed. Anne M. Oakley (Huguenot Society Publications, 48, 1969).

Acts of the Privy Council of England, ed. J. R. Dasent, vols. i–xi (1890–3).

Bibliotheca Reformatoria Neerlandica, ed. S. Cramer and F. Pijper, (The Hague, 1903–14).

Biografisch woordenboek van protestantsche godgeleerden in Nederland, ed. J. P. de Bie and J. Wosjes (The Hague, 1919–49).

Calendar of Patent Rolls, Edward VI, Philip and Mary, and Elizabeth (1924–).

Calendar of State Papers Domestic, Edward VI, Mary, and Elizabeth, 1547–1580, ed. R. Lemon (1856).

Calendar of State Papers Foreign, Edward VI and Mary, Elizabeth, ed. W. B. Turnbull, etc. (1861–1950).

Calendar of State Papers relating to the negotiations between England and Spain ... ed. R. Tyler, etc., vols. ix–xiii, *Elizabeth*, vol. 1 (1892–1954).

Calvin, *Thesaurus Epistolicus Calvinianus*, in *Joannis Calvini Opera*, ed. E. Cunitz and E. Baum (*Corpus Reformatorum*, 29–87, 1863–1900).

—— *Letters of John Calvin*, ed. J. Bonnet (Edinburgh, 1855–7).

—— *Lettres Anglaises*, ed. Albert-Marie Schmidt (Paris, 1959).

—— *Les Lettres à Jean Calvin de la Collection Saurrau*, ed. Rodolphe Peter and Jean Rott (Paris, 1972).

The Chronicle and Political Papers of King Edward VI, ed. W. K. Jordan (1966).

Coussemaker, E. de, *Troubles religieux du XVIᵉ siècle dans la Flandre maritime, 1560–1570* (Bruges, 1876).

Denizations, *Letters of Denization and Acts of Naturalization for Aliens in England, 1509–1603*, ed. W. Page (Huguenot Society Publications, 8, 1893).

D'Ewes, Sir Simon, *The Journals of all the Parliaments during the Reign of Queen Elizabeth, both of the House of Lords and House of Commons* (1682).

The Diary of Henry Machyn, Citizen and Merchant Taylor of London, 1550–1563, ed. J. G. Nichols (Camden Society, xlii, 1848).

A Discourse of the Common Weal of this Realm of England, ed. E. Lamond (Cambridge, 1929).

Die evangelischen Kirchenordnungen des 16. Jahrhunderts. ed. E. Sehling, vii. (Tübingen, 1963).

First and Second Prayer Books of Edward VI (Everyman's Library, 1913).

Foedera, Conventiones, Literae, et cuiscumque Generis Acta Publica, Inter Regis Angliae, ed. Thomas Rymer (1704–26).

Gorham, George C., *Gleanings of a few scattered ears during the period of the Reformation in England, 1533–1588* (1857).

Haag, E. and E., *La France Protestante*, 1st ed. (Paris, 1846–59), 2nd ed. (Paris, 1877–88).

Hessels, J. H. *Ecclesiae Londino-Batavae Archivum, Epistulae et Tractatus* (Cambridge, 1889–97).

Journals of the House of Commons, vol. 1 (1803).

Journals of the House of Lords, vol. 1 (n.d.).

Kerkeraads-protocollen der Nederduitsche vluchtelingen-kerk te Londen, 1560–63, ed. A. A. van Schelven (Historisch Genootschap te Utrecht, 3rd series, 43, 1921).

Kerkeraads-protocollen der Hollandsche gemeente te Londen, 1569–71, ed. A. Kuyper (Marnix Society, series 1, part 1, 1870).

Kervyn de Lettenhove, J. M. B. C., *Relations politiques des Pays-Bas et de l'Angleterre, sous le règne de Philippe II* (Brussels, 1888–1900).

Joannis a Lasco Opera tam edita quam inedita ed. A. Kuyper (Amsterdam, 1866).

Letters and Papers Foreign and Domestic of the reign of Henry VIII, ed. J. S. Brewer, *et al.*, 2nd ed. (1920–32).

Literary Remains of King Edward the Sixth, ed. J. G. Nichols, vol. 1, (Roxburghe Club, 74, 1857).

London and Middlesex Chantry Certificates, 1548, ed. C. J. Kitching (London Record Society, 16, 1980).

Micron, Martin *De Christlicke Ordinancien der Nederlantscher Ghemeinten te Londen*, ed. W. F. Dankbaar (The Hague, 1956).

Nieuw Nederlandsch Biografisch Woordenboek, ed. P. C. Molhuysen and P. J. Blok (Leiden, 1911–37).

Original Letters relative to the English Reformation, ed. H. Robinson, (Parker Society, 1846–7).
Pollanus, Liturgia Sacra, ed. A. C. Honders (Leiden, 1970).
Proceedings in the Parliaments of Elizabeth I, 1558–1581, ed. T. E. Hartley (Leicester, 1981).
Quellen zur Geschichte des Kirchlichen Unterrichts, ed. J. M. Reu, (Gütersloh, 1904–1935), vol. 8.
Remains of Archbishop Grindal, ed. W. Nicholson (Parker Society, 1843).
Returns of Aliens dwelling in the City and Suburbs of London, ed. R. E. G. and E. F. Kirk (Huguenot Society Publications, 10, 1900–8).
Returns of Strangers in the Metropolis, 1593, 1627, 1635, 1639, ed. I. Scouloudi (Huguenot Society Publications, 57, 1985).
Ruytinck, Symeon, *Gheschiedenissen ende handelingen die voornemelick aengaen de Nederduytsche natie ende gemeynten wonende in Engelant bysonder tot Londen*, ed. J. J. van Toorenenbergen (Marnix Society, series 3, part 1, 1873).
The Statutes of the Realm, ed. A. Luders etc. (1810–28).
Stow, J., *A Survey of London*, ed. C. L. Kingsford (Oxford, 1971).
Toute la forme et maniere du Ministere Ecclesiastique en l'Eglise des estrangers, dressee a Londres . . . (Emden, 1556).
Tudor Royal Proclamations, ed. P. L. Hughes and J. F. Larkin (1964–9).
Tudor Economic Documents, ed. R. H. Tawney and E. Powers (1924).
Wardens' Accounts of the Worshipful Company of Founders of the City of London, 1497–1681, ed. C. G. Parsloe (1964).
The Zurich Letters, ed. H. Robinson (Parker Society, 1842–5).

(2) Secondary Sources

Backhouse, M. F., 'The Official Start of Armed Resistance in the Low Countries: Boeschepe 12 July 1562', *Archiv für Reformationsgeschichte* 71 (1980).
——, 'De verspreiding van het Calvinisme in Vlaanderen in de XVIe eeuw', *De Franse Nederlanden*, 1982.
——, 'Guerilla War and Banditry in the Sixteenth Century: the Wood Beggars in the Westkwartier of Flanders (1567–1568)', *Archiv für Reformationsgeschichte*, 74 (1983).
Bauer, K., *Valérand Poullain* (Elberfeld, 1927).
Beeman, G. B., 'The Early History of the Strangers' Church, 1550–1561', *HS*, xv (1933–7).
Benedict, Philip, *Rouen during the Wars of Religion* (Cambridge, 1981).
Bense, J. F., *Anglo-Dutch Relations from the earliest Times to the Death of William the Third* (Oxford, 1925).
Bornkamm, Heinrich, 'Martin Bucer, der dritte deutsche Reformator', *Das Jahrhundert der Reformation* (Göttingen, 1966).

Briggs, E. R., 'An Apostle of the Incomplete Reformation: Jacopo Aconcio (1500–1567)', *HS*, xxii (1970–6).
—— 'Reflections on the first Century of the Huguenot Churches in England', *HS*, xxiii (1977–82).
Burn, J. S., *History of the French, Walloon, Dutch Refugees* (1846).
Bush, M. L., *The Government Policy of Protector Somerset* (1975).

Chambers, Bettye, 'The First French New Testament Printed in England?', *BHR*, 39 (1977).
——, 'Thomas Gualtier strikes again . . . and again?', *BHR*, 41 (1979).
Chitty, C. W., 'Aliens in England in the Sixteenth Century', *Race*, 8 (1966–7).
Clair, Colin, 'Refugee Printers and Publishers in Britain during the Tudor Period', *HS*, xxii (1970–6).
——, 'On the Printing of Certain Reformation Books', *The Library*, 5th series, xviii (1963).
Clark, Peter, ed., *The European Crisis of the 1590s* (1985).
Collinson, Patrick, *Archbishop Grindal, 1519–1583* (1979).
——, 'The Elizabethan Puritans and the Foreign Reformed Churches in London', *HS*, xx (1958–64).
Consitt, Frances, *The London Weavers' Company* (Oxford, 1933).
Crew, Phyllis Mack, *Calvinist Preaching and Iconoclasm in the Netherlands 1544–1569* (Cambridge, 1978).
Cross, F. W., *History of the Walloon and Huguenot Church at Canterbury* (Huguenot Society Publications, 15, 1898).
Cunningham, W., *Alien Immigrants to England* (1897).

Dalton, H., *Johannes a Lasco* (Gotha, 1881).
Davies, D. S., 'Acontius, Champion of Toleration and the Patent System', *Economic History Review*, vii (1936–7).
Davis, John F., *Heresy and Reformation in the South East of England, 1520–1559* (1983).
Decavele, Johan, *De Dageraad van de Reformatie in Vlaanderen, 1520–65*, (Brussels, 1975).
Denis, Philippe, *Les Églises D'Étrangers en Pays Rhénans (1538–1564)* (Paris, 1984).
——, 'Un combat aux frontières de l'Orthodoxie', *BHR*, 38 (1976).
——, 'Pierre Alexandre et la discipline ecclésiastique', *BHR*, 39 (1977).
——, 'John Veron: The First Known French Protestant in England', *HS*, 22 (1970–6).
——, '"Discipline" in the English Huguenot Churches of the Reformation', *HS*, 23 (1977–82).
Dollinger, Philippe, *The German Hansa* (1970).

Duff, E. G., *A Century of the English Book Trade* (1948).

Duke, Alastair, 'The Ambivalent Face of Calvinism in the Netherlands, 1561–1618', in Menna Prestwich (ed.), *International Calvinism, 1541–1715* (Oxford, 1985).

Dulken, J. T. C. van, *The Dutch Church, Austin Friars* (n.pl., n.d.). Pamphlet in the Guildhall Library, London.

Ebrard, F. C., *Die französisch-reformierte Gemeinde in Frankfurt am Main, 1554–1904* (Frankfurt, 1906).

Elkington, George, *The Coopers: Company and Craft* (1933).

Fast, H., *Heinrich Bullinger und die Täufer* (Neustadt, 1959).

Feldman, A. B., 'Dutch Exiles and Elizabethan Playwrights', *Notes and Queries*, 196 (1951).

Finlay, Roger, *Population and Metropolis* (Cambridge, 1981).

Gerretsen, J. H., *Micronius, zijn leven, zijn geschriften, zijn geestesrichting* (Nijmegen, 1895).

Gilmont, J. F., 'Un pseudonyme de Pierre Alexandre: Simon Alexius', *Bulletin de la Société d'Histoire du Protestantisme Belge*, v, 6 (1970–1).

Ginkel, A. van, *De Ouderling* (Amsterdam, 1975).

Giuseppi, M., 'Alien Merchants in England in the Fifteenth Century', *Transactions of the Royal Historical Society*, 9 (1895).

Goeters, W. G., 'Dokumenten van Adriaan van Haemstede', *NAK*, 5 (1908).

Hall, Basil, *John a Lasco, a Pole in Reformation England* (Friends of Dr Williams's Library, 25th Lecture, 1971).

Holmes, Martin, 'Evil May Day, 1517: the Story of a Riot', *History Today*, 15 (1965).

Hopf, Constantin, *Martin Bucer and the English Reformation* (Oxford, 1946).

Horst, I. B., *The Radical Brethren. Anabaptism and the English Reformation to 1558* (Nieuwkoop, 1972).

Isaacs, Frank, 'Egidius van der Erve and his English Printed Books', *The Library*, 4th series, xii (1931–2).

Jelsma, A. J., *Adriaan van Haemstede en zijn Martelaarsboek* (The Hague, 1970).

Johnson, A. F., 'English Books Printed Abroad', *The Library*, 5th series, iv (1949–50).

Jones, Norman L., *Faith by Statute. Parliament and the Settlement of Religion 1559* (1982).

Jonge, H. J. de, 'Caro in Spiritum', in I. B. Horst, etc., eds., *De Geest in het geding* (Alphen, 1978).

Jordan, W. K., *Edward VI: The Young King* (1968).

——, *Edward VI: The Threshold of Power* (1970).

Kayser, Rudolf, 'Johannes a Lasco und die Londoner Flüchtlings-gemeinde in Hamburg', *Zeitschrift des Vereins für hamburgische Geschichte*, 37 (1938).

Knappert, L., *Het Ontstaan en de Vestiging van het protestantisme in de Nederlanden* (Utrecht, 1924).

Koolman, J. ten D., 'Jan Utenhoves Besuch bei Heinrich Bullinger im Jahre 1549', *Zwingliana*, 14 (1974–8).

Kronenberg, M. E., 'Notes on English Printing in the Low Countries', *The Library*, 4th series, ix (1928–9).

Kruske, Richard, *Johannes a Lasco und der Sakramentsstreit* (Leipzig, 1901).

Kuyper, A., 'De Hollandsche gemeinte te Londen in 1570/71', in *Voor driehondert jaren* (Bronsveld, 1870).

Lenselink, S. J., *De Nederlandse Psalmberijmingen van de Souterliedekens tot Datheen* (Assen, 1959).

Lindeboom, J., *Austin Friars. History of the Dutch Reformed Church in London, 1550–1950* (The Hague, 1950).

Meiners, E., *Oostvrieschlandts kerkelijke Geschiedenisse* (Groningen, 1738–9).

Michotte, Oswald, *Un Réformateur, Pierre Alexandre* (Nessonvaux, 1913).

Nauta, D., and J. P. van Dooren, eds., *De Synode van Emden October 1571* (Kampen, 1971).

Neuser, Wilhelm, 'Die Aufnahme der Flüchtlinge aus England in Wesel (1553) und ihre Ausweisung trotz der Vermittlung Calvins und Melanchthons', in *Weseler Konvent, 1568–1968* (Düsseldorf, 1968).

Nevinson, J. L., 'Emanuel van Meteren, 1535–1612', *HS*, xix (1952–8).

Nijenhuis, W., *Adrianus Saravia* (Leiden, 1980).

——, 'Variants within Dutch Calvinism in the sixteenth century', *Low Countries History Yearbook*, 12 (1979).

Norwood, F. A., *The Reformation Refugees as an Economic Force* (Chicago, 1942).

——, 'The London Dutch Refugees in Search of a Home, 1553–1554', *American Historical Review*, 58 (1952–3).

——, 'The Strangers' "Model Churches" in Sixteenth-Century England', in F. H. Littell, ed., *Reformation Studies* (Richmond, Va., 1962).

Opie, John, 'The Anglicizing of John Hooper', *Archiv für Reformations-geschichte*, 59 (1968).

Parker, Geoffrey, *The Dutch Revolt* (1977).

Pascal, George, *Jean de Lasco. Son temps, sa vie, ses oeuvres* (Paris, 1894).

Pijper, F., *Jan Utenhove, zijn leven en zijne werken* (Leiden, 1883).

Primus, J. H., *The Vestments Controversy: An Historical Study of the Earliest Tensions within the Church of England in the Reigns of Edward VI and Elizabeth* (Kampen, 1960).

Rahlenbeck, C., 'Les réfugiés belges du seizième siècle en Angleterre', *Revue trimestrielle*, 2nd series, viii (1865).

Ramsay, G. D., *The City of London in International Politics at the Accession of Elizabeth Tudor* (Manchester, 1975).

Reusch, F. Heinrich, *Die Indices librorum prohibitorum des sechzehnten Jahrhunderts* (Tübingen, 1886).

Robson-Scott, W. D., 'Josua Maler's visit to England in 1551', *Modern Language Review*, xlv (1950).

Schelven, A. A. van, *De Nederduitsche vluchtelingenkerken der XVIe eeuw in Engeland en Duitschland in hunne beteekenis voor de Reformatie in de Nederlanden* (The Hague, 1908).

——, 'Karakter en Stand van Van Haemstede', *NAK*, 8 (1911).

——, 'Het begin van het gewapend verzet tegen Spanje in de 16e-eeuwsche Nederlanden', *Handelingen en Mededeelingen van de Maatschappij der Nederlandsche Letterkunde te Leiden*, (1914–15).

——, 'Johannes Engelram', *Stemmen des tijds*, v (1916).

Schickler, Baron Fernand de, *Les Églises du Refuge en Angleterre* (Paris, 1892).

Schilling, Heinz, *Niederländische Exulanten im 16. Jahrhundert. Ihre Stellung im Sozialgefüge und im religiösen Leben deutscher und englischer Städte* (Gütersloh, 1972).

Scouloudi, Irene, 'Alien Immigration into and Alien Communities in London, 1558–1640', *HS*, xvi (1937–41).

Smiles, Samuel, *The Huguenots: Their Settlements, Churches, and Industries in England and Ireland* (1867).

Smyth, C. H., *Cranmer and the Reformation under Edward VI* (Cambridge, 1926).

Sprengler-Ruppenthal, Anneliese, *Mysterium und Riten nach der Londoner Kirchenordnung der Niederländer*. Forschungen zur kirchlichen Rechtsgeschichte und zum Kirchenrecht, vol. 7 (Cologne, 1967).

——, 'Ausdehnung und Grenzen der Befugnisse der Diakonen in der Londoner niederländischen Gemeinde 1560–1564. Eine Studie zum Ämterrecht', *Jahrbuch der Gesellschaft für niedersächsische Kirchengeschichte*, 63 (1965).

Strype, John. *Ecclesiastical Memorials . . . of the Church of England under King Henry VIII, King Edward VI, and Queen Mary I* (Oxford, 1822).

——, *Memorials of . . . Archbishop Cranmer* (Oxford, 1840).

——, *The history of the life and acts of . . . Edmund Grindal* (Oxford, 1821).

Thirsk, Joan, *Economic Policy and Projects* (Oxford, 1978).

Thrupp, Sylvia L., 'Aliens in and around London in the Fifteenth Century', in A. E. J. Hollaender and William Kellaway, eds., *Studies in London History* (1969).

——, *The Merchant Class of Medieval London* (Ann Arbor, Michigan, 1948).

Trapman, J., 'Delenus en de Bijbel', *NAK*, 56 (1975–6).

Verduyn, W. D., *Emanuel van Meteren: Bijdrage tot de kennis van zijn leven, zijn tijd en het ontstaan van zijn geschiedwerk* (The Hague, 1926).

Verheyden, A. L. E., 'Une correspondance inédite adressée par les familles protestantes des Pays-Bas à leurs coreligionnaires d'Angleterre (11 nov. 1569–25 fév. 1570), *Bulletin de la Commission Royale d'Histoire*, 120 (1955).

——, 'Le Protestantisme à Nieuport au XVIᵉ siècle', *Bulletin de la Commission Royale d'Histoire*, 116 (1951).

Wijnman, H. F., 'Grepen uit de Geschiedenis van de Nederlandse Emigrantendrukkerijen te Emden', I, *Het Boek*, 36 (1963–4); II, *Het Boek*, 37 (1965–6).

——, 'Wouter Deelen', *Jaarboek Amstelodamum*, 27 (1930).

Williams, Lionel, 'Alien Immigrants in Relation to Industry and Society in Tudor England', *HS*, xix (1952–8).

Worman, Ernest, *Alien Members of the Book Trade* (1906).

Woodstra, Marten, *De Hollandsche Vreemdelingen-gemeente te Londen* (Groningen, 1908).

(C) UNPUBLISHED THESES

Bratchell, M. E., 'Alien Merchant Communities in London, 1500–50' (Cambridge Univ. Ph.D. thesis, 1974).

Denis, Philippe, 'Les Églises d'étrangers à Londres jusqu'à la mort de Calvin: de l'Église de Jean Lasco à l'établissement du calvinisme' (Liège Univ. mémoire de licence, 1973–4).

Loach, Jennifer, 'Opposition to the Crown in Parliament, 1553–1558' (Oxford Univ. D. Phil. thesis, 1974).

Scouloudi, Irene, 'Alien Immigration and alien communities in London 1558–1640' (London Univ. M.Sc.(Econ) thesis, 1936).

Took, Patricia M., 'Government and the Printing Trade' (London Univ. Ph.D. thesis, 1979).

Index